sweetness & lightning

10

Gido Amagakure

c o n t e n t s

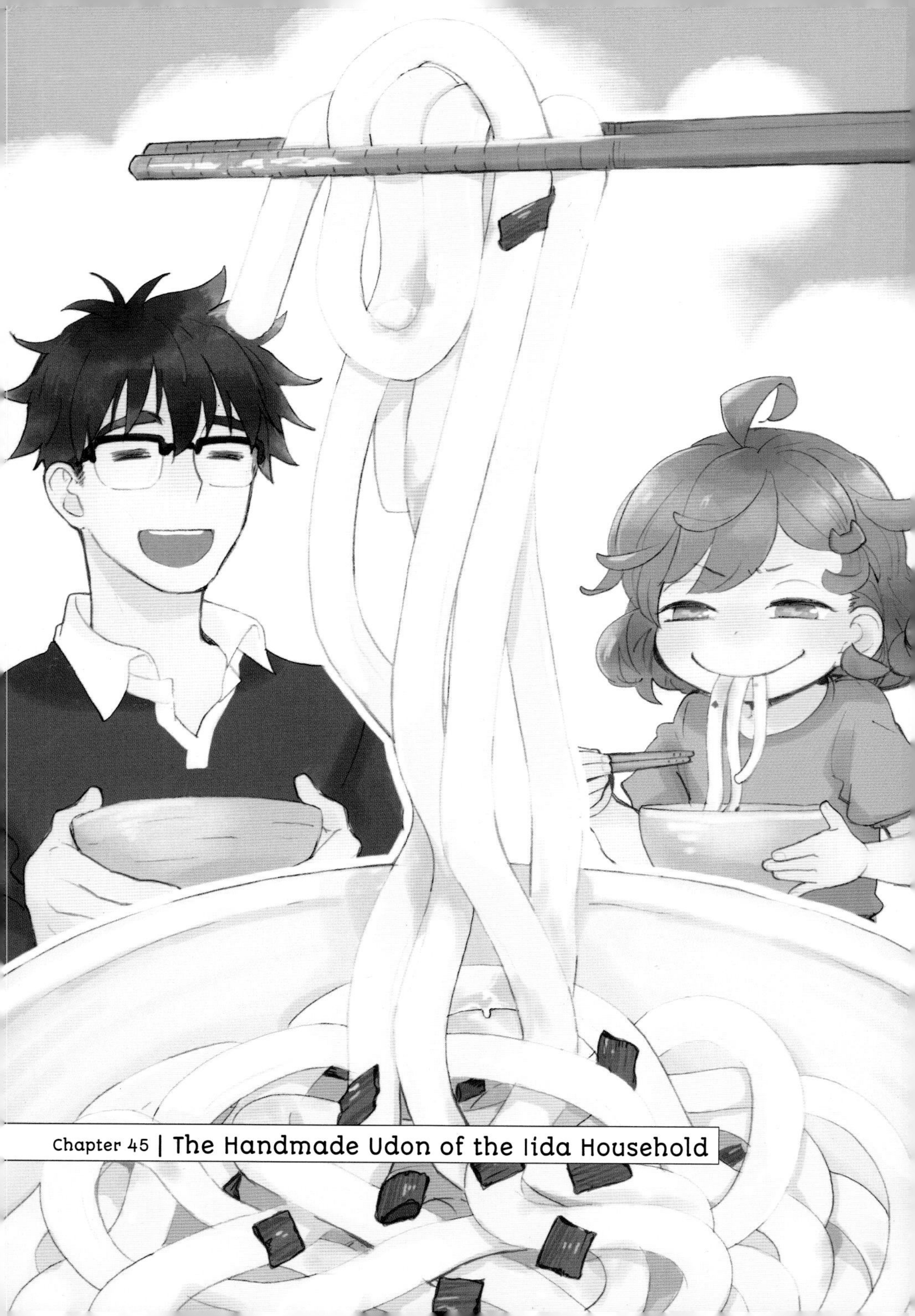

Chapter 45 | The Handmade Udon of the Iida Household

sweetness &
lightning

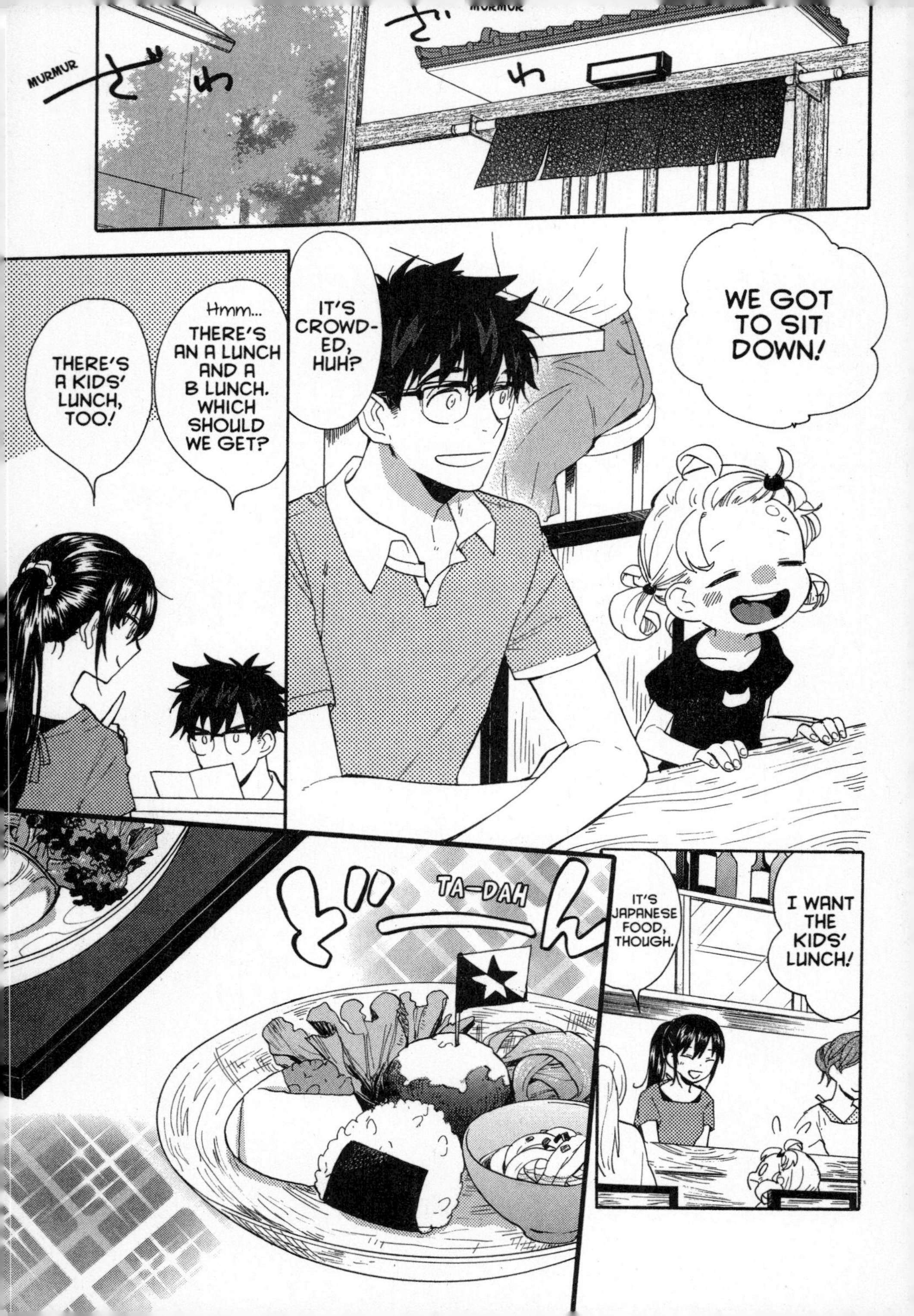
ざわ
MURMUR
ざわ
MURMUR
WE GOT TO SIT DOWN!
IT'S CROWDED, HUH?
Hmm... THERE'S AN A LUNCH AND A B LUNCH. WHICH SHOULD WE GET?
THERE'S A KIDS' LUNCH, TOO!
I WANT THE KIDS' LUNCH!
IT'S JAPANESE FOOD, THOUGH.
どーん
TA-DAH

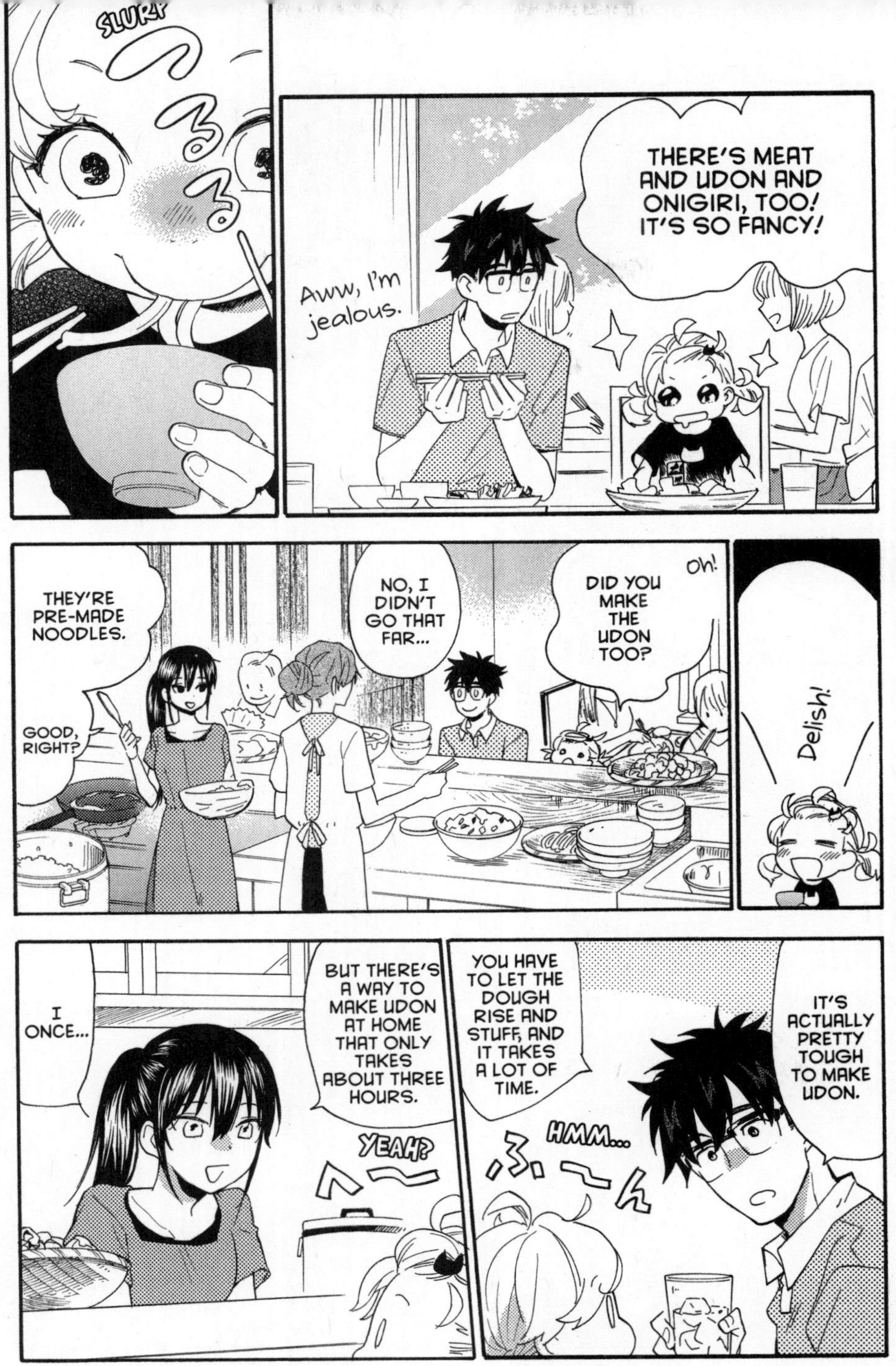
THERE'S MEAT AND UDON AND ONIGIRI, TOO! IT'S SO FANCY!
Aww, I'm jealous.
SLURP
つるる
Delish!
Oh!
DID YOU MAKE THE UDON TOO?
NO, I DIDN'T GO THAT FAR...
THEY'RE PRE-MADE NOODLES.
GOOD, RIGHT?
IT'S ACTUALLY PRETTY TOUGH TO MAKE UDON.
YOU HAVE TO LET THE DOUGH RISE AND STUFF, AND IT TAKES A LOT OF TIME.
HMM...
ふ〜ん
BUT THERE'S A WAY TO MAKE UDON AT HOME THAT ONLY TAKES ABOUT THREE HOURS.
YEAH?
へ〜
I ONCE...

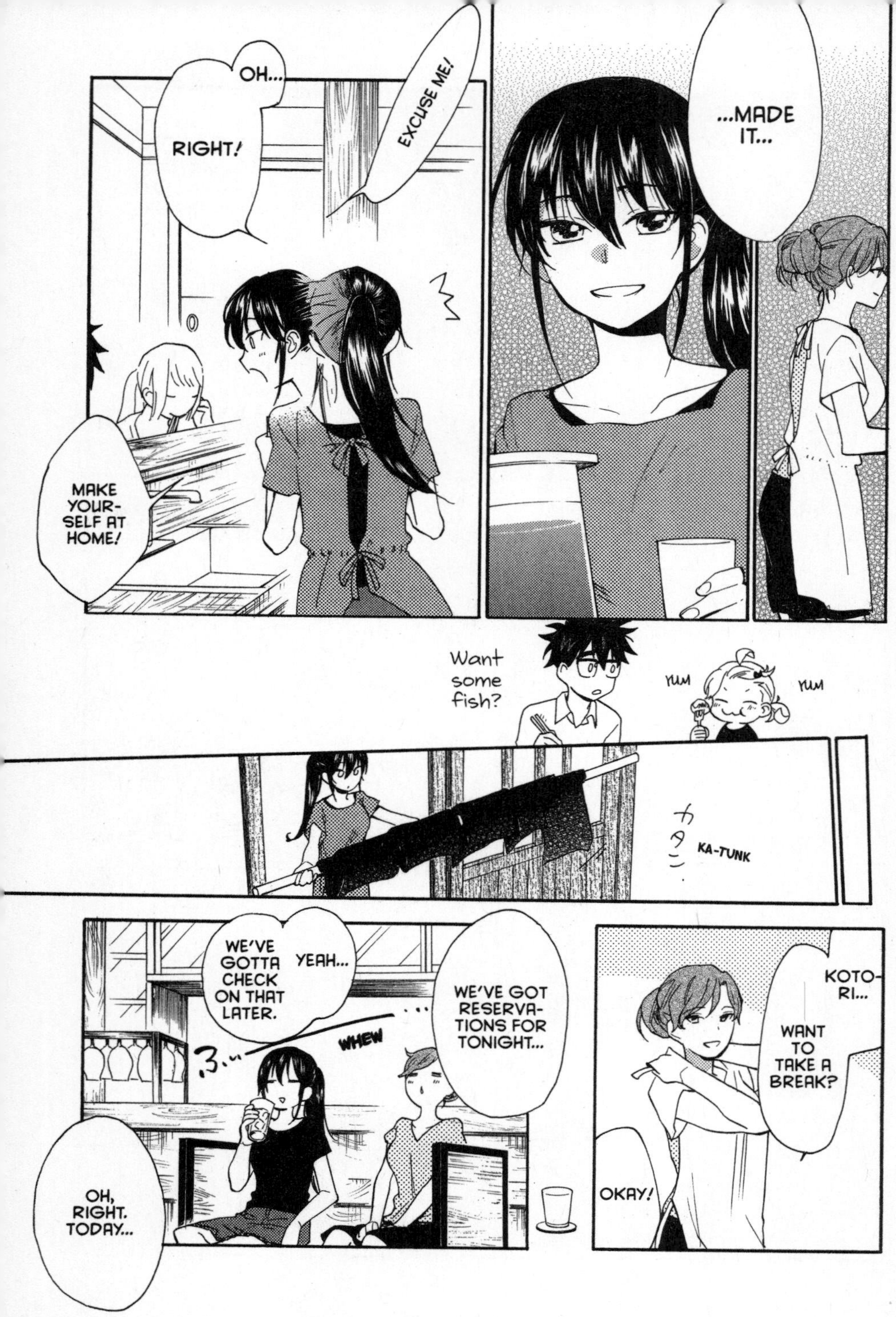
...MADE IT...
EXCUSE ME!
OH... RIGHT!
MAKE YOURSELF AT HOME!
YUM YUM
Want some fish?
カタン
KA-TUNK
KOTORI... WANT TO TAKE A BREAK?
OKAY!
WE'VE GOT RESERVATIONS FOR TONIGHT...
...
YEAH...
WE'VE GOTTA CHECK ON THAT LATER.
WHEW
ふぅ
OH, RIGHT. TODAY...

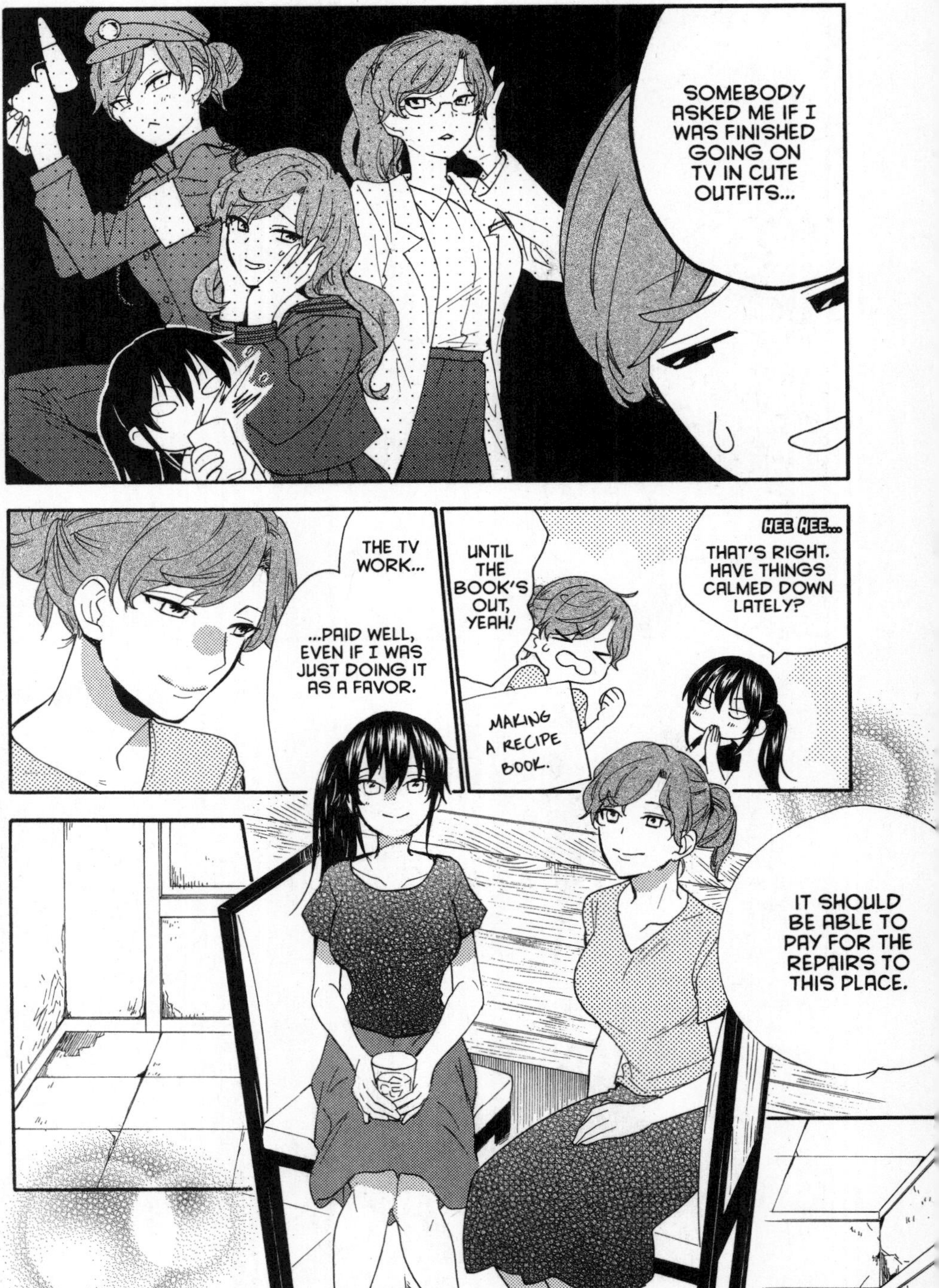
SOMEBODY ASKED ME IF I WAS FINISHED GOING ON TV IN CUTE OUTFITS...
HEE HEE...
THAT'S RIGHT. HAVE THINGS CALMED DOWN LATELY?
UNTIL THE BOOK'S OUT, YEAH!
MAKING A RECIPE BOOK.
THE TV WORK...
...PAID WELL, EVEN IF I WAS JUST DOING IT AS A FAVOR.
IT SHOULD BE ABLE TO PAY FOR THE REPAIRS TO THIS PLACE.

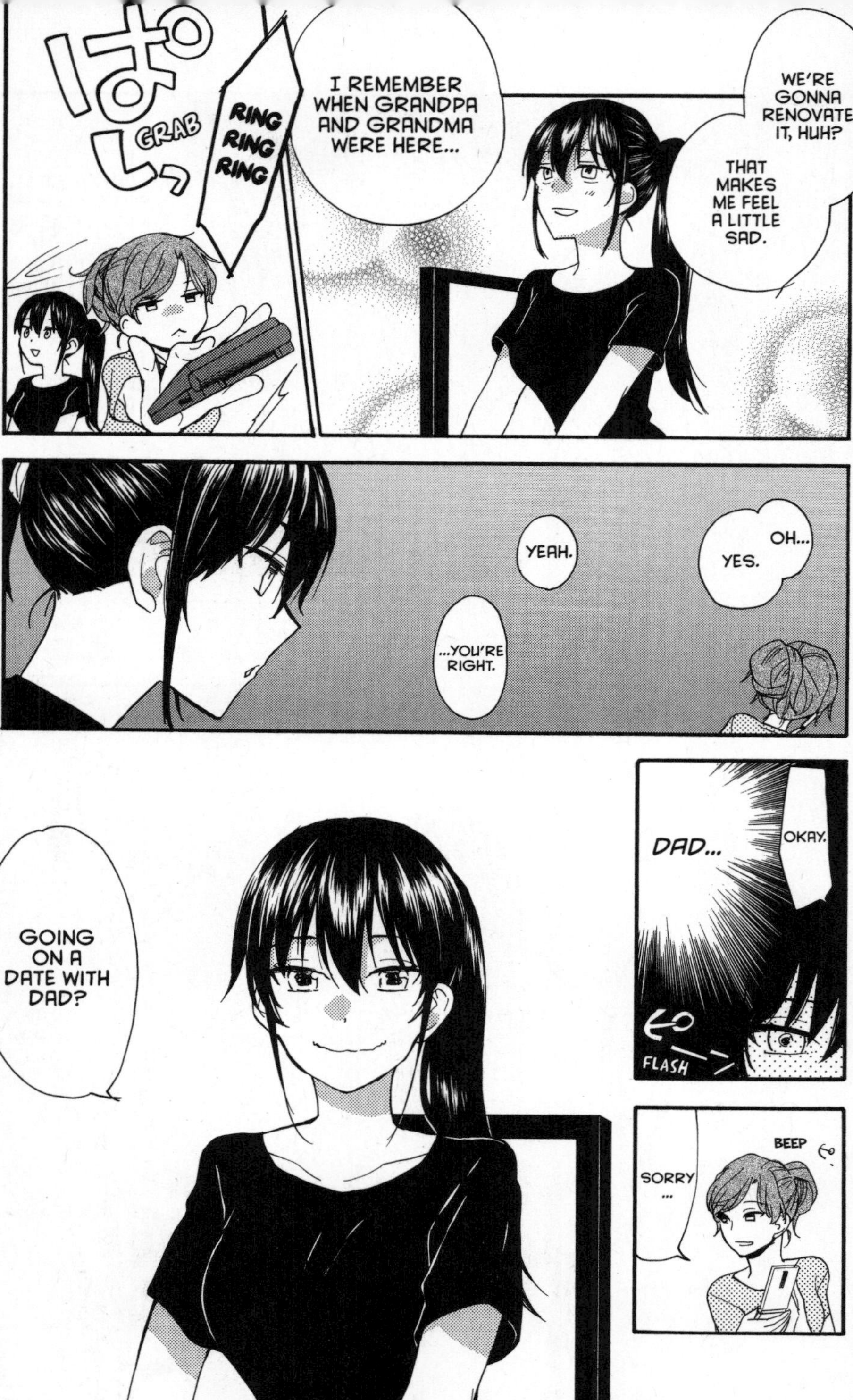
WE'RE GONNA RENOVATE IT, HUH?
THAT MAKES ME FEEL A LITTLE SAD.
I REMEMBER WHEN GRANDPA AND GRANDMA WERE HERE...
RING RING RING
ぱしっ
GRAB
OH... YES.
YEAH.
...YOU'RE RIGHT.
OKAY.
DAD...
FLASH
BEEP
SORRY ...
GOING ON A DATE WITH DAD?

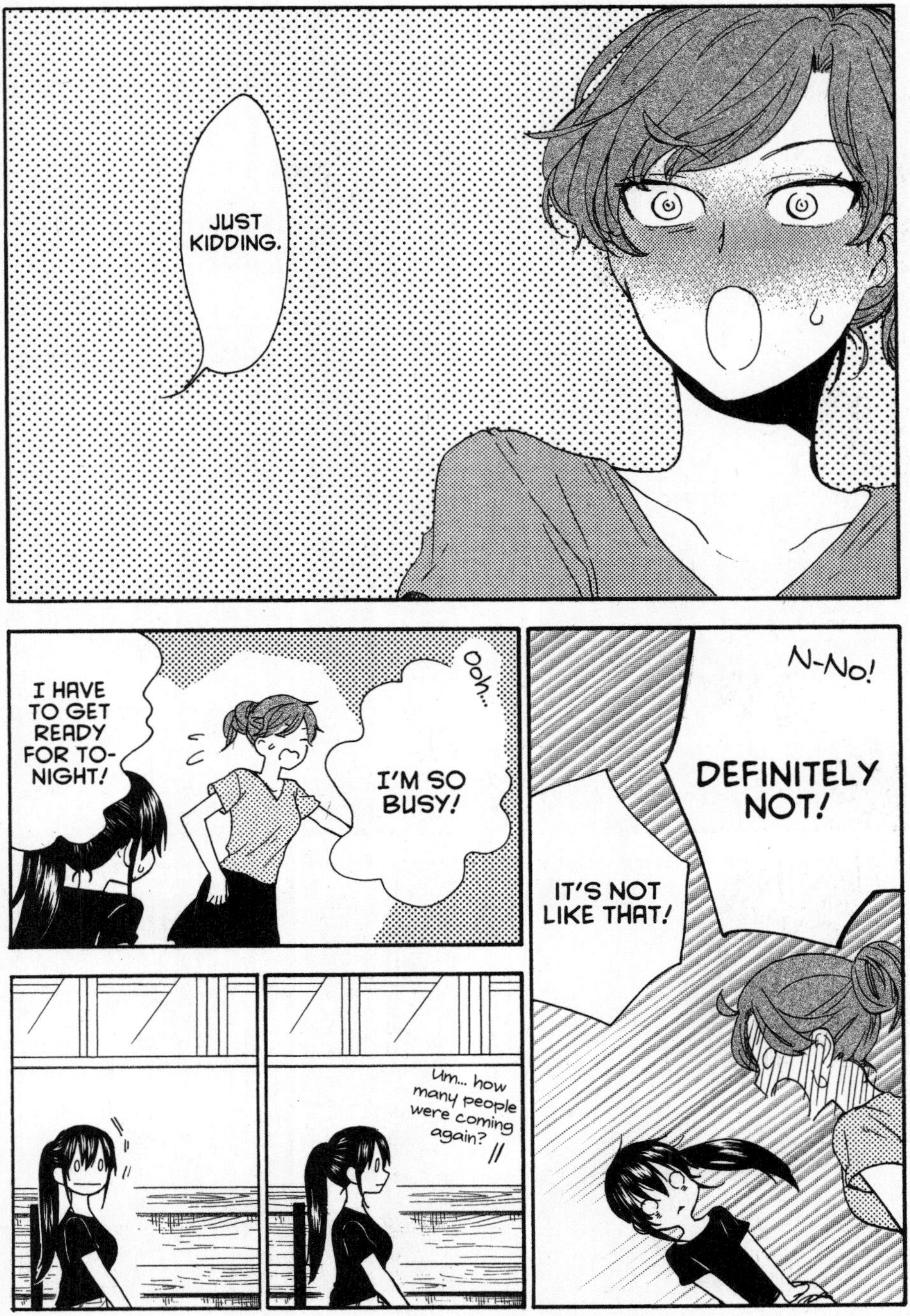
JUST KIDDING.
N-No!
DEFINITELY NOT!
IT'S NOT LIKE THAT!
Ooh...
I'M SO BUSY!
I HAVE TO GET READY FOR TO-NIGHT!
Um... how many people were coming again?

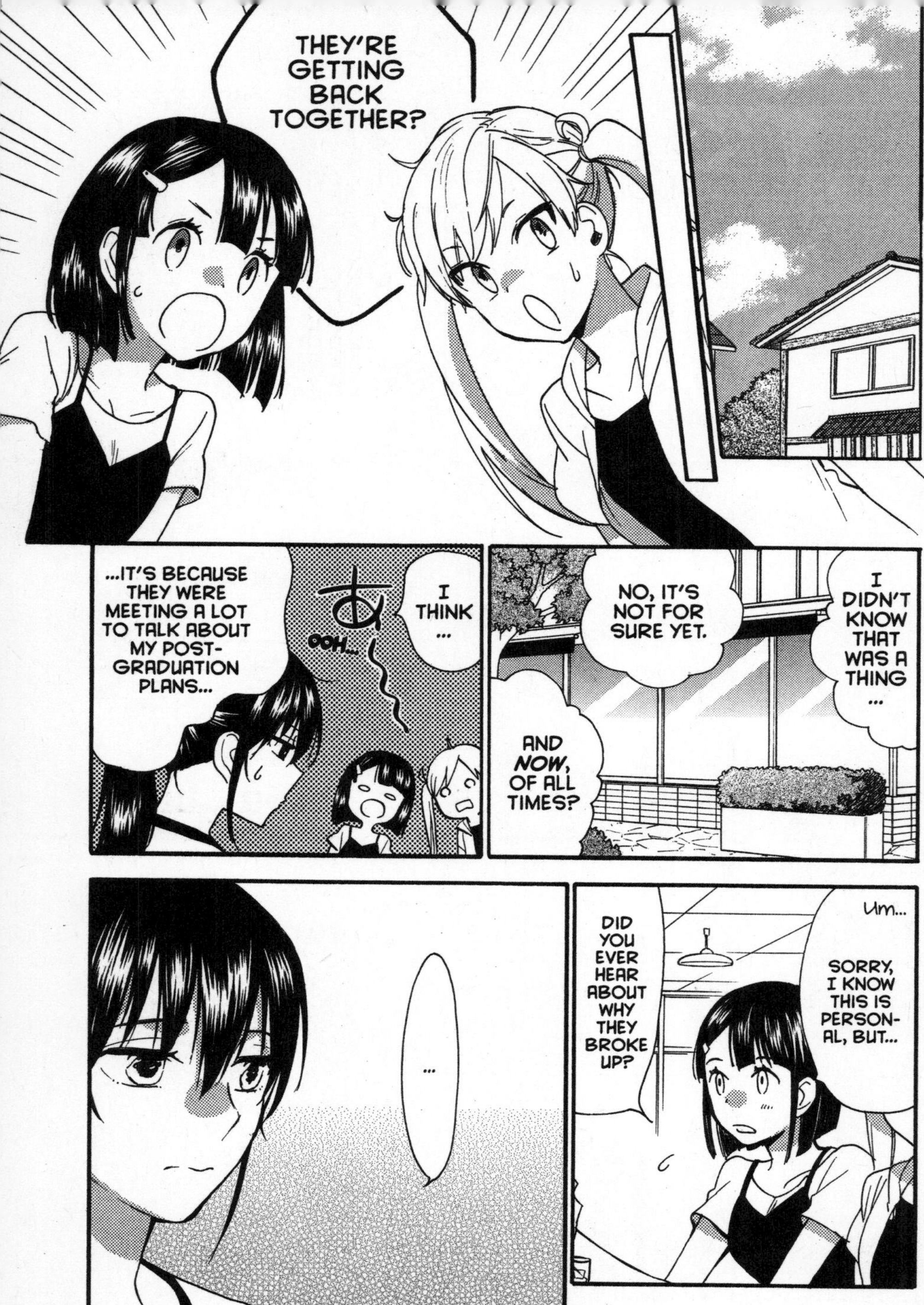
THEY'RE GETTING BACK TOGETHER?
I DIDN'T KNOW THAT WAS A THING...
NO, IT'S NOT FOR SURE YET.
AND *NOW*, OF ALL TIMES?
I THINK...
...IT'S BECAUSE THEY WERE MEETING A LOT TO TALK ABOUT MY POST-GRADUATION PLANS...
OOH...
Um...
SORRY, I KNOW THIS IS PERSONAL, BUT...
DID YOU EVER HEAR ABOUT WHY THEY BROKE UP?
...

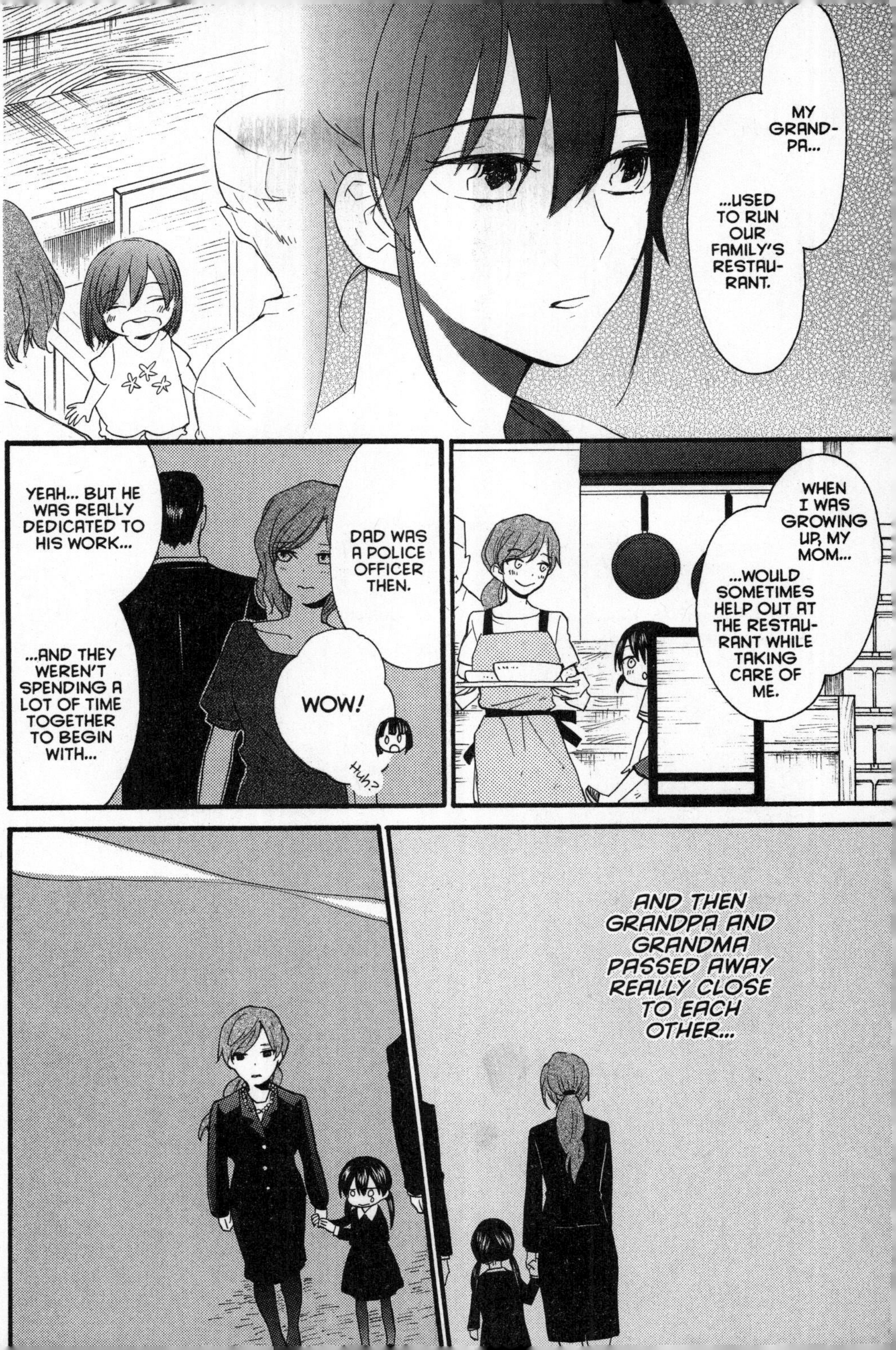
MY GRANDPA...
...USED TO RUN OUR FAMILY'S RESTAURANT.
WHEN I WAS GROWING UP, MY MOM...
...WOULD SOMETIMES HELP OUT AT THE RESTAURANT WHILE TAKING CARE OF ME.
DAD WAS A POLICE OFFICER THEN.
WOW!
Huh?
YEAH... BUT HE WAS REALLY DEDICATED TO HIS WORK...
...AND THEY WEREN'T SPENDING A LOT OF TIME TOGETHER TO BEGIN WITH...
AND THEN GRANDPA AND GRANDMA PASSED AWAY REALLY CLOSE TO EACH OTHER...

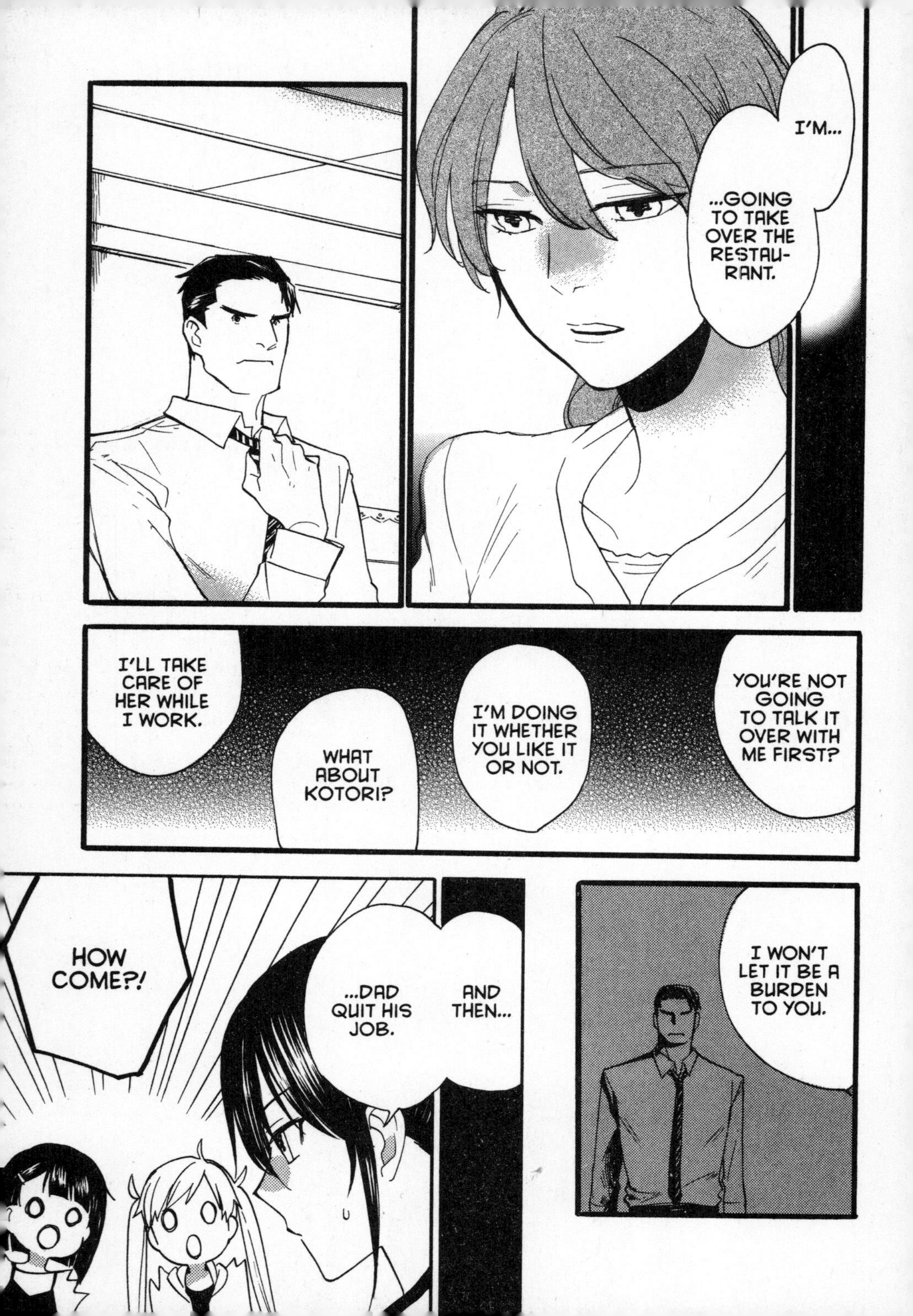
I'M...
...GOING TO TAKE OVER THE RESTAU-RANT.
YOU'RE NOT GOING TO TALK IT OVER WITH ME FIRST?
I'M DOING IT WHETHER YOU LIKE IT OR NOT.
WHAT ABOUT KOTORI?
I'LL TAKE CARE OF HER WHILE I WORK.
I WON'T LET IT BE A BURDEN TO YOU.
AND THEN...
...DAD QUIT HIS JOB.
HOW COME?!

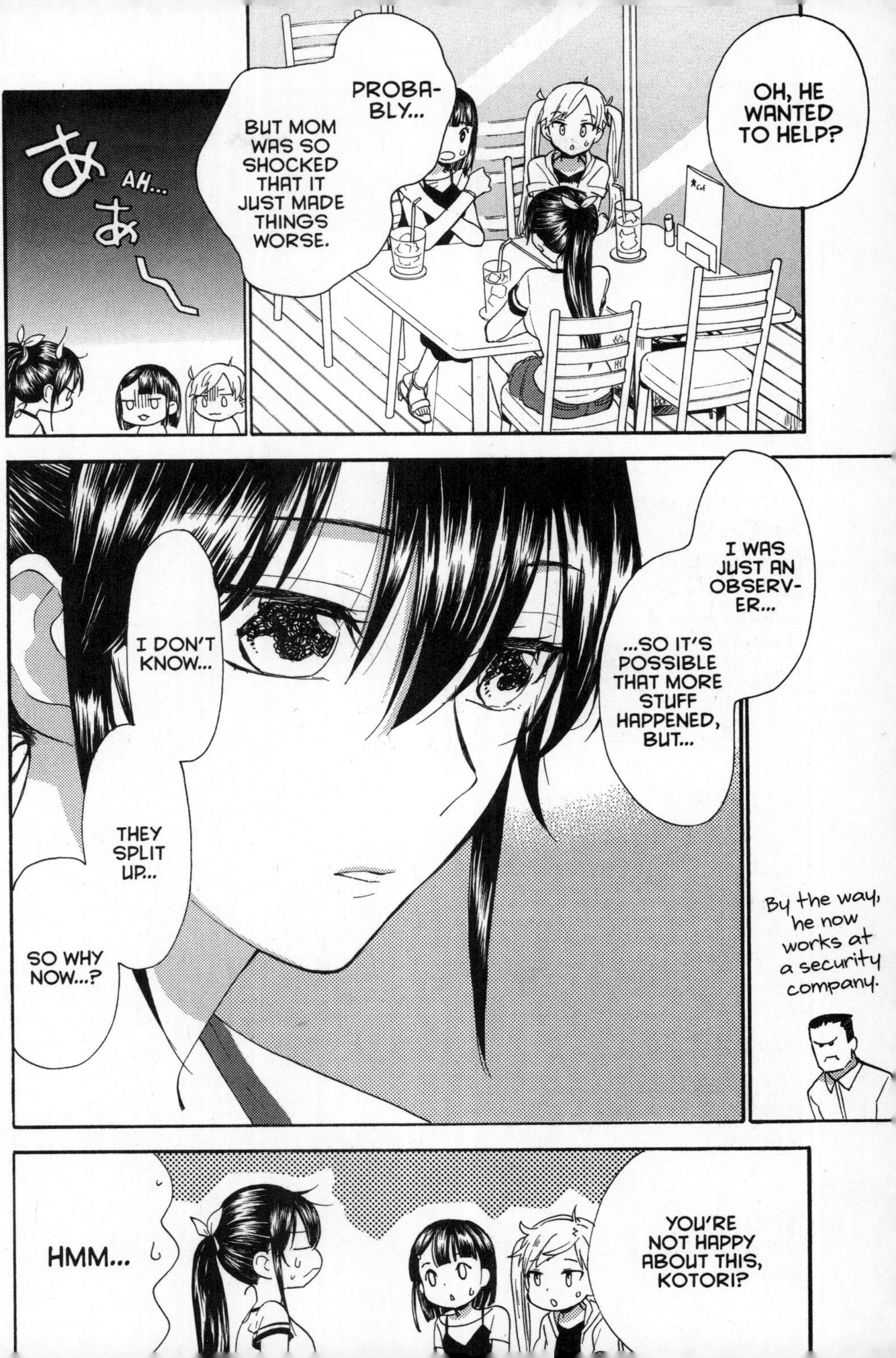
OH, HE WANTED TO HELP?
PROBA-BLY...
BUT MOM WAS SO SHOCKED THAT IT JUST MADE THINGS WORSE.
あぁ～
AH...
By the way, he now works at a security company.
I WAS JUST AN OBSERVER-ER...
...SO IT'S POSSIBLE THAT MORE STUFF HAPPENED, BUT...
I DON'T KNOW...
THEY SPLIT UP...
SO WHY NOW...?
YOU'RE NOT HAPPY ABOUT THIS, KOTORI?
HMM...

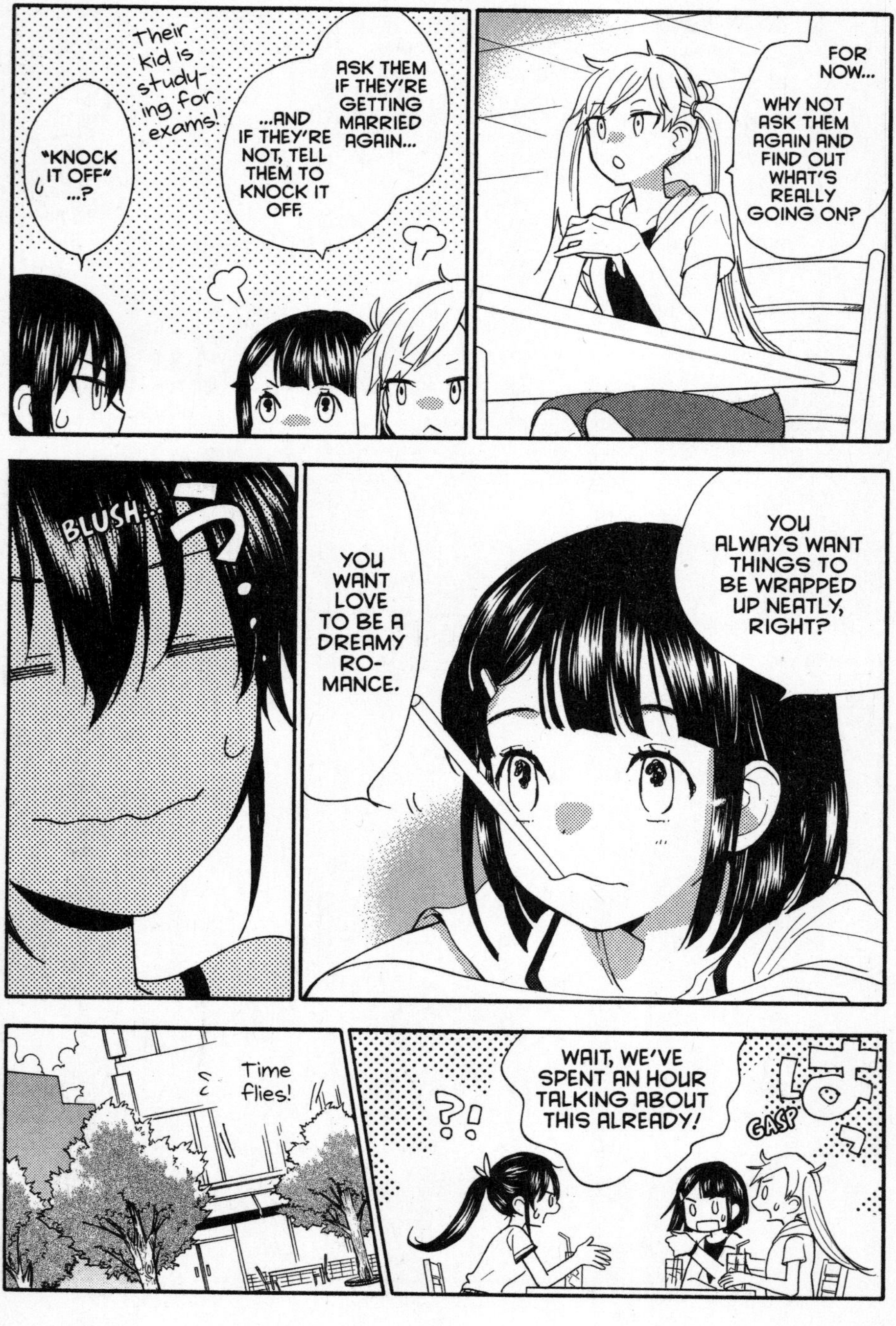
FOR NOW...
WHY NOT ASK THEM AGAIN AND FIND OUT WHAT'S REALLY GOING ON?
ASK THEM IF THEY'RE GETTING MARRIED AGAIN...
...AND IF THEY'RE NOT, TELL THEM TO KNOCK IT OFF.
Their kid is study-ing for exams!
"KNOCK IT OFF" ...?
YOU ALWAYS WANT THINGS TO BE WRAPPED UP NEATLY, RIGHT?
YOU WANT LOVE TO BE A DREAMY RO-MANCE.
BLUSH...
GASP
WAIT, WE'VE SPENT AN HOUR TALKING ABOUT THIS ALREADY!
?!
Time flies!

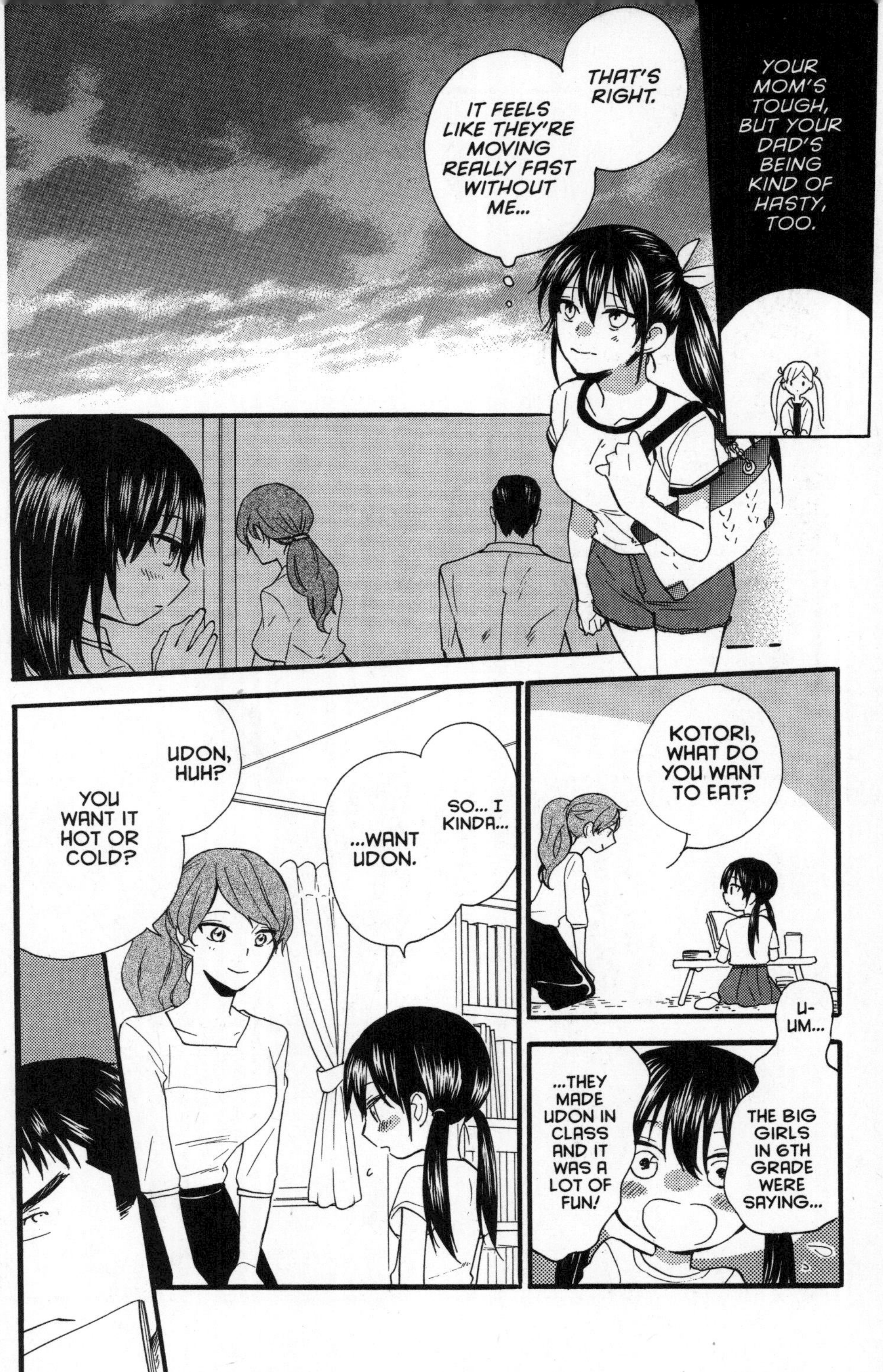
YOUR MOM'S TOUGH, BUT YOUR DAD'S BEING KIND OF HASTY, TOO.
THAT'S RIGHT.
IT FEELS LIKE THEY'RE MOVING REALLY FAST WITHOUT ME...
KOTORI, WHAT DO YOU WANT TO EAT?
U-UM...
THE BIG GIRLS IN 6TH GRADE WERE SAYING...
...THEY MADE UDON IN CLASS AND IT WAS A LOT OF FUN!
SO... I KINDA...
...WANT UDON.
UDON, HUH?
YOU WANT IT HOT OR COLD?

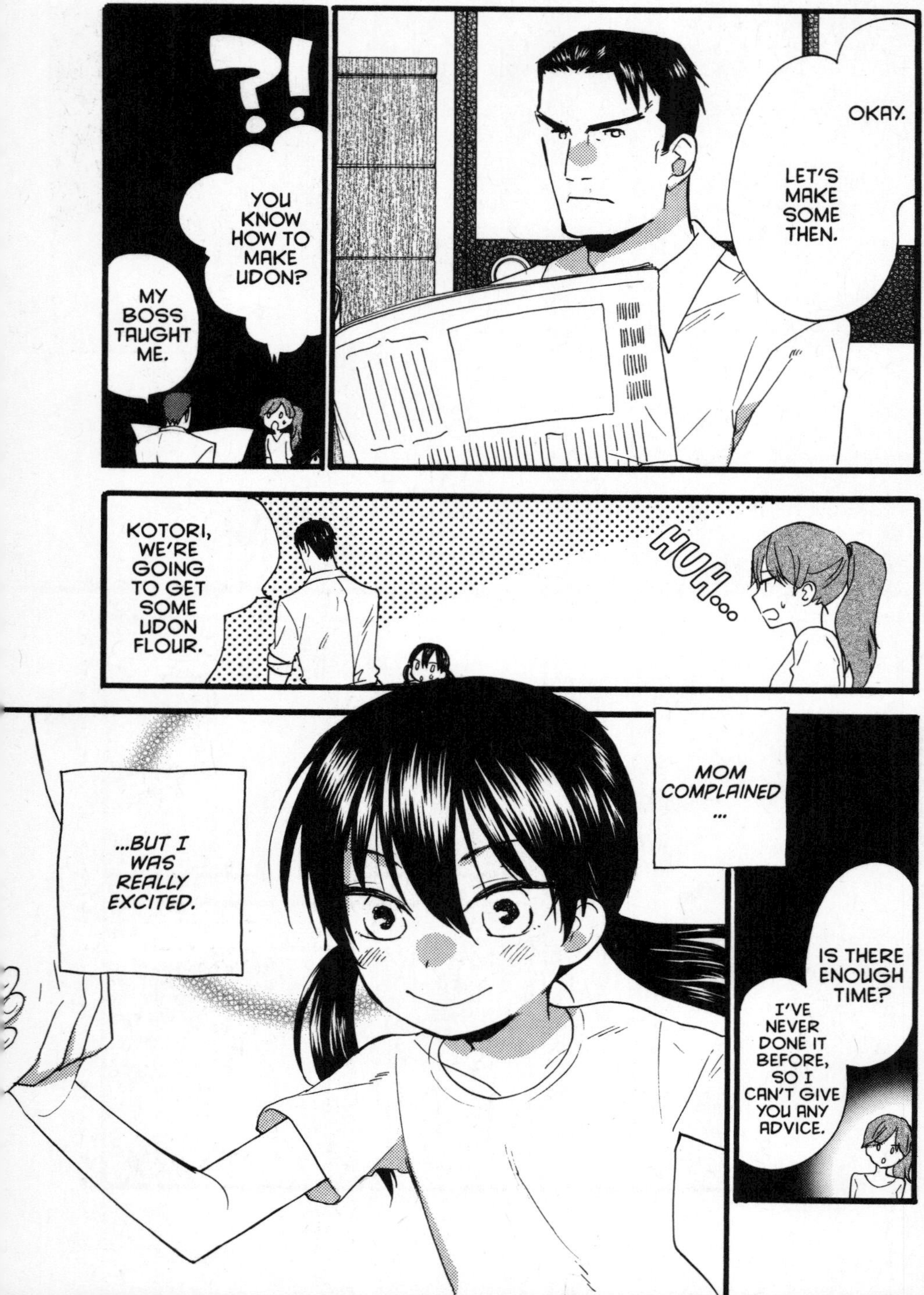
OKAY.
LET'S MAKE SOME THEN.
?!
YOU KNOW HOW TO MAKE UDON?
MY BOSS TAUGHT ME.
HUH...
KOTORI, WE'RE GOING TO GET SOME UDON FLOUR.
MOM COMPLAINED ...
IS THERE ENOUGH TIME?
I'VE NEVER DONE IT BEFORE, SO I CAN'T GIVE YOU ANY ADVICE.
...BUT I WAS REALLY EXCITED.

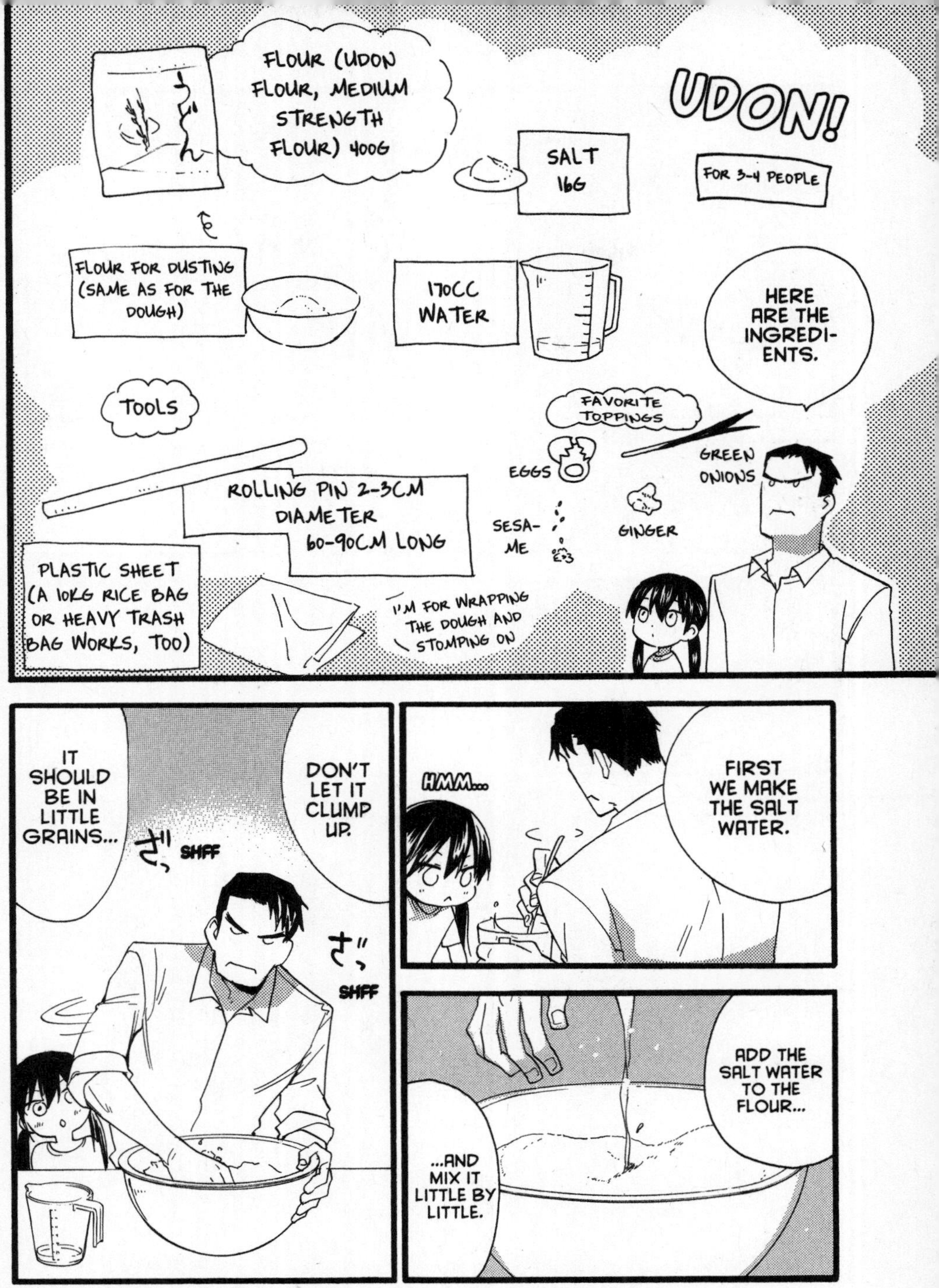
UDON!
FOR 3-4 PEOPLE
HERE ARE THE INGREDI-ENTS.
SALT 16G
FLOUR (UDON FLOUR, MEDIUM STRENGTH FLOUR) 400G
FAVORITE TOPPINGS
GREEN ONIONS
EGGS
GINGER
SESA-ME
170CC WATER
FLOUR FOR DUSTING (SAME AS FOR THE DOUGH)
TOOLS
ROLLING PIN 2-3CM DIAMETER 60-90CM LONG
I'M FOR WRAPPING THE DOUGH AND STOMPING ON
PLASTIC SHEET (A 10KG RICE BAG OR HEAVY TRASH BAG WORKS, TOO)
FIRST WE MAKE THE SALT WATER.
HMM...
ADD THE SALT WATER TO THE FLOUR...
...AND MIX IT LITTLE BY LITTLE.
DON'T LET IT CLUMP UP.
IT SHOULD BE IN LITTLE GRAINS...
SHFF
SHFF

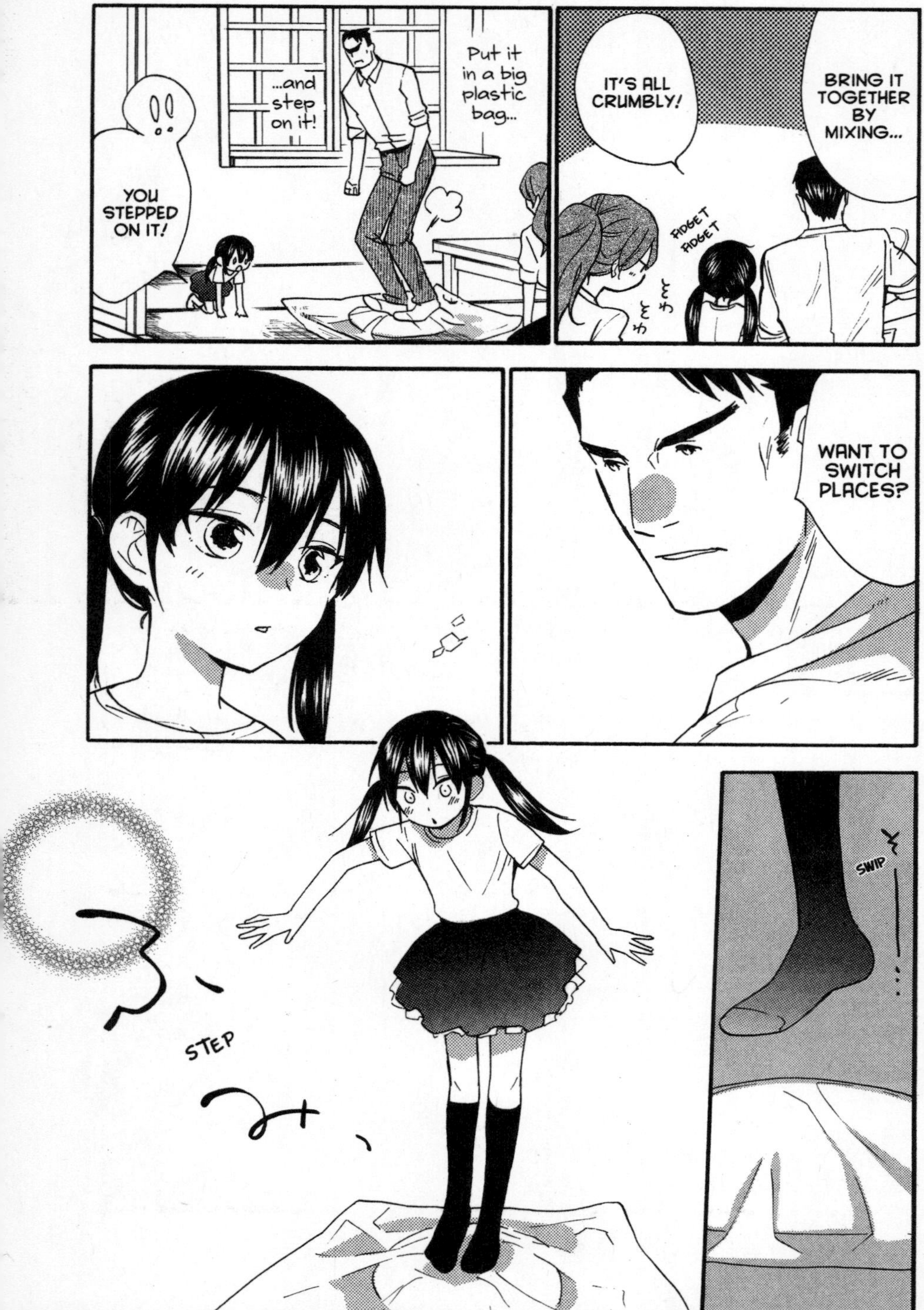
BRING IT TOGETHER BY MIXING...
IT'S ALL CRUMBLY!
FIDGET FIDGET
Put it in a big plastic bag...
...and step on it!
!!
YOU STEPPED ON IT!
WANT TO SWITCH PLACES?
SWIP
STEP

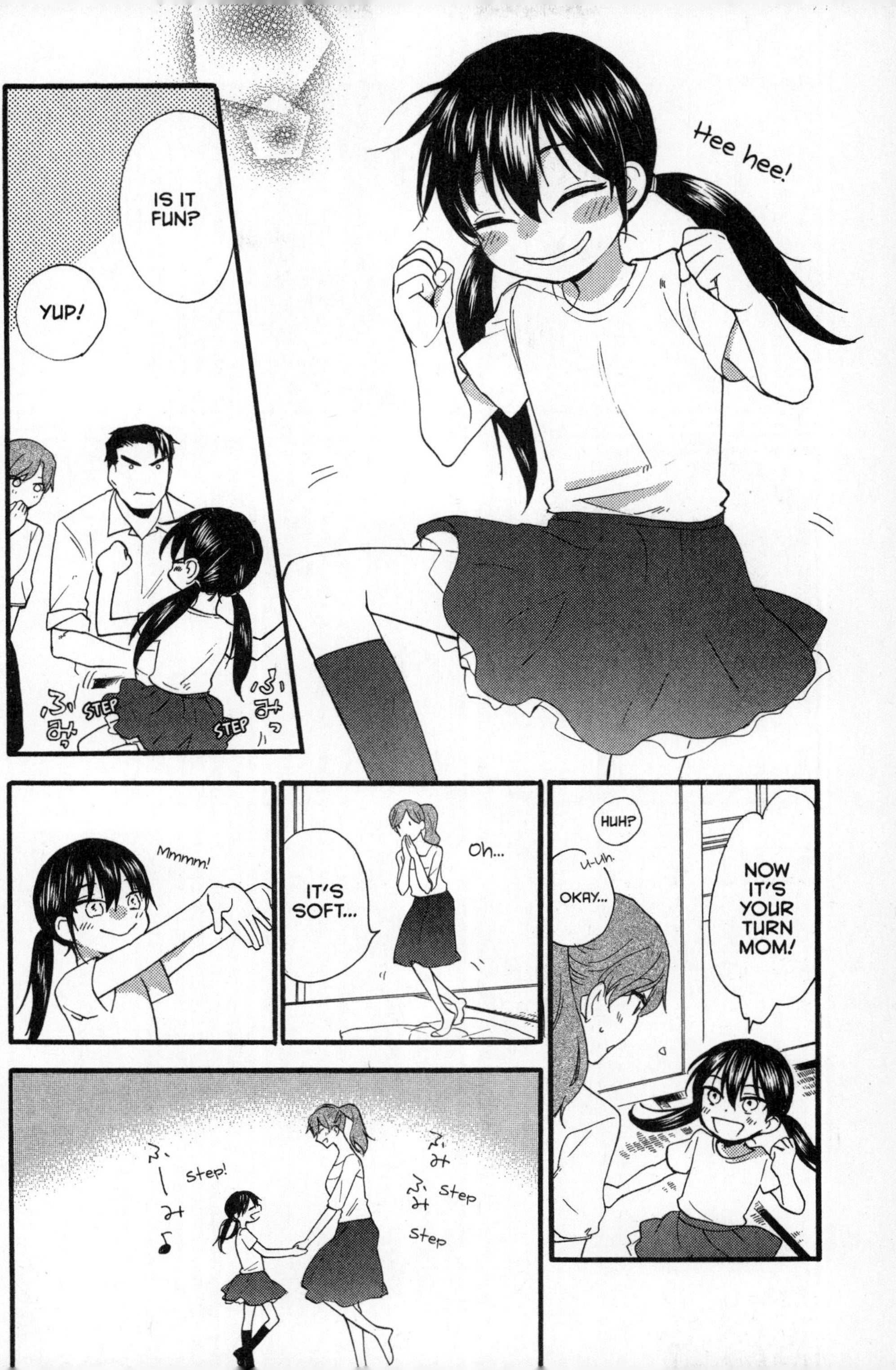
Hee hee!
IS IT FUN?
YUP!
ふみ
STEP
STEP
ふみ
NOW IT'S YOUR TURN MOM!
HUH?
U-UH.
OKAY...
Oh...
IT'S SOFT...
Mmmm!
ふみ
step
ふみ
step
ふーみ♪
step!

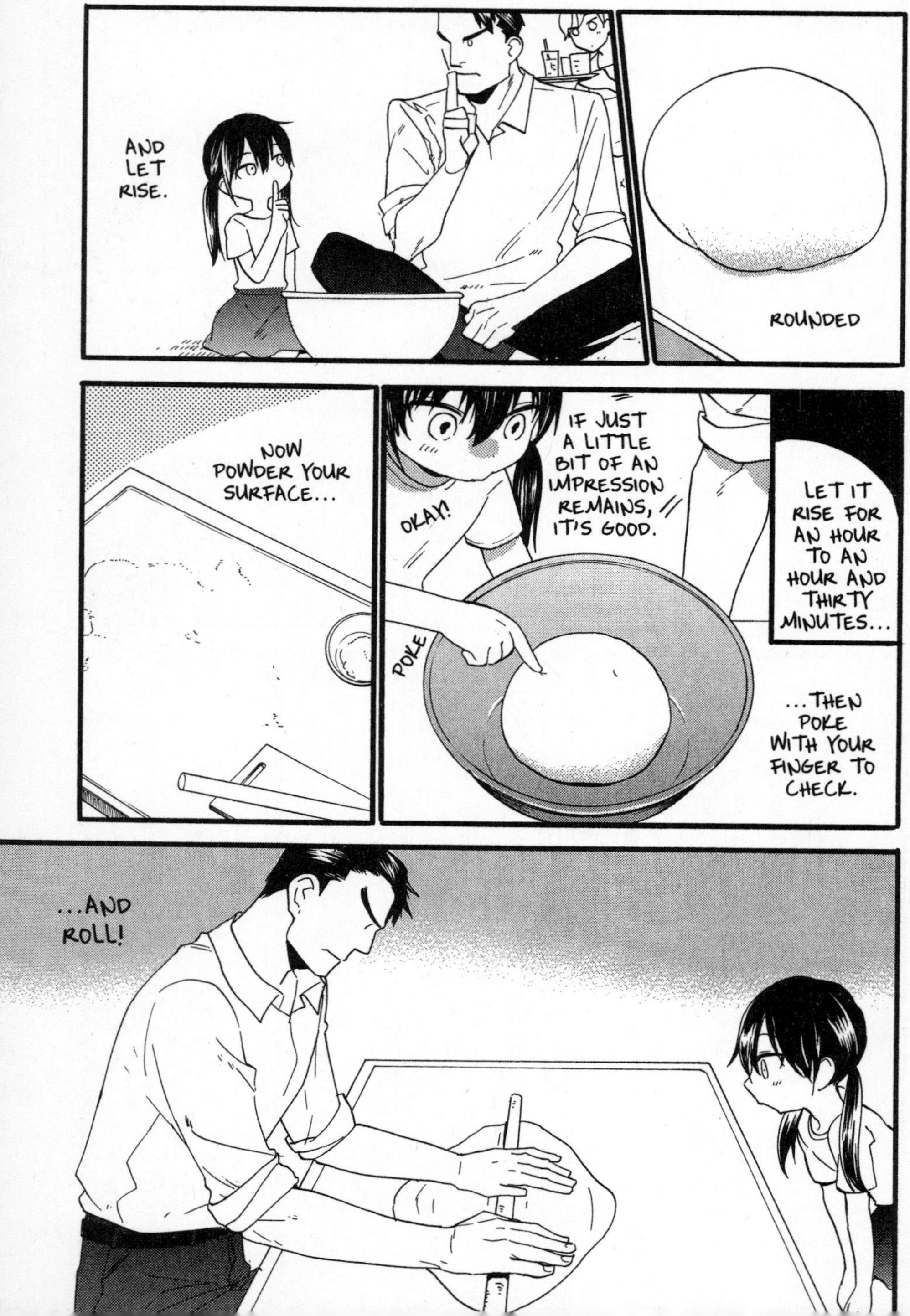
ROUNDED
AND LET RISE.
LET IT RISE FOR AN HOUR TO AN HOUR AND THIRTY MINUTES...
...THEN POKE WITH YOUR FINGER TO CHECK.
IF JUST A LITTLE BIT OF AN IMPRESSION REMAINS, IT'S GOOD.
OKAY!
POKE
NOW POWDER YOUR SURFACE...
...AND ROLL!

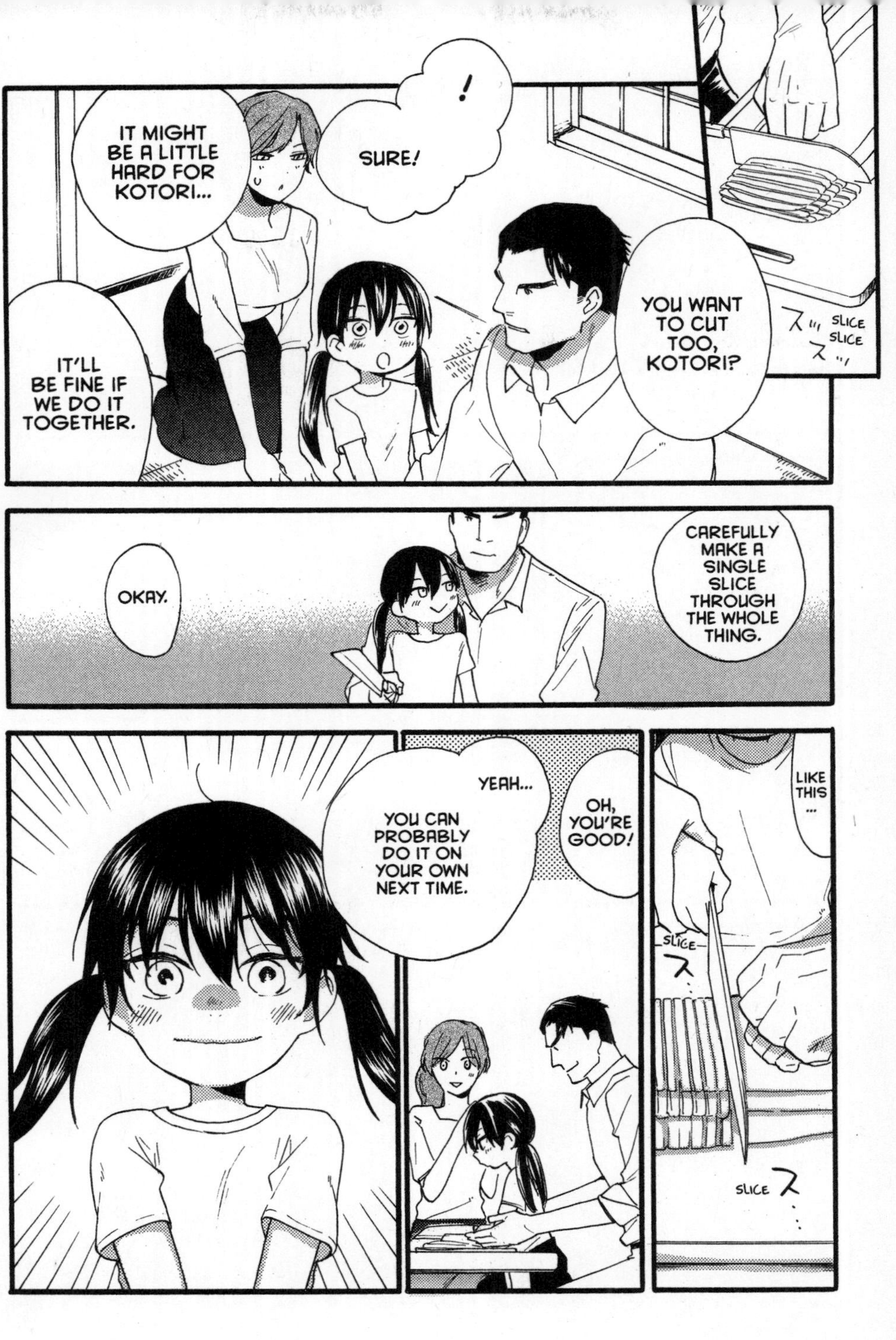
ス SLICE
ス SLICE
YOU WANT TO CUT TOO, KOTORI?
!
SURE!
IT MIGHT BE A LITTLE HARD FOR KOTORI...
IT'LL BE FINE IF WE DO IT TOGETHER.
CAREFULLY MAKE A SINGLE SLICE THROUGH THE WHOLE THING.
OKAY.
LIKE THIS...
SLICE ス...
SLICE ス...
OH, YOU'RE GOOD!
YEAH...
YOU CAN PROBABLY DO IT ON YOUR OWN NEXT TIME.

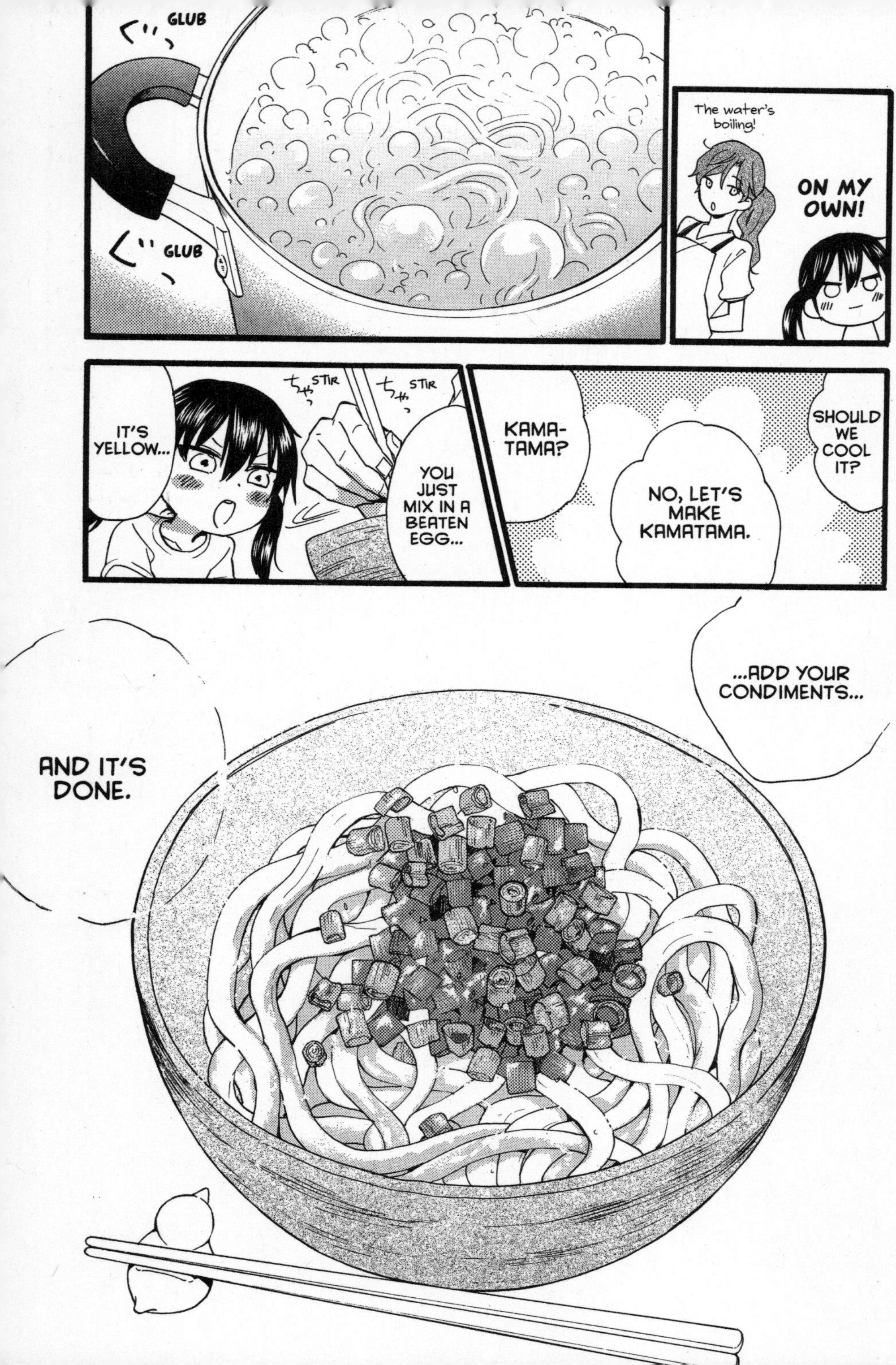
The water's boiling!
ON MY OWN!
GLUB
GLUB
SHOULD WE COOL IT?
NO, LET'S MAKE KAMATAMA.
KAMA-TAMA?
YOU JUST MIX IN A BEATEN EGG...
STIR
STIR
IT'S YELLOW...
...ADD YOUR CONDIMENTS...
AND IT'S DONE.

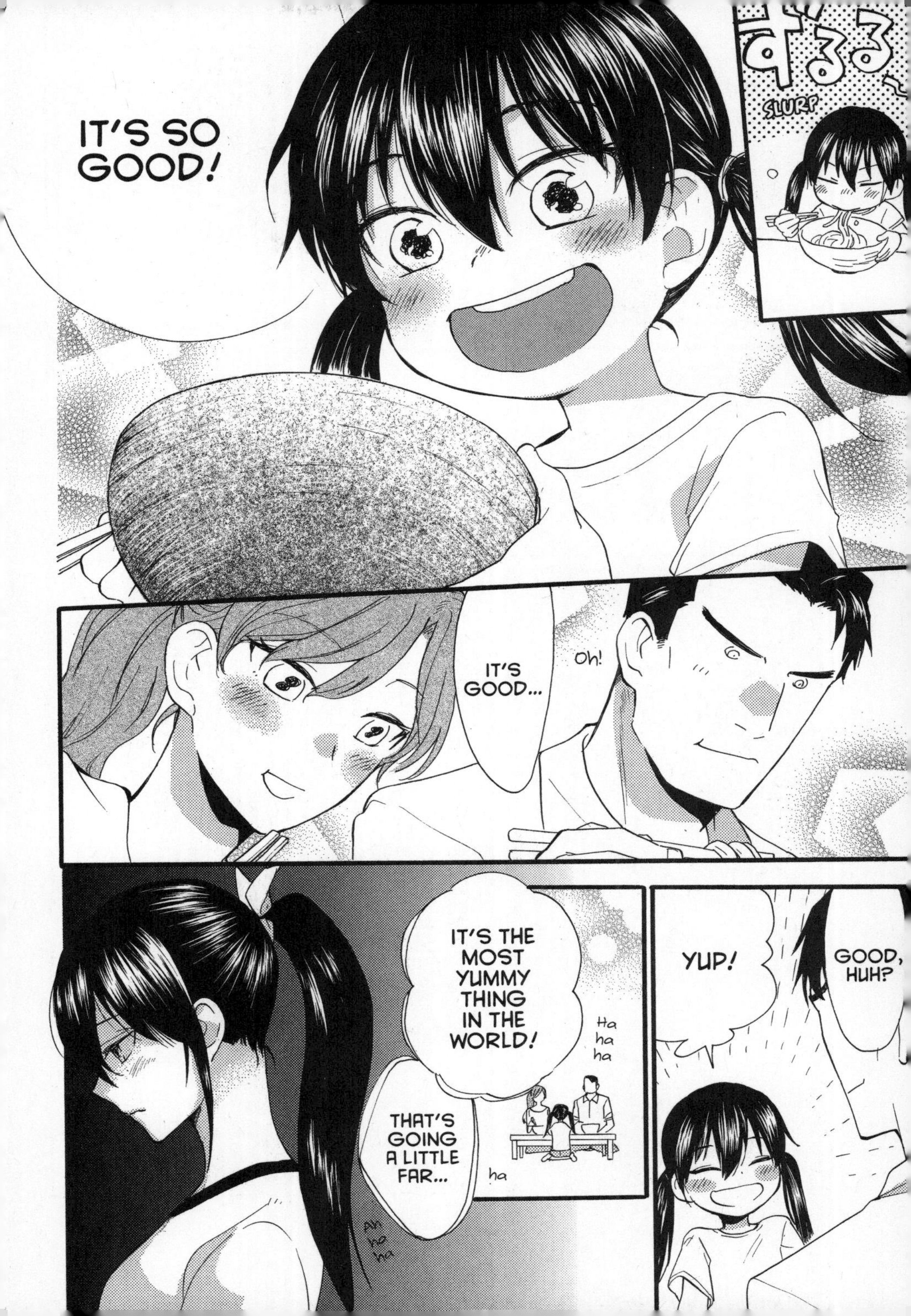
ずるる
SLURP
IT'S SO GOOD!
Oh!
IT'S GOOD...
GOOD, HUH?
YUP!
IT'S THE MOST YUMMY THING IN THE WORLD!
Ha ha ha
THAT'S GOING A LITTLE FAR...
ha
Ah ha ha

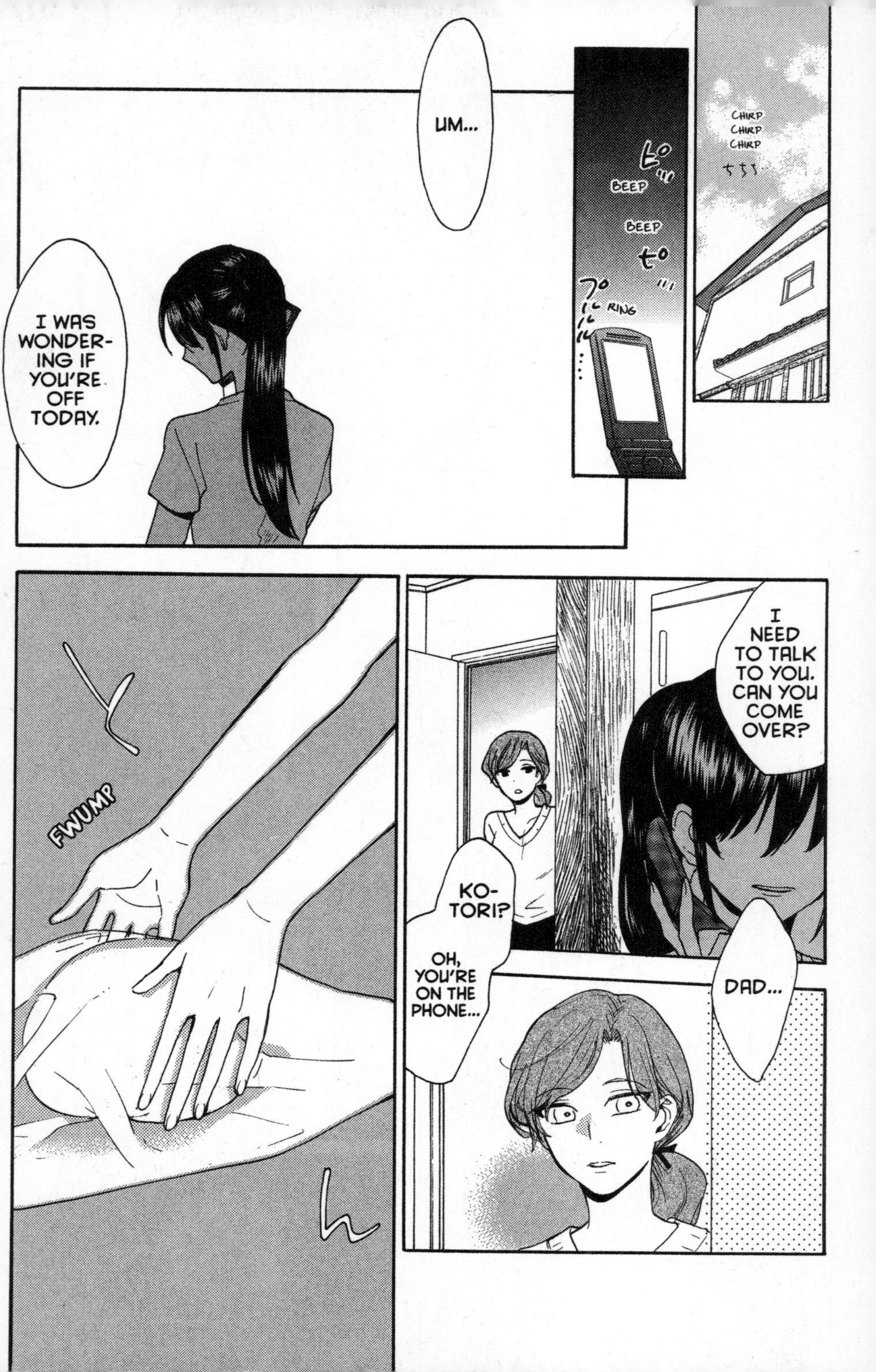
CHIRP
CHIRP
CHIRP
BEEP
BEEP
RING
UM...
I WAS WONDERING IF YOU'RE OFF TODAY.
I NEED TO TALK TO YOU. CAN YOU COME OVER?
KO-TORI?
DAD...
OH, YOU'RE ON THE PHONE...
FWUMP

HOOONK

I'M MAKING UDON.

RATTLE

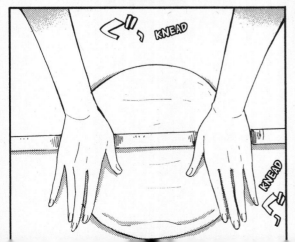

KNEAD

KNEAD

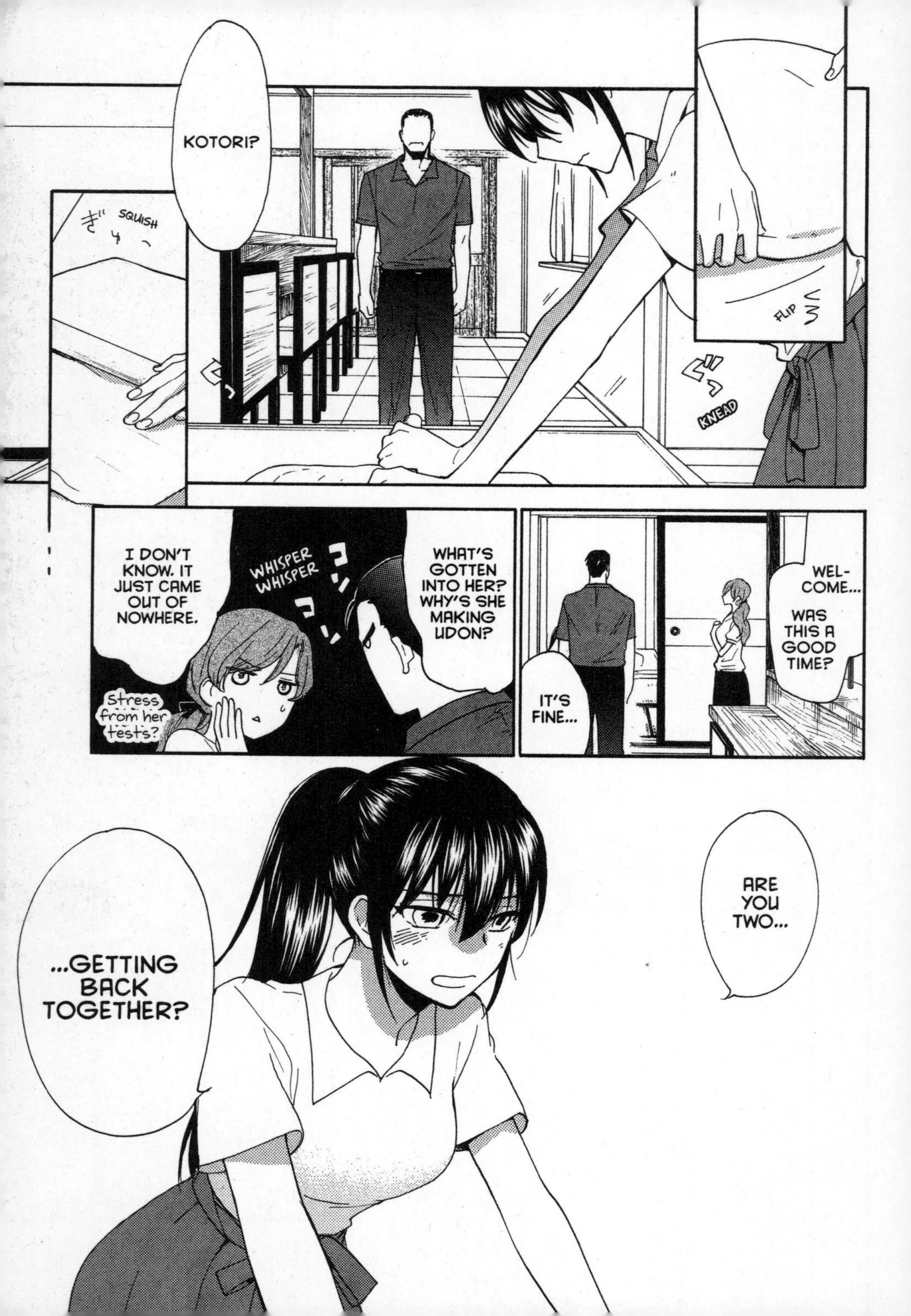
FLIP
KOTORI?
KNEAD
SQUISH
WEL-COME... WAS THIS A GOOD TIME?
IT'S FINE...
WHAT'S GOTTEN INTO HER? WHY'S SHE MAKING UDON?
WHISPER WHISPER
I DON'T KNOW. IT JUST CAME OUT OF NOWHERE.
Stress from her tests?
ARE YOU TWO...
...GETTING BACK TOGETHER?

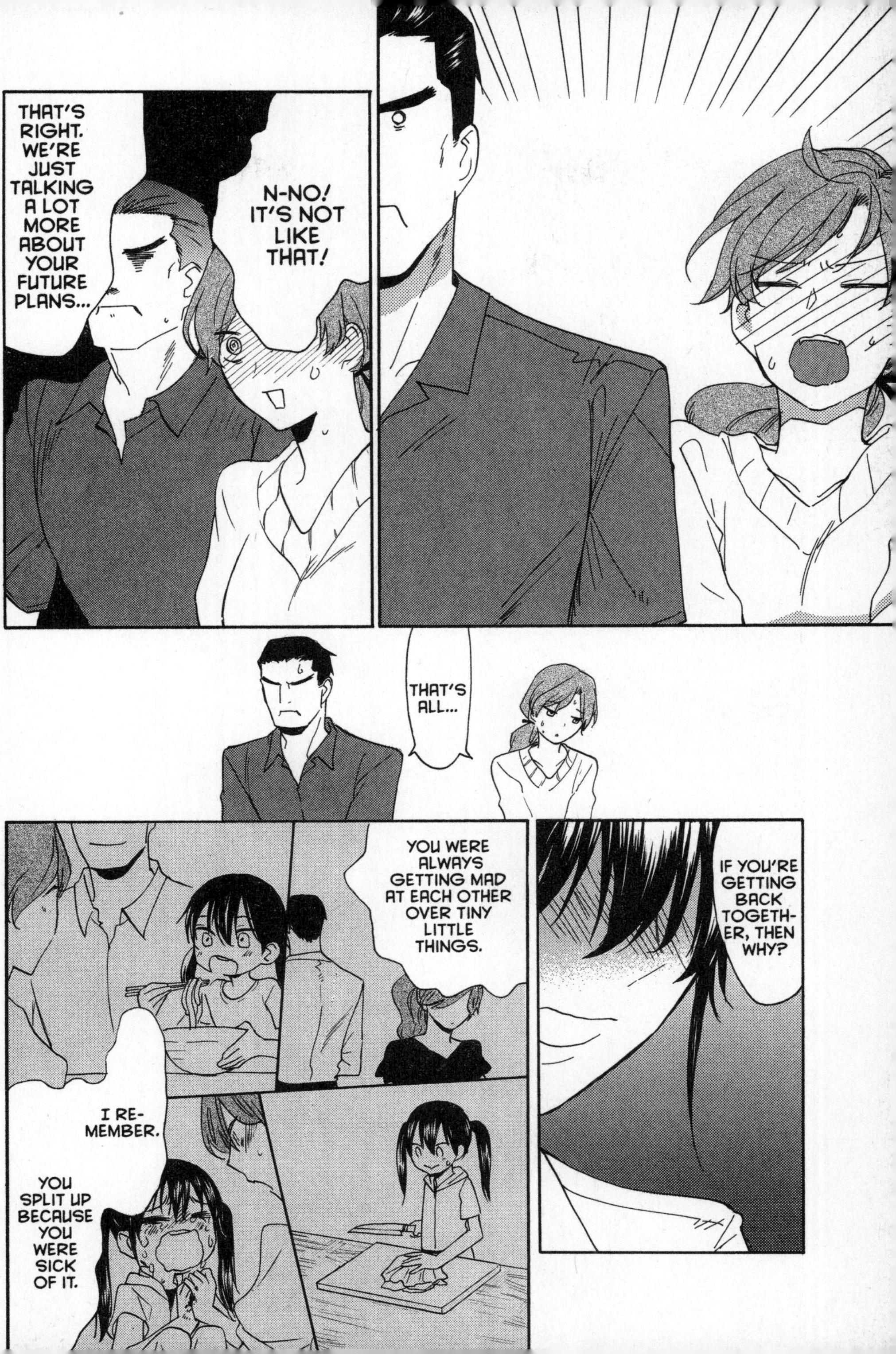
N-NO! IT'S NOT LIKE THAT!
THAT'S RIGHT. WE'RE JUST TALKING A LOT MORE ABOUT YOUR FUTURE PLANS...
THAT'S ALL...
IF YOU'RE GETTING BACK TOGETHER, THEN WHY?
YOU WERE ALWAYS GETTING MAD AT EACH OTHER OVER TINY LITTLE THINGS.
I REMEMBER.
YOU SPLIT UP BECAUSE YOU WERE SICK OF IT.

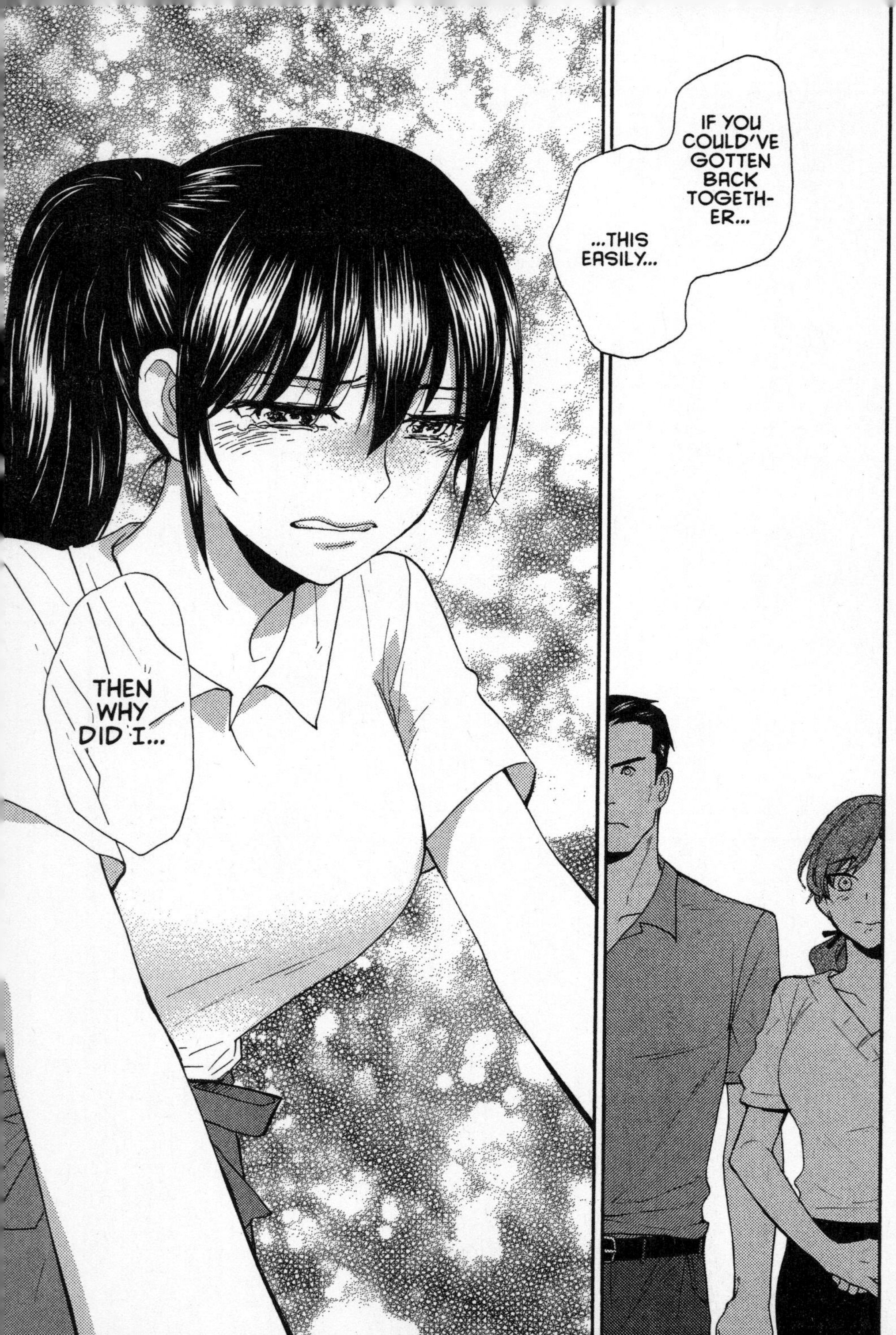
IF YOU COULD'VE GOTTEN BACK TOGETH-ER...
...THIS EASILY...
THEN WHY DID I...

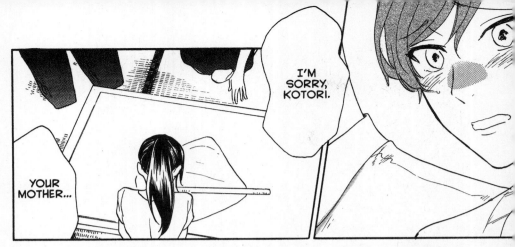

I'M SORRY, KOTORI.

YOUR MOTHER...

I...

HE WAS THE ONE PERSON I JUST COULDN'T GET ALONG WITH.

...

FEELINGS I COULD CONTROL WITH OTHER PEOPLE...

...I COULDN'T CONTROL WITH HIM, AND I GOT SO FRUSTRATED...

I TURNED INTO THIS AWFUL PERSON...

...AND I HATED IT SO MUCH...

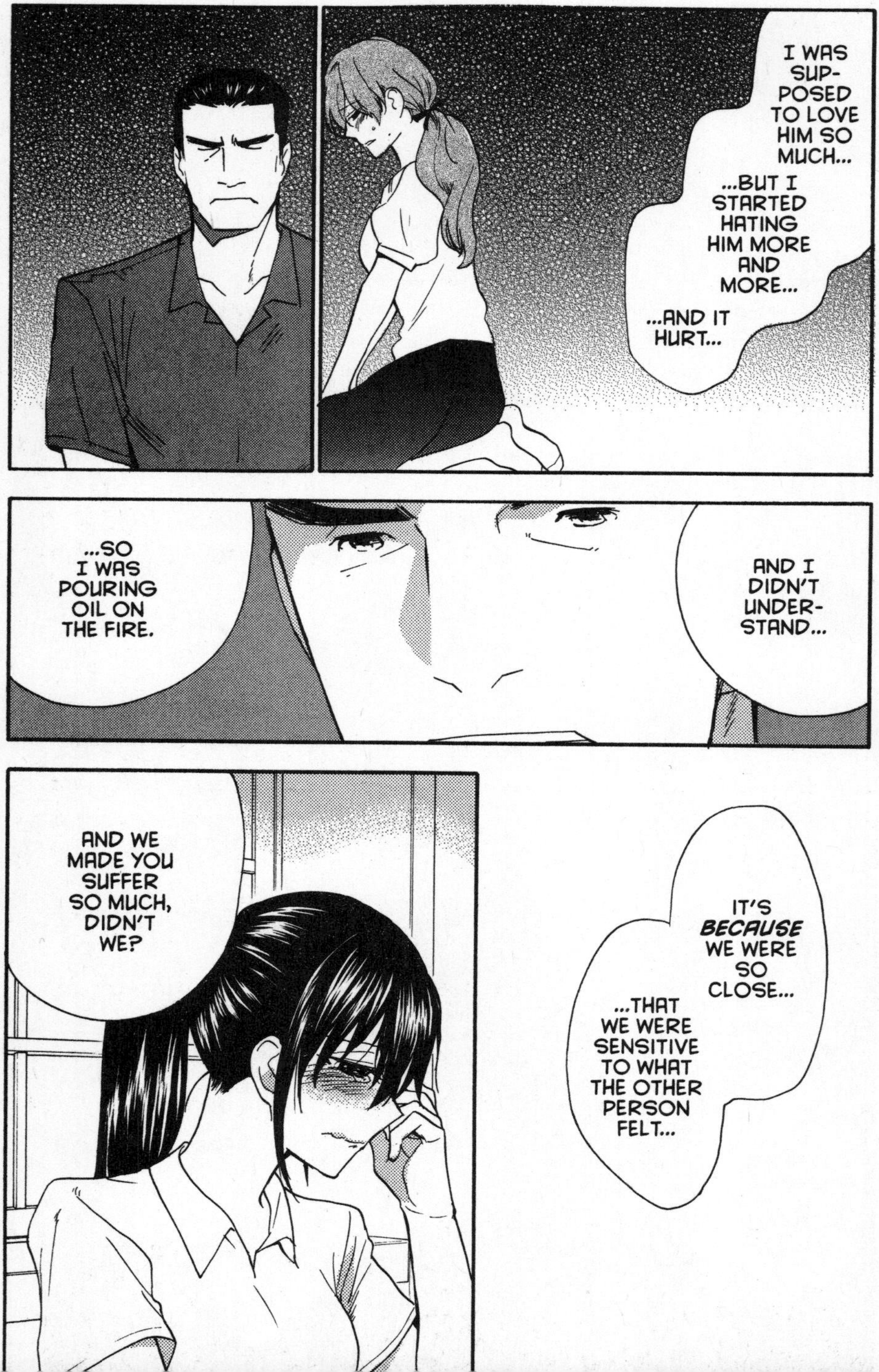
I WAS SUP-POSED TO LOVE HIM SO MUCH...
...BUT I STARTED HATING HIM MORE AND MORE...
...AND IT HURT...
AND I DIDN'T UNDER-STAND...
...SO I WAS POURING OIL ON THE FIRE.
IT'S *BECAUSE* WE WERE SO CLOSE...
...THAT WE WERE SENSITIVE TO WHAT THE OTHER PERSON FELT...
AND WE MADE YOU SUFFER SO MUCH, DIDN'T WE?

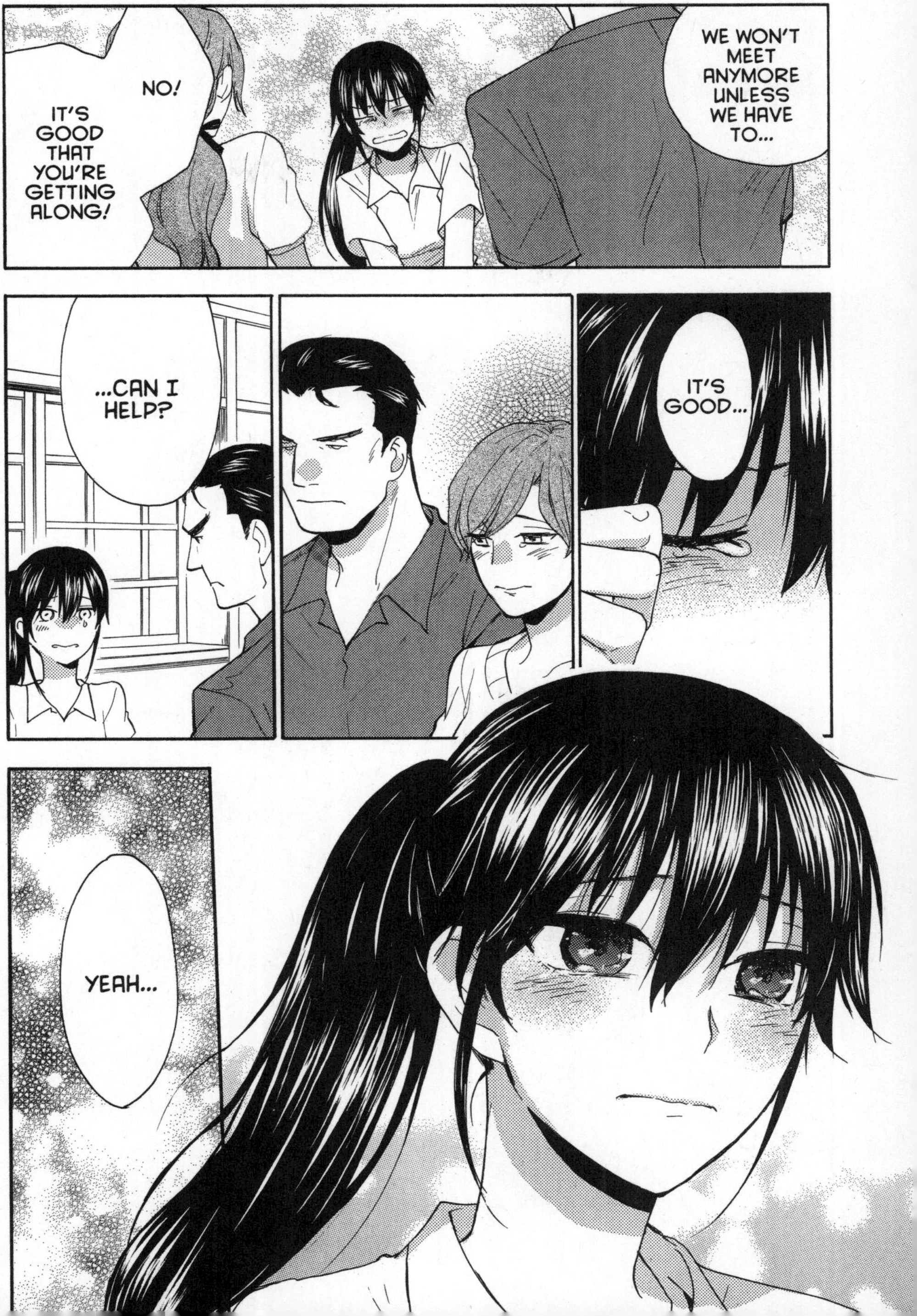
WE WON'T MEET ANYMORE UNLESS WE HAVE TO...
NO!
IT'S GOOD THAT YOU'RE GETTING ALONG!
IT'S GOOD...
...CAN I HELP?
YEAH...

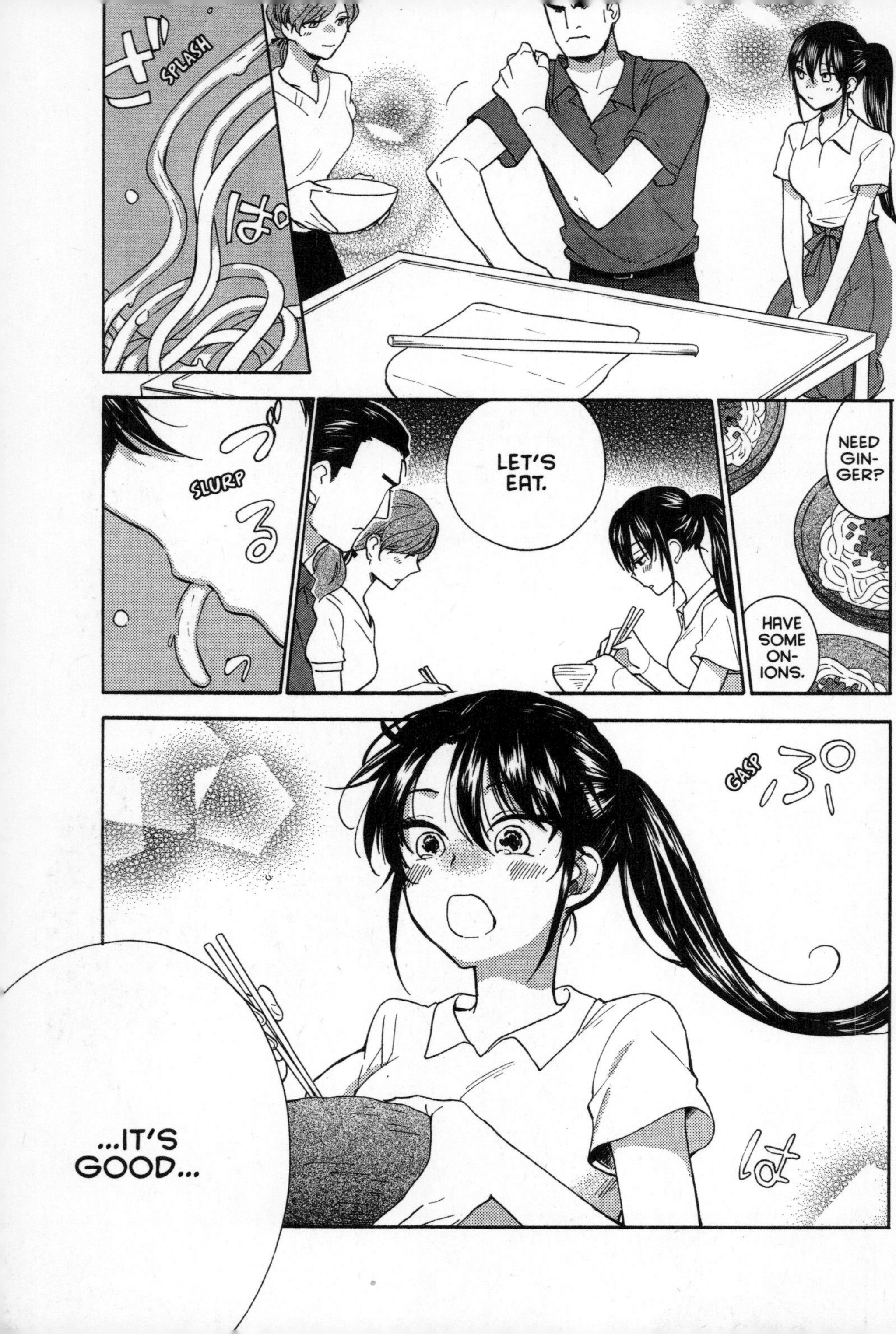
SPLASH
NEED GIN-GER?
HAVE SOME ON-IONS.
LET'S EAT.
SLURP
GASP
...IT'S GOOD...

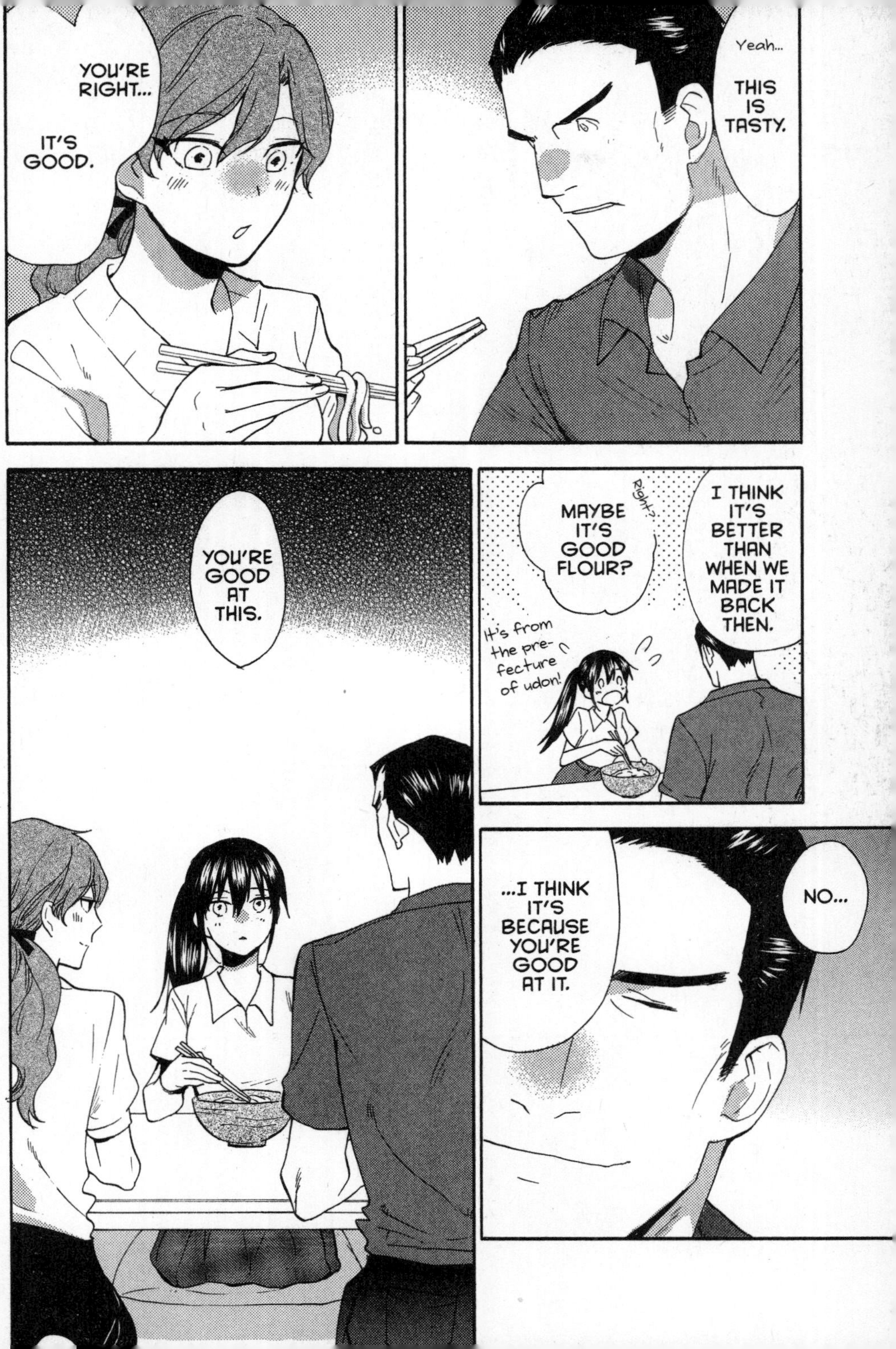
Yeah...
THIS IS TASTY.
YOU'RE RIGHT...
IT'S GOOD.
I THINK IT'S BETTER THAN WHEN WE MADE IT BACK THEN.
Right?
MAYBE IT'S GOOD FLOUR?
It's from the pre-fecture of udon!
NO...
...I THINK IT'S BECAUSE YOU'RE GOOD AT IT.
YOU'RE GOOD AT THIS.

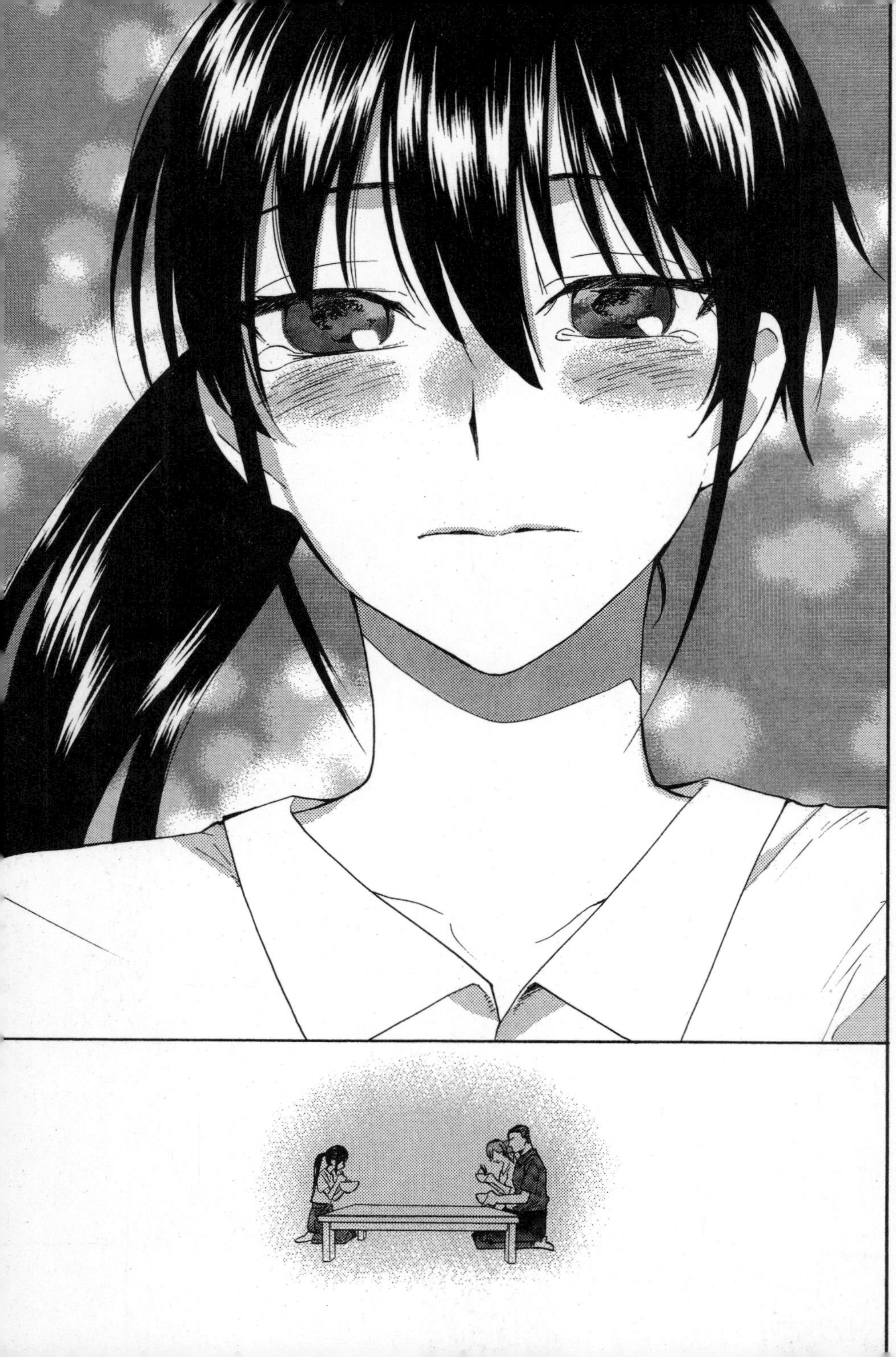

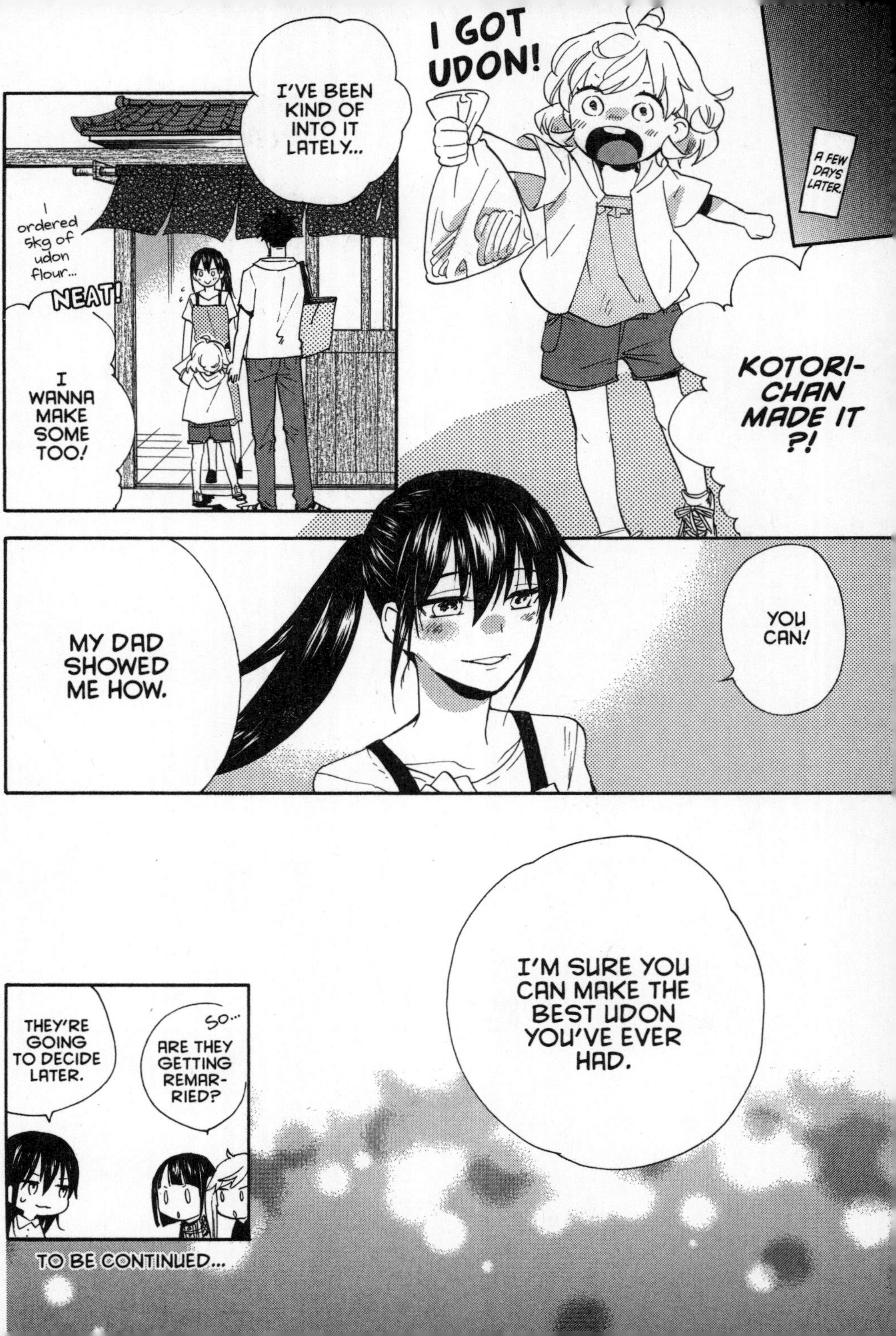
A FEW DAYS LATER.
I GOT UDON!
KOTORI-CHAN MADE IT?!
I'VE BEEN KIND OF INTO IT LATELY...
I ordered 5kg of udon flour...
NEAT!
I WANNA MAKE SOME TOO!
YOU CAN!
MY DAD SHOWED ME HOW.
I'M SURE YOU CAN MAKE THE BEST UDON YOU'VE EVER HAD.
SO...
ARE THEY GETTING REMAR-RIED?
THEY'RE GOING TO DECIDE LATER.
TO BE CONTINUED...

UDON

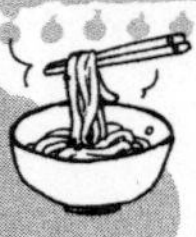

There's an illustration for this on the next page!

☆ Ingredients ☆ (serves 3-4)

- → 400g flour (udon flour or medium-strength flour)
- → 16g salt
- → 165cc water
- → Flour for dusting (same flour used for dough)
- → Rolling pin 2-3cm diameter, 60-90cm long
- → Vinyl sheet (can substitute with 10kg rice bag or thick garbage bag)

Directions

If the room temperature is about 20°C

1. Add the salt to the water. Stir until completely dissolved.
2. Sieve the flour.
3. Add (2) to (1) gradually and mix together, making sure that all the flour is combine with the water.
   ☆POINT☆ Do not knead. Large lumps will gradually get smaller until the entire mix looks like bread crumbs.
4. Clump (3) together and cover in plastic wrap. Let sit for 10 minutes.
5. Wrap (4) in the vinyl sheet. Knead by stepping on it evenly for 4-5 minutes.
6. Turn the dough over. Fold the left and right side inwards, folding it into three. Then fold the top and bottom, creating a square shape.
7. Lay the dough back down on the vinyl sheet, folded side down. Step on it for 4-5 minutes. Repeat steps (6) and (7) again.
8. Turn the dough over and fold the square into itself. Transfer the dough to a bowl. Roll the edges to the center, making the dough round.
9. Seal the dough in a resealable bag. Let rest for 2-3 hours.
10. Dust the top of the dough with flour. Push and stretch the dough while dusting with flour.
11. Roll the dough with a rolling pin into a 1cm thick circle. Continue to dust with an appropriate amount of flour for the following steps.
12. Roll out the dough moving from the center to one edge.
13. Roll out the dough in the same way on the opposite corner, creating a diamond shape.
14. Turn the dough 90 degrees and roll out one corner in the same way. Then turn the dough around and do the same to the final corner until the dough is a square.
15. Wind the dough around the rolling pin from one corner.
16. Roll the dough wrapped rolling pin while pushing down. Repeat this 7-8 times.
17. Un-roll the dough.
18. Follow steps (15) to (17) with the other three corners.
19. Move the edge of the dough towards you and repeat steps (15) to (18). Roll out to a thickness of 3-4mm.
20. Make sure the dough is an even thickness.
21. Dust the dough with flour and wrap the dough around the rolling pin.
22. Fold the dough back in on itself in a mountain on a chopping board.
23. Dust with flour and cut into 3-5mm thick strips.
24. Gather them in a bundle (about 15 strips) and strike them against the chopping board.

Dust with flour so the cut noodles don't stick together.

Dashi and Soy Sauce Soup Stock

☆ Ingredients ☆ (serves 3-4)

- → 50cc soy sauce
- → 25cc mirin
- → 5g bonito flakes

Directions

1. Combine the soy sauce and mirin on the stove. Once it simmers lower the heat and add the bonito flakes.
2. Simmer for 1 minute then turn off the heat. Let rest.
3. Once the stock has cooled run the stock through a sieve. Squeeze the clumps through the sieve.

KAMATAMA UDON

★ Ingredients ★ Serves 1

150g Udon (uncooked)
1 tablespoon dashi soy sauce soup stock
Sprinkle sesame seeds
1 egg
Sprinkle of green onions

Directions

1. Boil a pan full of water and add the udon. Boil the udon for 10-12 minutes (for 15-20 minutes if you want them nice and fat).

★ ☆ Point If you don't use **10 times** the udon's weight of water then the center of the noodles might not cook. The time it takes to boil depends on the thickness. You can check if it's cooked by eating it!

2. Crack egg into a warmed bowl and stir.
3. Drain the udon, add to the bowl from step (2), and mix well.
4. Add seasonings and dashi soy sauce soup stock and you're done!

WHEN YOU NEED TO KNEAD THE UDON

Let the dough from step (9) sit...
(10) Dust the top of the dough with flour.
Stretch out.
(11) Roll out a 1cm thick circle...
...with...
a rolling pin!
(12) ★ Regularly dust with flour!
Roll from the center out.
Push down hard as you roll.
(13)
This half is stretched out. Turn 180 degrees.
Now do the same to this half!
Then...
...it looks like a long diamond!
(14) Turn 90 degrees
Roll out the top half in the same way.
Turn 180 degrees
Roll out this half too.
So now it's a giant square!
(15)
Wrap one corner around the rolling pin.
Curl the dough all the way around.
(16) Bring it towards you
Roll the dough while pressing down with both hands.
Bring it towards you again. Do this 7-8 times.
(17) Roll the dough over 180 degrees.
Bringing the rolling pin towards you.
Lay out the dough
(18) Repeat steps (15) to (17) with the other three corners.
(19)
Place a part in front of you
Repeat steps (15) to (18) until the dough is about 3-4mm thick.
(20)
Use the rolling pin to fold the dough into a little pile.
About at wide as this
☆ Cut the dough into 3-5mm thick strips as you sprinkle it with flour!

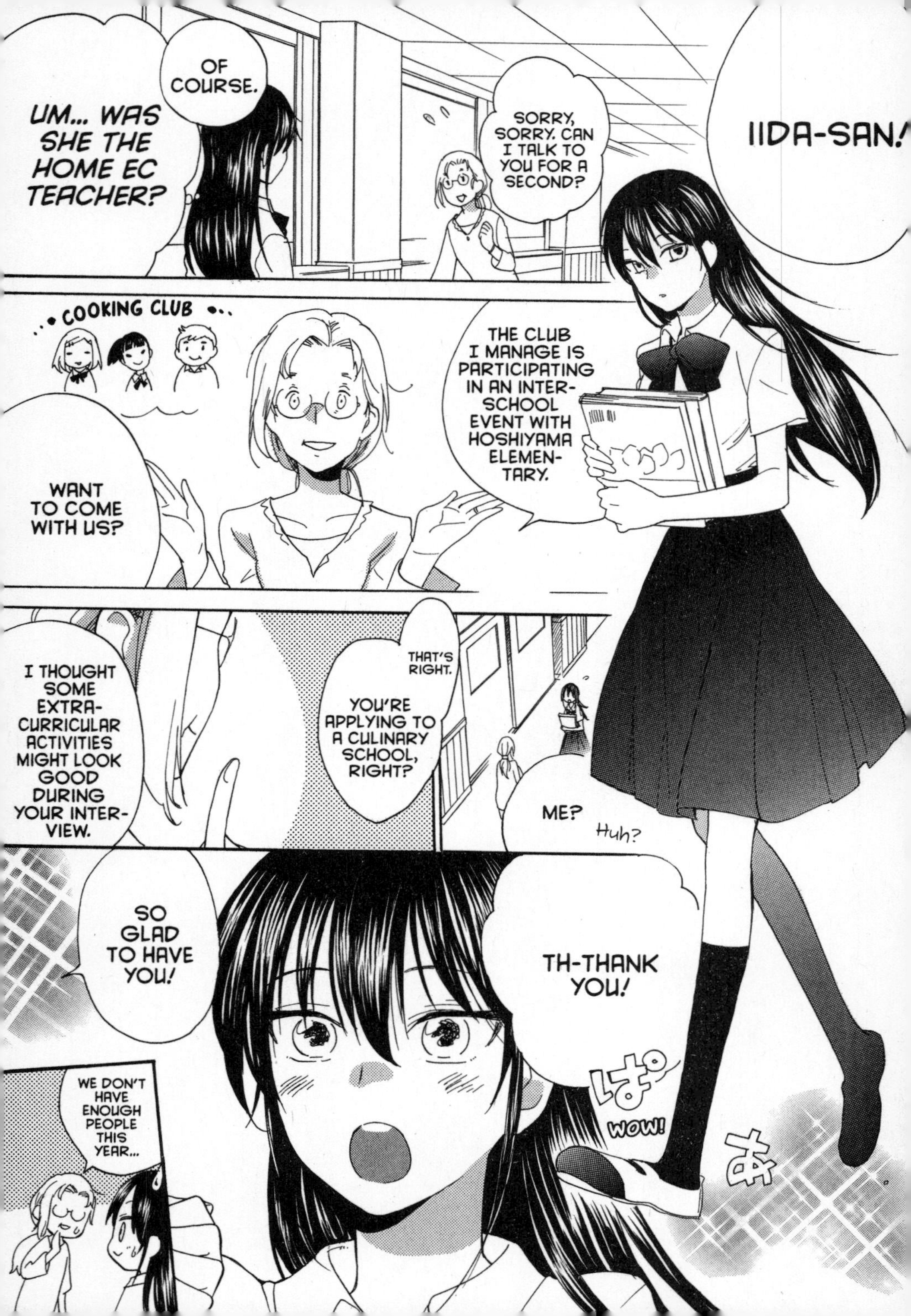
IIDA-SAN!
SORRY, SORRY. CAN I TALK TO YOU FOR A SECOND?
OF COURSE.
UM... WAS SHE THE HOME EC TEACHER?
THE CLUB I MANAGE IS PARTICIPATING IN AN INTER-SCHOOL EVENT WITH HOSHIYAMA ELEMENTARY.
...COOKING CLUB...
WANT TO COME WITH US?
ME?
Huh?
THAT'S RIGHT.
YOU'RE APPLYING TO A CULINARY SCHOOL, RIGHT?
I THOUGHT SOME EXTRA-CURRICULAR ACTIVITIES MIGHT LOOK GOOD DURING YOUR INTER-VIEW.
TH-THANK YOU!
ぱ
WOW!
あ
SO GLAD TO HAVE YOU!
WE DON'T HAVE ENOUGH PEOPLE THIS YEAR...

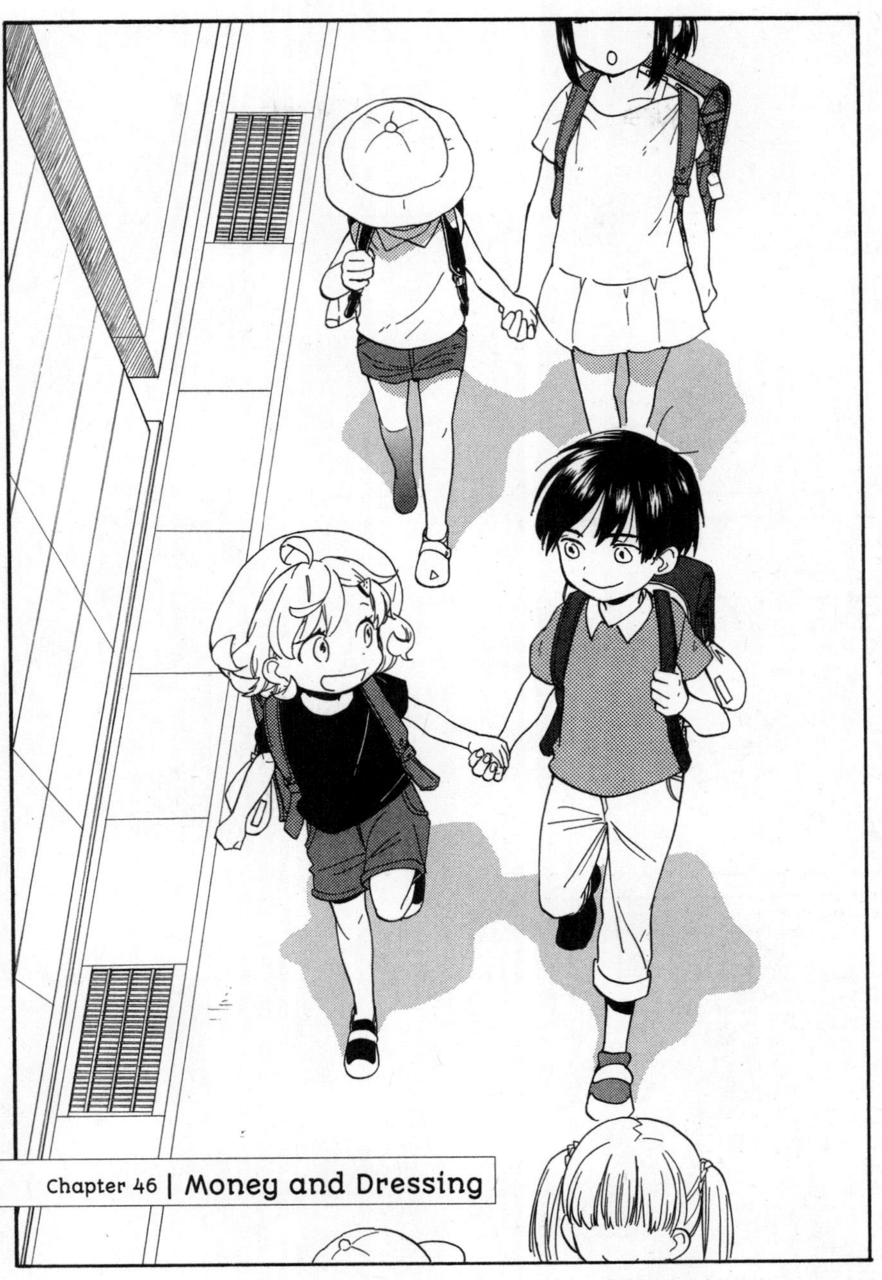
Chapter 46 | Money and Dressing

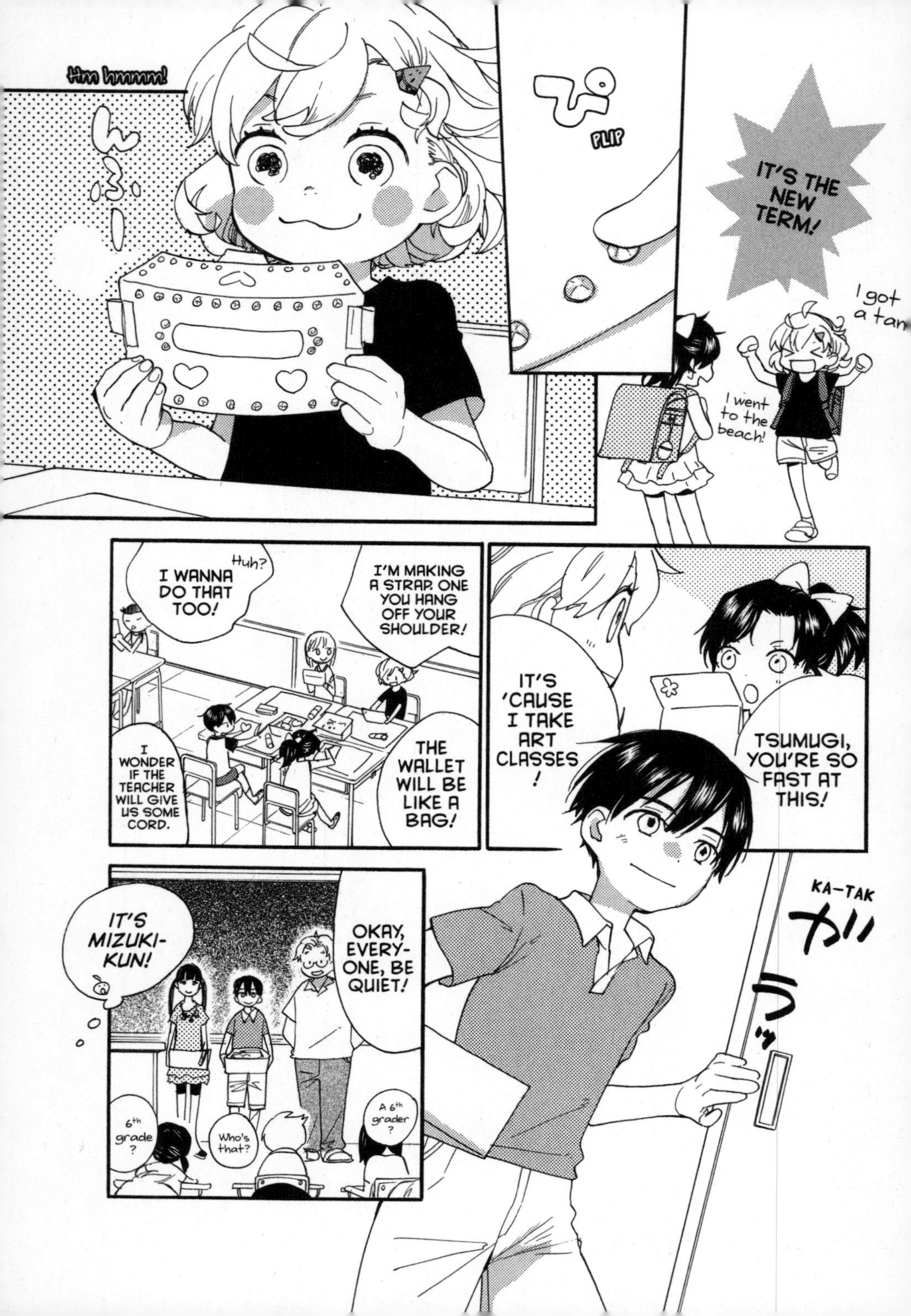

IT'S THE NEW TERM!
I got a tan
I went to the beach!
PLIP
Hm hmmm!
TSUMUGI, YOU'RE SO FAST AT THIS!
IT'S 'CAUSE I TAKE ART CLASSES!
I'M MAKING A STRAP. ONE YOU HANG OFF YOUR SHOULDER!
Huh?
I WANNA DO THAT TOO!
THE WALLET WILL BE LIKE A BAG!
I WONDER IF THE TEACHER WILL GIVE US SOME CORD.
KA-TAK
OKAY, EVERYONE, BE QUIET!
IT'S MIZUKI-KUN!
A 6th grader?
Who's that?
6th grade?

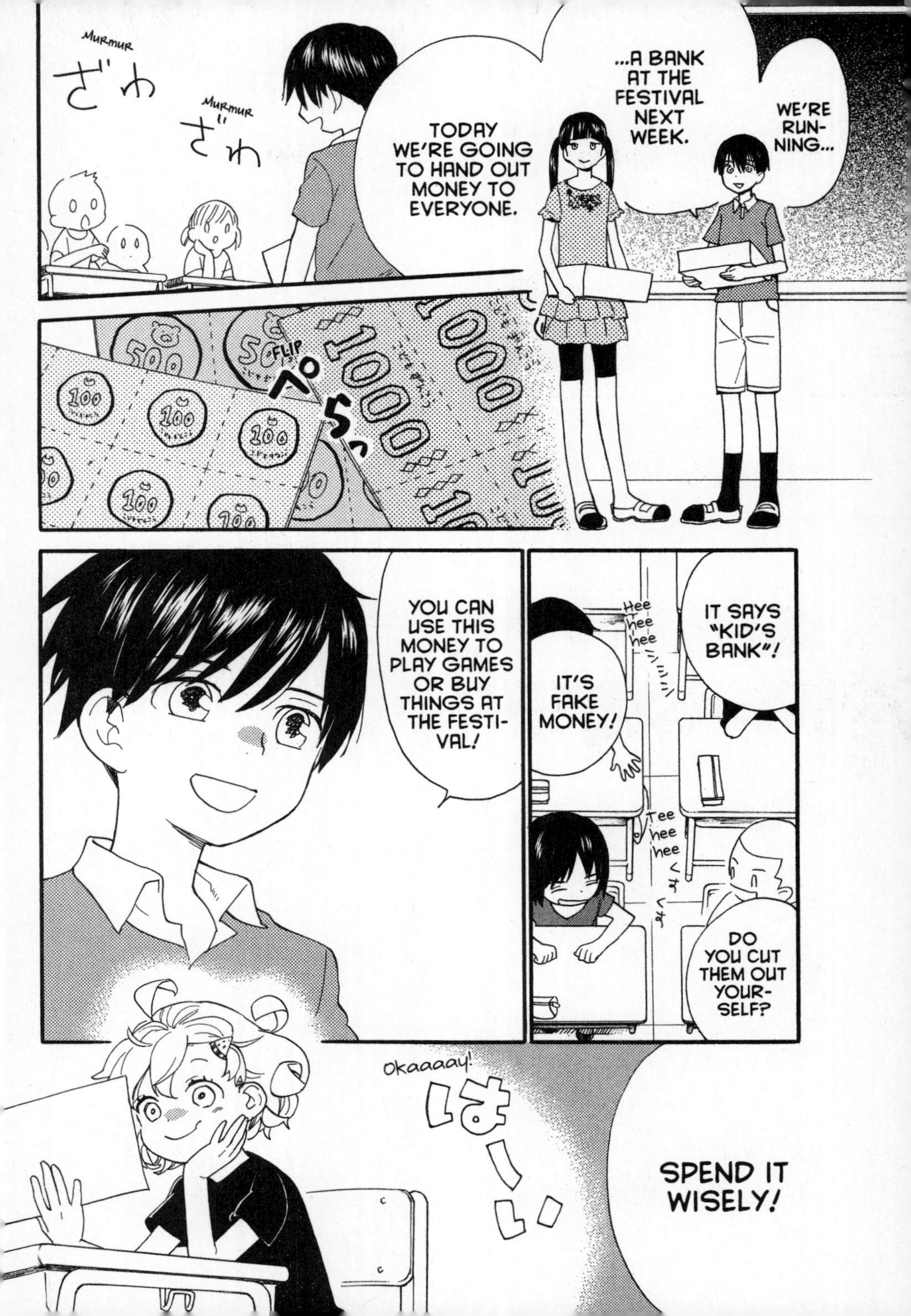
We're running...
...a bank at the festival next week.
Today we're going to hand out money to everyone.
Murmur ざわ
Murmur ざわ
Flip ぺらっ
It says "Kid's Bank"!
Hee hee hee
It's fake money!
Tee hee hee くすくす
Do you cut them out yourself?
You can use this money to play games or buy things at the festi-val!
Spend it wisely!
Okaaaay! はーい

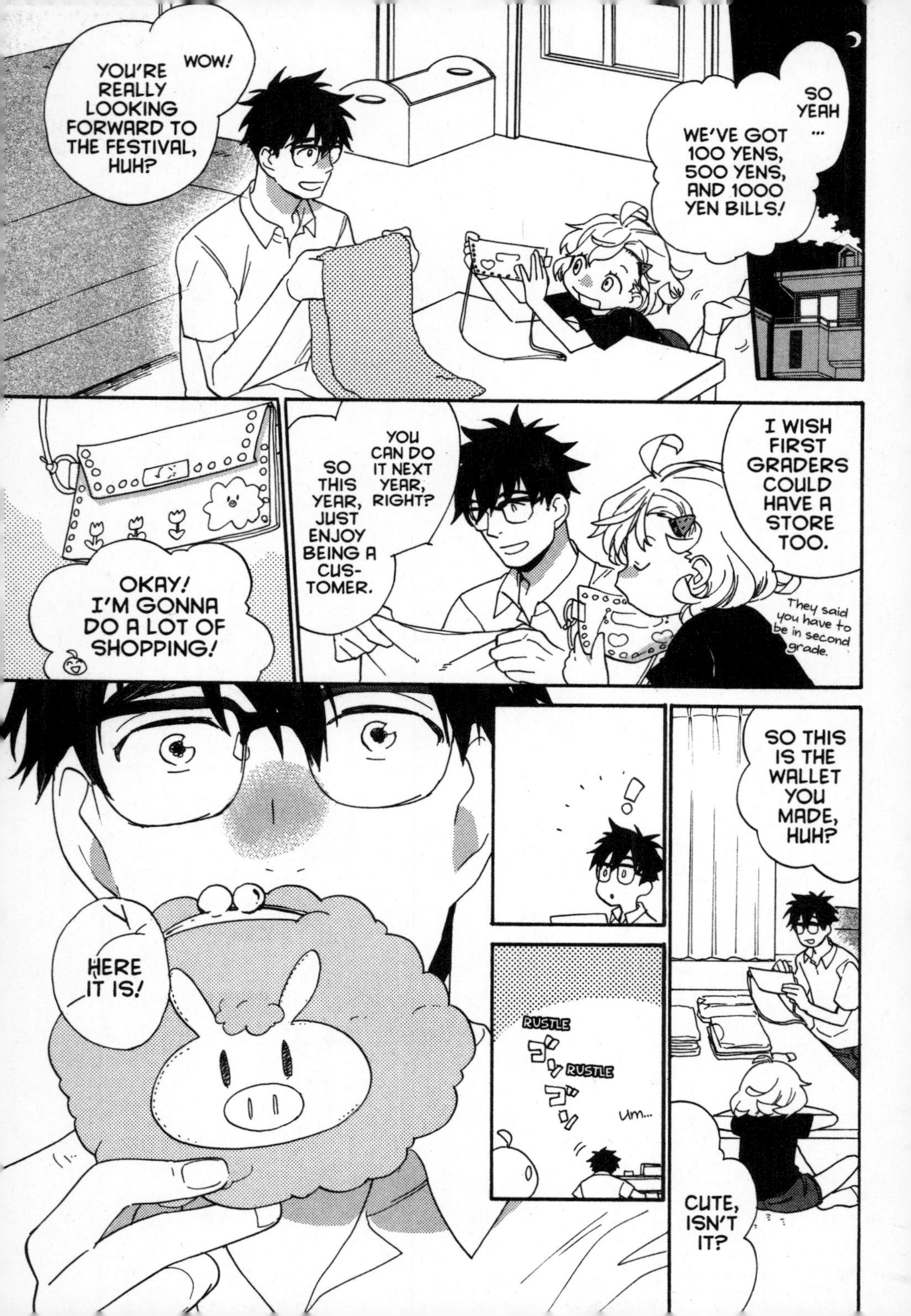
SO YEAH ...
WE'VE GOT 100 YENS, 500 YENS, AND 1000 YEN BILLS!
WOW!
YOU'RE REALLY LOOKING FORWARD TO THE FESTIVAL, HUH?
I WISH FIRST GRADERS COULD HAVE A STORE TOO.
They said you have to be in second grade.
YOU CAN DO IT NEXT YEAR, RIGHT?
SO THIS YEAR, JUST ENJOY BEING A CUS-TOMER.
OKAY! I'M GONNA DO A LOT OF SHOPPING!
SO THIS IS THE WALLET YOU MADE, HUH?
CUTE, ISN'T IT?
!
RUSTLE
RUSTLE
um...
HERE IT IS!

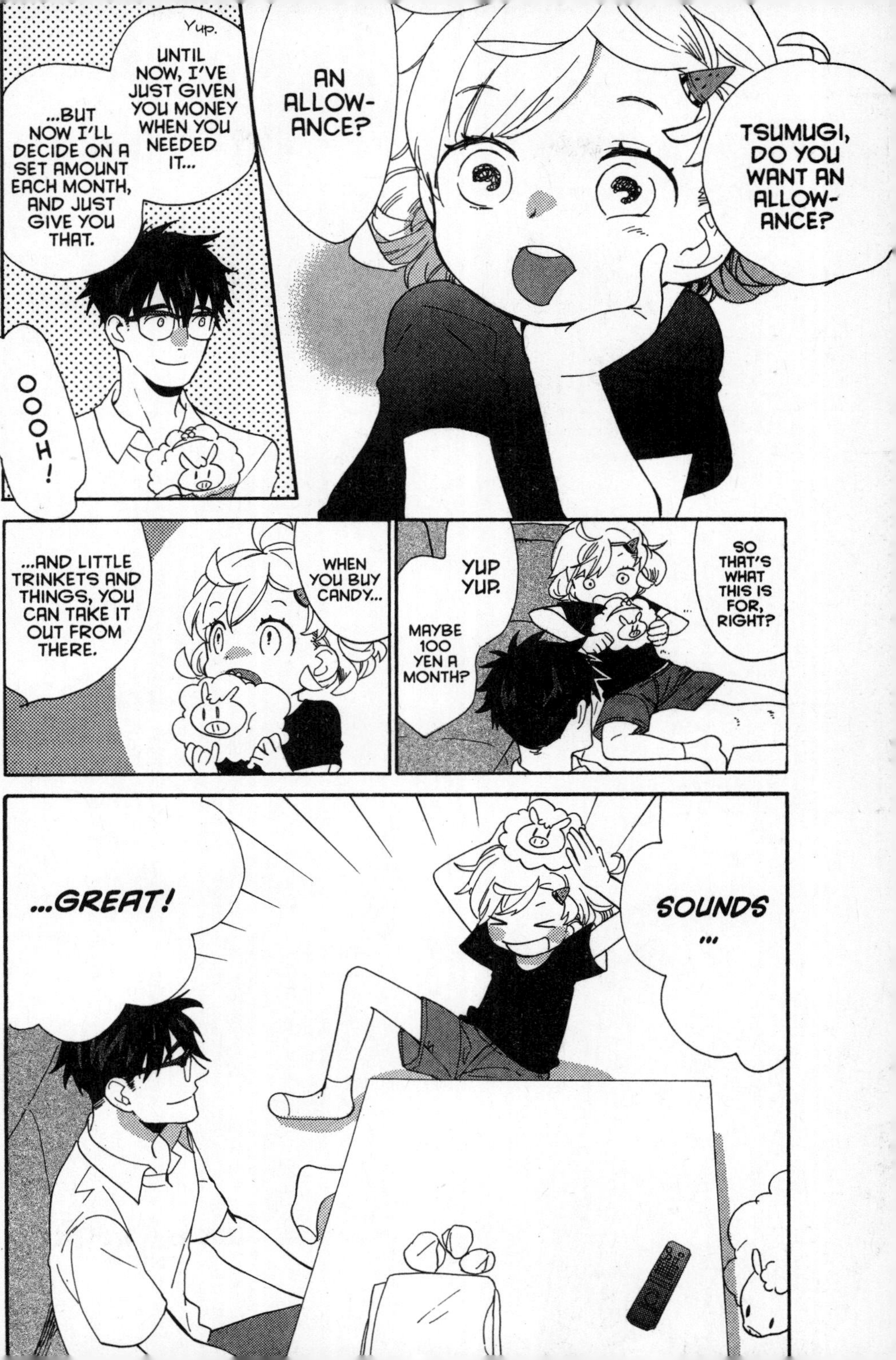
TSUMUGI, DO YOU WANT AN ALLOWANCE?
AN ALLOWANCE?
Yup.
UNTIL NOW, I'VE JUST GIVEN YOU MONEY WHEN YOU NEEDED IT...
...BUT NOW I'LL DECIDE ON A SET AMOUNT EACH MONTH, AND JUST GIVE YOU THAT.
OOOH!
SO THAT'S WHAT THIS IS FOR, RIGHT?
YUP YUP.
MAYBE 100 YEN A MONTH?
WHEN YOU BUY CANDY...
...AND LITTLE TRINKETS AND THINGS, YOU CAN TAKE IT OUT FROM THERE.
SOUNDS...
...GREAT!

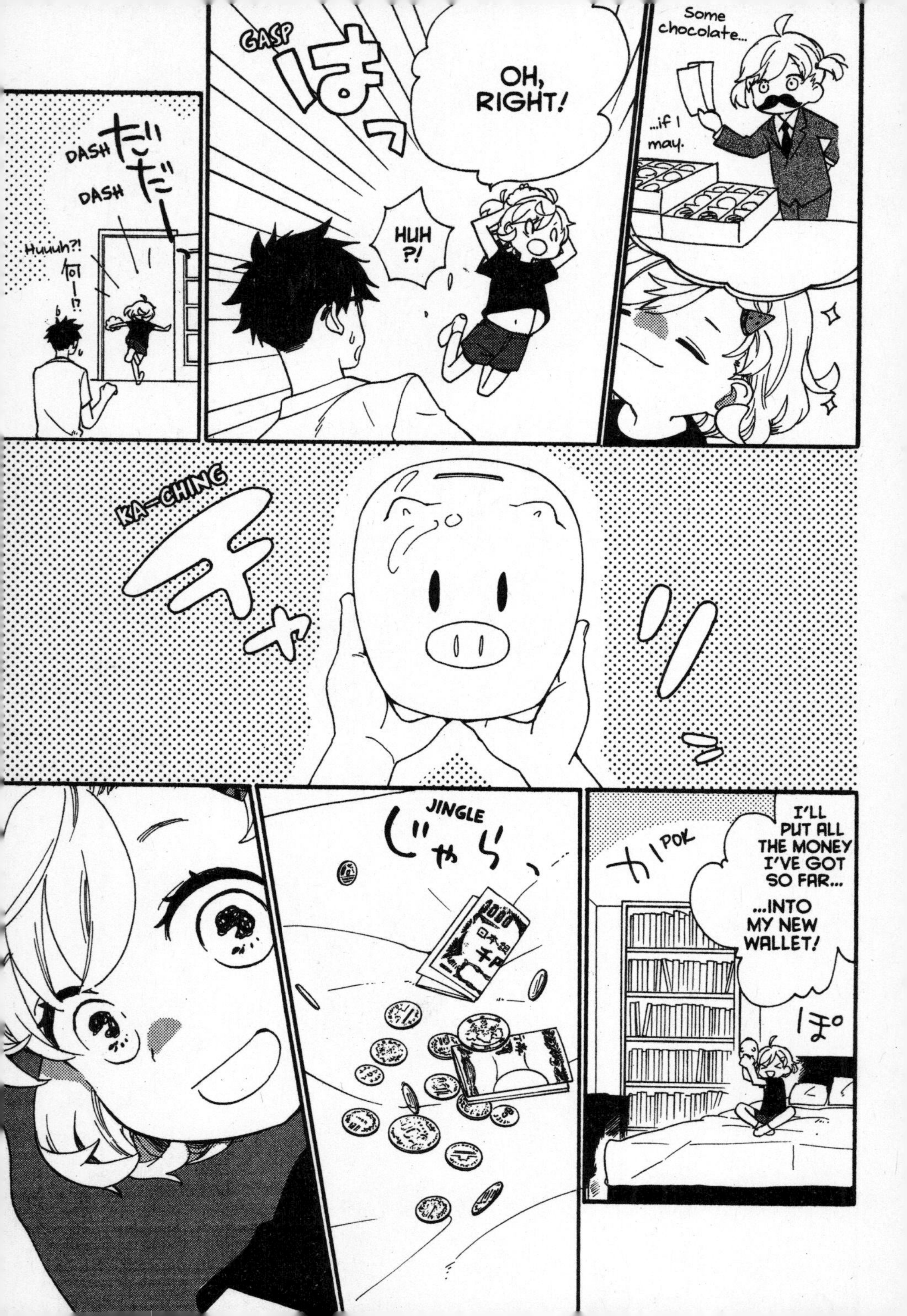
Some chocolate...
...if I may.
GASP
はっ
OH, RIGHT!
HUH?!
DASH
だだー
DASH
Huuuh?!
何ー!?
KA-CHING
チャリ
POK
I'LL PUT ALL THE MONEY I'VE GOT SO FAR...
...INTO MY NEW WALLET!
ぽ
JINGLE
じゃら

THERE'S
SO MUCH...

さっ Shuffle
さっ Shuffle

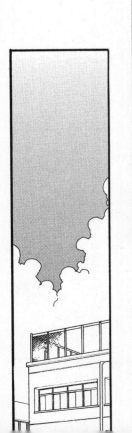

AM I
SUPER-
RICH?

AM I
RICH?

Yahooooo!! いやっほ——

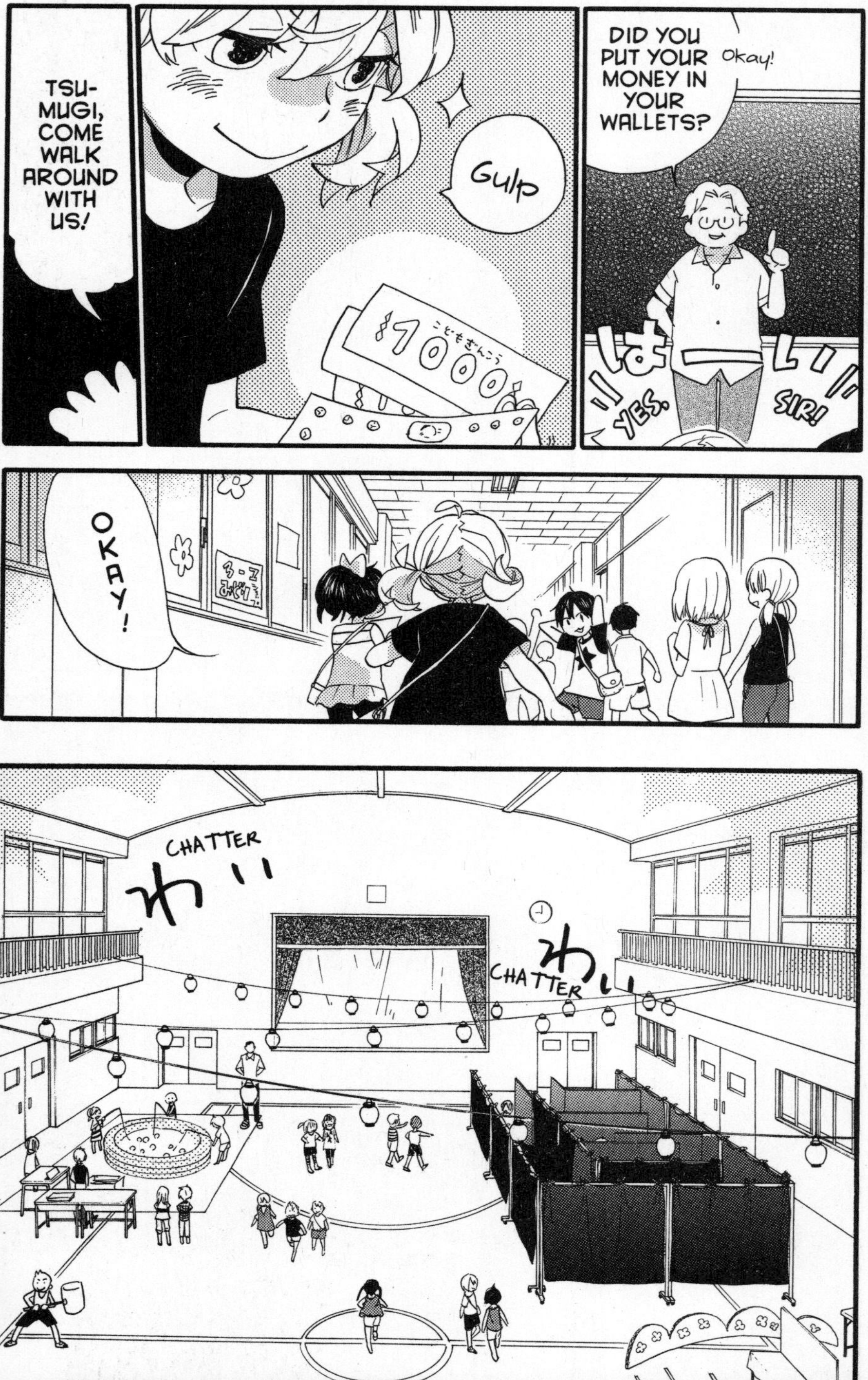
DID YOU PUT YOUR MONEY IN YOUR WALLETS?
Okay!
はーい
YES, SIR!
Gulp
こどもぎんこう
1000
TSU-MUGI, COME WALK AROUND WITH US!
OKAY!
CHATTER
わい
CHATTER
わい

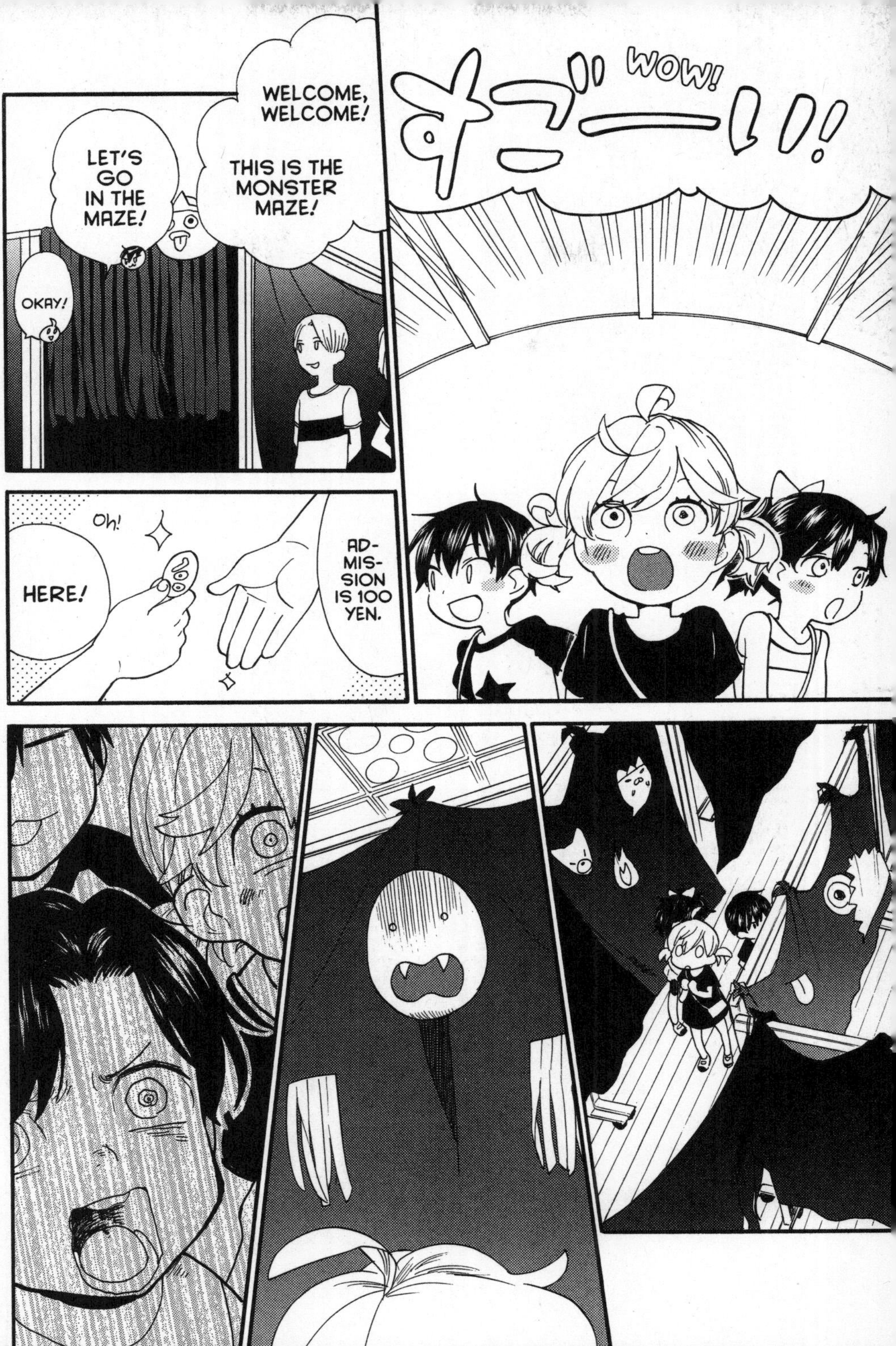

すごーい!!
WOW!
WELCOME, WELCOME!
THIS IS THE MONSTER MAZE!
LET'S GO IN THE MAZE!
OKAY!
ADMISSION IS 100 YEN.
Oh!
HERE!

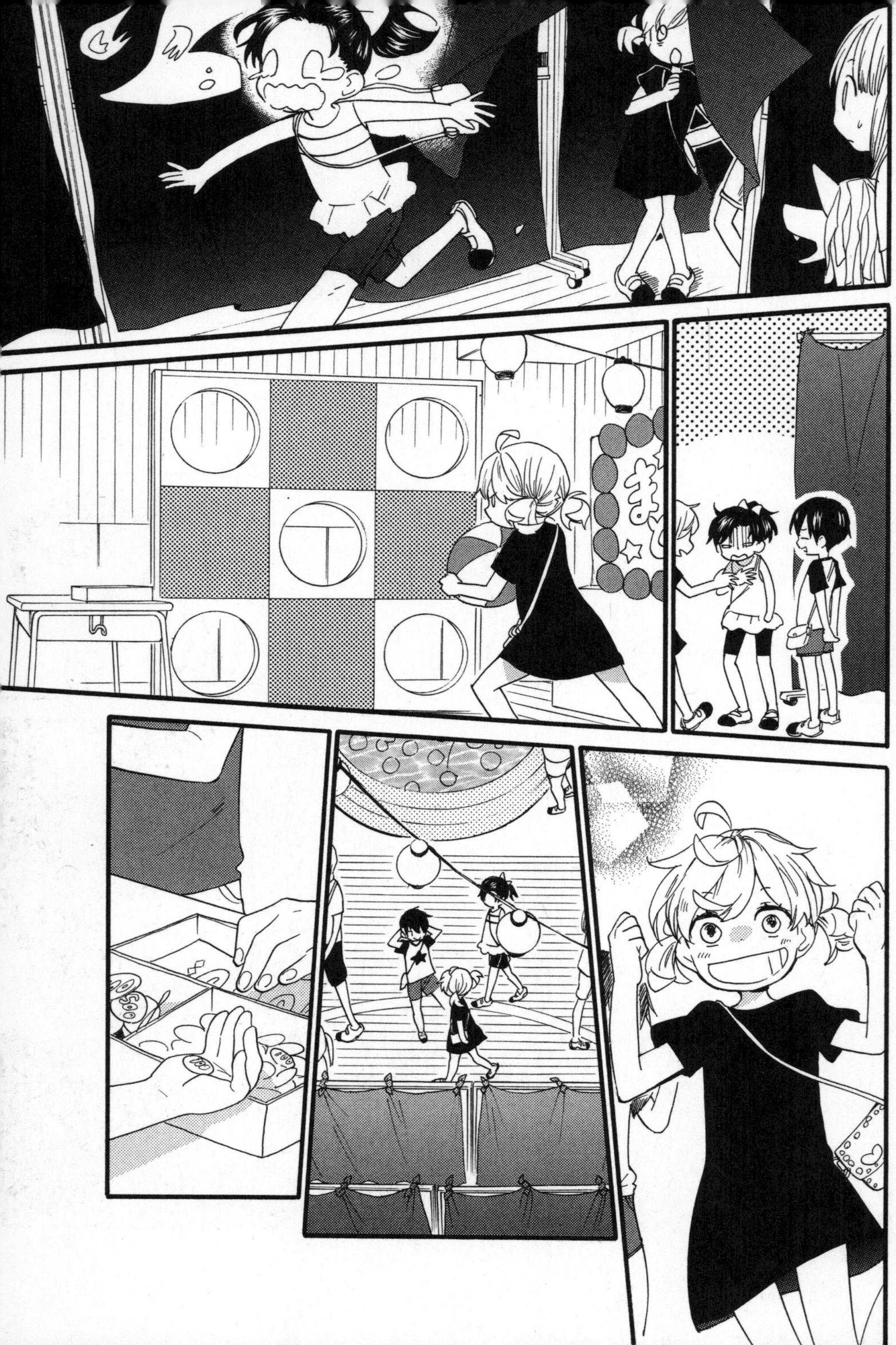

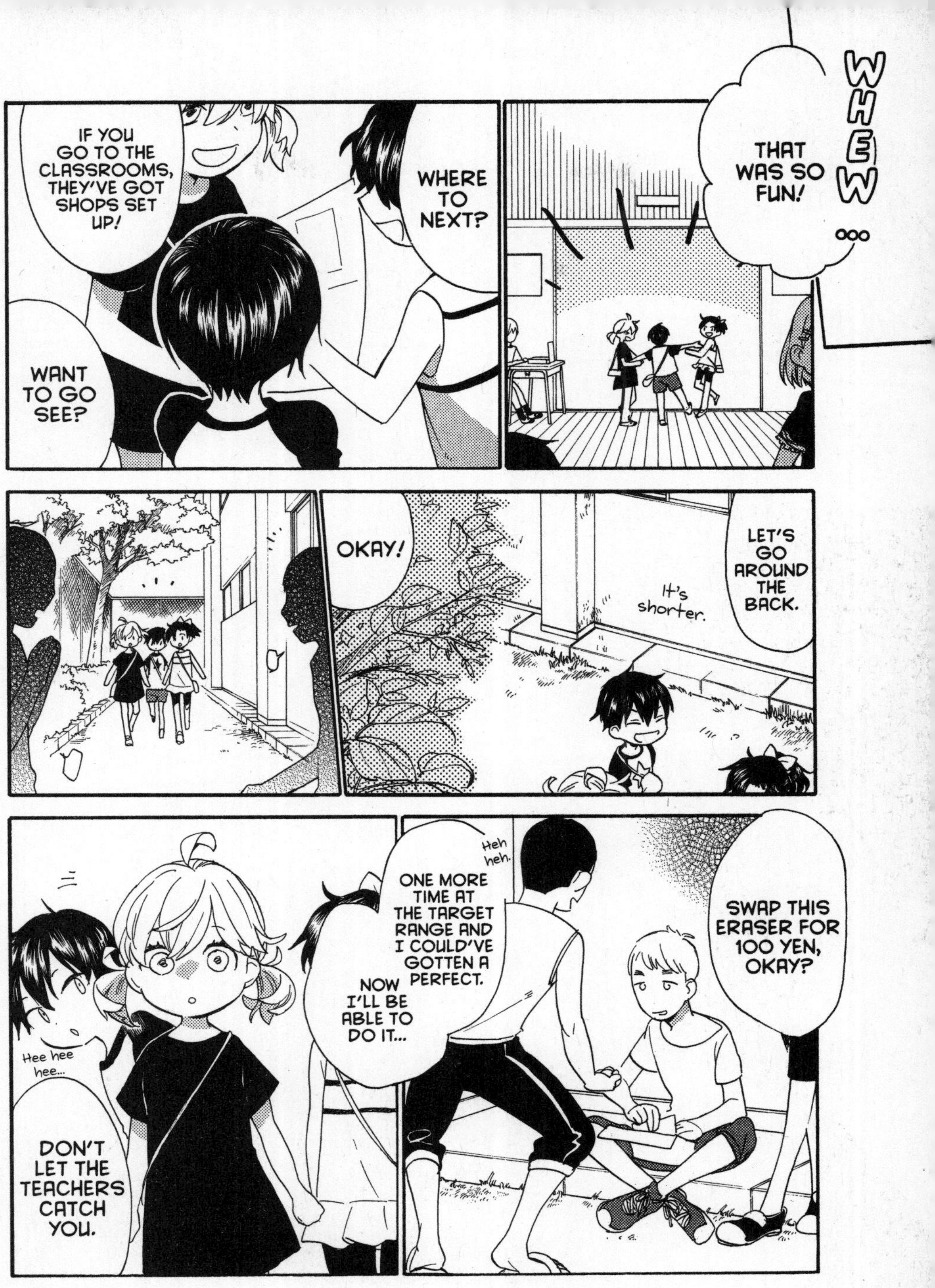
WHEW...
THAT WAS SO FUN!
WHERE TO NEXT?
IF YOU GO TO THE CLASSROOMS, THEY'VE GOT SHOPS SET UP!
WANT TO GO SEE?
LET'S GO AROUND THE BACK.
It's shorter.
OKAY!
SWAP THIS ERASER FOR 100 YEN, OKAY?
Heh heh.
ONE MORE TIME AT THE TARGET RANGE AND I COULD'VE GOTTEN A PERFECT.
NOW I'LL BE ABLE TO DO IT...
Hee hee hee...
DON'T LET THE TEACHERS CATCH YOU.

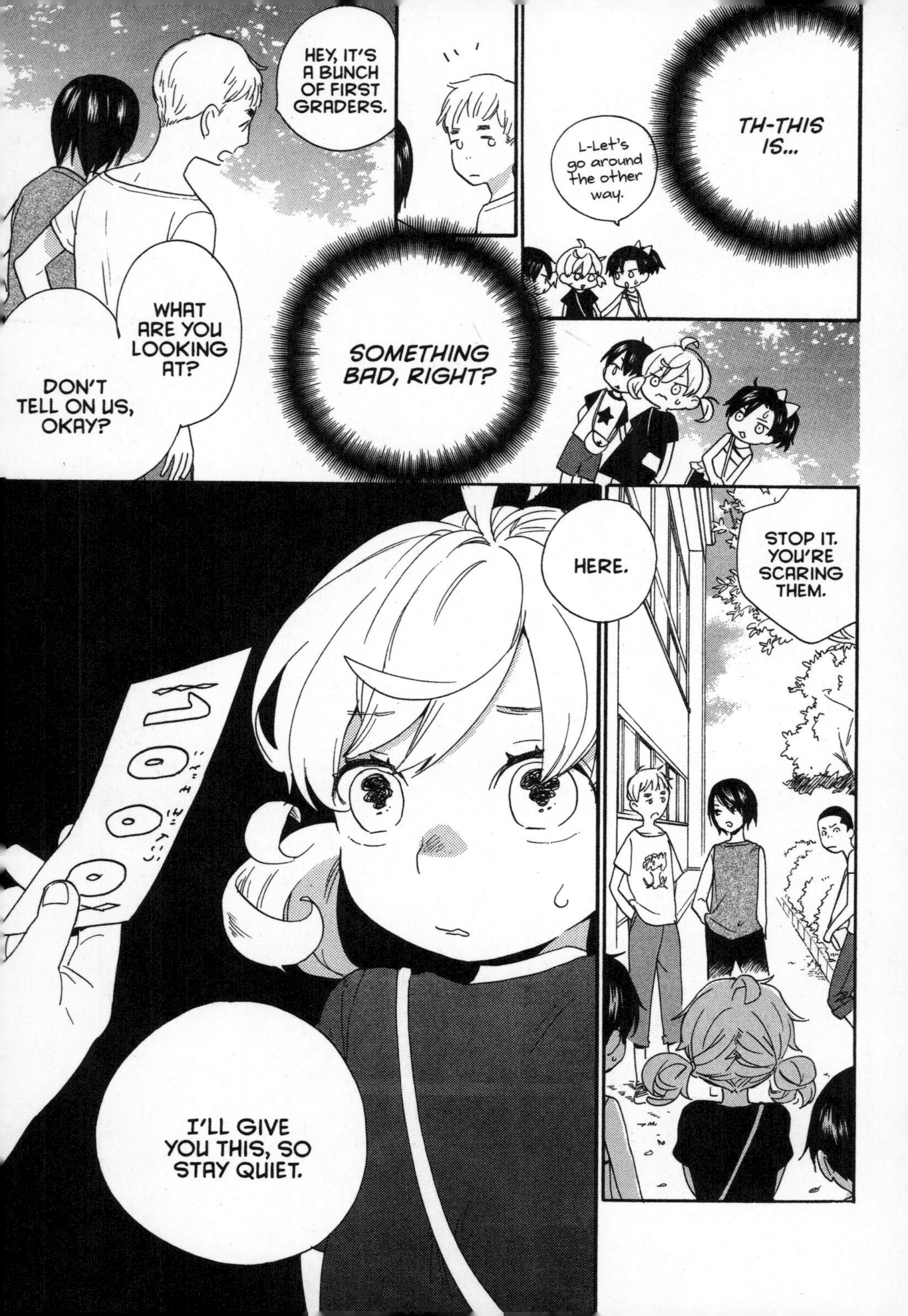
TH-THIS IS...
L-Let's go around the other way.
SOMETHING BAD, RIGHT?
HEY, IT'S A BUNCH OF FIRST GRADERS.
WHAT ARE YOU LOOKING AT?
DON'T TELL ON US, OKAY?
STOP IT. YOU'RE SCARING THEM.
HERE.
I'LL GIVE YOU THIS, SO STAY QUIET.

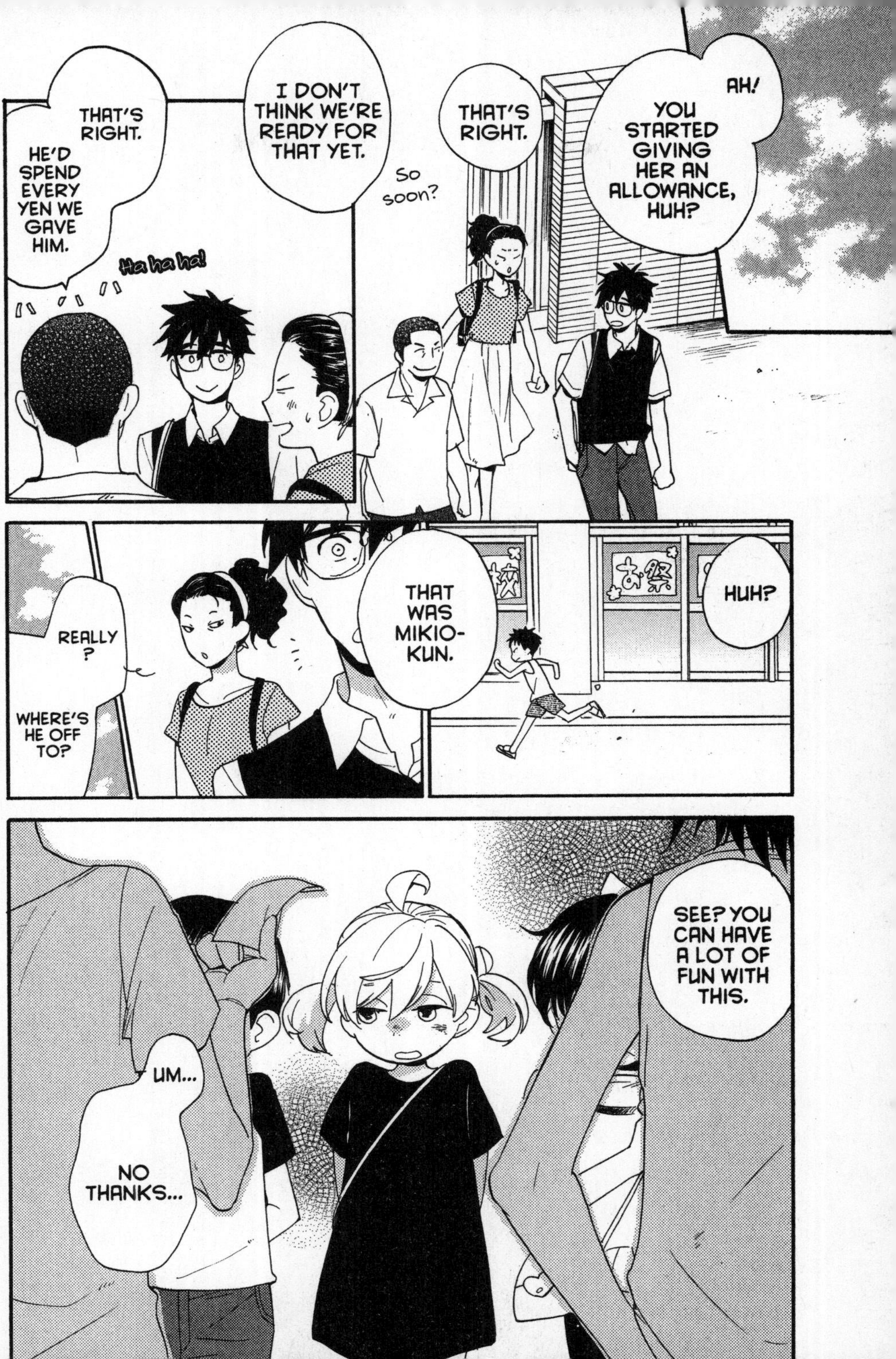
AH!
YOU STARTED GIVING HER AN ALLOWANCE, HUH?
THAT'S RIGHT.
So soon?
I DON'T THINK WE'RE READY FOR THAT YET.
THAT'S RIGHT.
HE'D SPEND EVERY YEN WE GAVE HIM.
Ha ha ha!
HUH?
THAT WAS MIKIO-KUN.
REALLY?
WHERE'S HE OFF TO?
SEE? YOU CAN HAVE A LOT OF FUN WITH THIS.
UM...
NO THANKS...

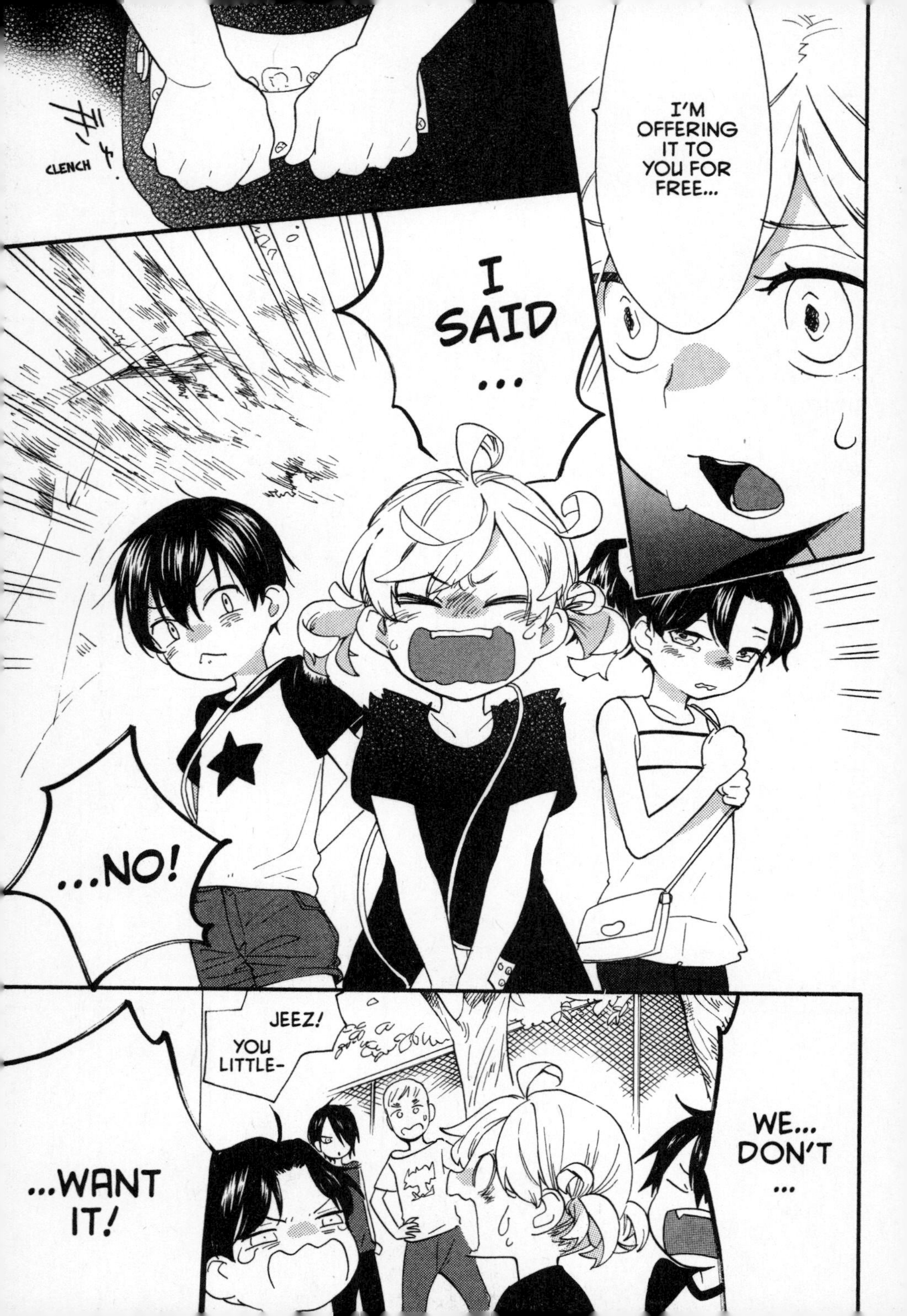
I'M OFFERING IT TO YOU FOR FREE...
CLENCH
I SAID ...
...NO!
WE... DON'T ...
...WANT IT!
JEEZ! YOU LITTLE-

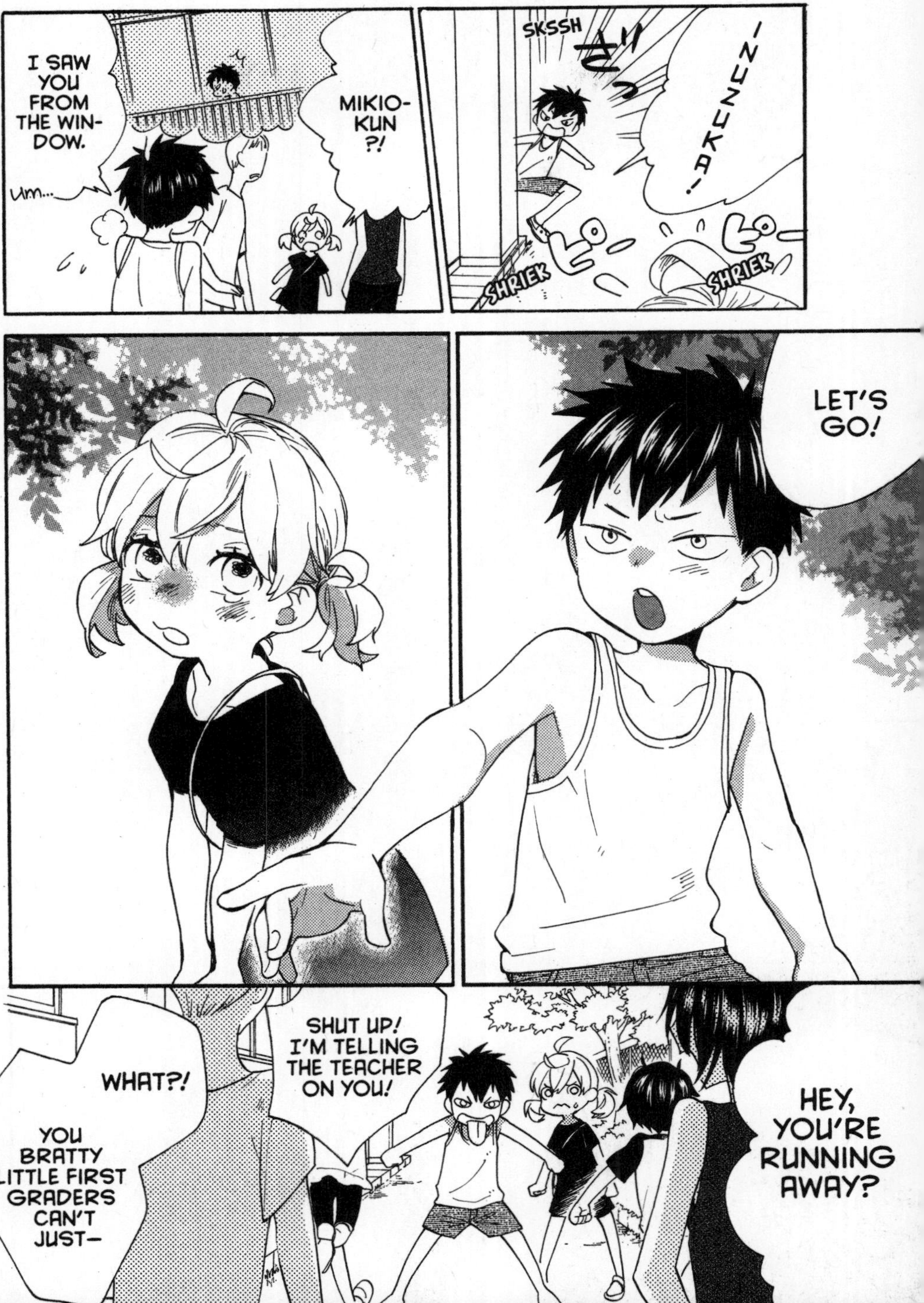
SKSSH
INUZUKA!
SHRIEK
SHRIEK
MIKIO-KUN?!
I SAW YOU FROM THE WIN-DOW.
um...
LET'S GO!
HEY, YOU'RE RUNNING AWAY?
SHUT UP! I'M TELLING THE TEACHER ON YOU!
WHAT?!
YOU BRATTY LITTLE FIRST GRADERS CAN'T JUST—

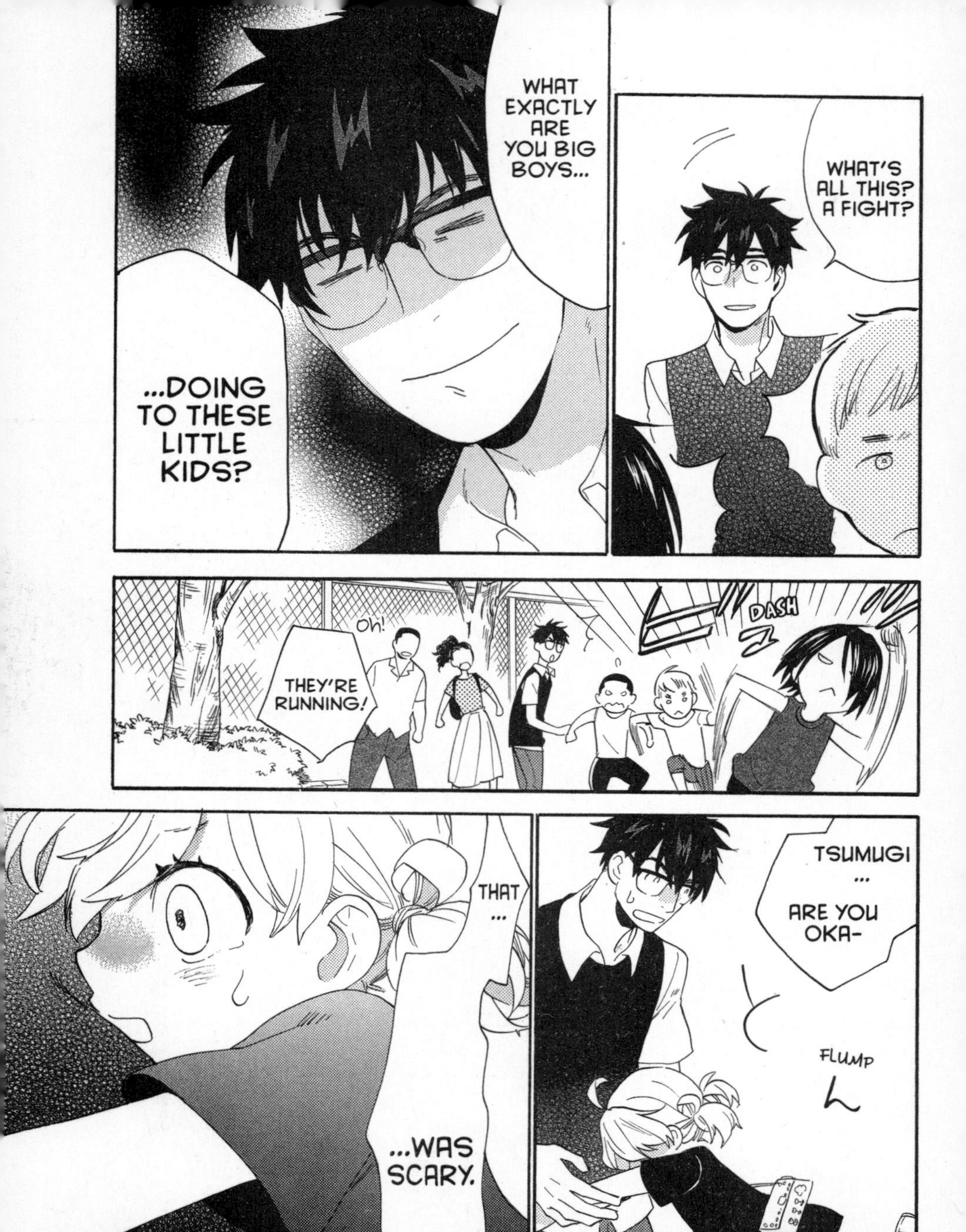
WHAT'S ALL THIS? A FIGHT?
WHAT EXACTLY ARE YOU BIG BOYS...
...DOING TO THESE LITTLE KIDS?
DASH
Oh!
THEY'RE RUNNING!
TSUMUGI ... ARE YOU OKA-
FLUMP
THAT ...
...WAS SCARY.

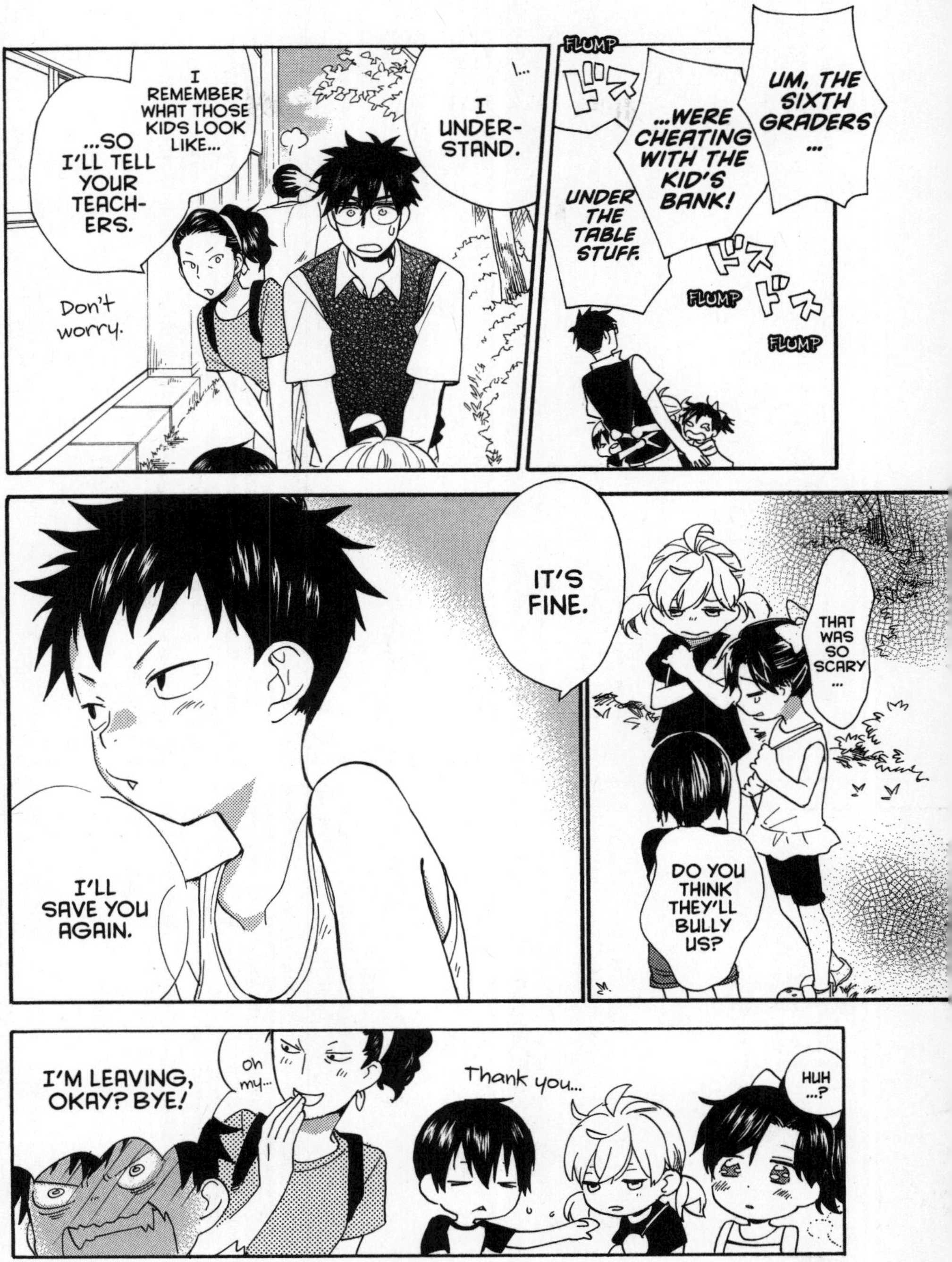
UM, THE SIXTH GRADERS ...
...WERE CHEATING WITH THE KID'S BANK!
UNDER THE TABLE STUFF.
FLUMP
ドス
FLUMP
ドス
FLUMP
ドス
I...
I UNDERSTAND.
I REMEMBER WHAT THOSE KIDS LOOK LIKE...
...SO I'LL TELL YOUR TEACHERS.
Don't worry.
THAT WAS SO SCARY ...
DO YOU THINK THEY'LL BULLY US?
IT'S FINE.
I'LL SAVE YOU AGAIN.
HUH ...?
Thank you...
Oh my...
I'M LEAVING, OKAY? BYE!

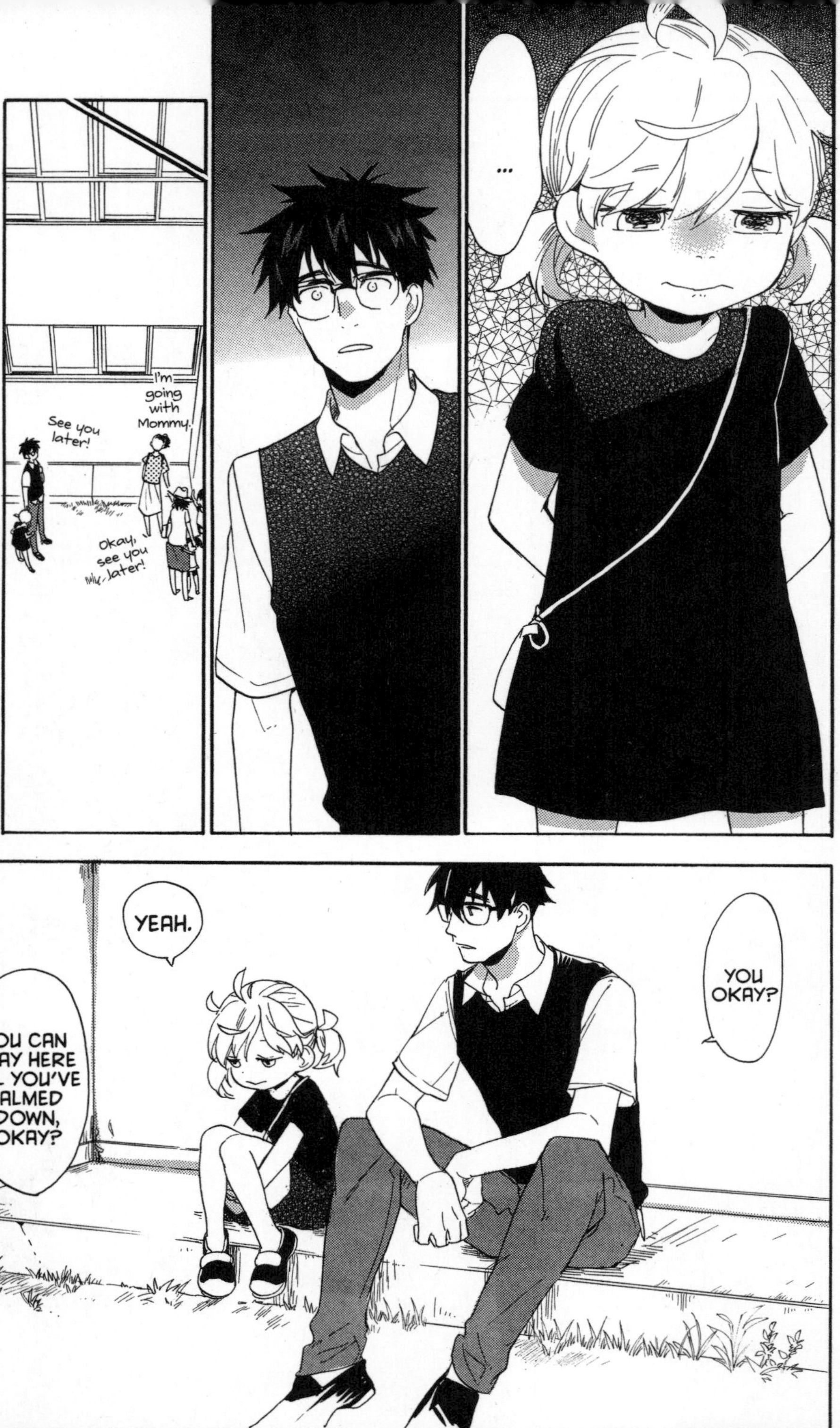
...
I'm going with Mommy.
See you later!
Okay, see you later!
YOU OKAY?
YEAH.
YOU CAN STAY HERE TILL YOU'VE CALMED DOWN, OKAY?

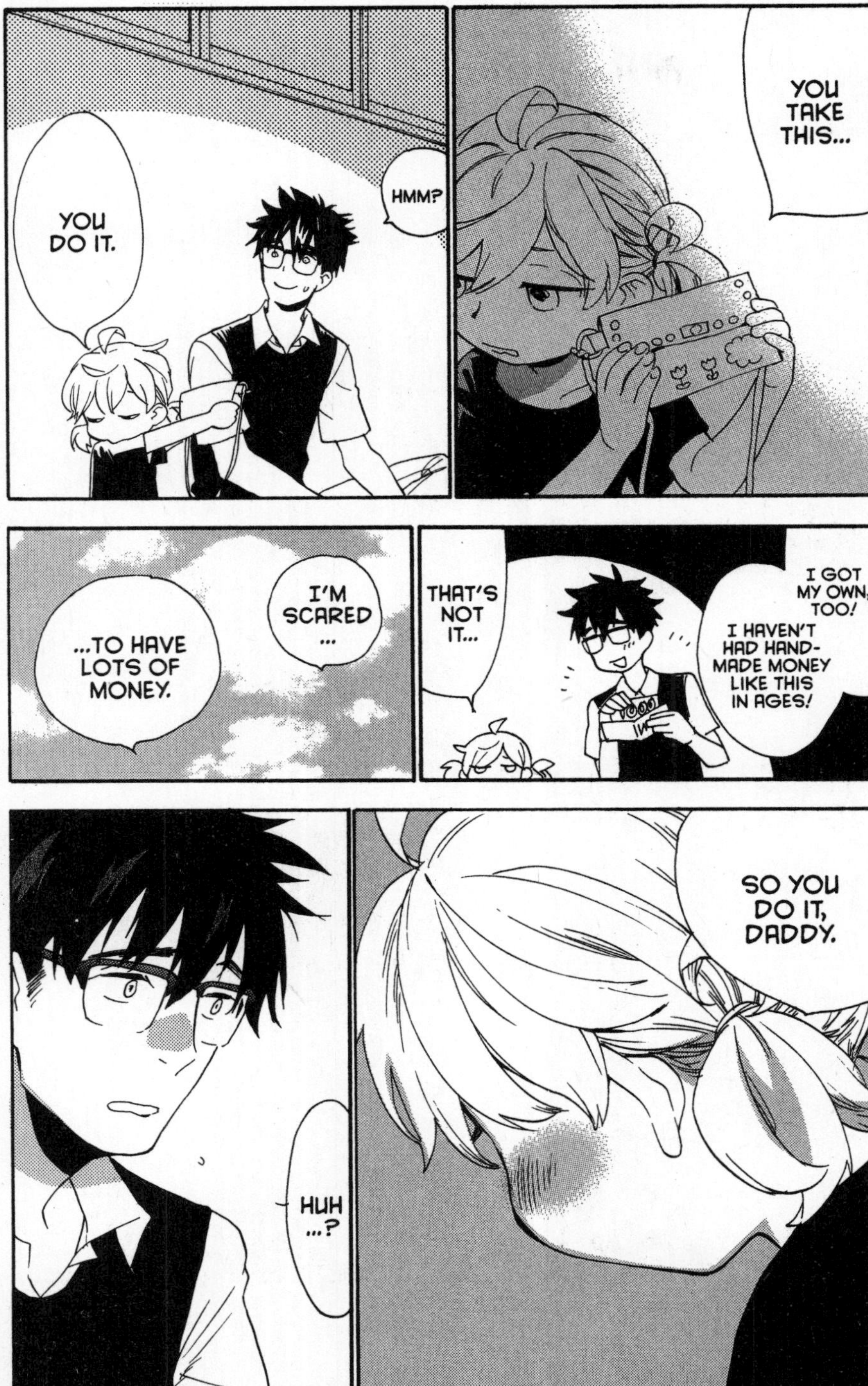
YOU TAKE THIS...
HMM?
YOU DO IT.
I GOT MY OWN, TOO!
I HAVEN'T HAD HAND-MADE MONEY LIKE THIS IN AGES!
THAT'S NOT IT...
I'M SCARED ...
...TO HAVE LOTS OF MONEY.
SO YOU DO IT, DADDY.
HUH ...?

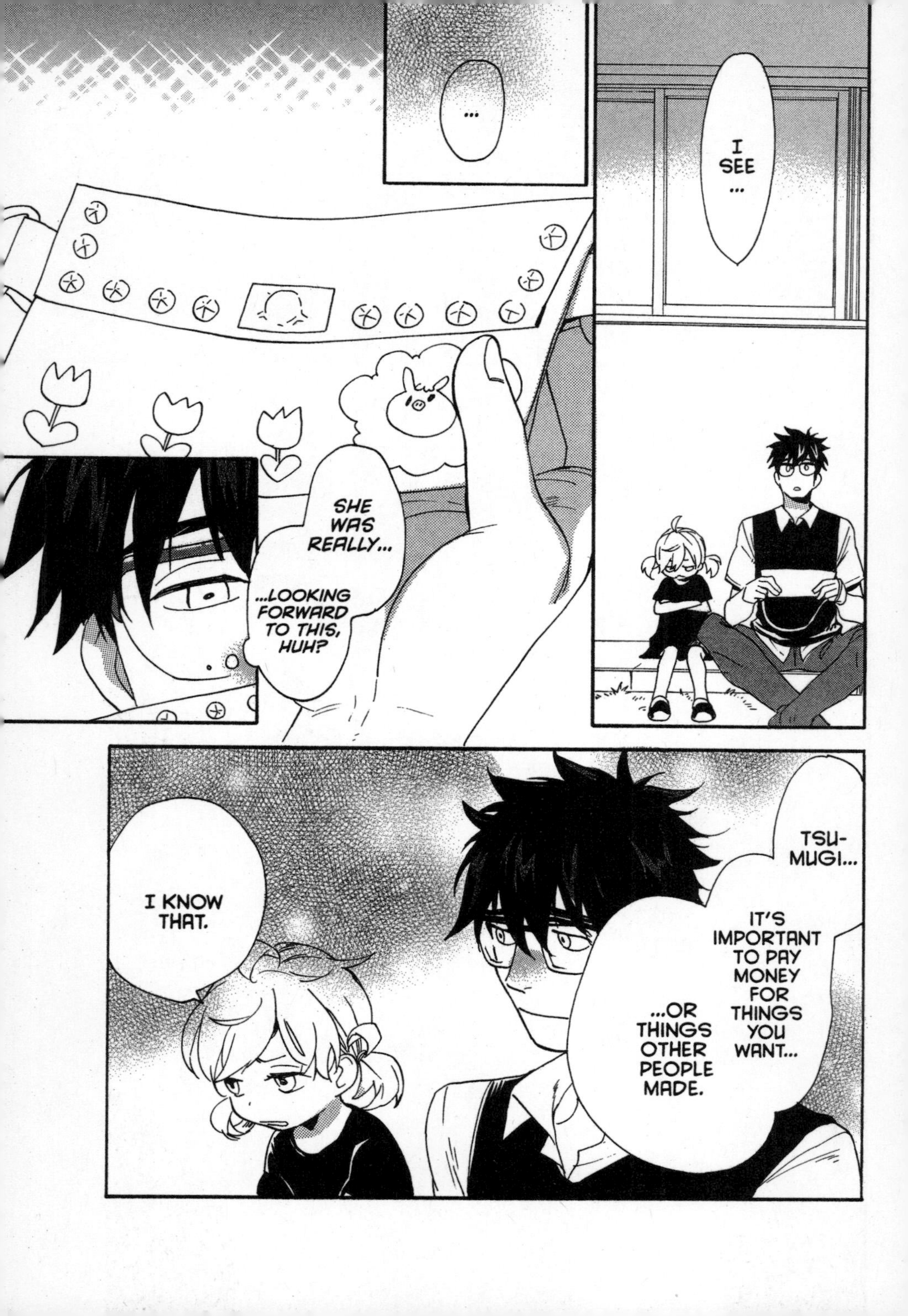

I SEE ...
...
SHE WAS REALLY...
...LOOKING FORWARD TO THIS, HUH?
TSU-MUGI...
IT'S IMPORTANT TO PAY MONEY FOR THINGS YOU WANT...
...OR THINGS OTHER PEOPLE MADE.
I KNOW THAT.

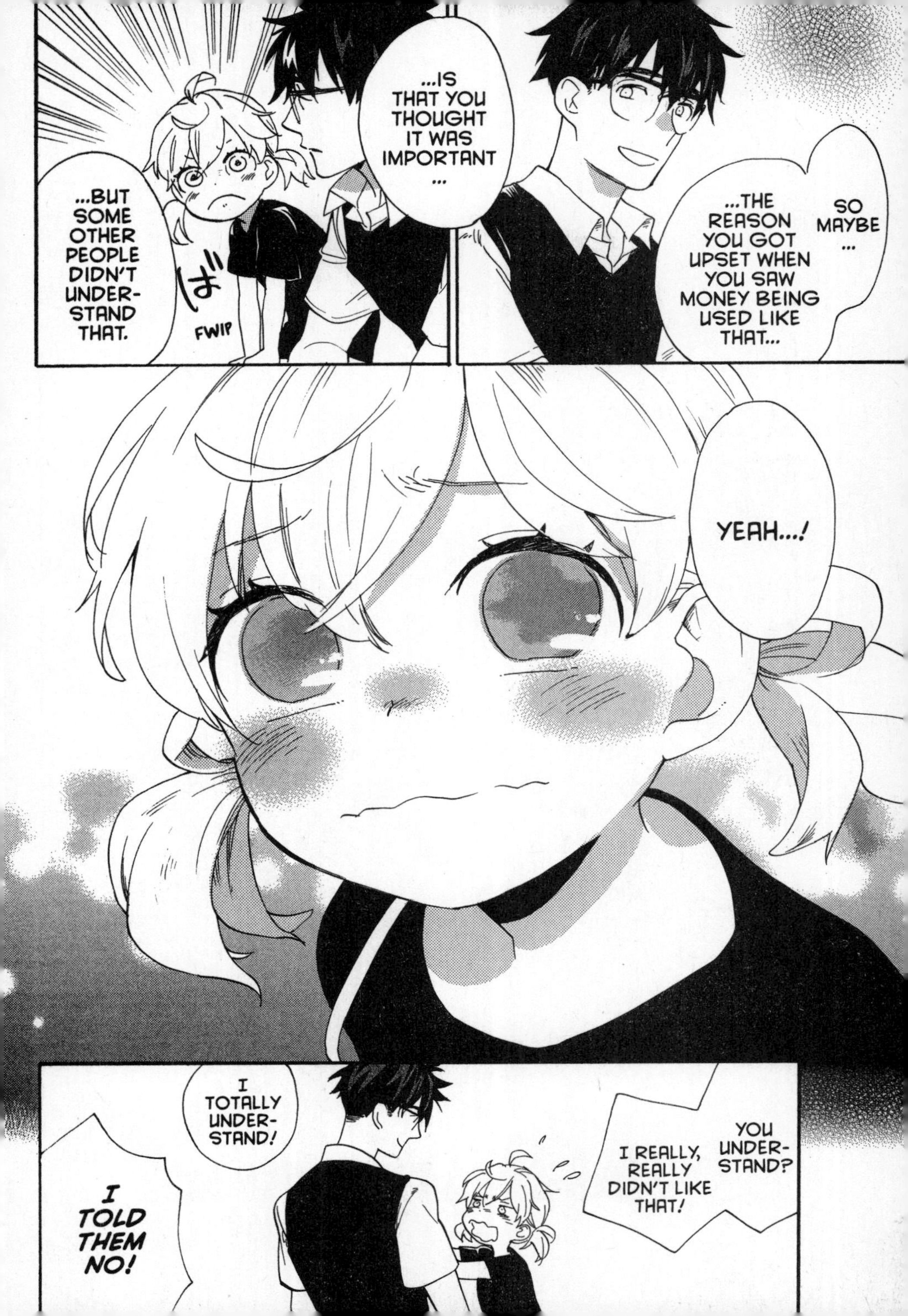
SO MAYBE ...
...THE REASON YOU GOT UPSET WHEN YOU SAW MONEY BEING USED LIKE THAT...
...IS THAT YOU THOUGHT IT WAS IMPORTANT ...
...BUT SOME OTHER PEOPLE DIDN'T UNDER-STAND THAT.
ば
FWIP
YEAH...!
YOU UNDER-STAND?
I REALLY, REALLY DIDN'T LIKE THAT!
I TOTALLY UNDER-STAND!
I TOLD THEM NO!

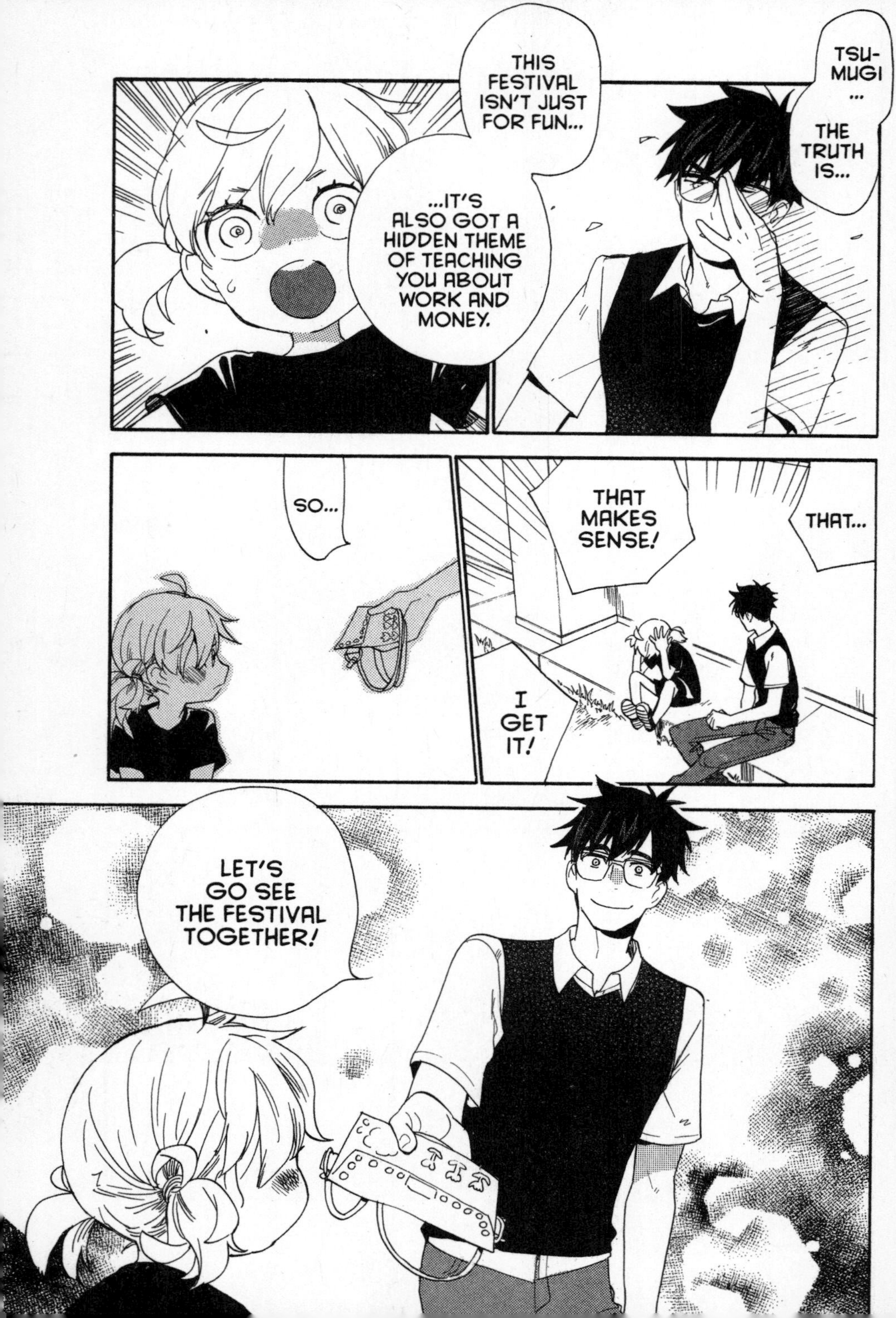
TSU-MUGI... THE TRUTH IS...
THIS FESTIVAL ISN'T JUST FOR FUN...
...IT'S ALSO GOT A HIDDEN THEME OF TEACHING YOU ABOUT WORK AND MONEY.
THAT...
THAT MAKES SENSE!
I GET IT!
SO...
LET'S GO SEE THE FESTIVAL TOGETHER!

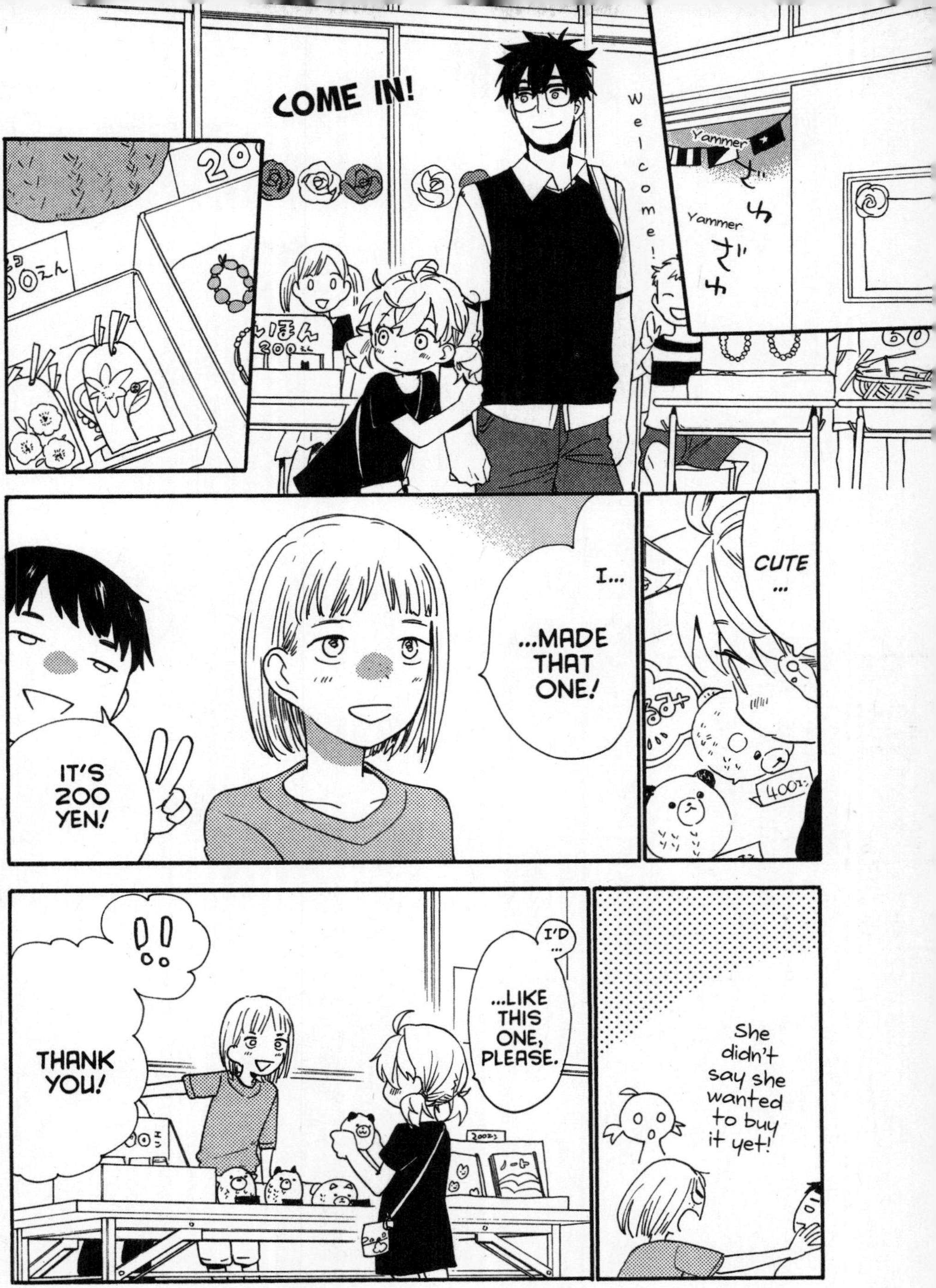
Yammer
Yammer
Welcome!
COME IN!
CUTE...
I...
...MADE THAT ONE!
IT'S 200 YEN!
She didn't say she wanted to buy it yet!
I'D...
...LIKE THIS ONE, PLEASE.
!!
THANK YOU!

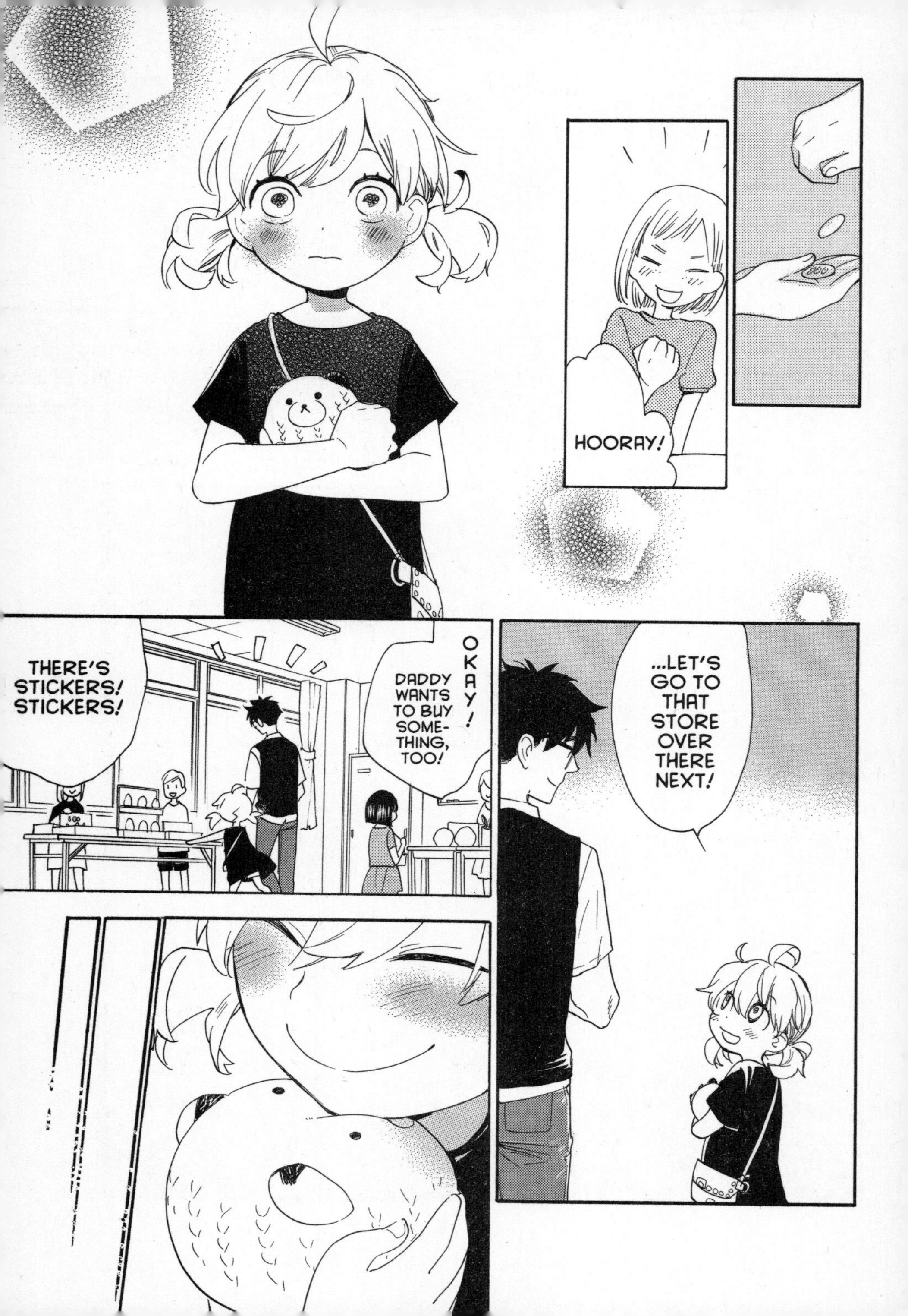
HOORAY!
...LET'S GO TO THAT STORE OVER THERE NEXT!
OKAY!
DADDY WANTS TO BUY SOME-THING, TOO!
THERE'S STICKERS! STICKERS!

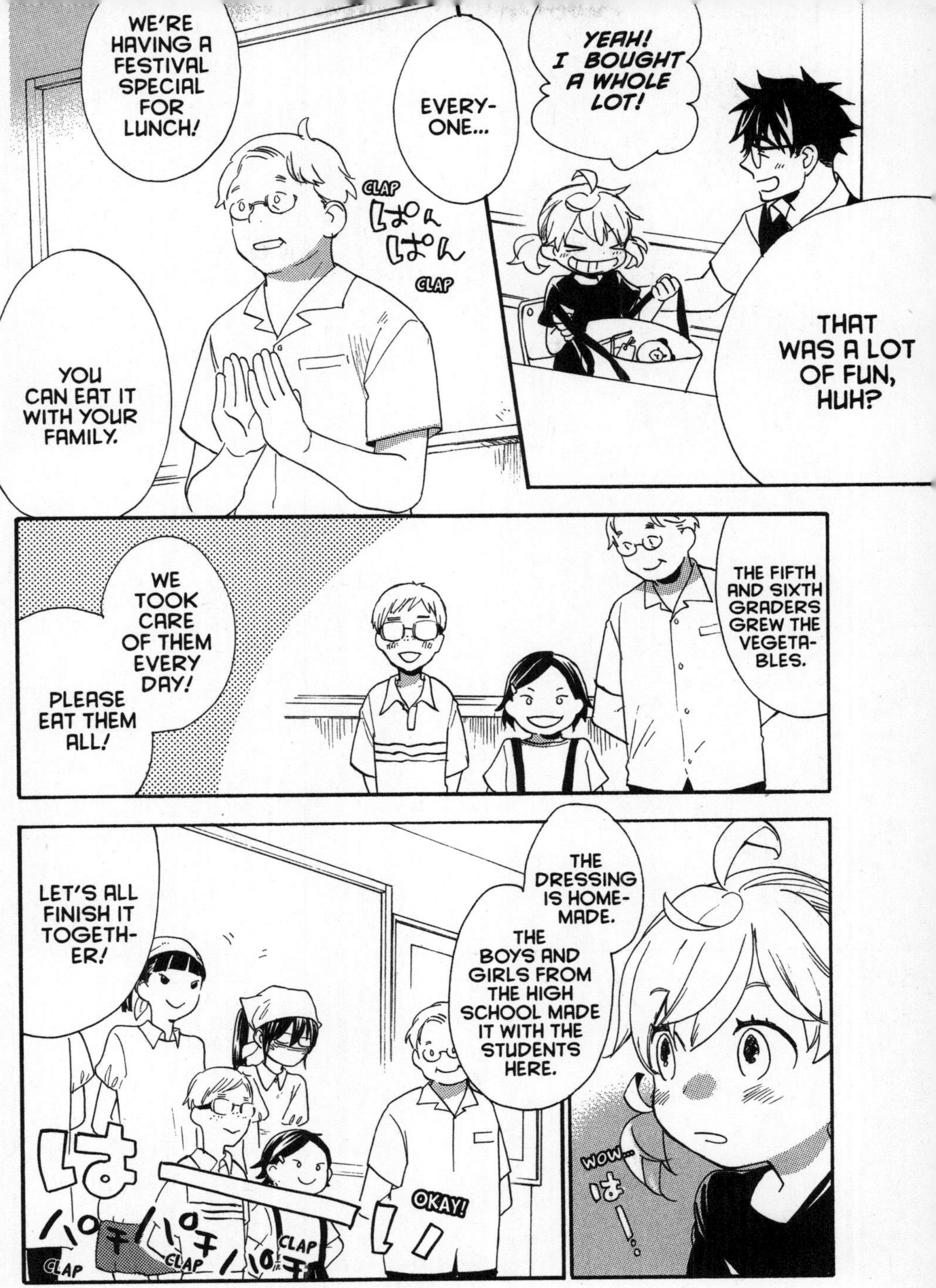
THAT WAS A LOT OF FUN, HUH?
YEAH! I BOUGHT A WHOLE LOT!
EVERY-ONE...
WE'RE HAVING A FESTIVAL SPECIAL FOR LUNCH!
CLAP ぱん
ぱん CLAP
YOU CAN EAT IT WITH YOUR FAMILY.
THE FIFTH AND SIXTH GRADERS GREW THE VEGETA-BLES.
WE TOOK CARE OF THEM EVERY DAY!
PLEASE EAT THEM ALL!
THE DRESSING IS HOME-MADE.
THE BOYS AND GIRLS FROM THE HIGH SCHOOL MADE IT WITH THE STUDENTS HERE.
WOW... は～。
LET'S ALL FINISH IT TOGETH-ER!
はーい! OKAY!
パチパチパチ CLAP CLAP CLAP

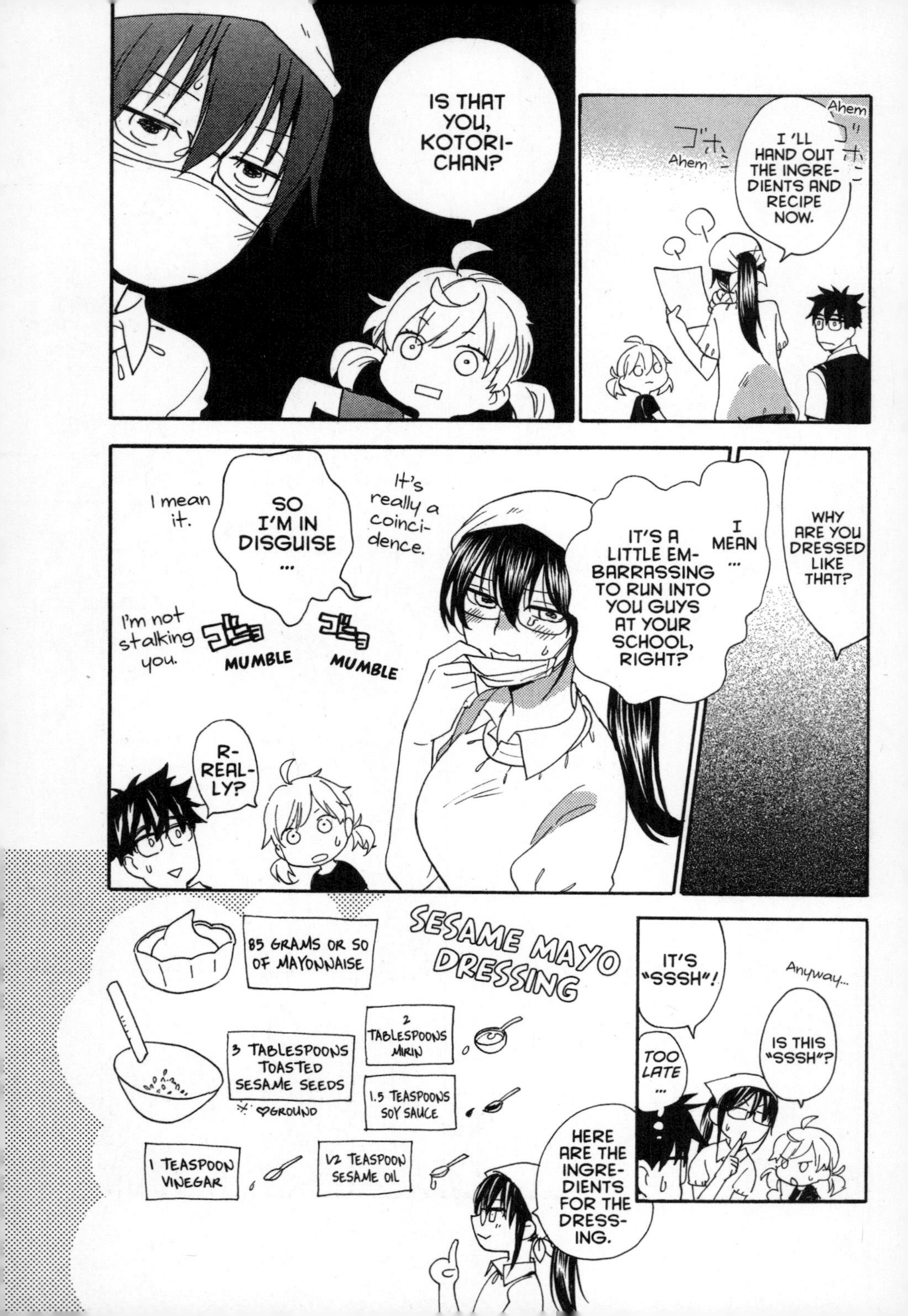

Ahem
Ahem
I'LL HAND OUT THE INGREDIENTS AND RECIPE NOW.
IS THAT YOU, KOTORI-CHAN?
WHY ARE YOU DRESSED LIKE THAT?
I MEAN ...
IT'S A LITTLE EMBARRASSING TO RUN INTO YOU GUYS AT YOUR SCHOOL, RIGHT?
It's really a coincidence.
SO I'M IN DISGUISE ...
I mean it.
MUMBLE
MUMBLE
I'm not stalking you.
R-REALLY?
IT'S "SSSH"!
Anyway...
IS THIS "SSSH"?
TOO LATE ...
SESAME MAYO DRESSING
85 GRAMS OR SO OF MAYONNAISE
2 TABLESPOONS MIRIN
3 TABLESPOONS TOASTED SESAME SEEDS
※ ♡GROUND
1.5 TEASPOONS SOY SAUCE
1/2 TEASPOON SESAME OIL
1 TEASPOON VINEGAR
HERE ARE THE INGREDIENTS FOR THE DRESSING.

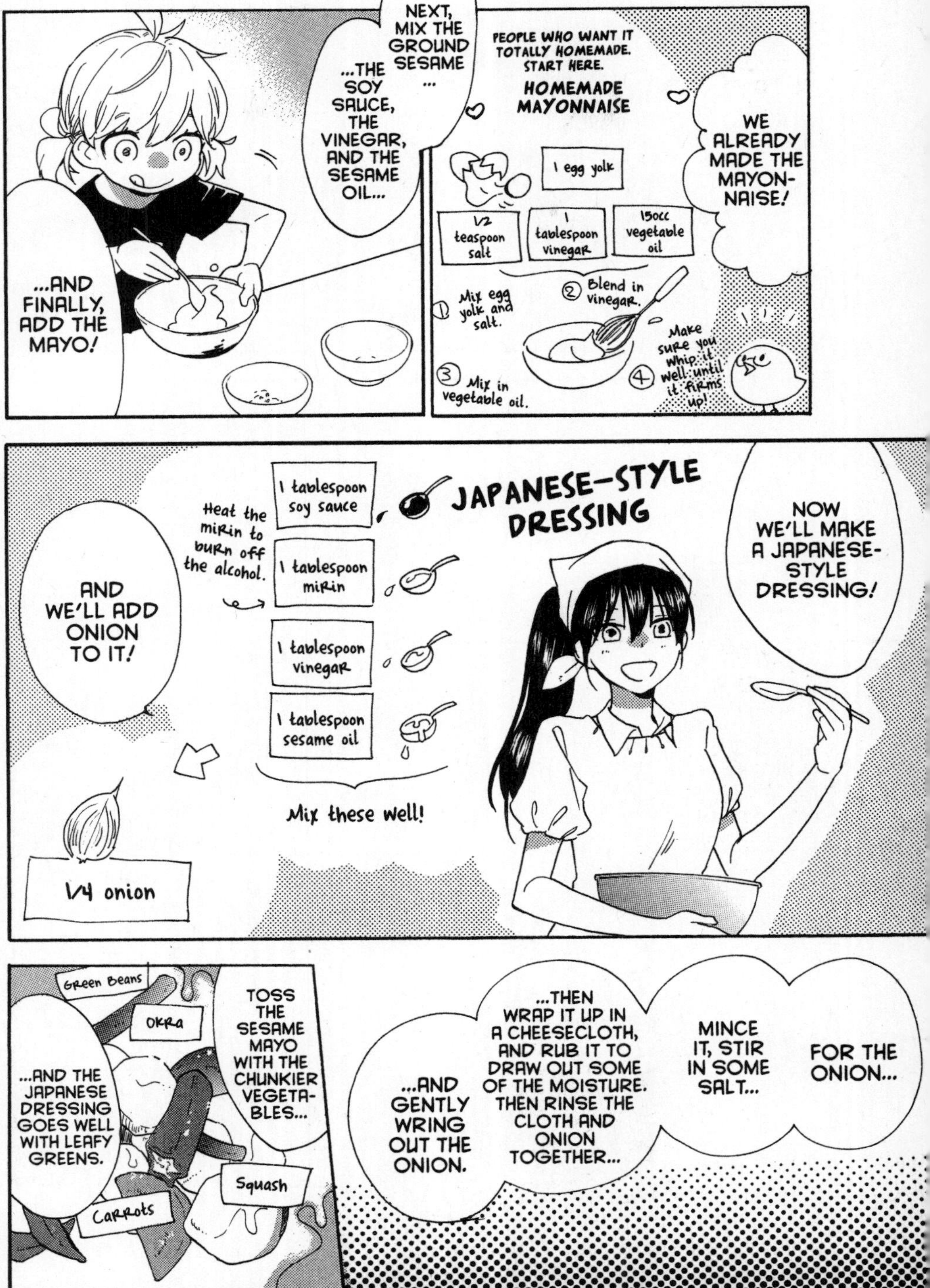
WE ALREADY MADE THE MAYONNAISE!
PEOPLE WHO WANT IT TOTALLY HOMEMADE. START HERE.
HOMEMADE MAYONNAISE
1 egg yolk
1/2 teaspoon salt
1 tablespoon vinegar
150cc vegetable oil
① Mix egg yolk and salt.
② Blend in vinegar.
③ Mix in vegetable oil.
④ Make sure you whip it well until it firms up!
NEXT, MIX THE GROUND SESAME ...
...THE SOY SAUCE, THE VINEGAR, AND THE SESAME OIL...
...AND FINALLY, ADD THE MAYO!
NOW WE'LL MAKE A JAPANESE-STYLE DRESSING!
JAPANESE-STYLE DRESSING
1 tablespoon soy sauce
1 tablespoon mirin
Heat the mirin to burn off the alcohol.
1 tablespoon vinegar
1 tablespoon sesame oil
Mix these well!
AND WE'LL ADD ONION TO IT!
1/4 onion
FOR THE ONION...
MINCE IT, STIR IN SOME SALT...
...THEN WRAP IT UP IN A CHEESECLOTH, AND RUB IT TO DRAW OUT SOME OF THE MOISTURE. THEN RINSE THE CLOTH AND ONION TOGETHER...
...AND GENTLY WRING OUT THE ONION.
TOSS THE SESAME MAYO WITH THE CHUNKIER VEGETABLES...
...AND THE JAPANESE DRESSING GOES WELL WITH LEAFY GREENS.
Green Beans
Okra
Squash
Carrots

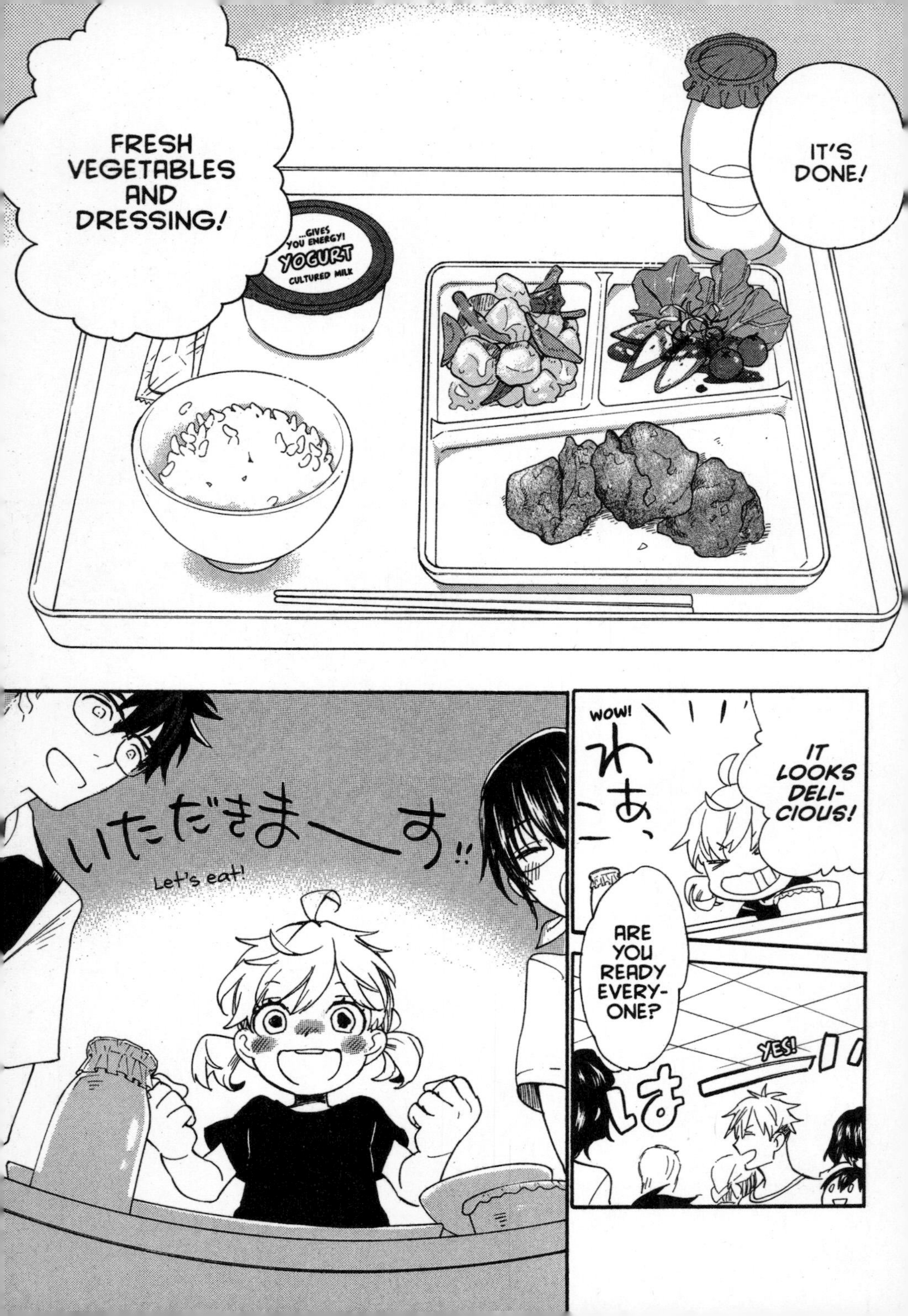
IT'S DONE!
FRESH VEGETABLES AND DRESSING!
...GIVES YOU ENERGY! YOGURT CULTURED MILK
WOW!
わあ、
IT LOOKS DELICIOUS!
ARE YOU READY EVERYONE?
YES!
はーー
いただきまーす!!
Let's eat!

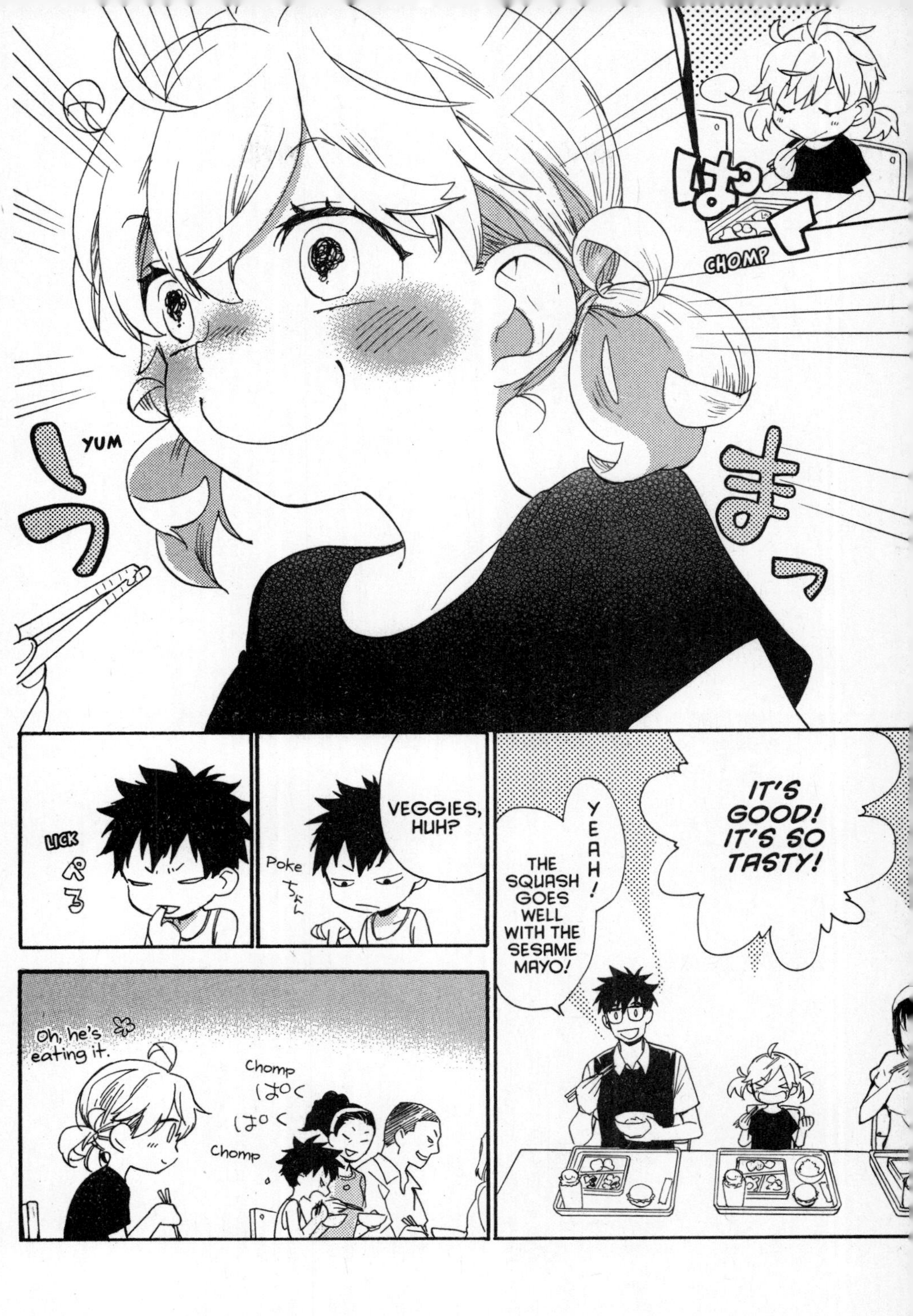
CHOMP
YUM
IT'S GOOD! IT'S SO TASTY!
YEAH!
THE SQUASH GOES WELL WITH THE SESAME MAYO!
VEGGIES, HUH?
Poke
LICK
ぺろ
Oh, he's eating it.
Chomp
ぱく
ぱく
Chomp

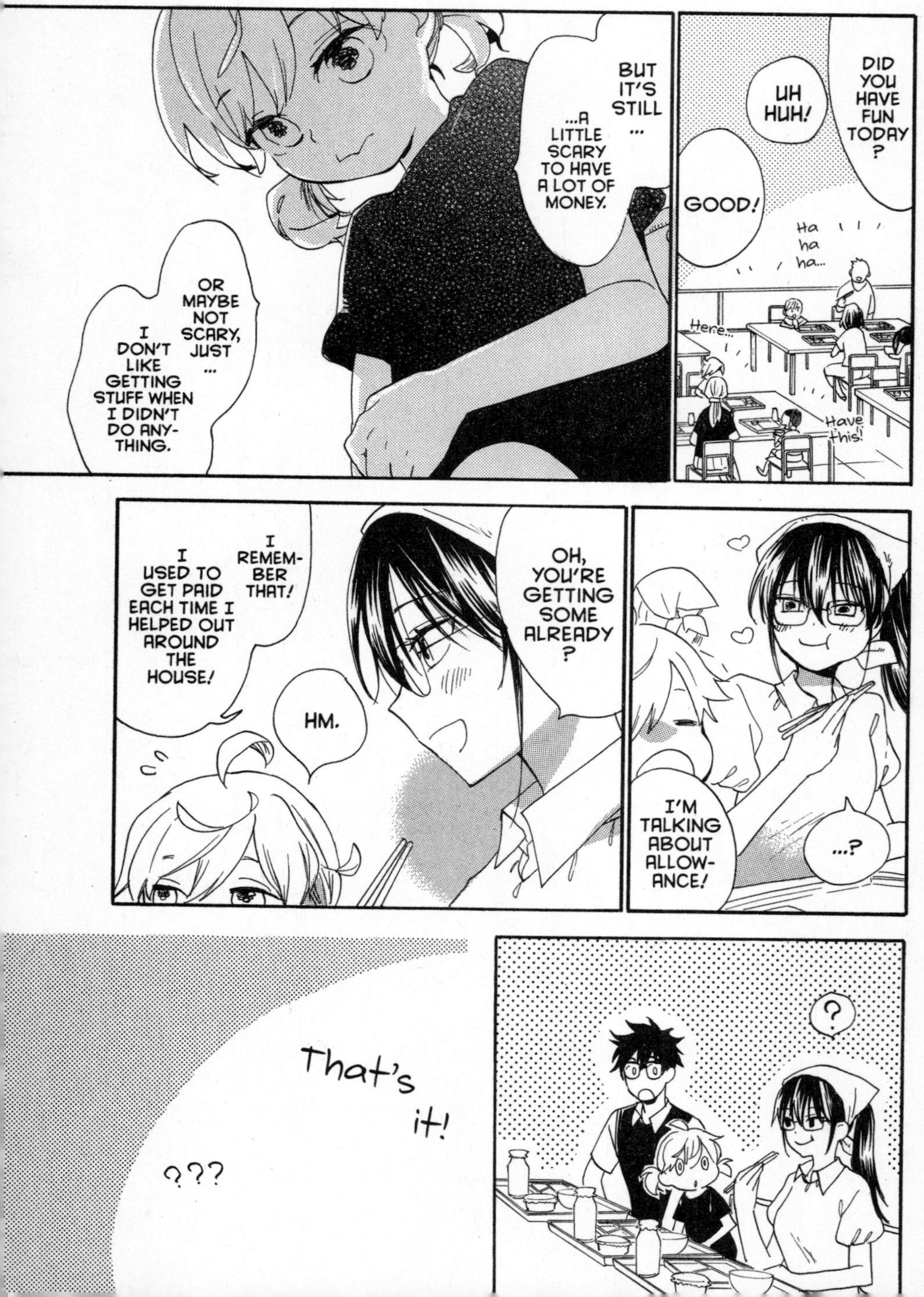
DID YOU HAVE FUN TODAY?
UH HUH!
GOOD!
Ha ha ha...
Here...
Have this!
BUT IT'S STILL...
...A LITTLE SCARY TO HAVE A LOT OF MONEY.
OR MAYBE NOT SCARY, JUST...
I DON'T LIKE GETTING STUFF WHEN I DIDN'T DO ANYTHING.
I'M TALKING ABOUT ALLOWANCE!
...?
OH, YOU'RE GETTING SOME ALREADY?
I REMEMBER THAT!
I USED TO GET PAID EACH TIME I HELPED OUT AROUND THE HOUSE!
HM.
?
That's it!
???

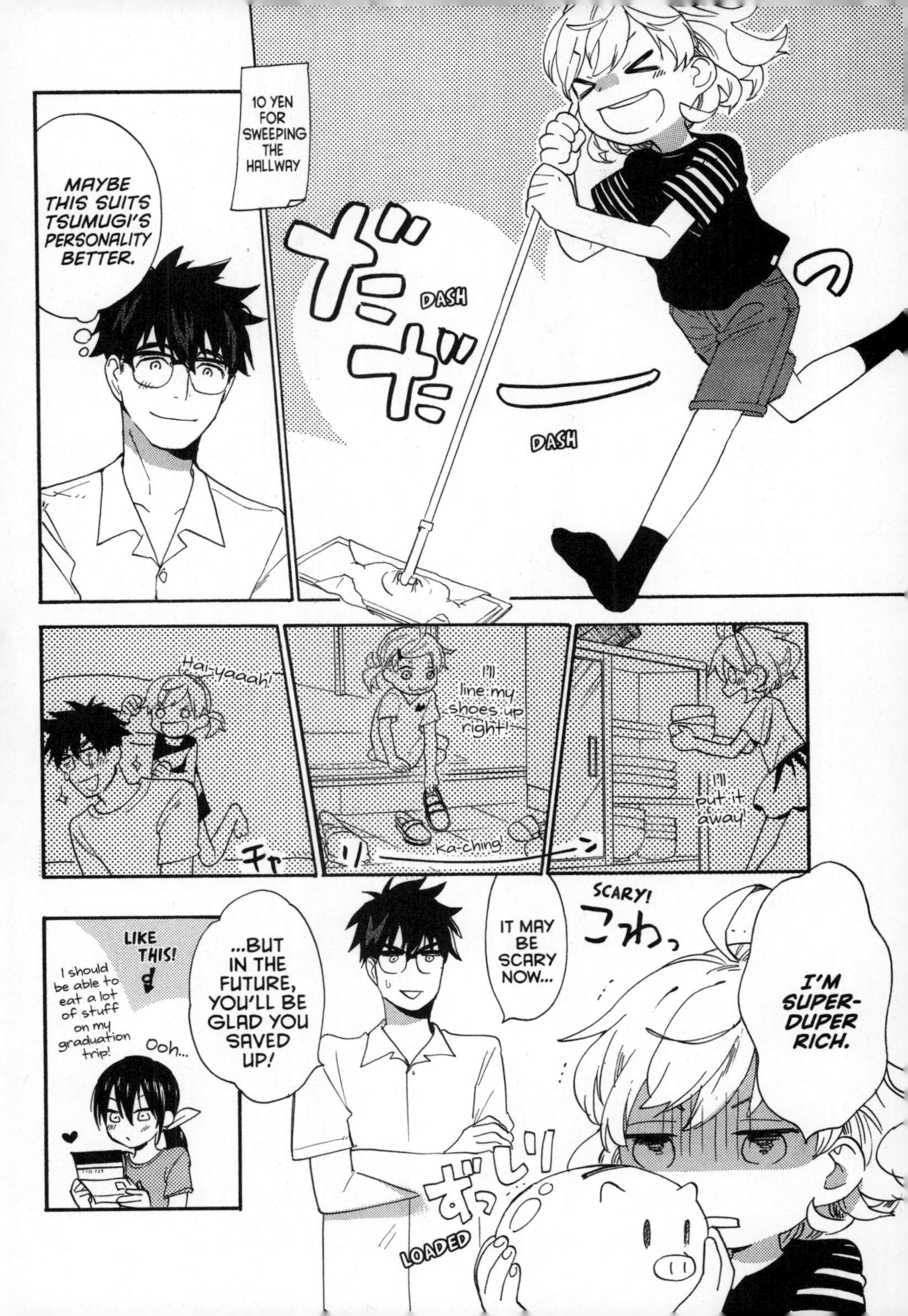
10 YEN FOR SWEEPING THE HALLWAY
ダ
DASH
ダー
DASH
MAYBE THIS SUITS TSUMUGI'S PERSONALITY BETTER.
I'll put it away!
I'll line my shoes up right!
ka-ching!
Hai-yaaah!
チャ
SCARY!
こわっ
I'M SUPER-DUPER RICH.
ずっしり
LOADED
IT MAY BE SCARY NOW...
...BUT IN THE FUTURE, YOU'LL BE GLAD YOU SAVED UP!
LIKE THIS!
I should be able to eat a lot of stuff on my graduation trip!
Ooh...

HOMEMADE MAYONNAISE

☆ Ingredients ☆ (Makes about 170g)

- →1 egg yolk
- →1 tablespoon vinegar
- →½ teaspoon salt
- →150cc salad oil

Directions

1. Mix the salt and the egg yolk.
2. Add the vinegar to (1) and mix until the salt has completely dissolved.
3. Mix (2) well while gradually adding the salad oil. Whisk until the mixture has emulsified and peaks form.

SESAME MAYO DRESSING

☆ Ingredients ☆

- →60-80g mayonnaise
- →2 tablespoons mirin
- →1 teaspoon vinegar
- →3 tablespoons sesame seeds
- →1.5 teaspoons soy sauce
- →½ teaspoon sesame oil

Directions

1. Simmer the mirin until about half is left. Remove from heat and let cool.
2. Crush the sesame seeds. Mix the seeds, (1), soy sauce, vinegar and sesame oil together.
3. Add mayonnaise to (2) until desired consistency.

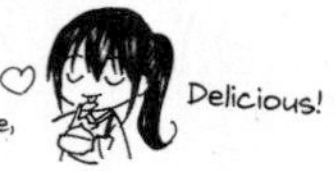
Delicious!

JAPANESE STYLE SALAD DRESSING

☆ Ingredients ☆

- →1 tablespoon soy sauce
- →½ tablespoon vinegar
- →1 tablespoon mirin
- →½ tablespoon sesame oil

Directions

1. Simmer the mirin then let cool.
2. Combine all the ingredients together.

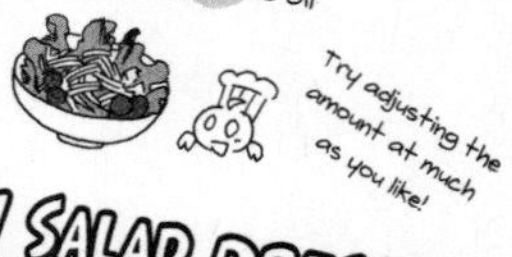
Try adjusting the amount at much as you like!

JAPANESE STYLE GREEN ONION SALAD DRESSING

☆ Ingredients ☆

- →¼ (50g) green onion
- →½ teaspoon salt

Directions

1. Dice the green onion into tiny pieces, add salt and mix.
2. Press (1) through a sieve until all the slime has been removed. Mix (2) well while gradually adding the salad oil. Whisk until the mixture has emulsified and peaks form. Rinse the sieve in some water, then dry.
3. Mix (2) to the Japanese dressing.
4. Season with (a tiny amount) of salt.

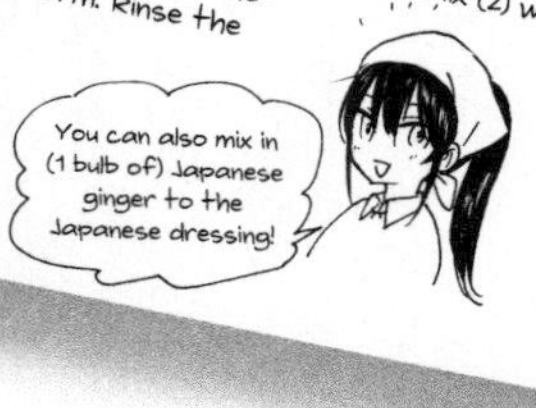
You can also mix in (1 bulb of) Japanese ginger to the Japanese dressing!

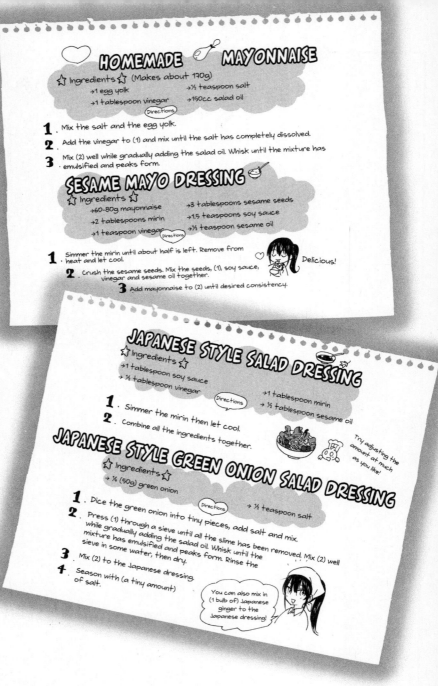

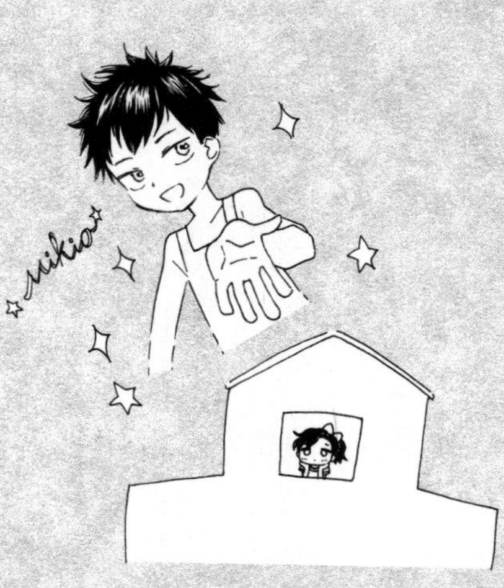
mikio

Chapter 47 | Celebratory Sukiyaki

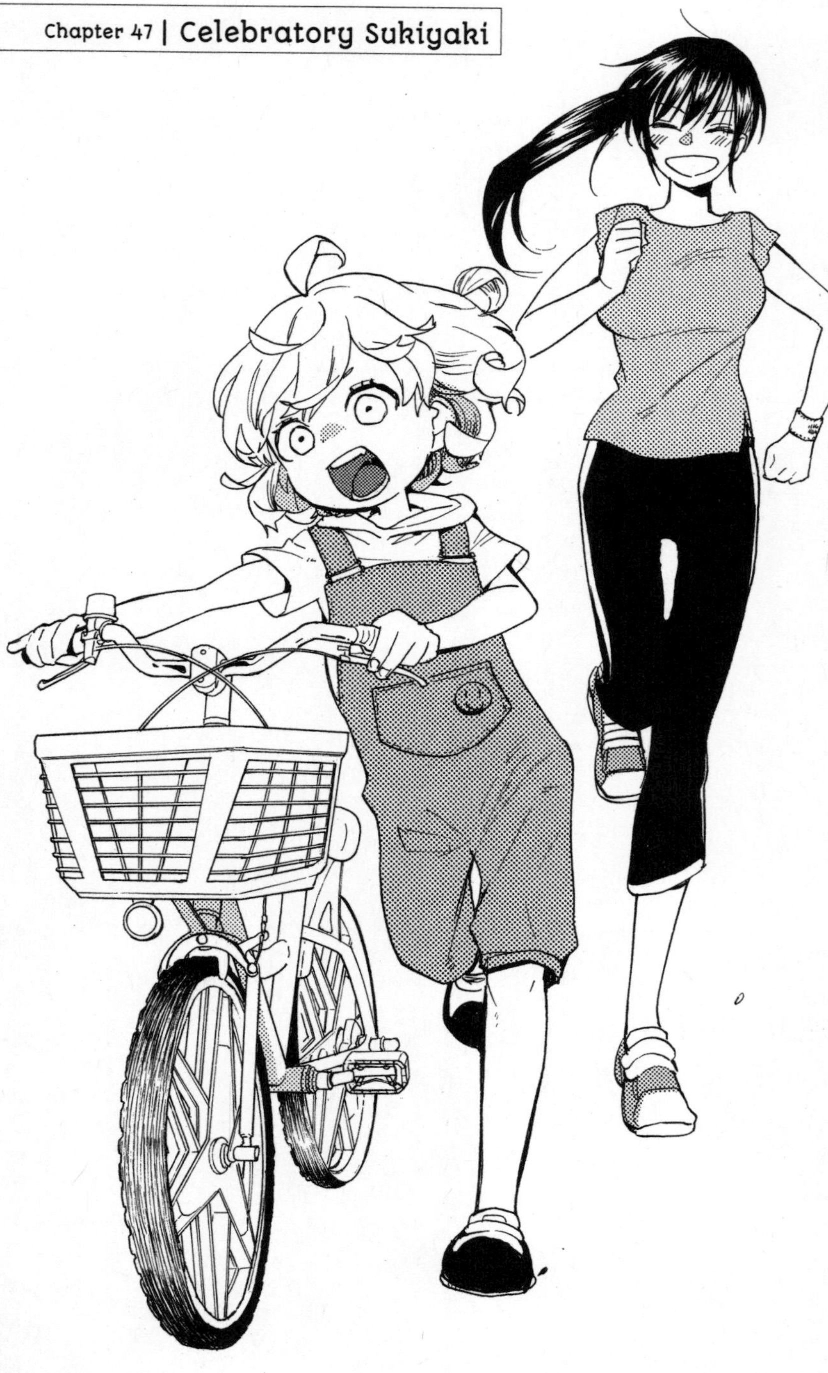

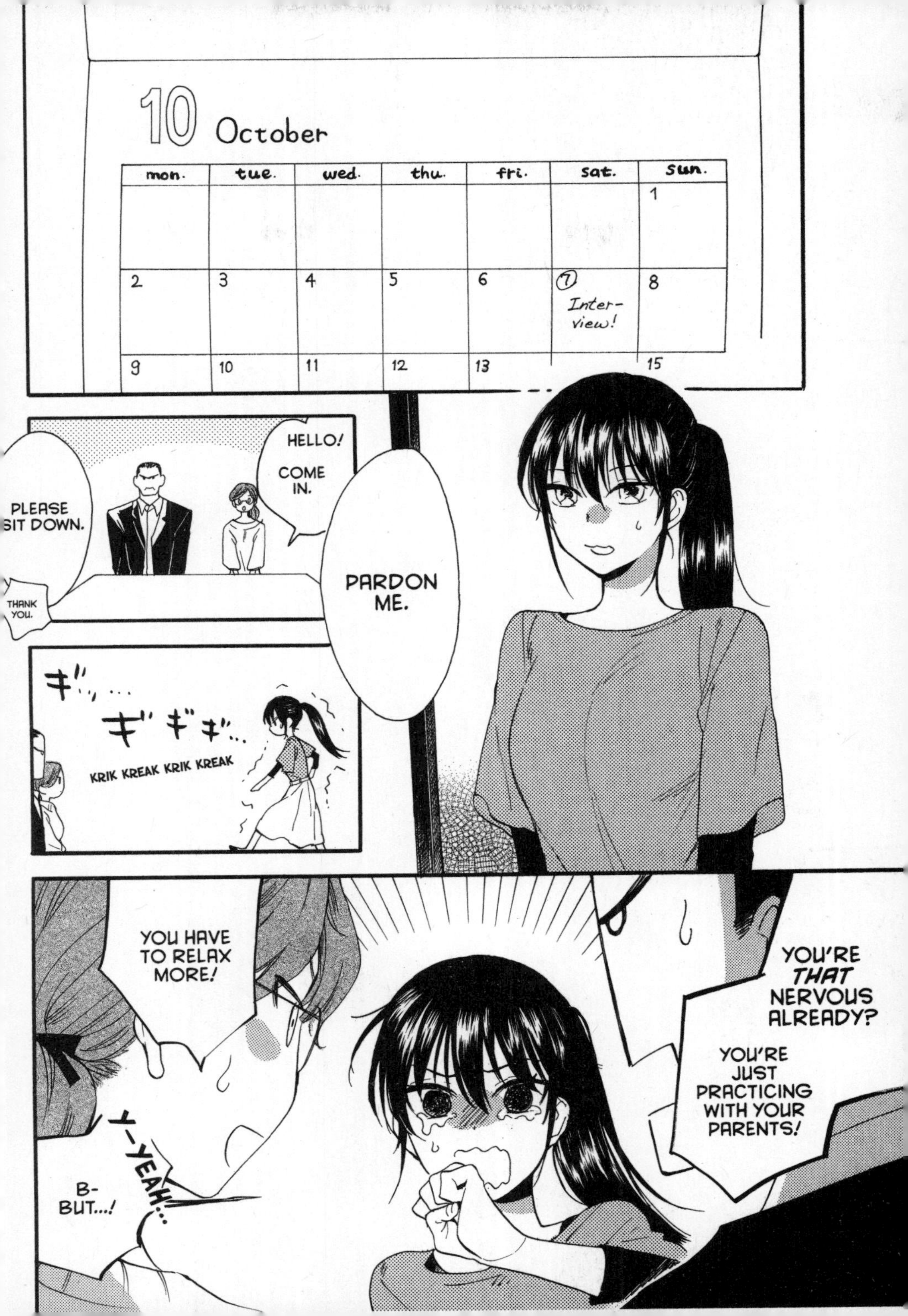
10 October
mon. tue. wed. thu. fri. sat. sun.
1
2 3 4 5 6 7 8
Inter-view!
9 10 11 12 13 15
PARDON ME.
HELLO! COME IN.
PLEASE SIT DOWN.
THANK YOU.
ギ‥…
ギギギ…
KRIK KREAK KRIK KREAK
YOU'RE THAT NERVOUS ALREADY?
YOU'RE JUST PRACTICING WITH YOUR PARENTS!
YOU HAVE TO RELAX MORE!
Y-YEAH…
B-BUT…!

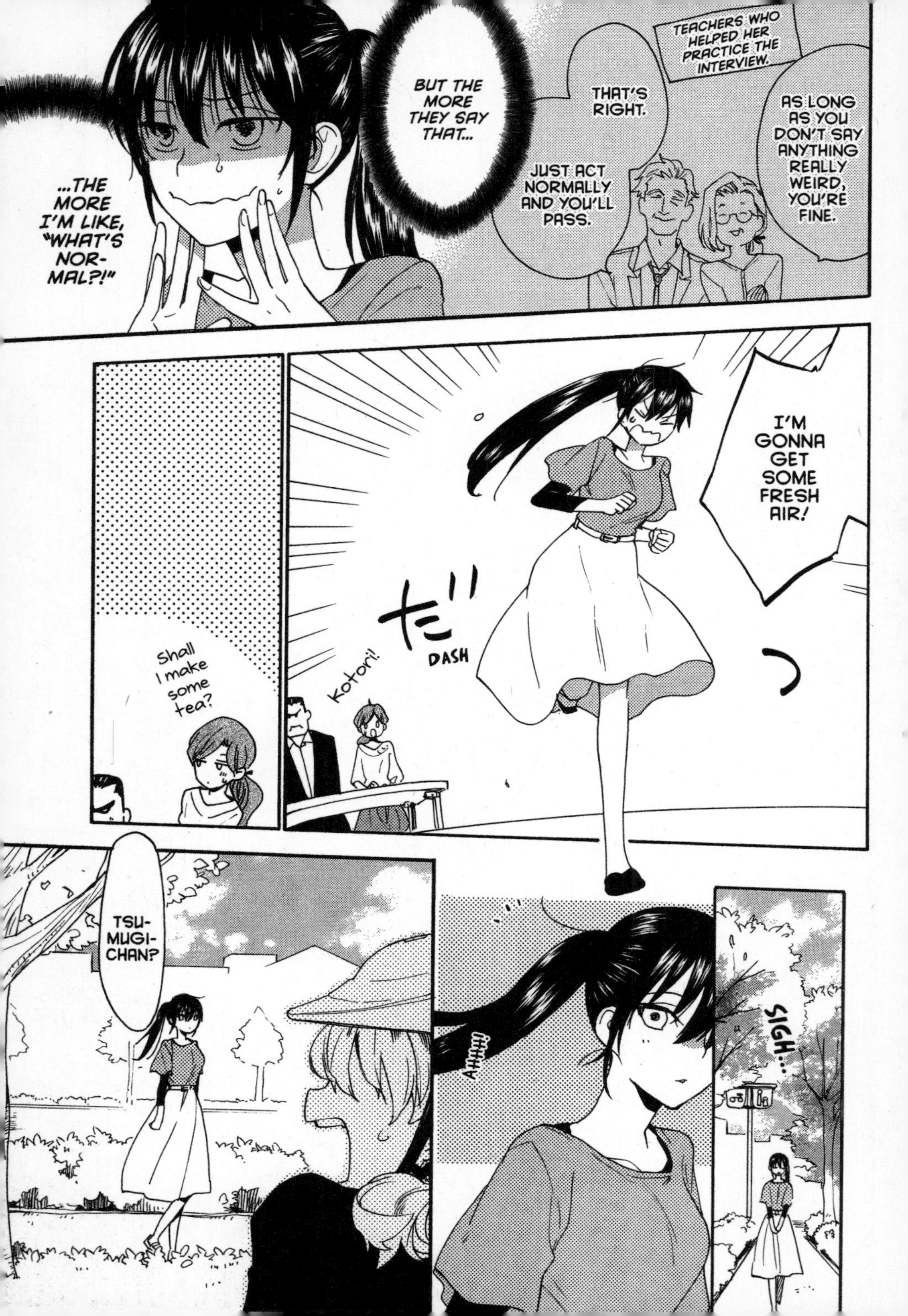
TEACHERS WHO HELPED HER PRACTICE THE INTERVIEW.
AS LONG AS YOU DON'T SAY ANYTHING REALLY WEIRD, YOU'RE FINE.
THAT'S RIGHT.
JUST ACT NORMALLY AND YOU'LL PASS.
BUT THE MORE THEY SAY THAT...
...THE MORE I'M LIKE, "WHAT'S NOR-MAL?!"
I'M GONNA GET SOME FRESH AIR!
だッ
DASH
Kotori!
Shall I make some tea?
SIGH...
AHHHH!!
TSU-MUGI-CHAN?

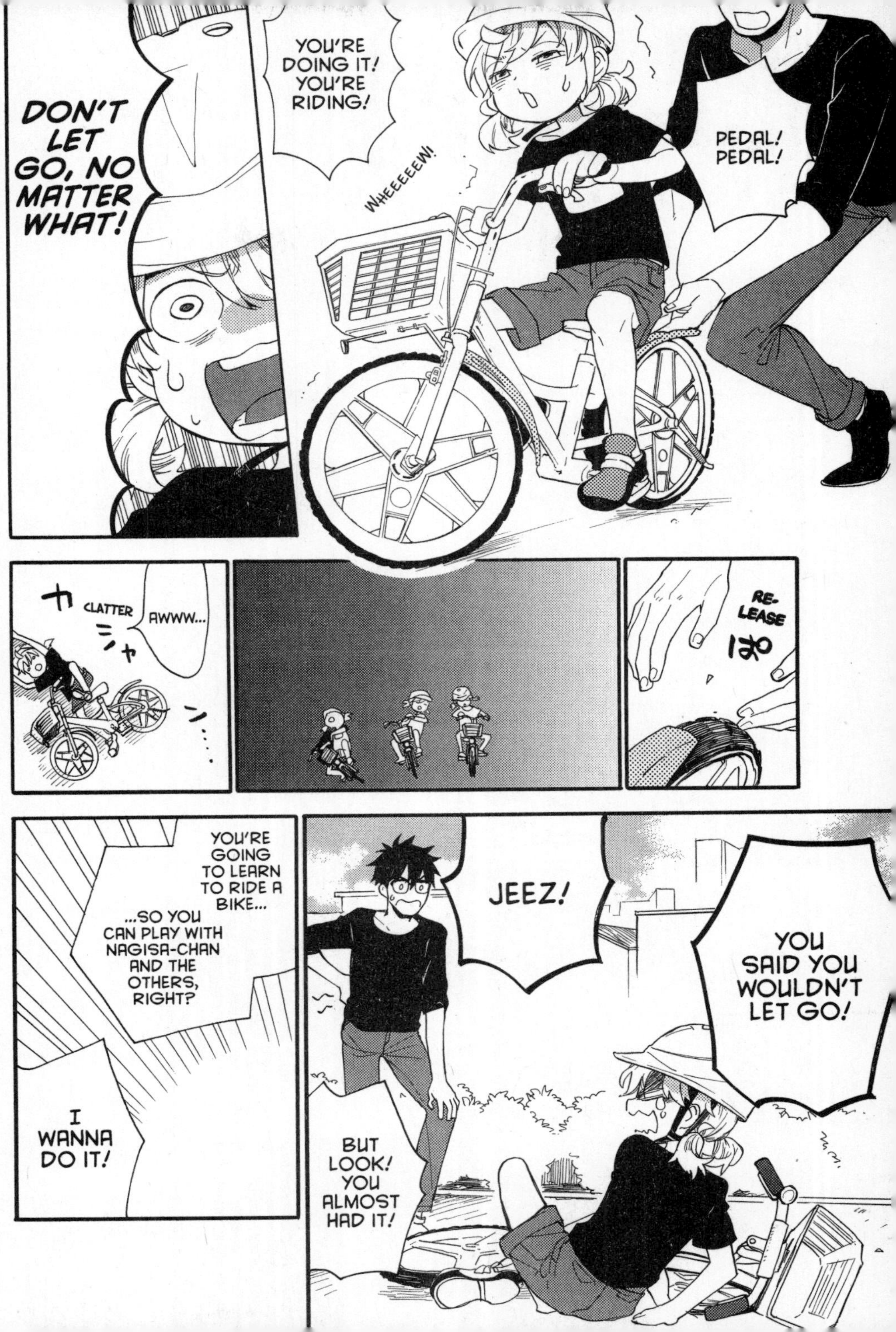
PEDAL! PEDAL!
YOU'RE DOING IT! YOU'RE RIDING!
WHEEEEEW!
DON'T LET GO, NO MATTER WHAT!
RE-LEASE
ぱっ
AWWW...
CLATTER
ガシャン
YOU SAID YOU WOULDN'T LET GO!
JEEZ!
BUT LOOK! YOU ALMOST HAD IT!
YOU'RE GOING TO LEARN TO RIDE A BIKE...
...SO YOU CAN PLAY WITH NAGISA-CHAN AND THE OTHERS, RIGHT?
I WANNA DO IT!

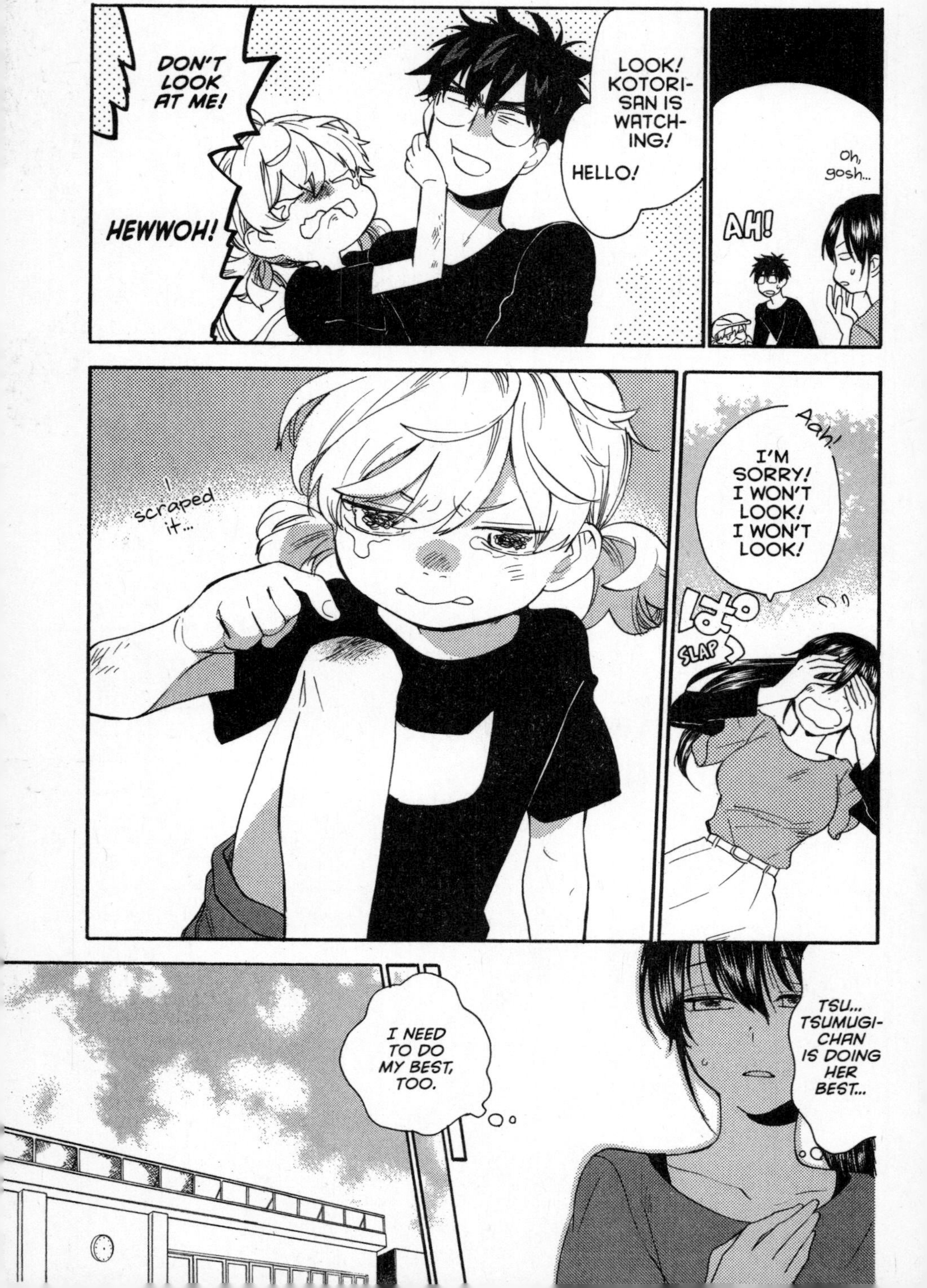
Oh, gosh...
AH!
LOOK! KOTORI-SAN IS WATCHING!
HELLO!
DON'T LOOK AT ME!
HEWWOH!
Aah!
I'M SORRY! I WON'T LOOK! I WON'T LOOK!
ぱっ
SLAP
I scraped it...
TSU... TSUMUGI-CHAN IS DOING HER BEST...
I NEED TO DO MY BEST, TOO.

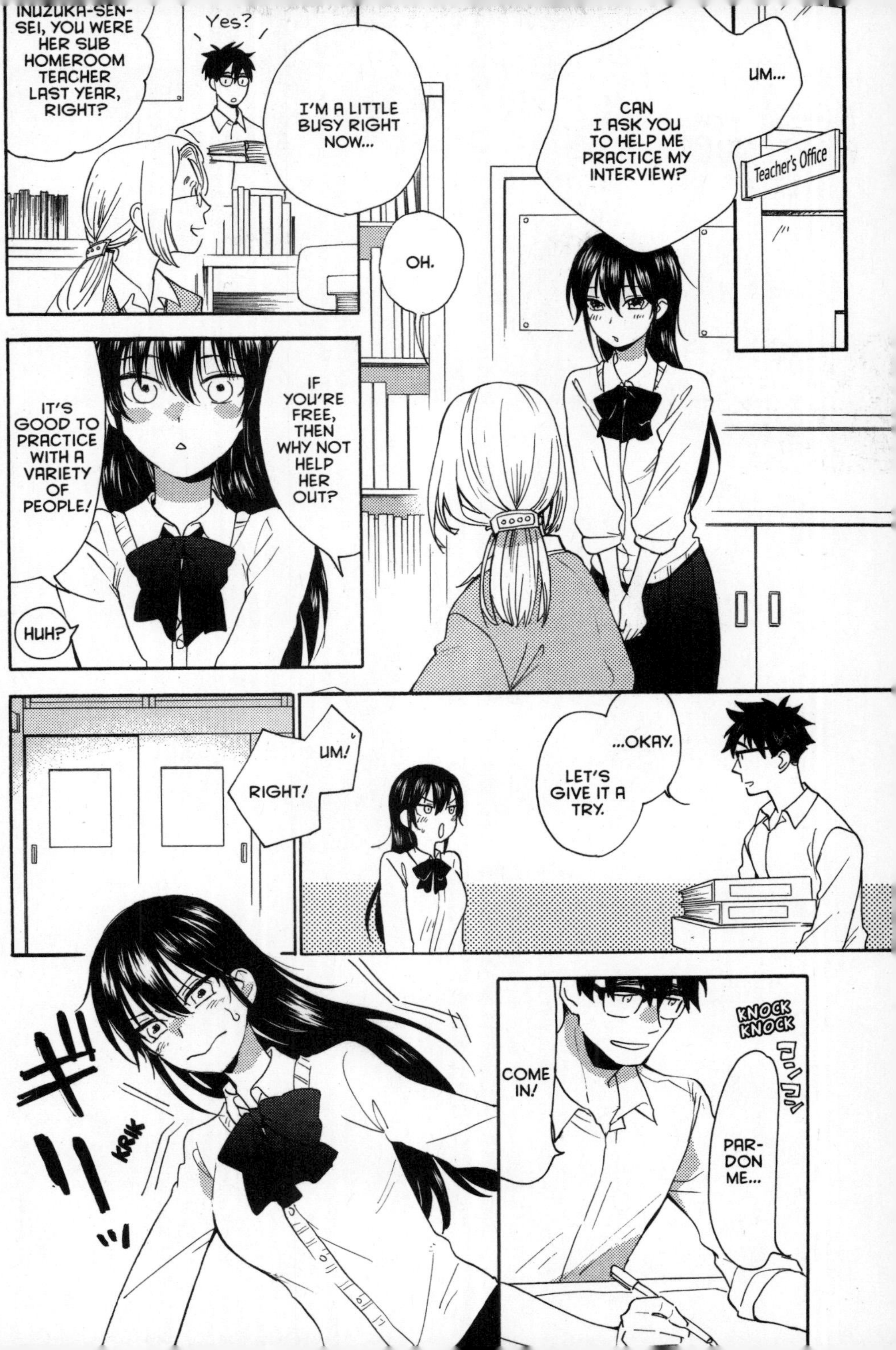
UM...
CAN I ASK YOU TO HELP ME PRACTICE MY INTERVIEW?
Teacher's Office
I'M A LITTLE BUSY RIGHT NOW...
OH.
INUZUKA-SENSEI, YOU WERE HER SUB HOMEROOM TEACHER LAST YEAR, RIGHT?
Yes?
IF YOU'RE FREE, THEN WHY NOT HELP HER OUT?
IT'S GOOD TO PRACTICE WITH A VARIETY OF PEOPLE!
HUH?
...OKAY.
LET'S GIVE IT A TRY.
UM!
RIGHT!
KNOCK KNOCK
PARDON ME...
COME IN!
KRIK

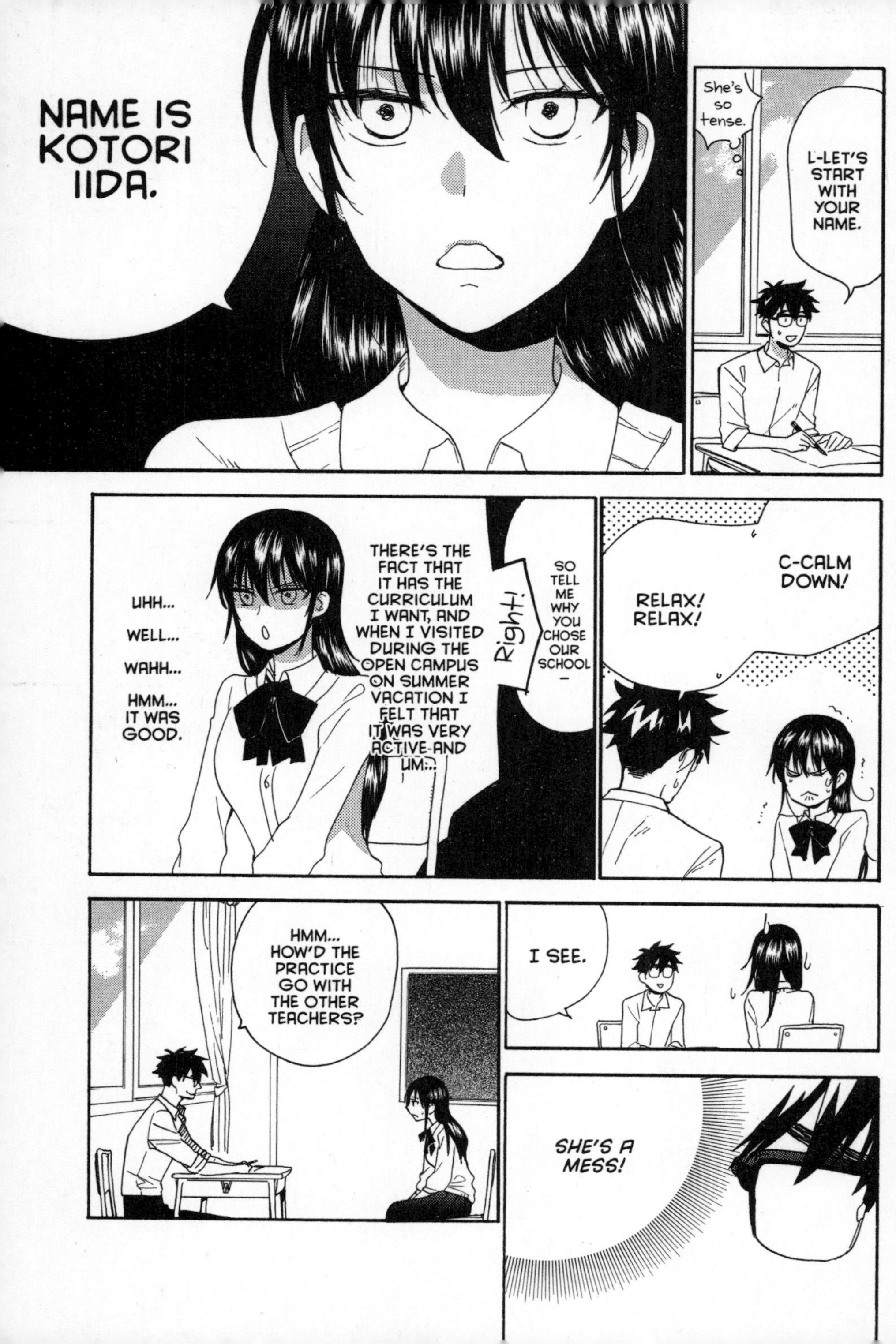
She's so tense.
L-LET'S START WITH YOUR NAME.
NAME IS KOTORI IIDA.
C-CALM DOWN!
RELAX! RELAX!
SO TELL ME WHY YOU CHOSE OUR SCHOOL—
Right!
THERE'S THE FACT THAT IT HAS THE CURRICULUM I WANT, AND WHEN I VISITED DURING THE OPEN CAMPUS ON SUMMER VACATION I FELT THAT IT WAS VERY ACTIVE-AND UM...
UHH... WELL... WAHH... HMM... IT WAS GOOD.
I SEE.
SHE'S A MESS!
HMM... HOW'D THE PRACTICE GO WITH THE OTHER TEACHERS?

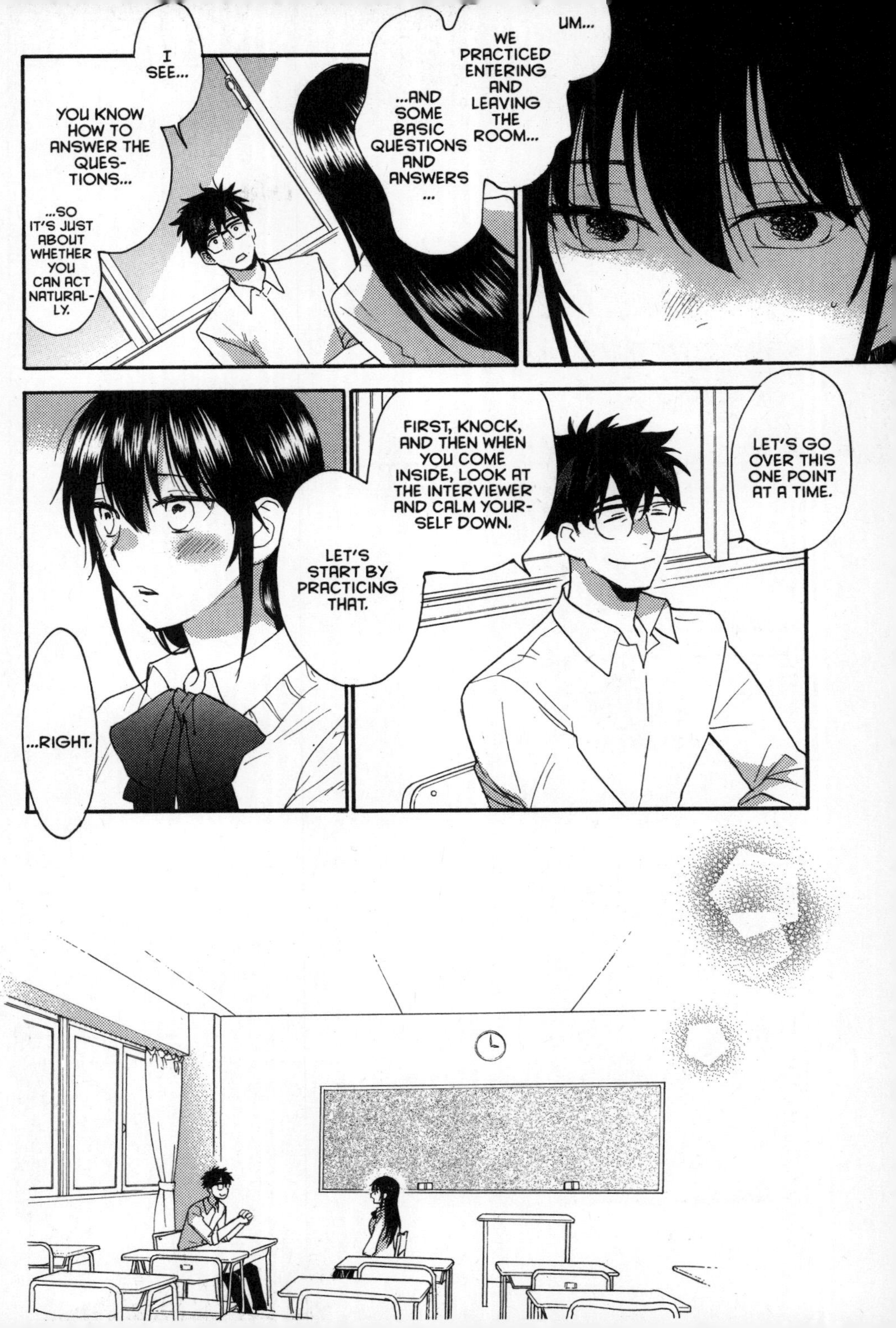
UM...
WE PRACTICED ENTERING AND LEAVING THE ROOM...
...AND SOME BASIC QUESTIONS AND ANSWERS...
I SEE...
YOU KNOW HOW TO ANSWER THE QUESTIONS...
...SO IT'S JUST ABOUT WHETHER YOU CAN ACT NATURALLY.
LET'S GO OVER THIS ONE POINT AT A TIME.
FIRST, KNOCK, AND THEN WHEN YOU COME INSIDE, LOOK AT THE INTERVIEWER AND CALM YOURSELF DOWN.
LET'S START BY PRACTICING THAT.
...RIGHT.

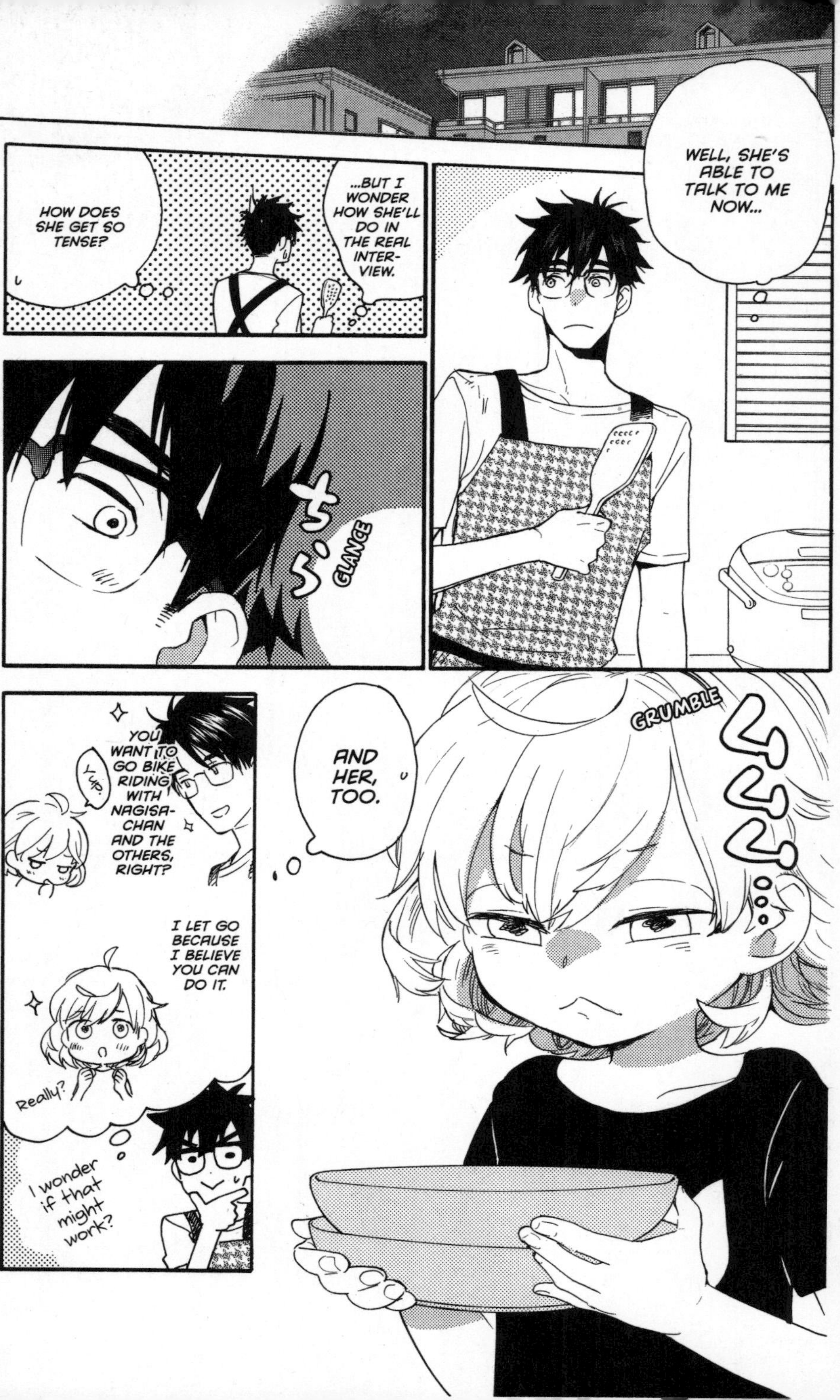
WELL, SHE'S ABLE TO TALK TO ME NOW...
...BUT I WONDER HOW SHE'LL DO IN THE REAL INTERVIEW.
HOW DOES SHE GET SO TENSE?
ちら
GLANCE
AND HER, TOO.
ムムム...
GRUMBLE
YOU WANT TO GO BIKE RIDING WITH NAGISA-CHAN AND THE OTHERS, RIGHT?
I LET GO BECAUSE I BELIEVE YOU CAN DO IT.
Really?
I wonder if that might work?

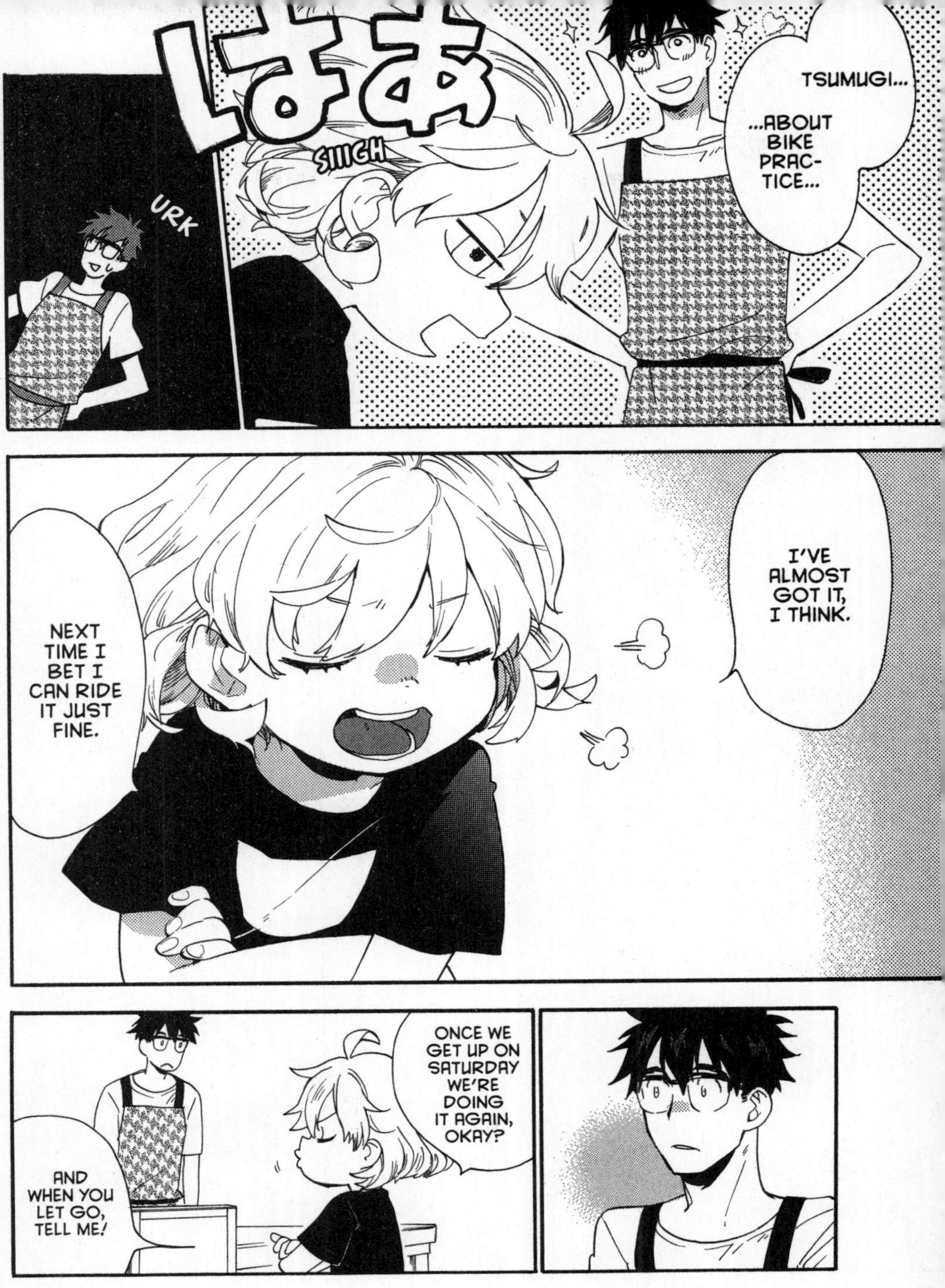
TSUMUGI...
...ABOUT BIKE PRAC-TICE...
SIIIGH
URK
I'VE ALMOST GOT IT, I THINK.
NEXT TIME I BET I CAN RIDE IT JUST FINE.
ONCE WE GET UP ON SATURDAY WE'RE DOING IT AGAIN, OKAY?
AND WHEN YOU LET GO, TELL ME!

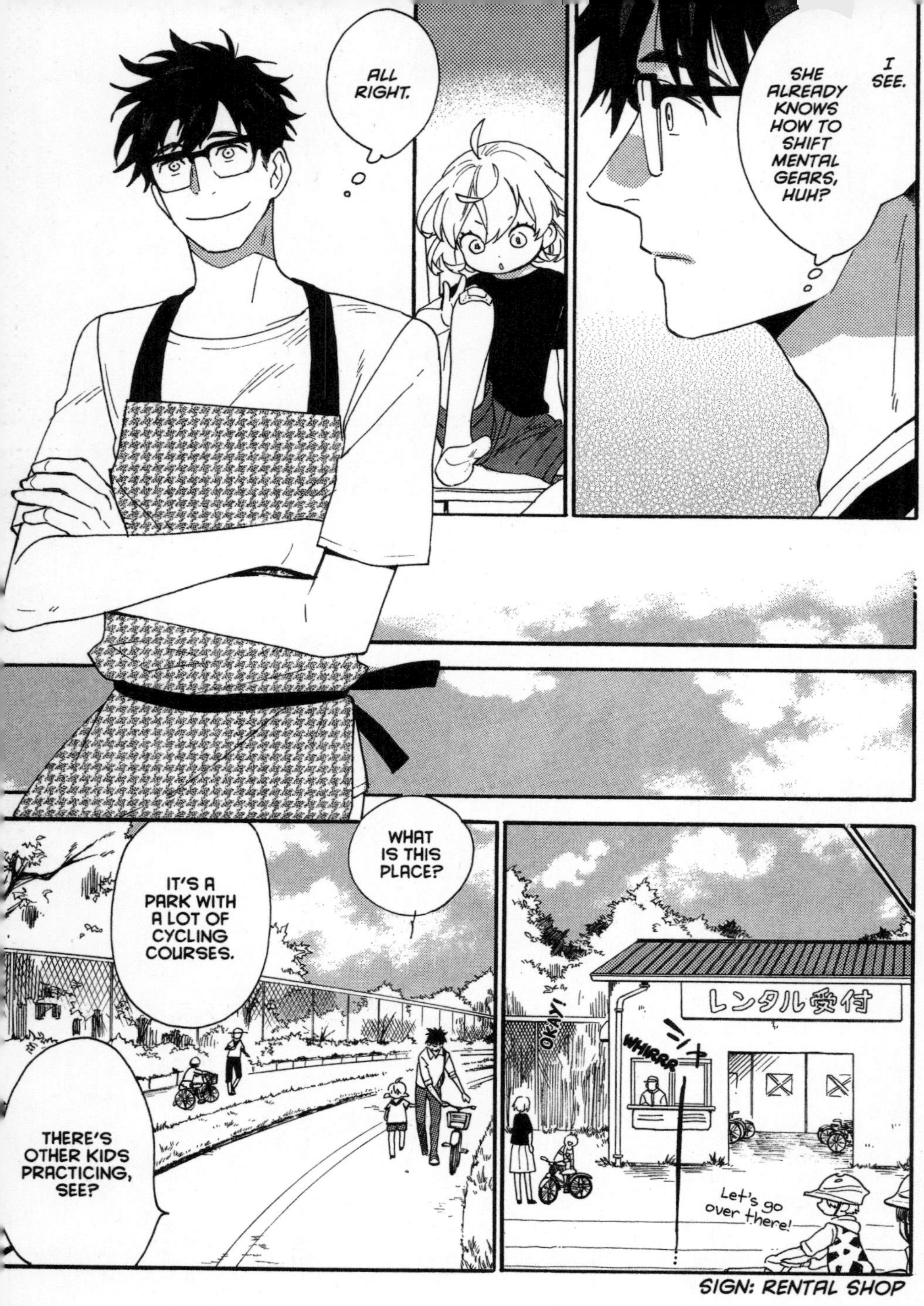
I SEE.
SHE ALREADY KNOWS HOW TO SHIFT MENTAL GEARS, HUH?
ALL RIGHT.
レンタル受付
WHIRRR
OKAY!
Let's go over there!
WHAT IS THIS PLACE?
IT'S A PARK WITH A LOT OF CYCLING COURSES.
THERE'S OTHER KIDS PRACTICING, SEE?

SIGN: RENTAL SHOP

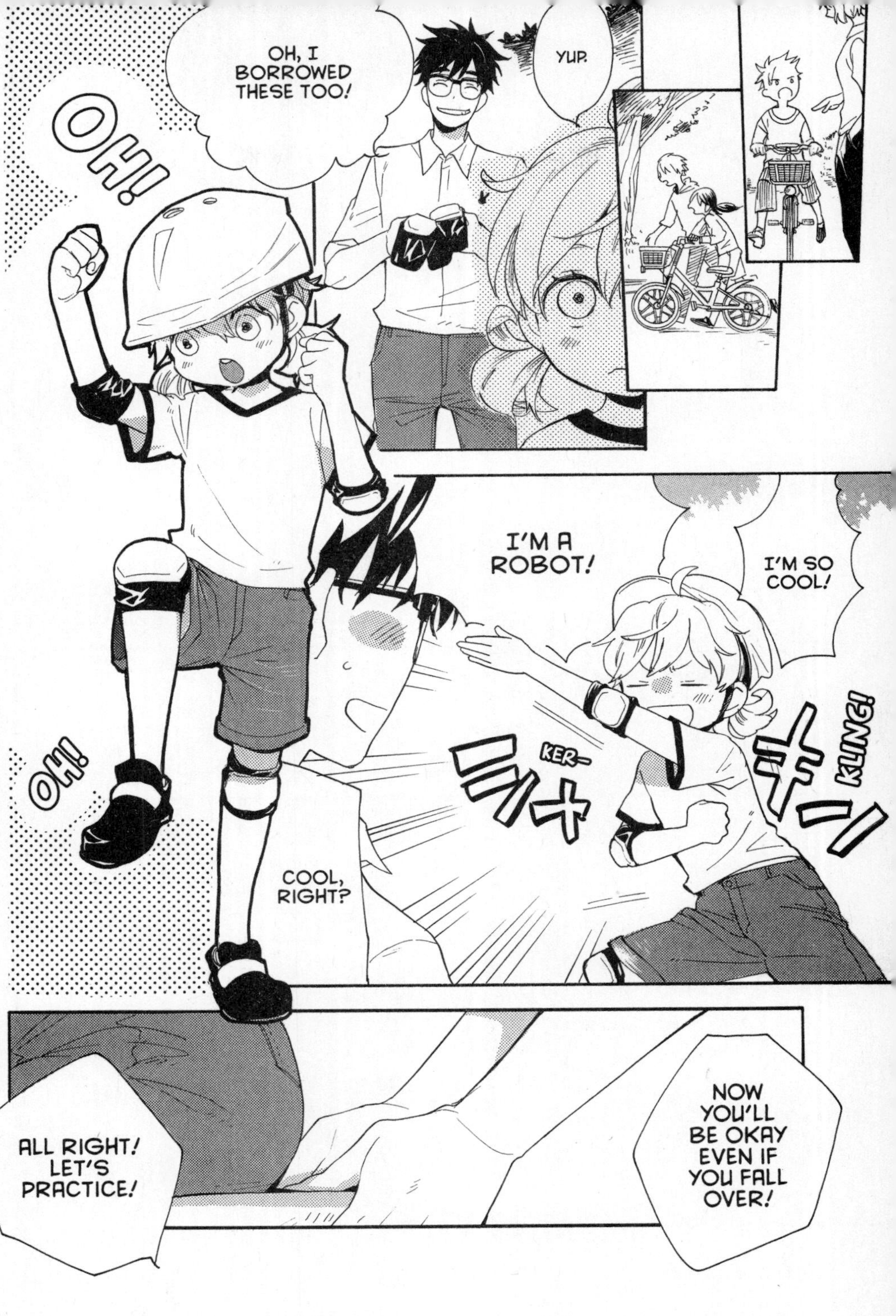
YUP.
OH, I BORROWED THESE TOO!
OH!
I'M SO COOL!
I'M A ROBOT!
KLING!
KER-
COOL, RIGHT?
OH!
NOW YOU'LL BE OKAY EVEN IF YOU FALL OVER!
ALL RIGHT! LET'S PRACTICE!

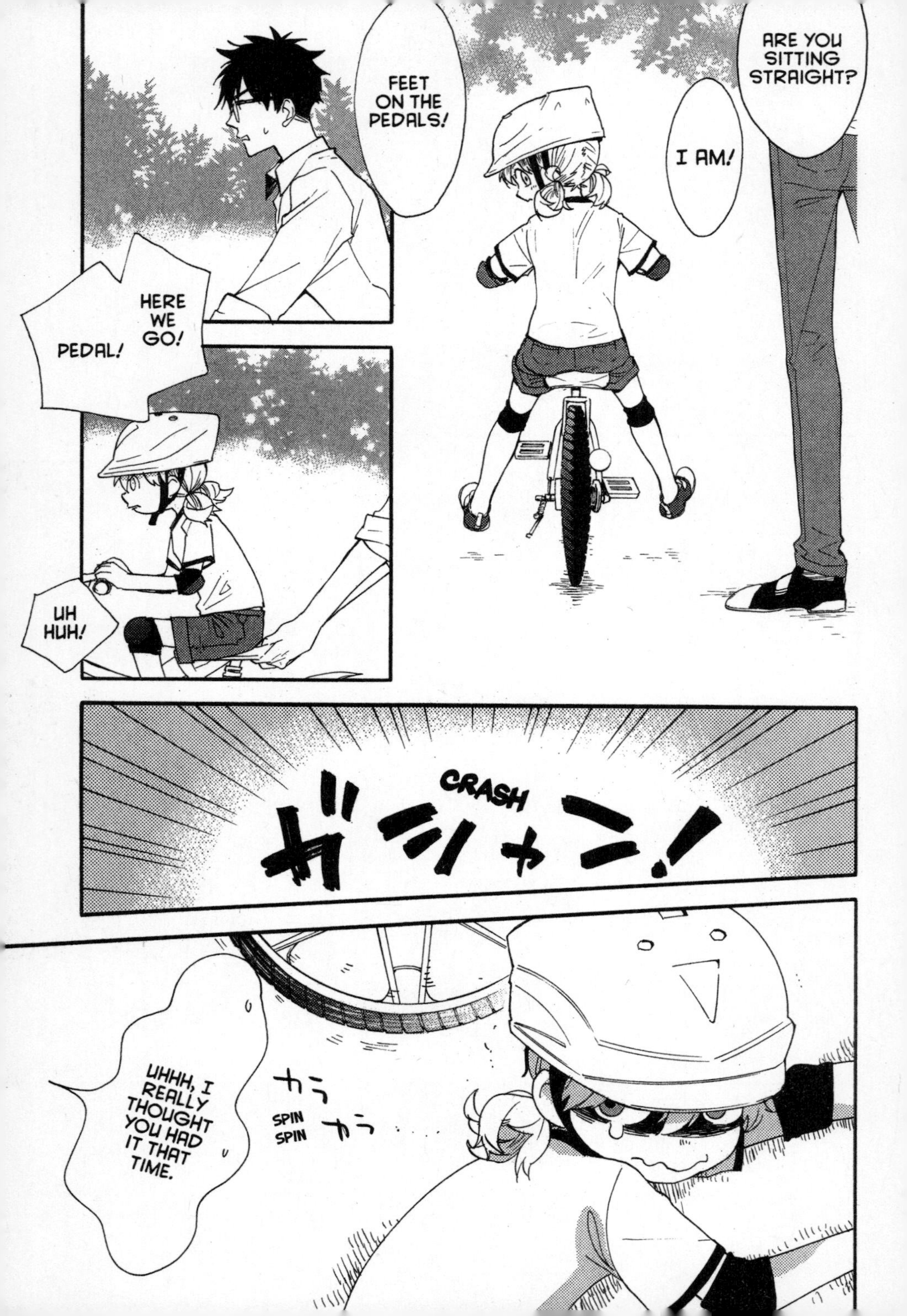
ARE YOU SITTING STRAIGHT?
I AM!
FEET ON THE PEDALS!
HERE WE GO!
PEDAL!
UH HUH!
CRASH
ガシャン!
カラ
カラ
SPIN SPIN
UHHH, I REALLY THOUGHT YOU HAD IT THAT TIME.

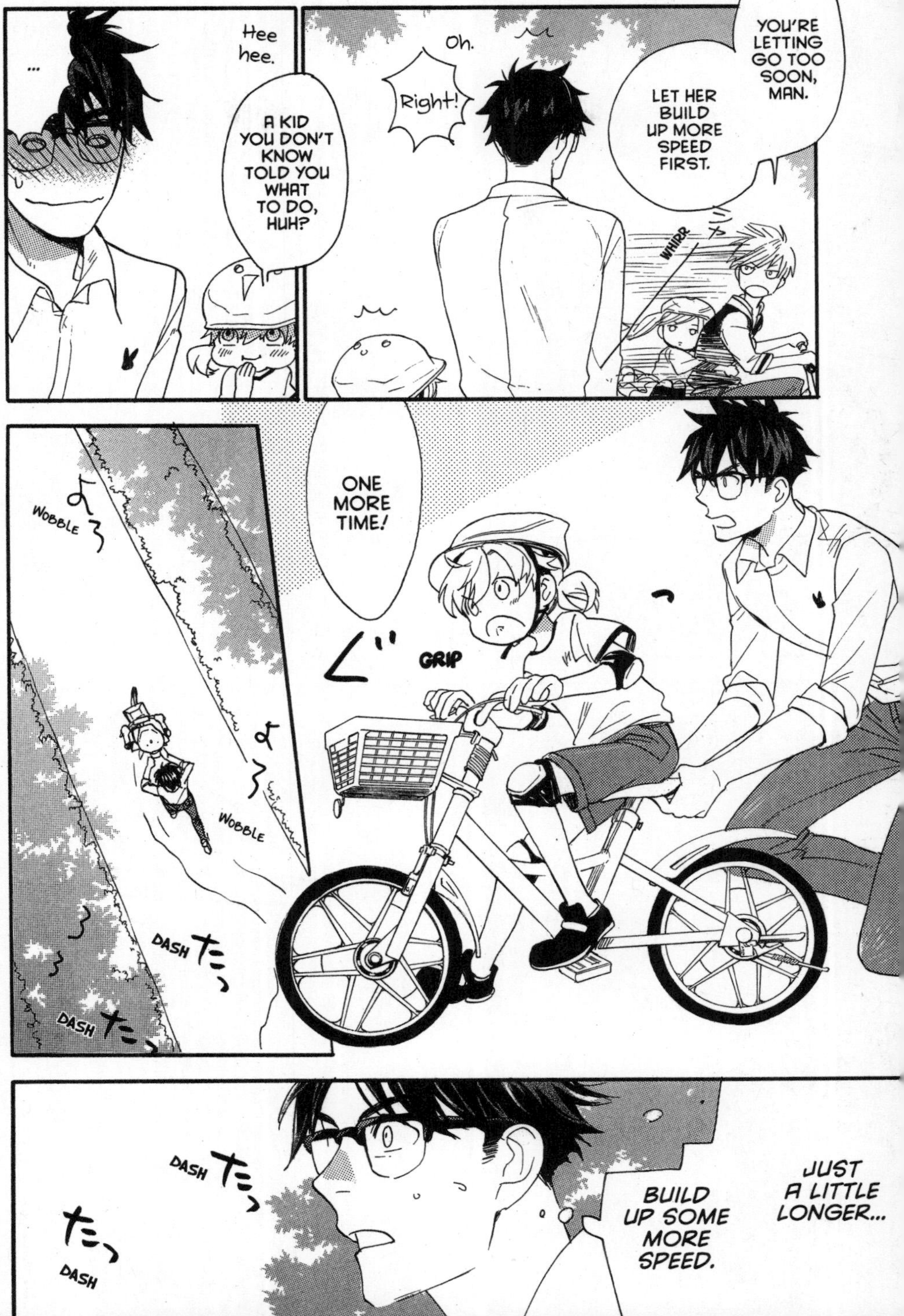
YOU'RE LETTING GO TOO SOON, MAN.
LET HER BUILD UP MORE SPEED FIRST.
WHIRR
Oh.
Right!
Hee hee.
A KID YOU DON'T KNOW TOLD YOU WHAT TO DO, HUH?
...
ONE MORE TIME!
GRIP
WOBBLE
WOBBLE
DASH
DASH
JUST A LITTLE LONGER...
BUILD UP SOME MORE SPEED.
DASH
DASH

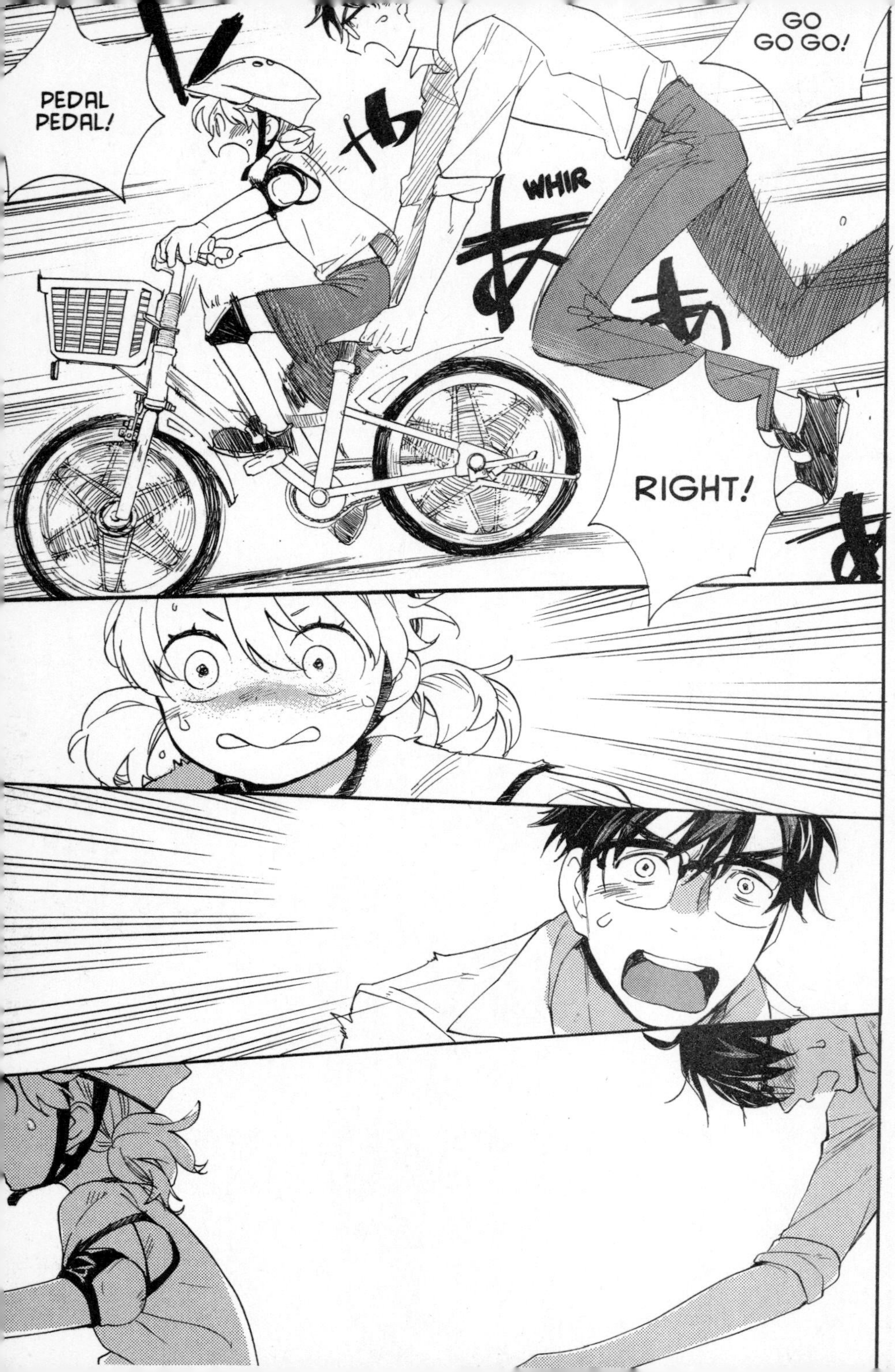
GO GO GO!
PEDAL PEDAL!
WHIR
RIGHT!

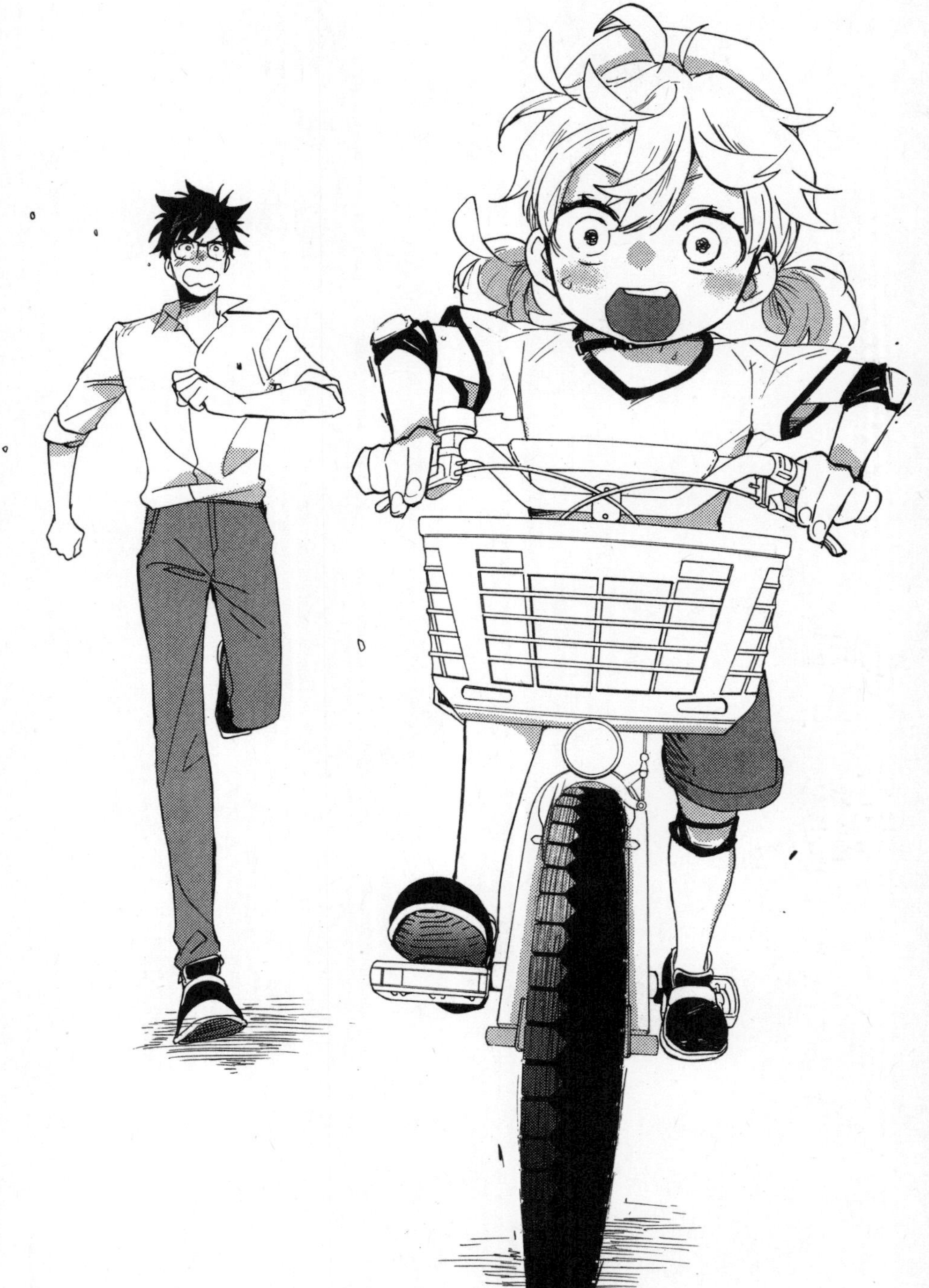

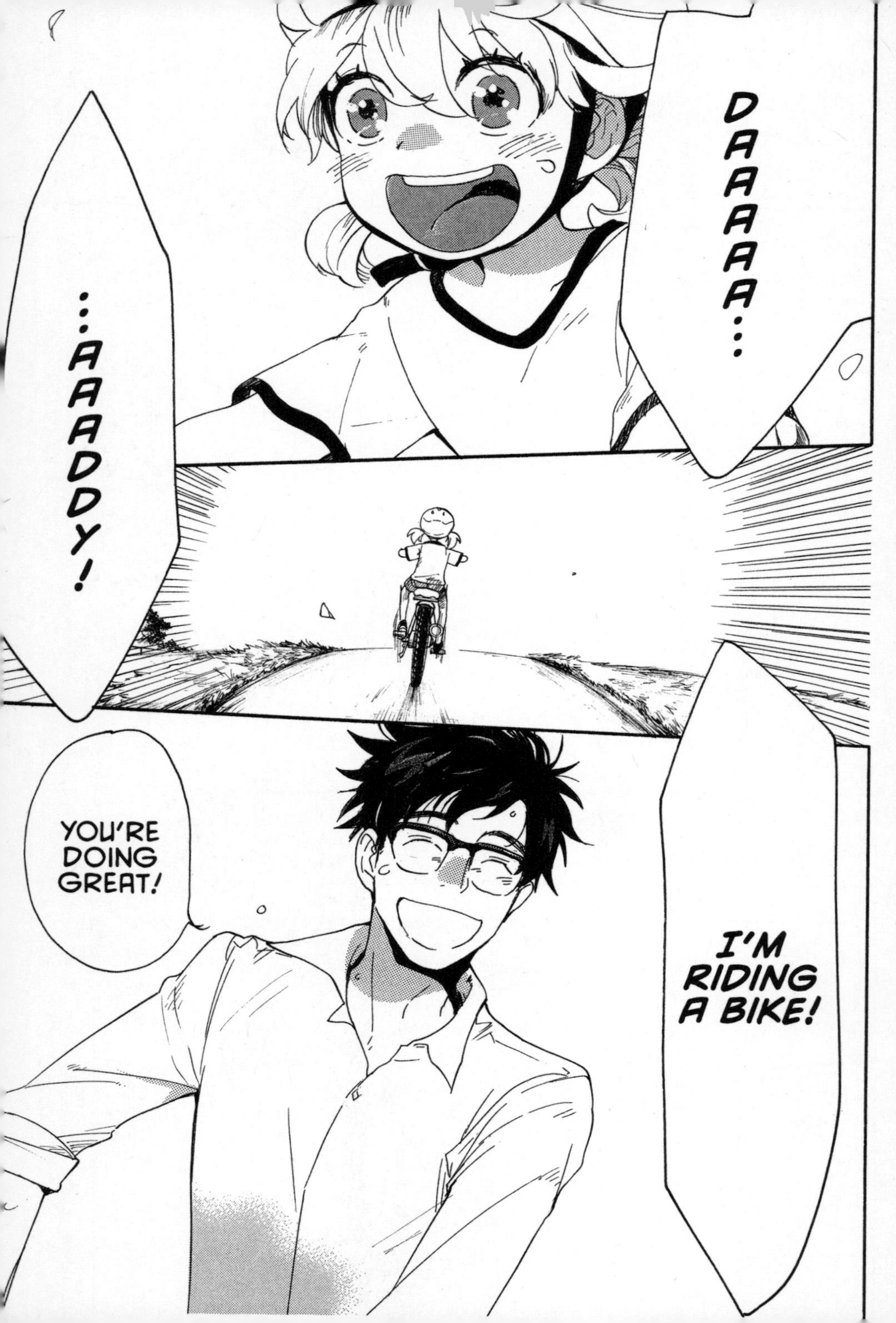
DAAAAAAA...
...AAAADDY!
I'M RIDING A BIKE!
YOU'RE DOING GREAT!

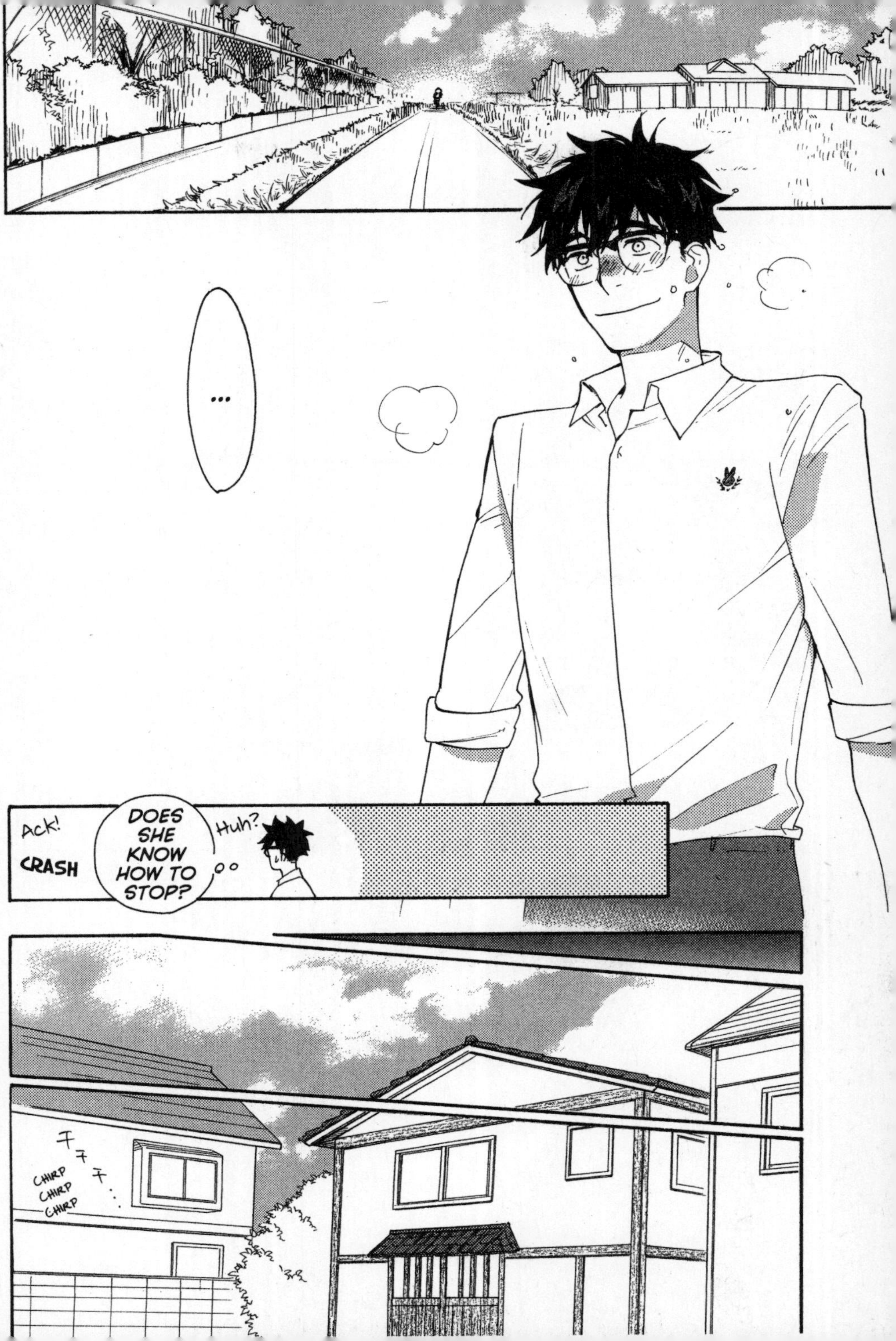
...
Huh?
DOES SHE KNOW HOW TO STOP?
Ack!
CRASH
チチチ...
CHIRP CHIRP CHIRP

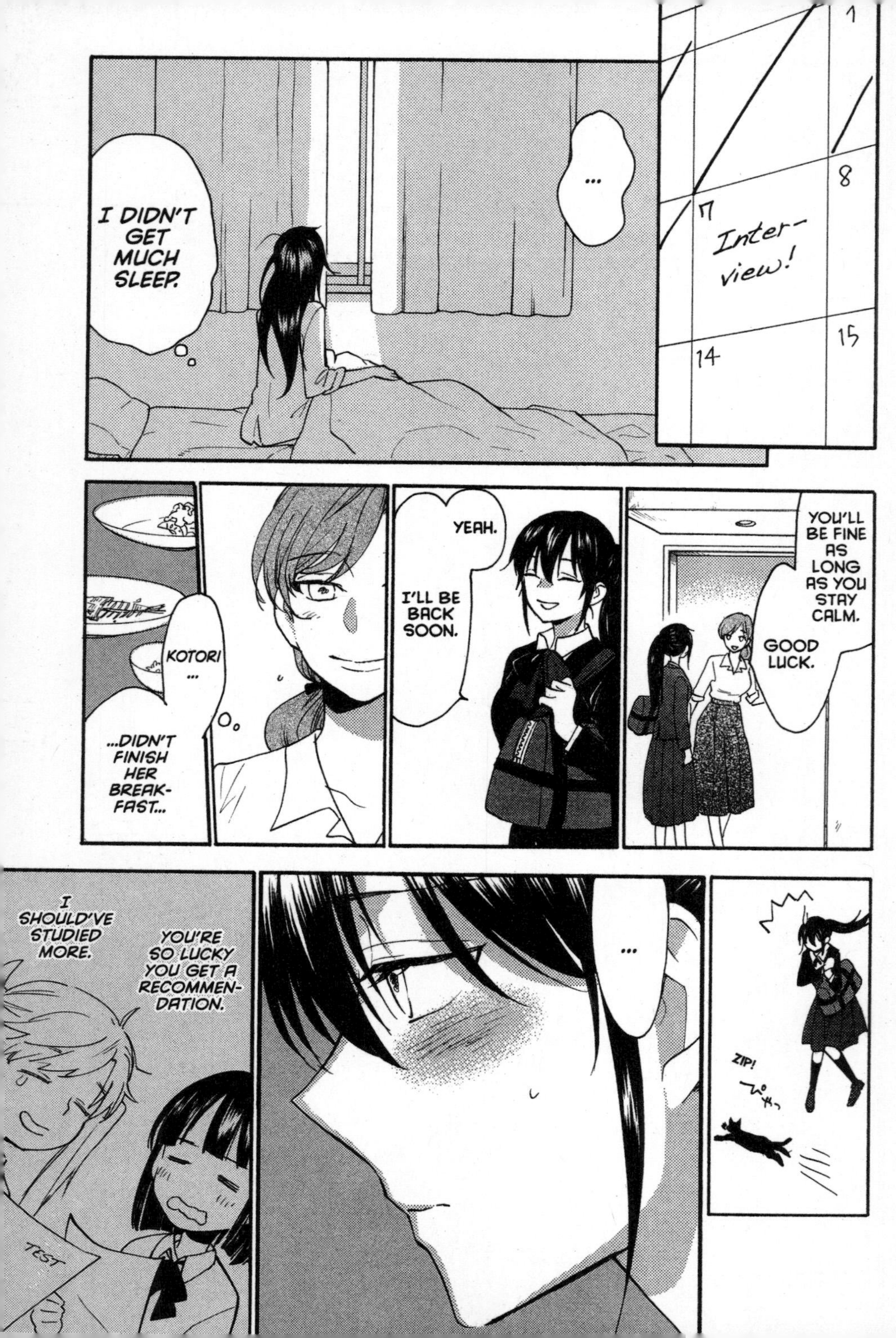
1
8
7
Inter-view!
15
14
...
I DIDN'T GET MUCH SLEEP.
YOU'LL BE FINE AS LONG AS YOU STAY CALM.
GOOD LUCK.
YEAH.
I'LL BE BACK SOON.
KOTORI ...
...DIDN'T FINISH HER BREAKFAST...
ZIP!
...
YOU'RE SO LUCKY YOU GET A RECOMMENDATION.
I SHOULD'VE STUDIED MORE.
TEST

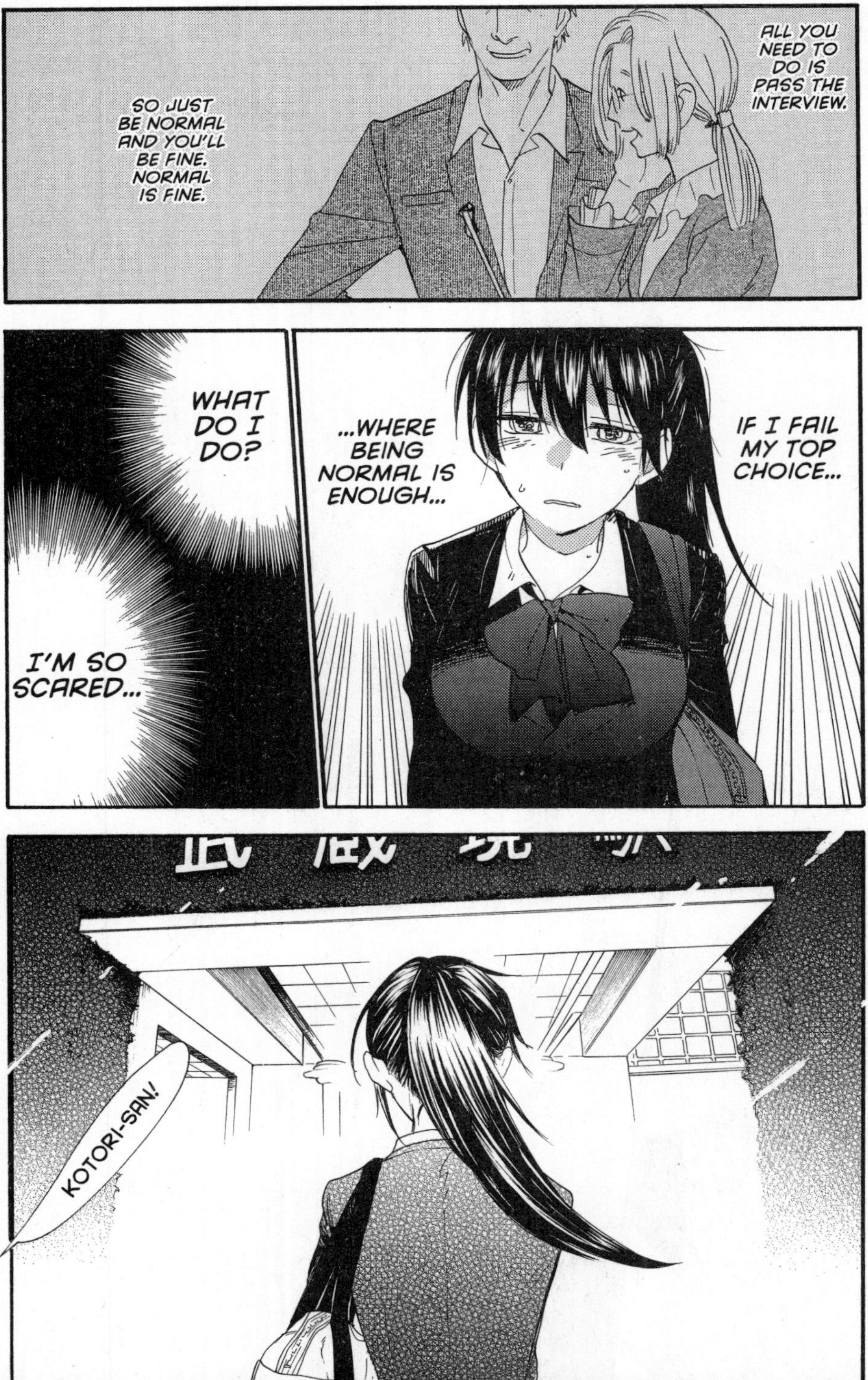
ALL YOU NEED TO DO IS PASS THE INTERVIEW.
SO JUST BE NORMAL AND YOU'LL BE FINE. NORMAL IS FINE.
IF I FAIL MY TOP CHOICE...
...WHERE BEING NORMAL IS ENOUGH...
WHAT DO I DO?
I'M SO SCARED...
KOTORI-SAN!

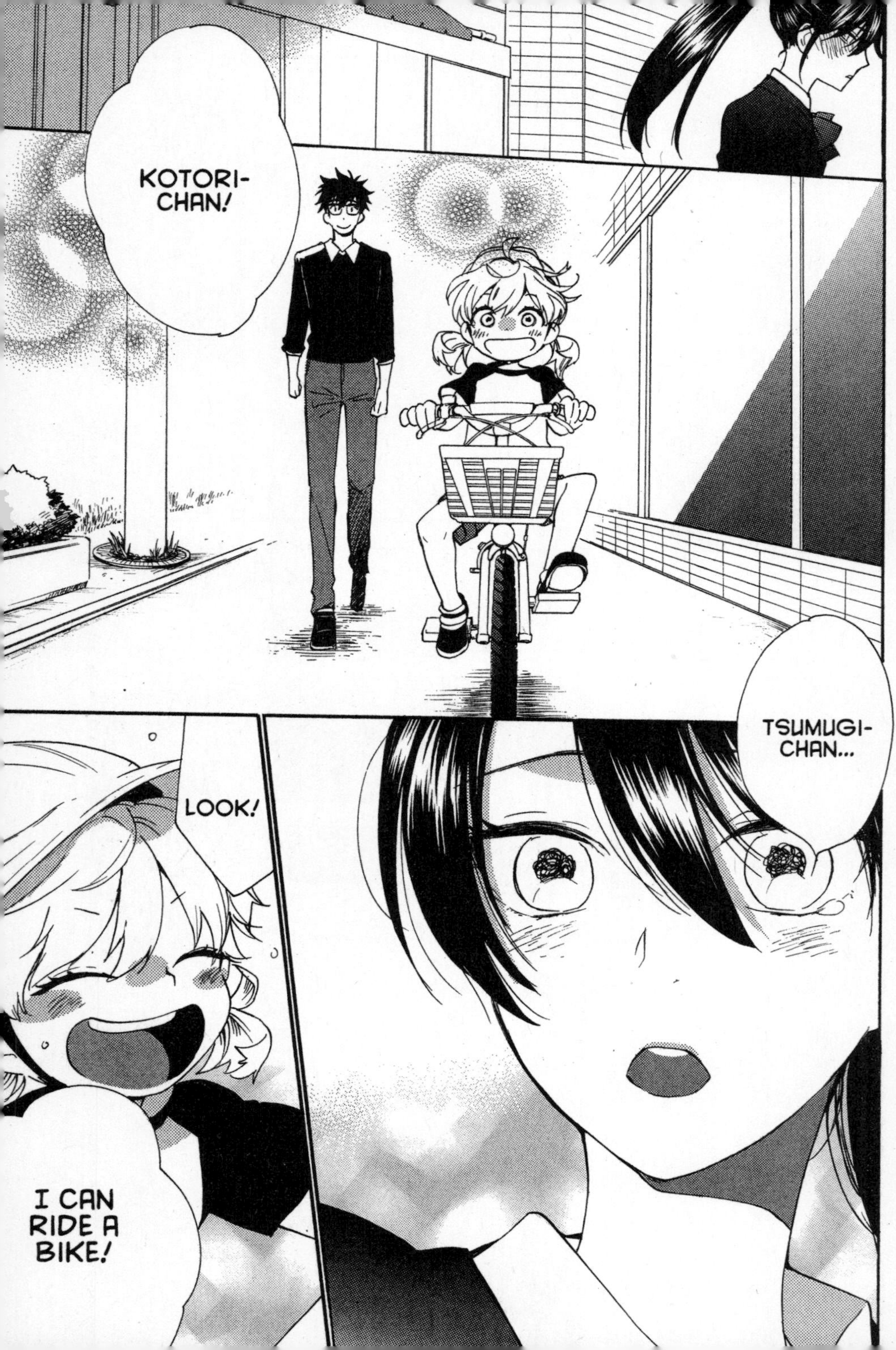
KOTORI-CHAN!
TSUMUGI-CHAN...
LOOK!
I CAN RIDE A BIKE!

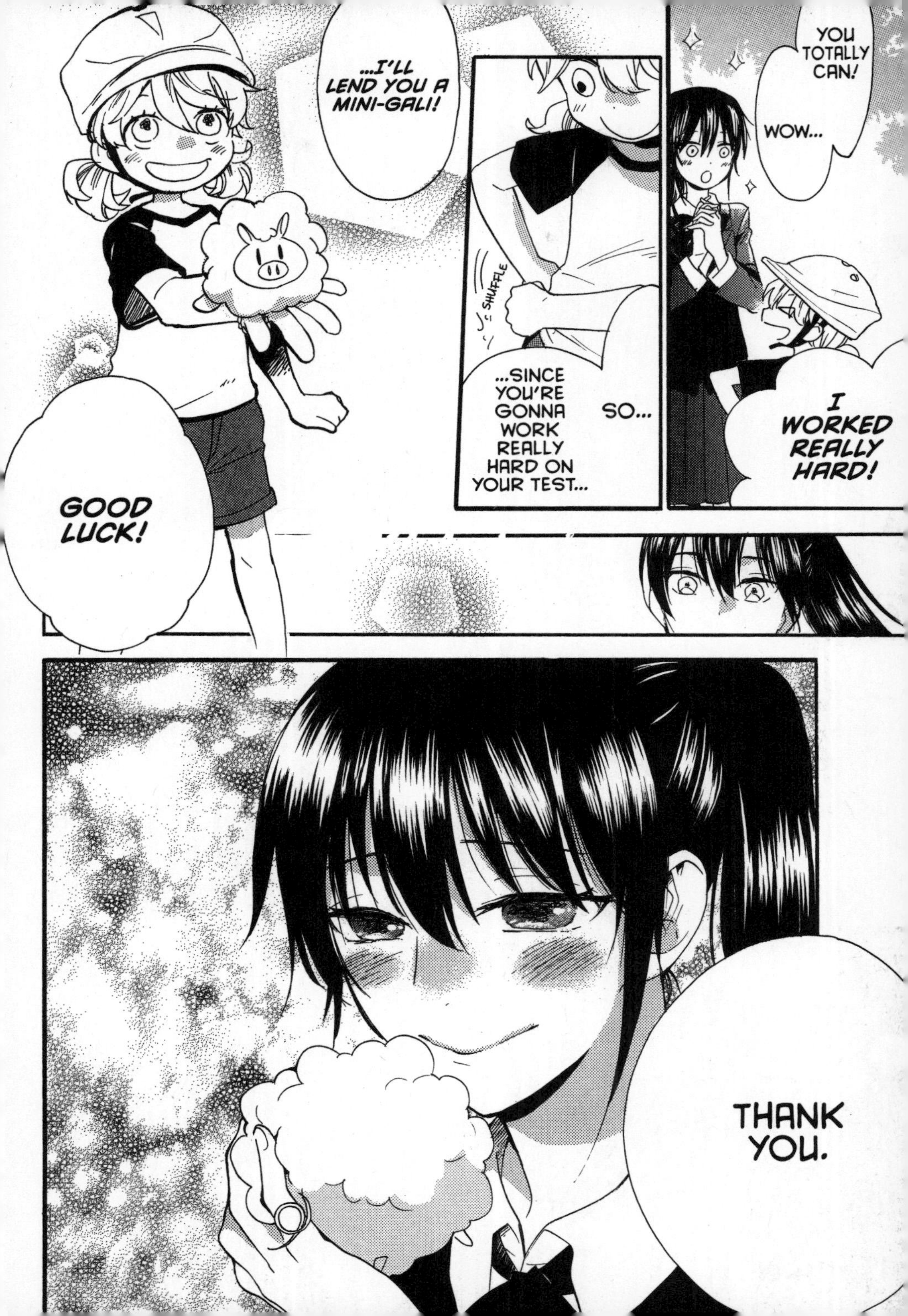
YOU TOTALLY CAN!
WOW...
I WORKED REALLY HARD!
SO...
...SINCE YOU'RE GONNA WORK REALLY HARD ON YOUR TEST...
SHUFFLE
...I'LL LEND YOU A MINI-GALI!
GOOD LUCK!
THANK YOU.

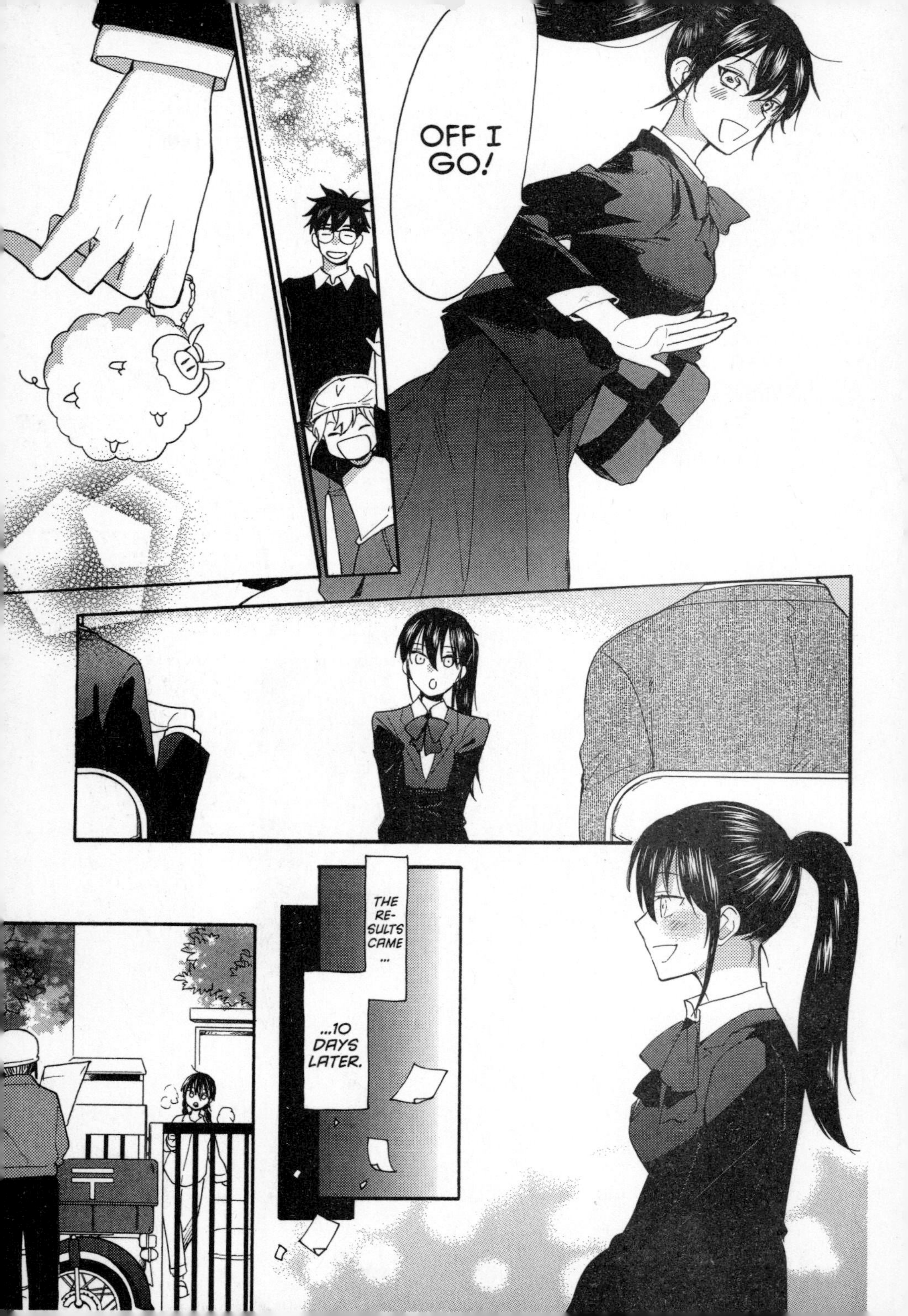
OFF I GO!
THE RE-SULTS CAME...
...10 DAYS LATER.

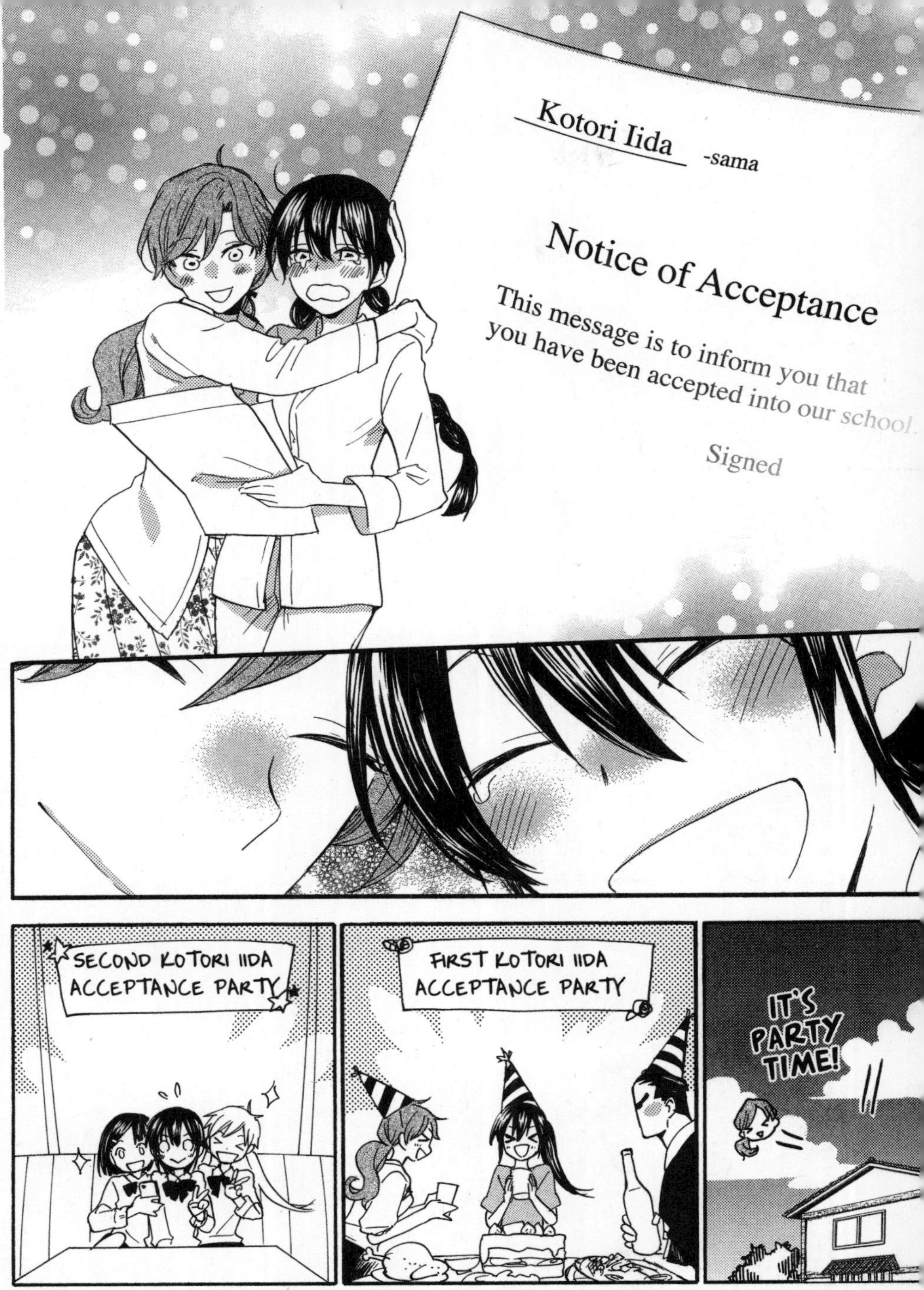
Kotori Iida -sama
Notice of Acceptance
This message is to inform you that you have been accepted into our school.
Signed
IT'S PARTY TIME!
FIRST KOTORI IIDA ACCEPTANCE PARTY
SECOND KOTORI IIDA ACCEPTANCE PARTY

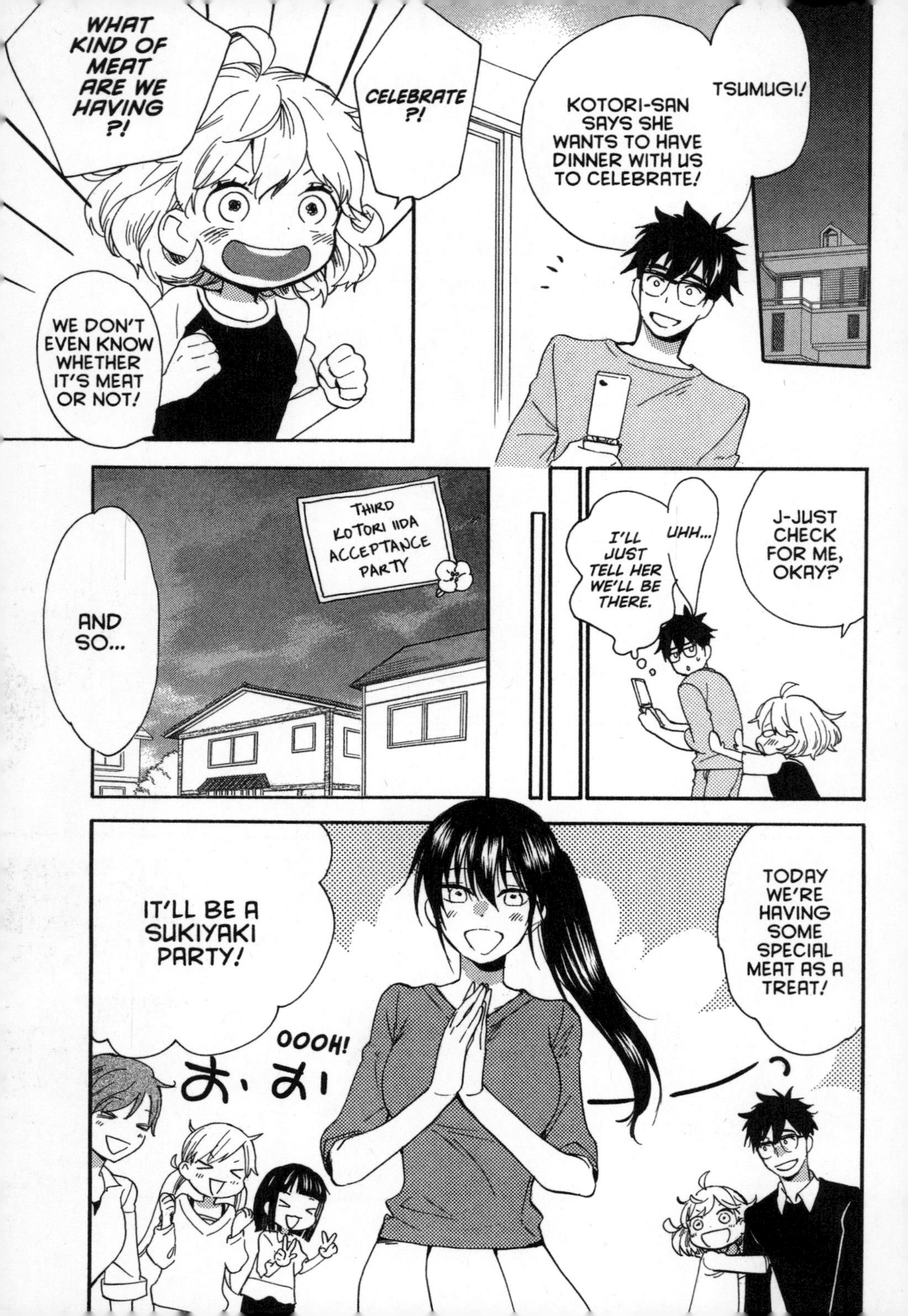
TSUMUGI!
KOTORI-SAN SAYS SHE WANTS TO HAVE DINNER WITH US TO CELEBRATE!
CELEBRATE?!
WHAT KIND OF MEAT ARE WE HAVING?!
WE DON'T EVEN KNOW WHETHER IT'S MEAT OR NOT!
J-JUST CHECK FOR ME, OKAY?
UHH...
I'LL JUST TELL HER WE'LL BE THERE.
AND SO...
THIRD KOTORI IIDA ACCEPTANCE PARTY
TODAY WE'RE HAVING SOME SPECIAL MEAT AS A TREAT!
IT'LL BE A SUKIYAKI PARTY!
OOOH!

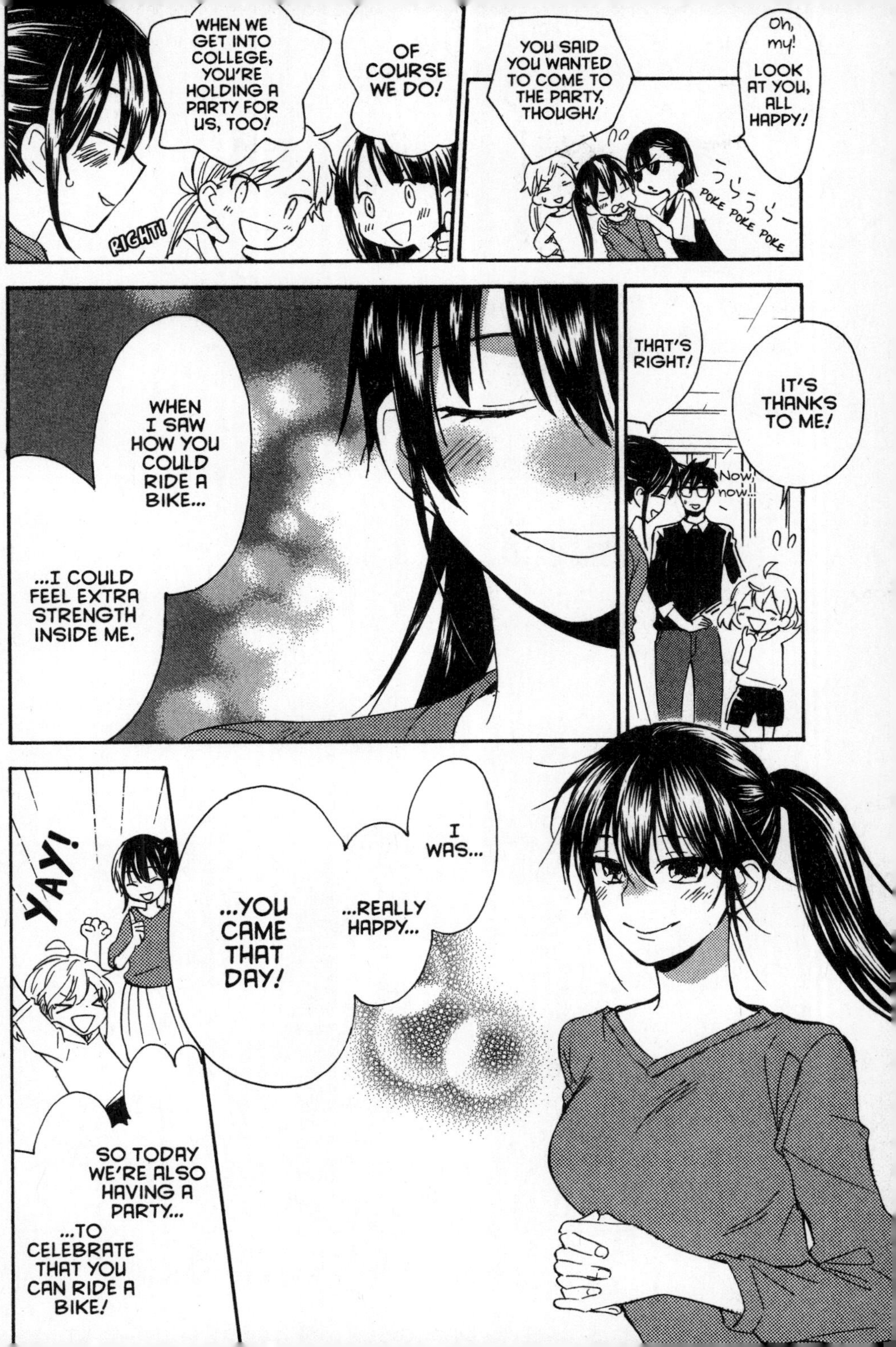
Oh, my!
LOOK AT YOU, ALL HAPPY!
YOU SAID YOU WANTED TO COME TO THE PARTY, THOUGH!
POKE POKE POKE
OF COURSE WE DO!
WHEN WE GET INTO COLLEGE, YOU'RE HOLDING A PARTY FOR US, TOO!
RIGHT!
THAT'S RIGHT!
IT'S THANKS TO ME!
Now, now..!
WHEN I SAW HOW YOU COULD RIDE A BIKE...
...I COULD FEEL EXTRA STRENGTH INSIDE ME.
I WAS...
...REALLY HAPPY...
...YOU CAME THAT DAY!
YAY!
SO TODAY WE'RE ALSO HAVING A PARTY...
...TO CELEBRATE THAT YOU CAN RIDE A BIKE!

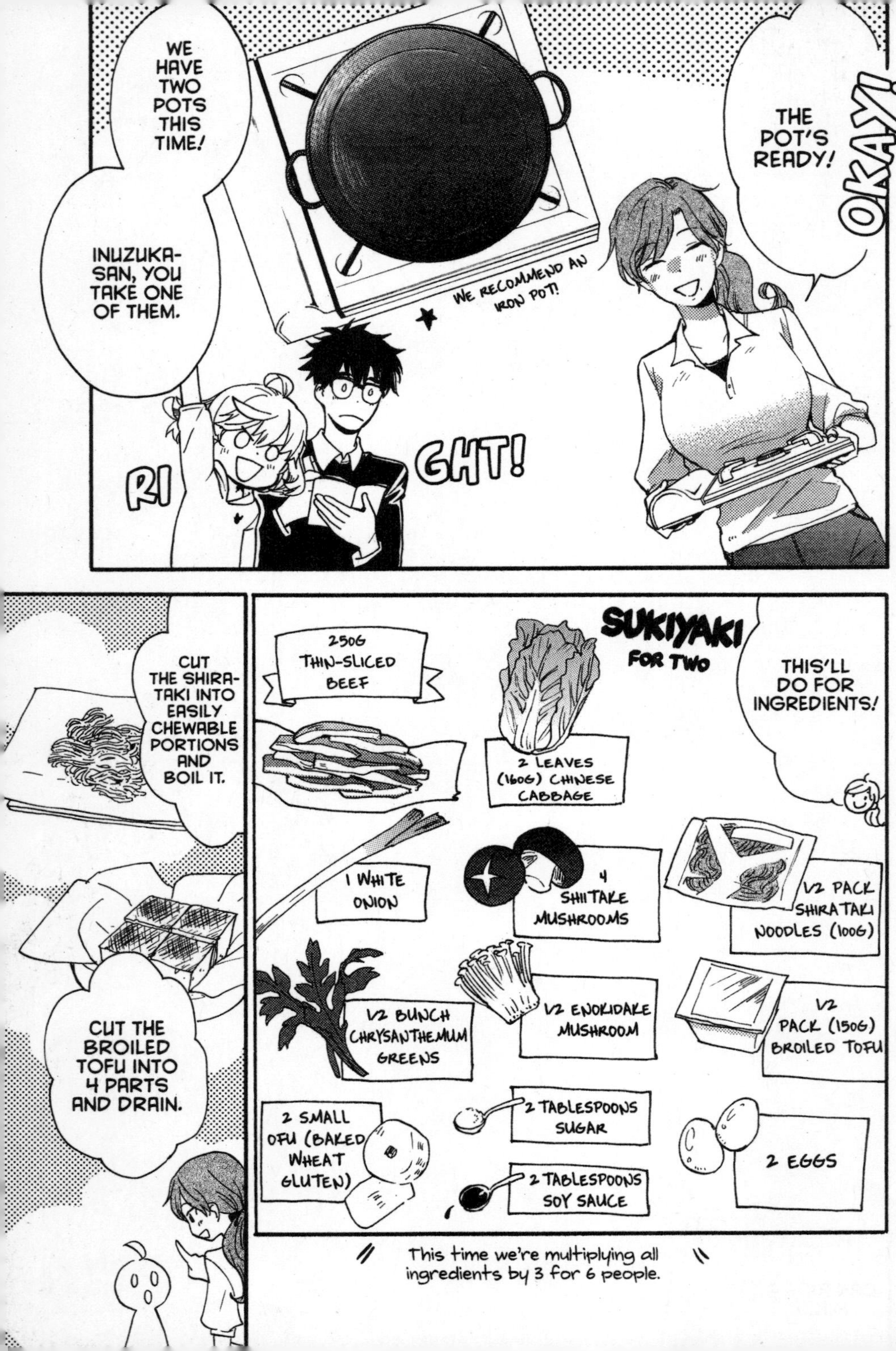
THE POT'S READY!
OKAY!
WE HAVE TWO POTS THIS TIME!
INUZUKA-SAN, YOU TAKE ONE OF THEM.
WE RECOMMEND AN IRON POT!
RI GHT!
THIS'LL DO FOR INGREDIENTS!
SUKIYAKI FOR TWO
250G THIN-SLICED BEEF
2 LEAVES (160G) CHINESE CABBAGE
1/2 PACK SHIRATAKI NOODLES (100G)
4 SHIITAKE MUSHROOMS
1 WHITE ONION
1/2 PACK (150G) BROILED TOFU
1/2 ENOKIDAKE MUSHROOM
1/2 BUNCH CHRYSANTHEMUM GREENS
2 EGGS
2 TABLESPOONS SUGAR
2 TABLESPOONS SOY SAUCE
2 SMALL OFU (BAKED WHEAT GLUTEN)
This time we're multiplying all ingredients by 3 for 6 people.
CUT THE SHIRATAKI INTO EASILY CHEWABLE PORTIONS AND BOIL IT.
CUT THE BROILED TOFU INTO 4 PARTS AND DRAIN.

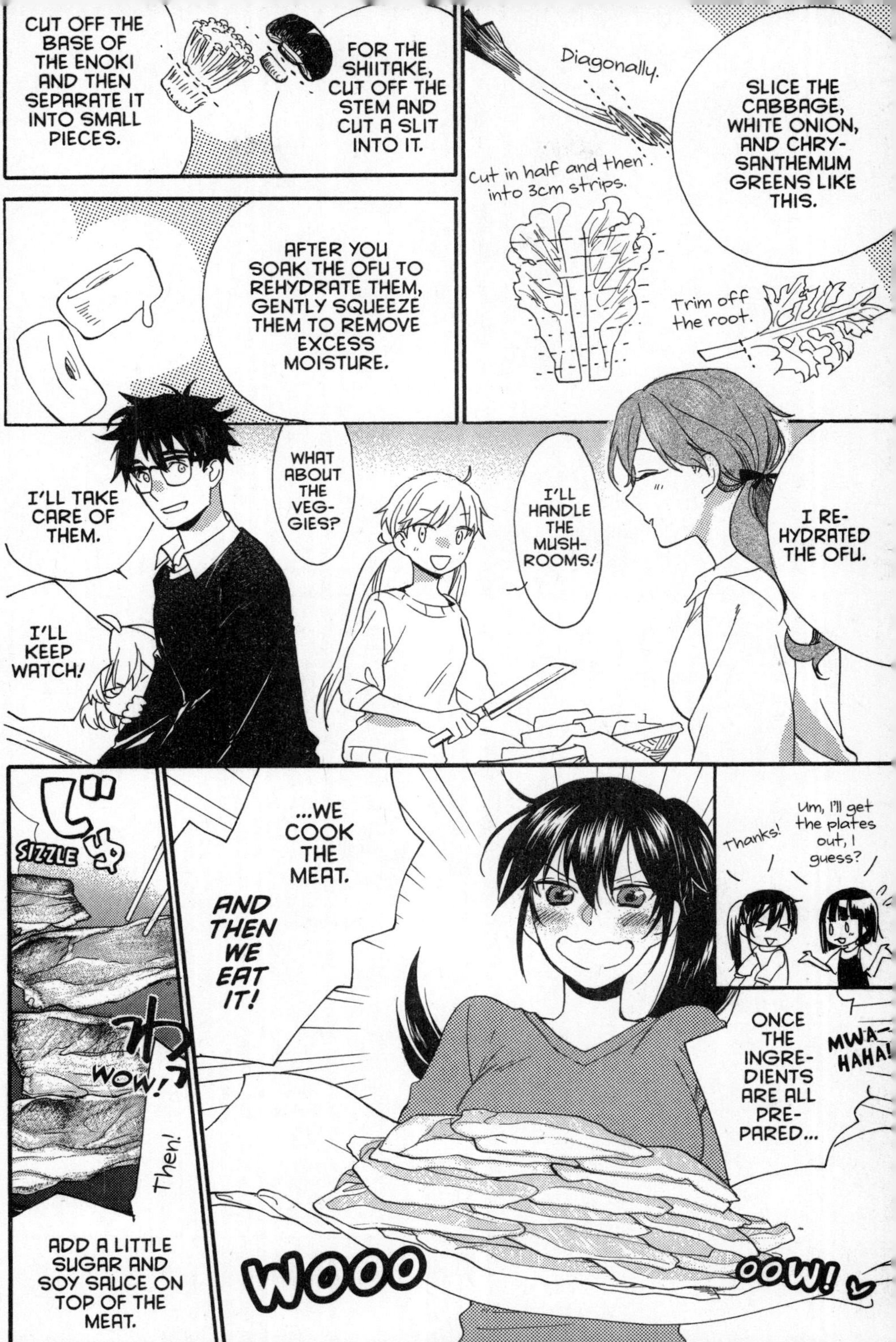
SLICE THE CABBAGE, WHITE ONION, AND CHRYSANTHEMUM GREENS LIKE THIS.
Diagonally.
Cut in half and then into 3cm strips.
Trim off the root.
FOR THE SHIITAKE, CUT OFF THE STEM AND CUT A SLIT INTO IT.
CUT OFF THE BASE OF THE ENOKI AND THEN SEPARATE IT INTO SMALL PIECES.
AFTER YOU SOAK THE OFU TO REHYDRATE THEM, GENTLY SQUEEZE THEM TO REMOVE EXCESS MOISTURE.
I REHYDRATED THE OFU.
I'LL HANDLE THE MUSHROOMS!
WHAT ABOUT THE VEGGIES?
I'LL TAKE CARE OF THEM.
I'LL KEEP WATCH!
Um, I'll get the plates out, I guess?
Thanks!
MWAHAHA!
ONCE THE INGREDIENTS ARE ALL PREPARED...
...WE COOK THE MEAT.
AND THEN WE EAT IT!
WOOO
OOW!
SIZZLE
WOW!
Then!
ADD A LITTLE SUGAR AND SOY SAUCE ON TOP OF THE MEAT.

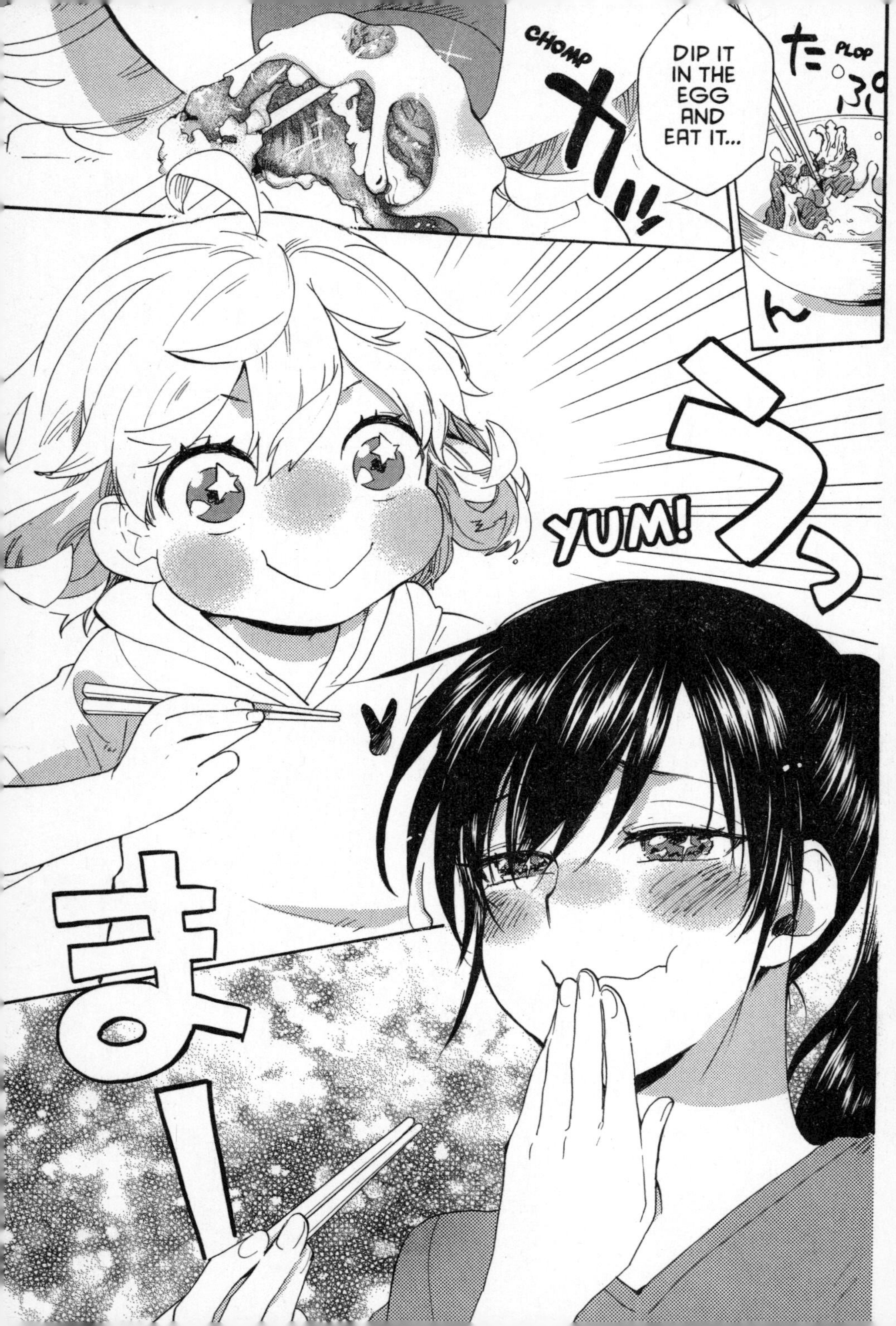
たぷん
PLOP
DIP IT IN THE EGG AND EAT IT...
カッ
CHOMP
うまっ!
YUM!

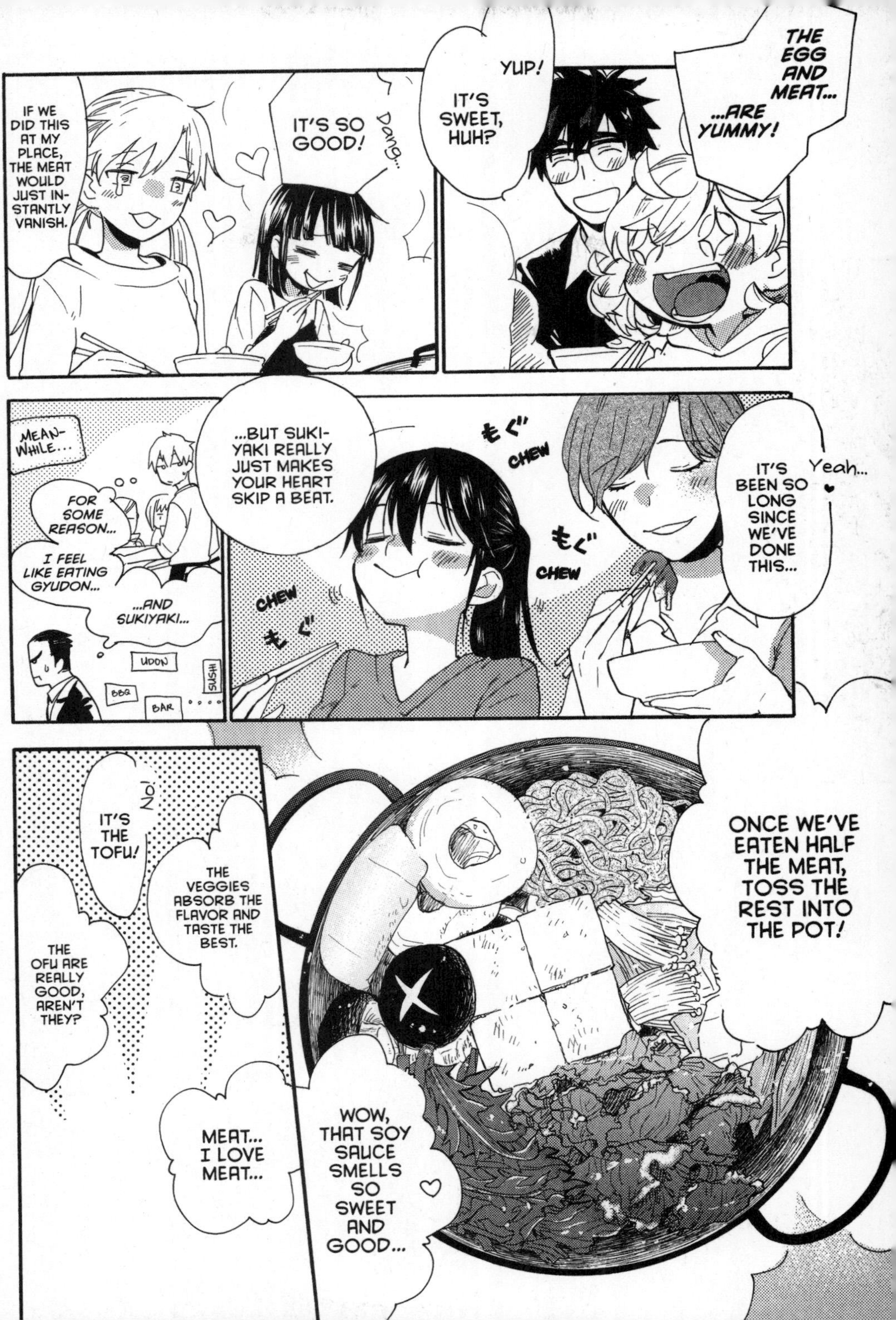
THE EGG AND MEAT... ...ARE YUMMY!
YUP!
IT'S SWEET, HUH?
Dang...
IT'S SO GOOD!
IF WE DID THIS AT MY PLACE, THE MEAT WOULD JUST INSTANTLY VANISH.
Yeah...
IT'S BEEN SO LONG SINCE WE'VE DONE THIS...
もぐ CHEW
もぐ CHEW
...BUT SUKIYAKI REALLY JUST MAKES YOUR HEART SKIP A BEAT.
CHEW もぐ
MEAN-WHILE...
FOR SOME REASON...
I FEEL LIKE EATING GYUDON...
...AND SUKIYAKI...
UDON
SUSHI
BBQ
BAR
ONCE WE'VE EATEN HALF THE MEAT, TOSS THE REST INTO THE POT!
WOW, THAT SOY SAUCE SMELLS SO SWEET AND GOOD...
MEAT... I LOVE MEAT...
NO!
IT'S THE TOFU!
THE VEGGIES ABSORB THE FLAVOR AND TASTE THE BEST.
THE OFU ARE REALLY GOOD, AREN'T THEY?

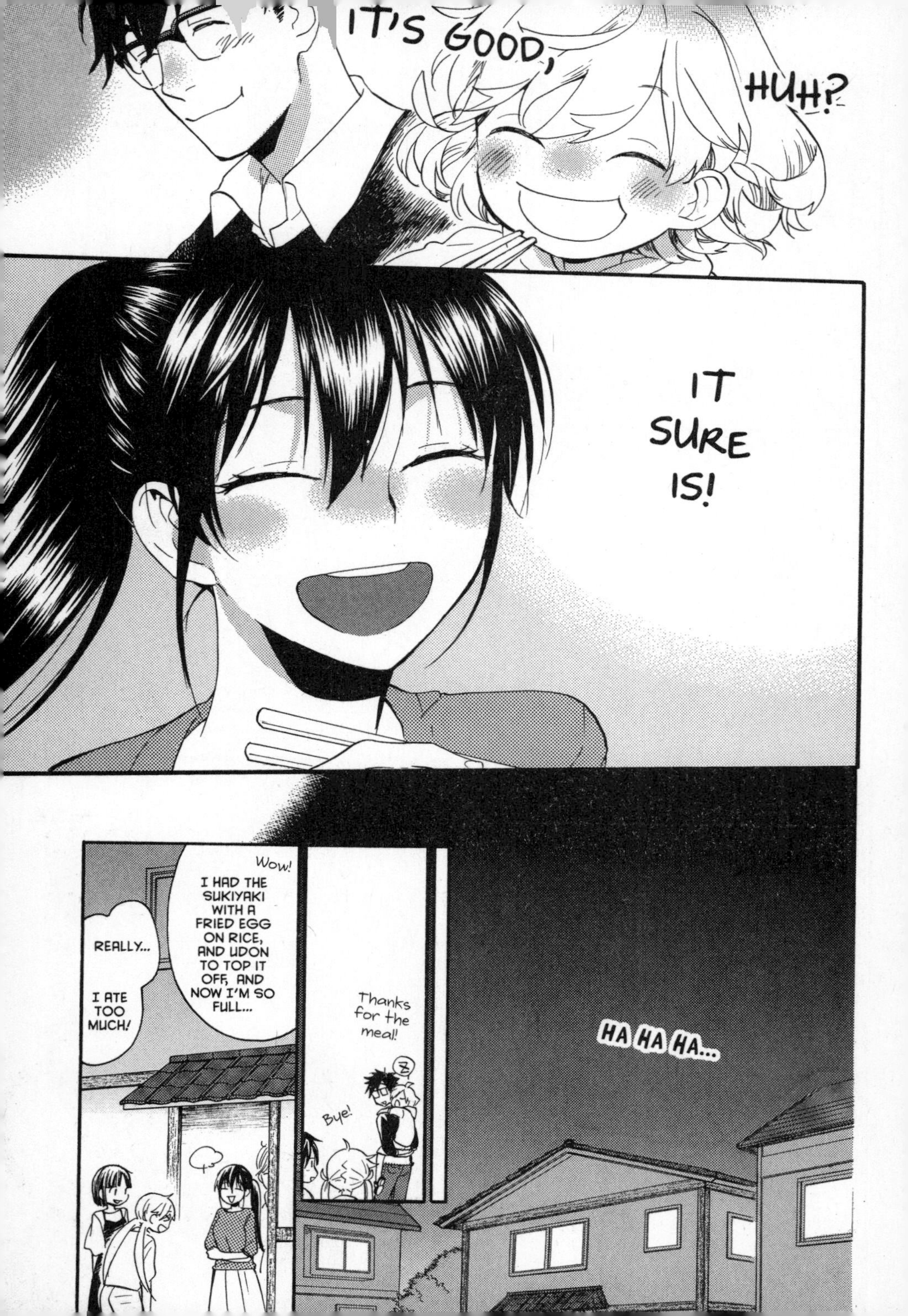
IT'S GOOD,
HUH?
IT SURE IS!
HA HA HA...
Thanks for the meal!
Bye!
Wow!
I HAD THE SUKIYAKI WITH A FRIED EGG ON RICE, AND UDON TO TOP IT OFF, AND NOW I'M SO FULL...
REALLY...
I ATE TOO MUCH!

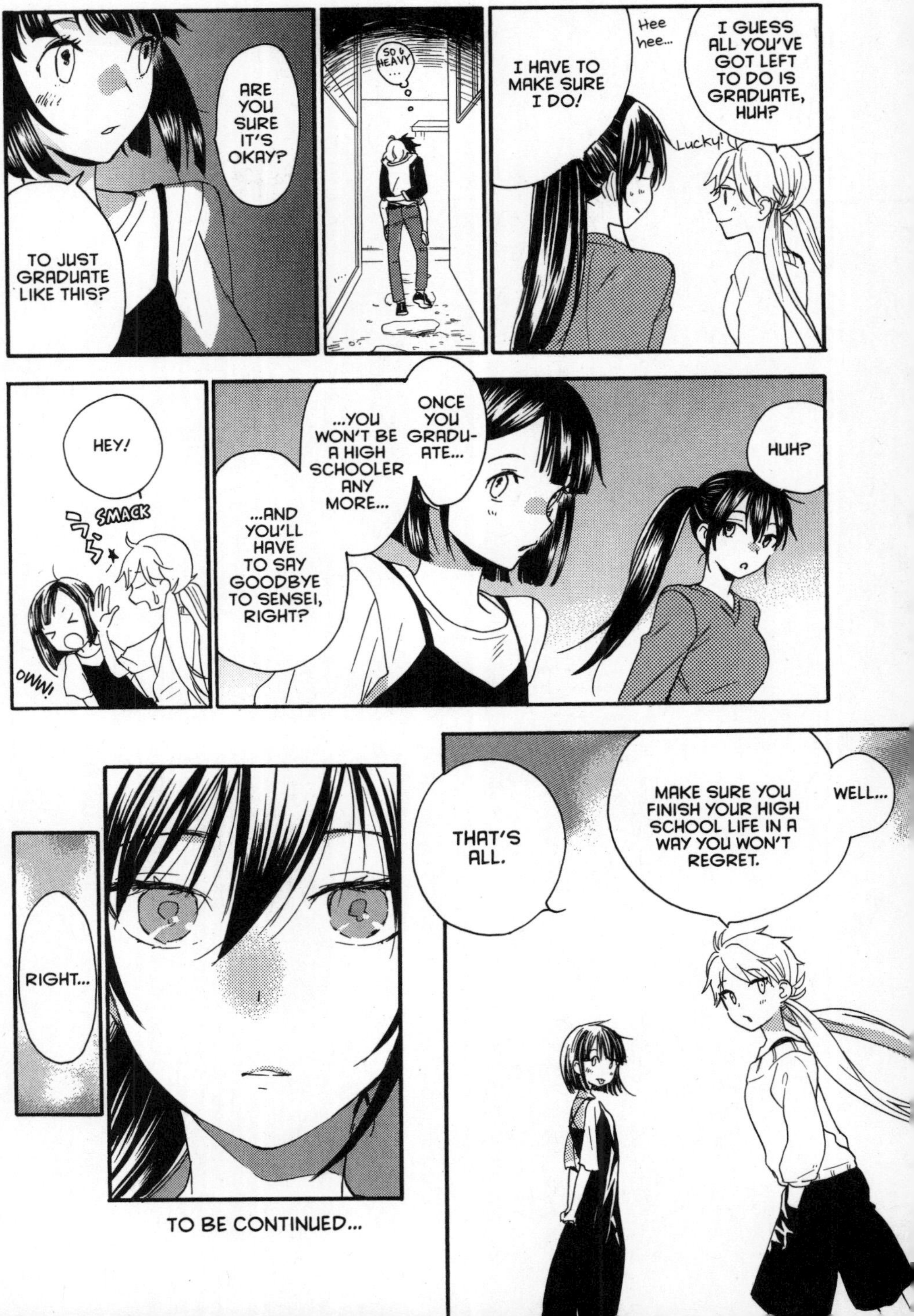
I GUESS ALL YOU'VE GOT LEFT TO DO IS GRADUATE, HUH?
Hee hee...
I HAVE TO MAKE SURE I DO!
Lucky!
SO HEAVY...
ARE YOU SURE IT'S OKAY?
TO JUST GRADUATE LIKE THIS?
HUH?
ONCE YOU GRADU-ATE...
...YOU WON'T BE A HIGH SCHOOLER ANY MORE...
...AND YOU'LL HAVE TO SAY GOODBYE TO SENSEI, RIGHT?
HEY!
SMACK
OWW!
WELL...
MAKE SURE YOU FINISH YOUR HIGH SCHOOL LIFE IN A WAY YOU WON'T REGRET.
THAT'S ALL.
RIGHT...

TO BE CONTINUED...

SUKIYAKI

☆Ingredients☆ (Serves 2)
- → 250g thin sliced beef
- → 50g shungiku
- → 160g nappa cabbage
- → 4 shiitake mushrooms
- → 1 green onion
- → ½ package enoki mushrooms
- → ½ package (100g) shirataki (konnyaku noodles)
- → 150g fried tofu
- → 2 small pieces yaki-fu (roasted gluten)
- → 2 eggs
- → 3.5 tablespoon sugar
- → 2 1/3 tablespoon soy sauce

Preparation

1. Cut the shirataki into easily eaten sizes. Boil for 3 minutes and drain. Rehydrate the yaki-fu in water. Squeeze lightly to drain water. Cut fried tofu into 4 pieces and drain.

2. Cut nappa cabbage length ways and then slice into 3cm pieces. Cut green onion on the diagonal and remove large stems from the shungiku.

3. Score an 'x' on the caps of the shiitake mushrooms. Separate the enoki mushrooms into little bunches.

4. Fry about half the meat in a nabe pot with oil. Add 1 tablespoon of sugar and 2 teaspoons of soy sauce, then turn stir to mix.

5. Put the nappa cabbage in an empty nabe pot. Then add the shiitake mushrooms, green onion, fried tofu, and shirataki mushroom one by one as they cook. Cover everything in 1.5 tablespoon of sugar and 1 tablespoon of soy sauce.

> Dip the cooked meat in some whipped egg and enjoy.

6. Once the vegetables are cooked through add the remaining meat. Cover with 1 tablespoon of sugar and 2 tablespoons of soy sauce, then stir to mix.

7. Add the enoki mushrooms, yaki-fu, and shungiku,

> Once it's all cooked dip it in some whisked egg and eat!

> This looks delicious

★POINT★
Cook everything on a medium to high heat.
Turn the heat to low if it looks like it's about to burn!

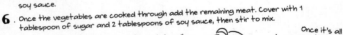

It's fine,
it's fine.

Chapter 48 | Roe and Love and Get-Togethers

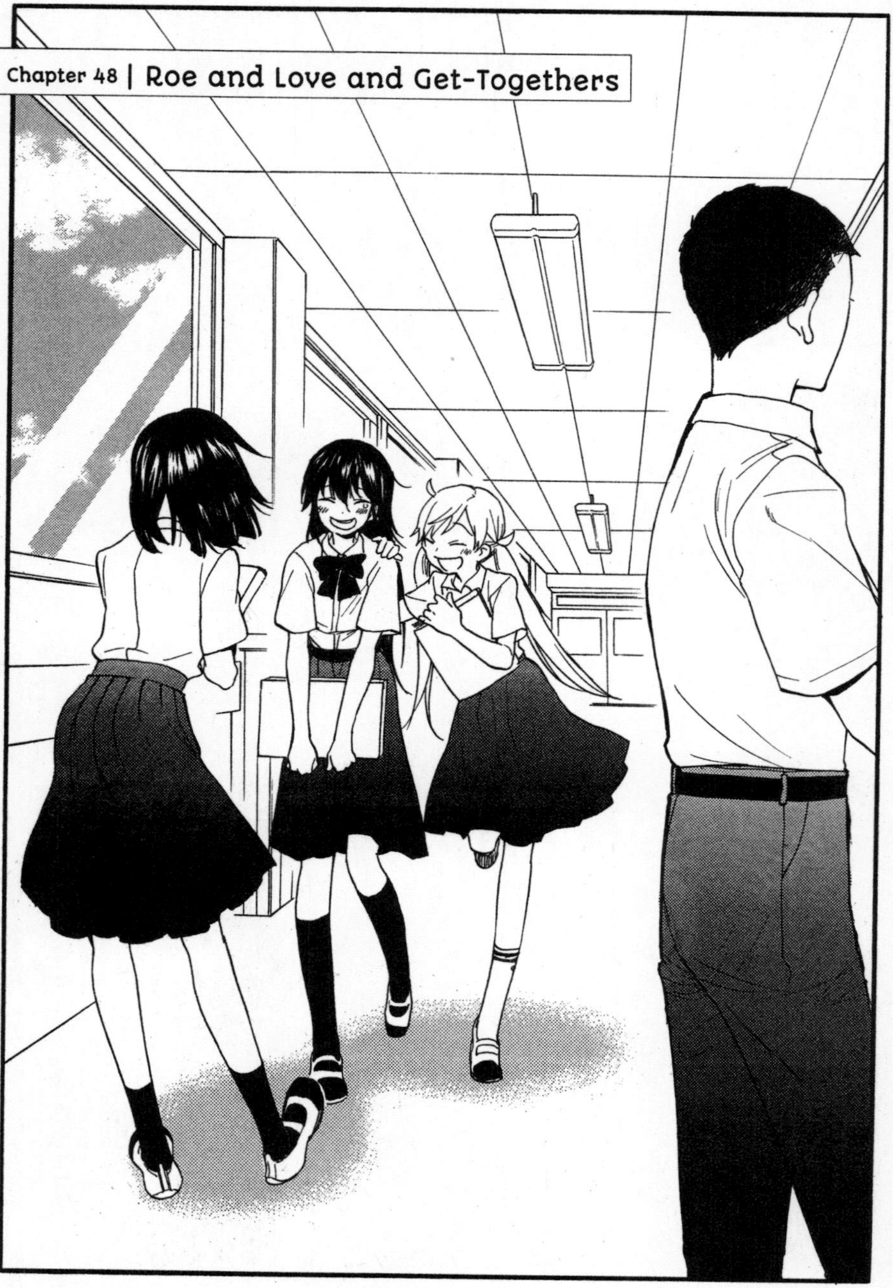

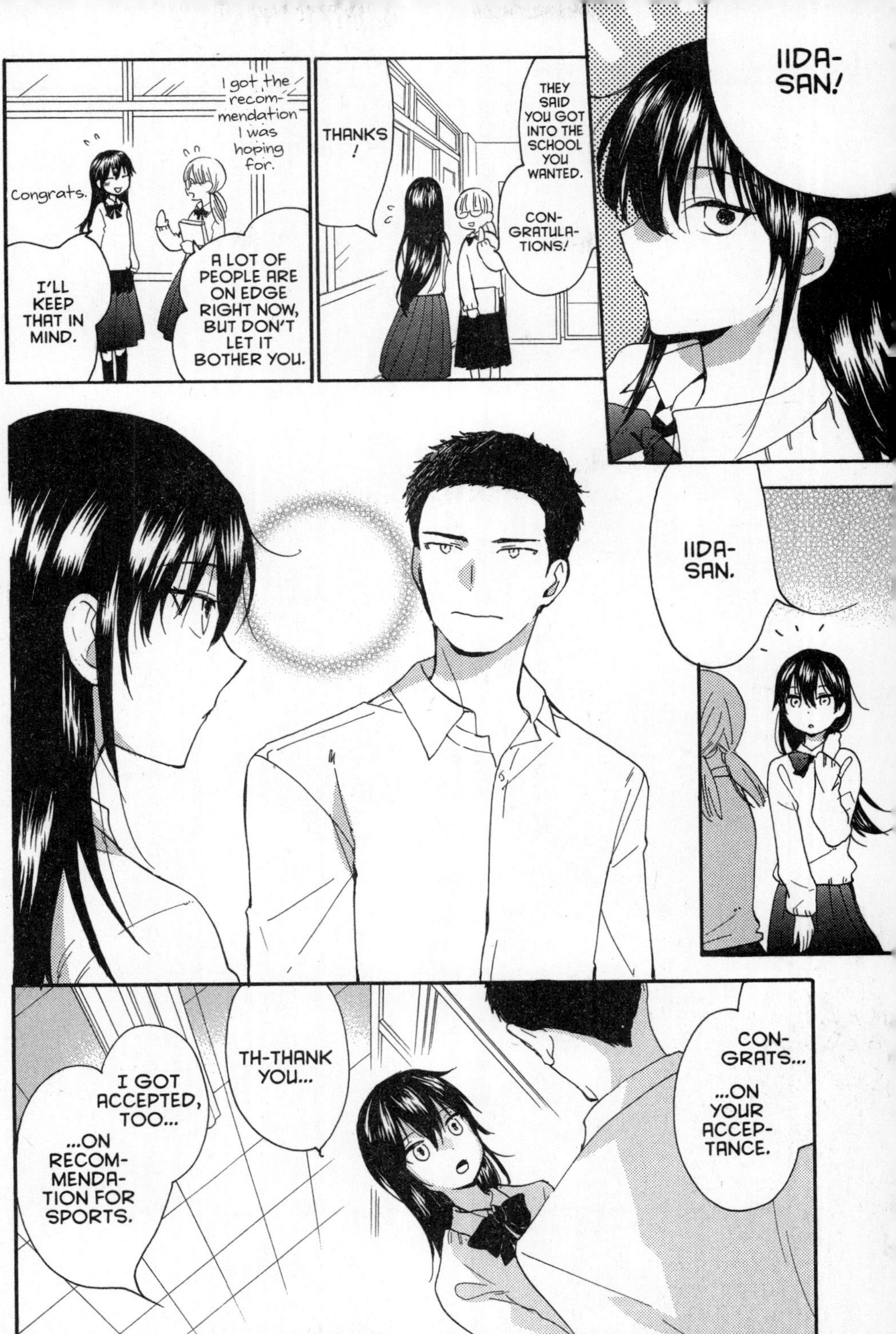
IIDA-SAN!
THEY SAID YOU GOT INTO THE SCHOOL YOU WANTED.
CONGRATULATIONS!
THANKS!
I got the recommendation I was hoping for.
Congrats.
A LOT OF PEOPLE ARE ON EDGE RIGHT NOW, BUT DON'T LET IT BOTHER YOU.
I'LL KEEP THAT IN MIND.
IIDA-SAN.
CONGRATS...
...ON YOUR ACCEPTANCE.
TH-THANK YOU...
I GOT ACCEPTED, TOO...
...ON RECOMMENDATION FOR SPORTS.

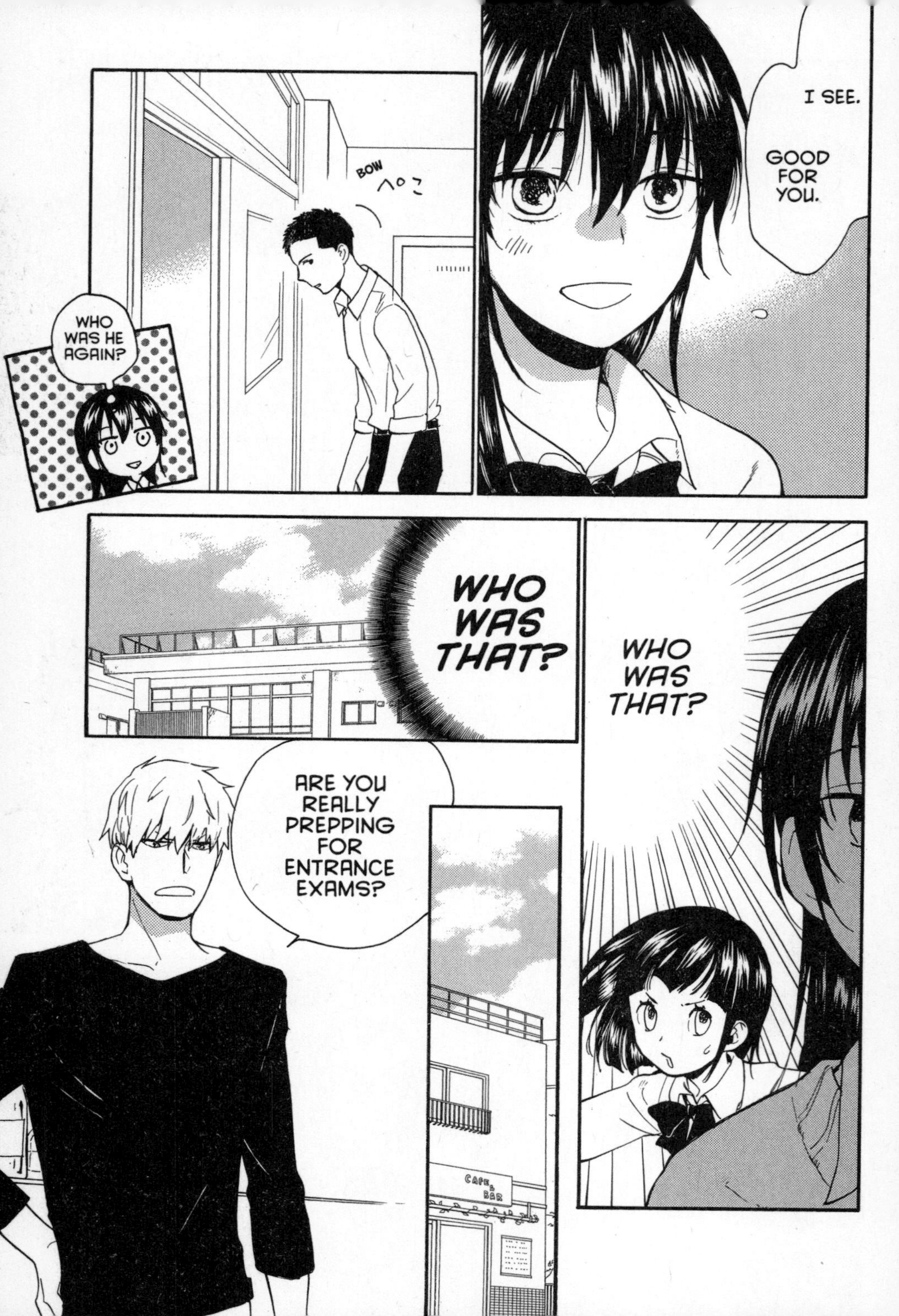
I SEE.
GOOD FOR YOU.
BOW
へこ
WHO WAS HE AGAIN?
WHO WAS THAT?
WHO WAS THAT?
ARE YOU REALLY PREPPING FOR ENTRANCE EXAMS?
CAFE & BAR

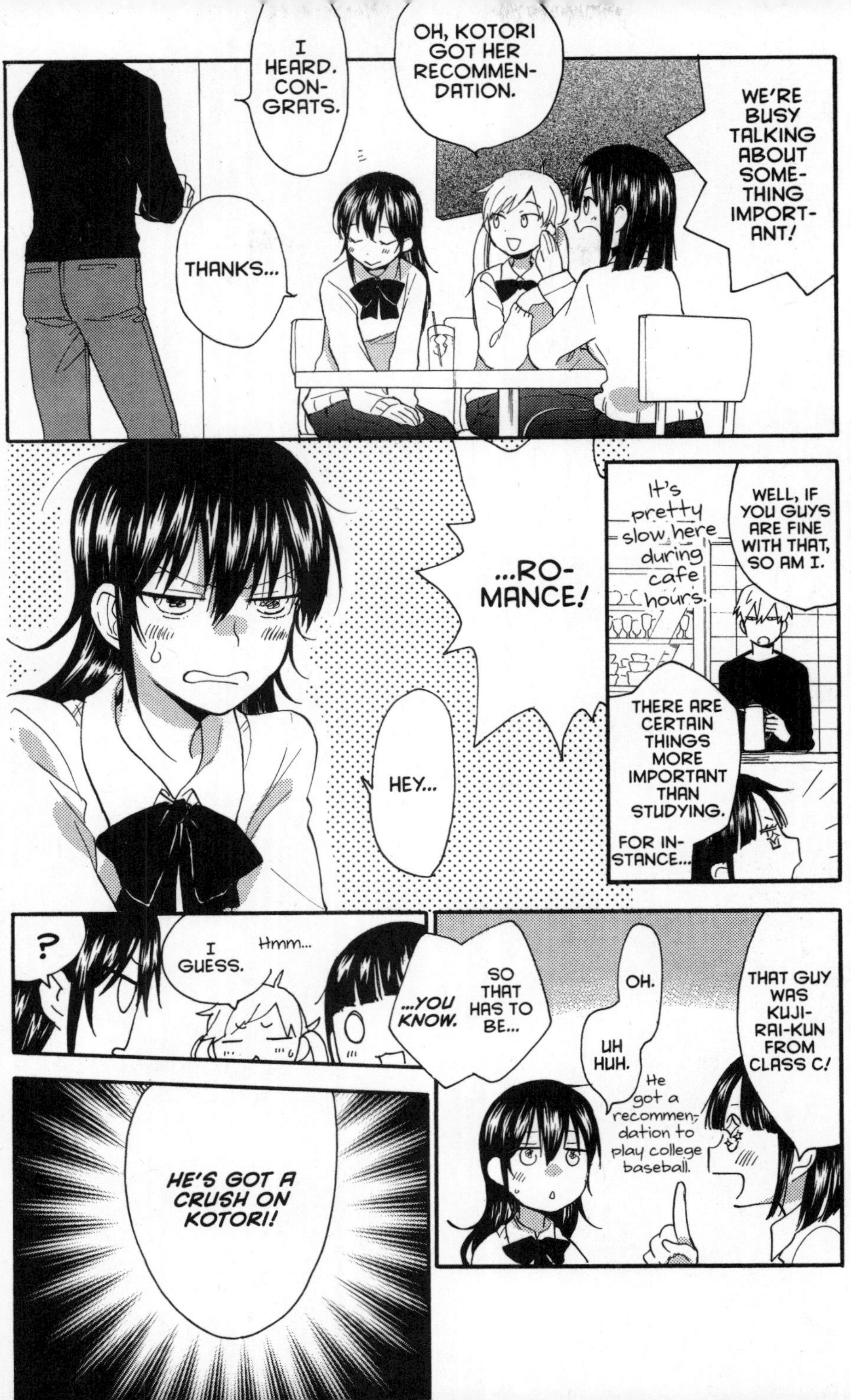
WE'RE BUSY TALKING ABOUT SOME-THING IMPORT-ANT!
OH, KOTORI GOT HER RECOMMEN-DATION.
I HEARD. CON-GRATS.
THANKS...
WELL, IF YOU GUYS ARE FINE WITH THAT, SO AM I.
It's pretty slow here during cafe hours.
THERE ARE CERTAIN THINGS MORE IMPORTANT THAN STUDYING.
FOR IN-STANCE...
...RO-MANCE!
HEY...
THAT GUY WAS KUJI-RAI-KUN FROM CLASS C!
OH.
UH HUH.
He got a recommen-dation to play college baseball.
SO THAT HAS TO BE...
...YOU KNOW.
Hmm...
I GUESS.
?
HE'S GOT A CRUSH ON KOTORI!

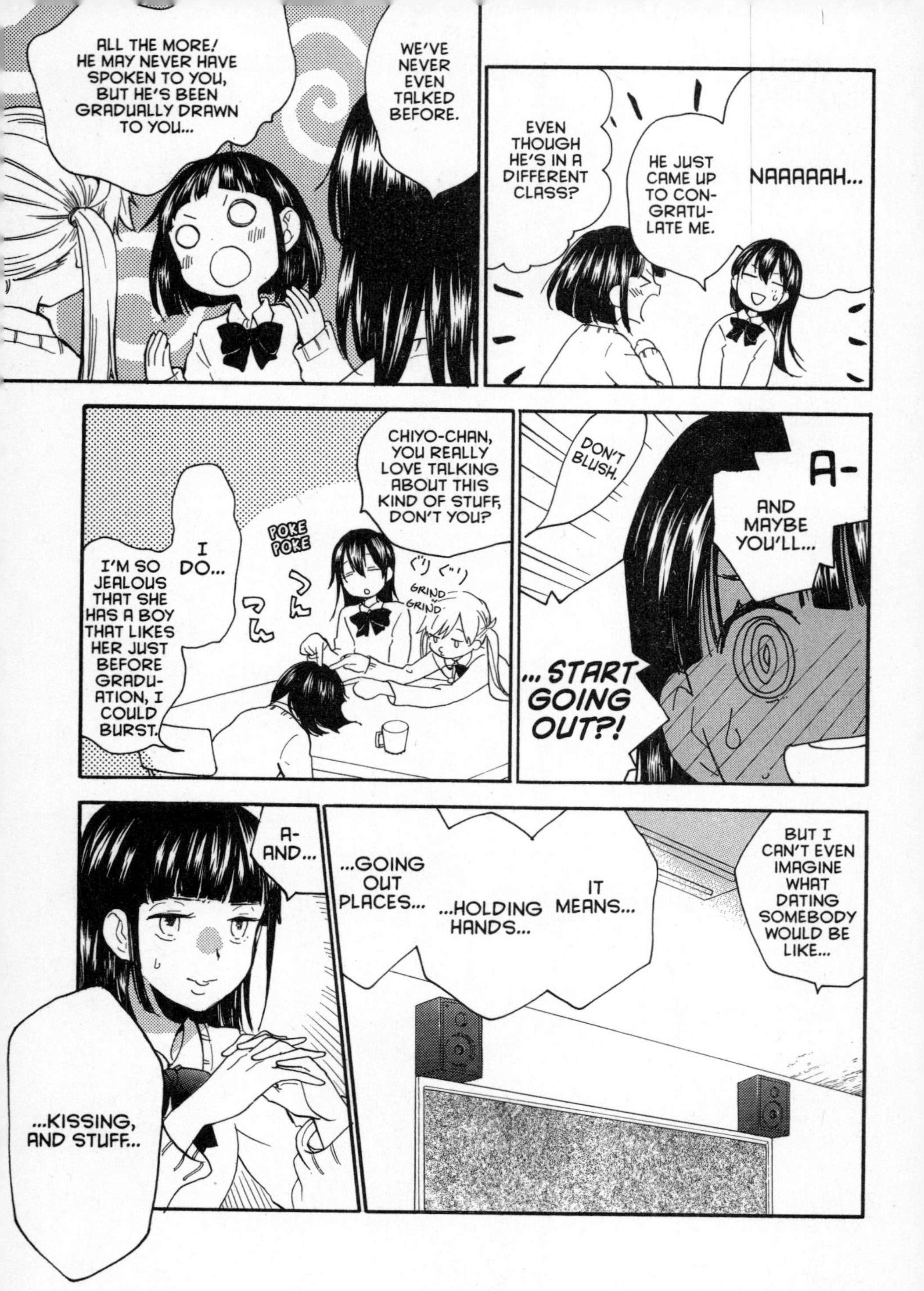
NAAAAAH...
HE JUST CAME UP TO CON-GRATU-LATE ME.
EVEN THOUGH HE'S IN A DIFFERENT CLASS?
WE'VE NEVER EVEN TALKED BEFORE.
ALL THE MORE! HE MAY NEVER HAVE SPOKEN TO YOU, BUT HE'S BEEN GRADUALLY DRAWN TO YOU...
A-
AND MAYBE YOU'LL...
DON'T BLUSH.
...START GOING OUT?!
CHIYO-CHAN, YOU REALLY LOVE TALKING ABOUT THIS KIND OF STUFF, DON'T YOU?
POKE POKE
GRIND GRIND
I DO...
I'M SO JEALOUS THAT SHE HAS A BOY THAT LIKES HER JUST BEFORE GRADU-ATION, I COULD BURST.
BUT I CAN'T EVEN IMAGINE WHAT DATING SOMEBODY WOULD BE LIKE...
IT MEANS...
...HOLDING HANDS...
...GOING OUT PLACES...
A- AND...
...KISSING, AND STUFF...

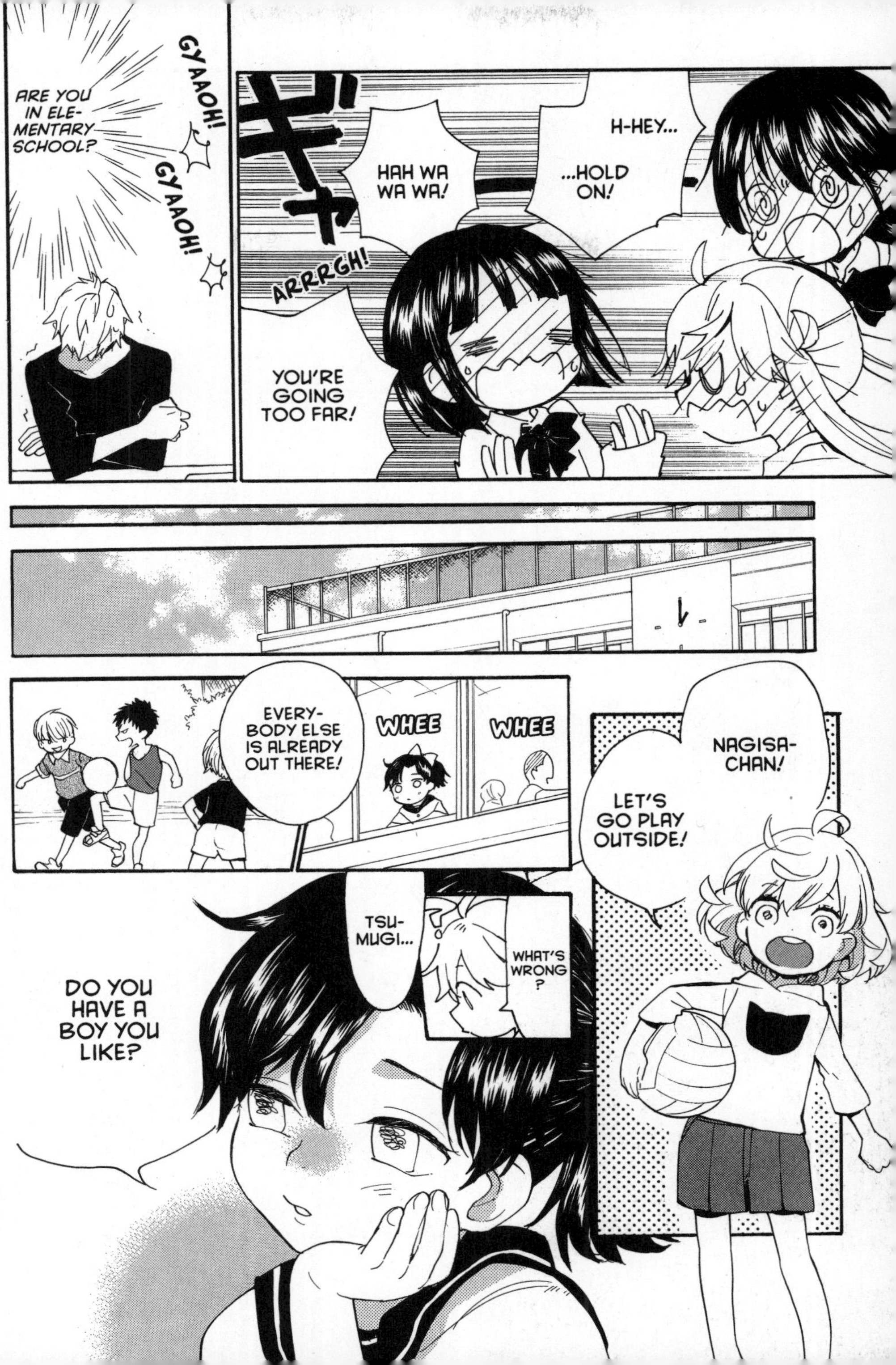
H-HEY...
...HOLD ON!
HAH WA WA WA!
ギャー
ARRRGH!
YOU'RE GOING TOO FAR!
GYAAOH!
GYAAOH!
ARE YOU IN ELE-MENTARY SCHOOL?
NAGISA-CHAN!
LET'S GO PLAY OUTSIDE!
WHEE
WHEE
EVERY-BODY ELSE IS ALREADY OUT THERE!
TSU-MUGI...
WHAT'S WRONG?
DO YOU HAVE A BOY YOU LIKE?

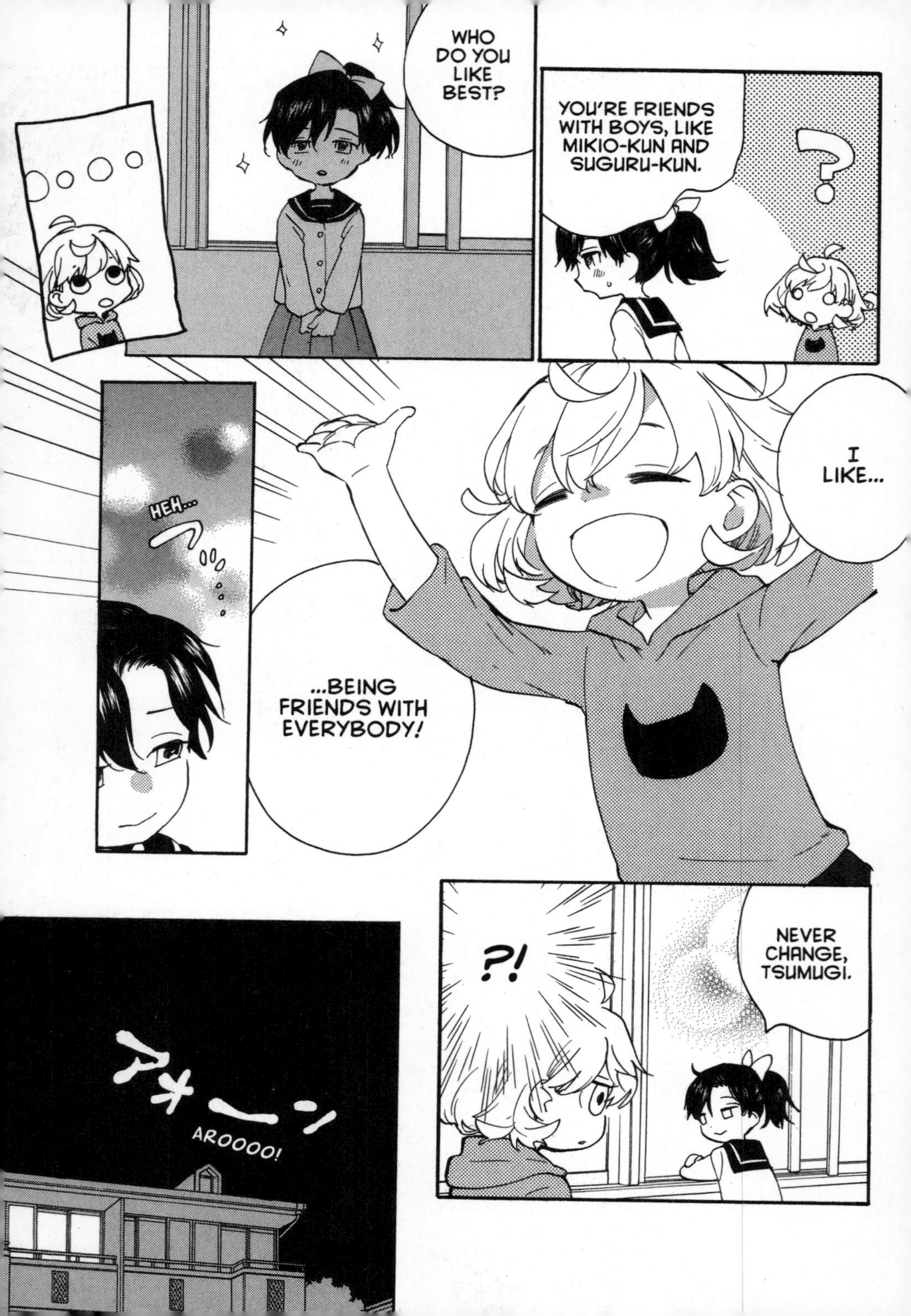
YOU'RE FRIENDS WITH BOYS, LIKE MIKIO-KUN AND SUGURU-KUN.
?
WHO DO YOU LIKE BEST?
I LIKE...
...BEING FRIENDS WITH EVERYBODY!
HEH...
NEVER CHANGE, TSUMUGI.
?!
アオーン
AROOOO!

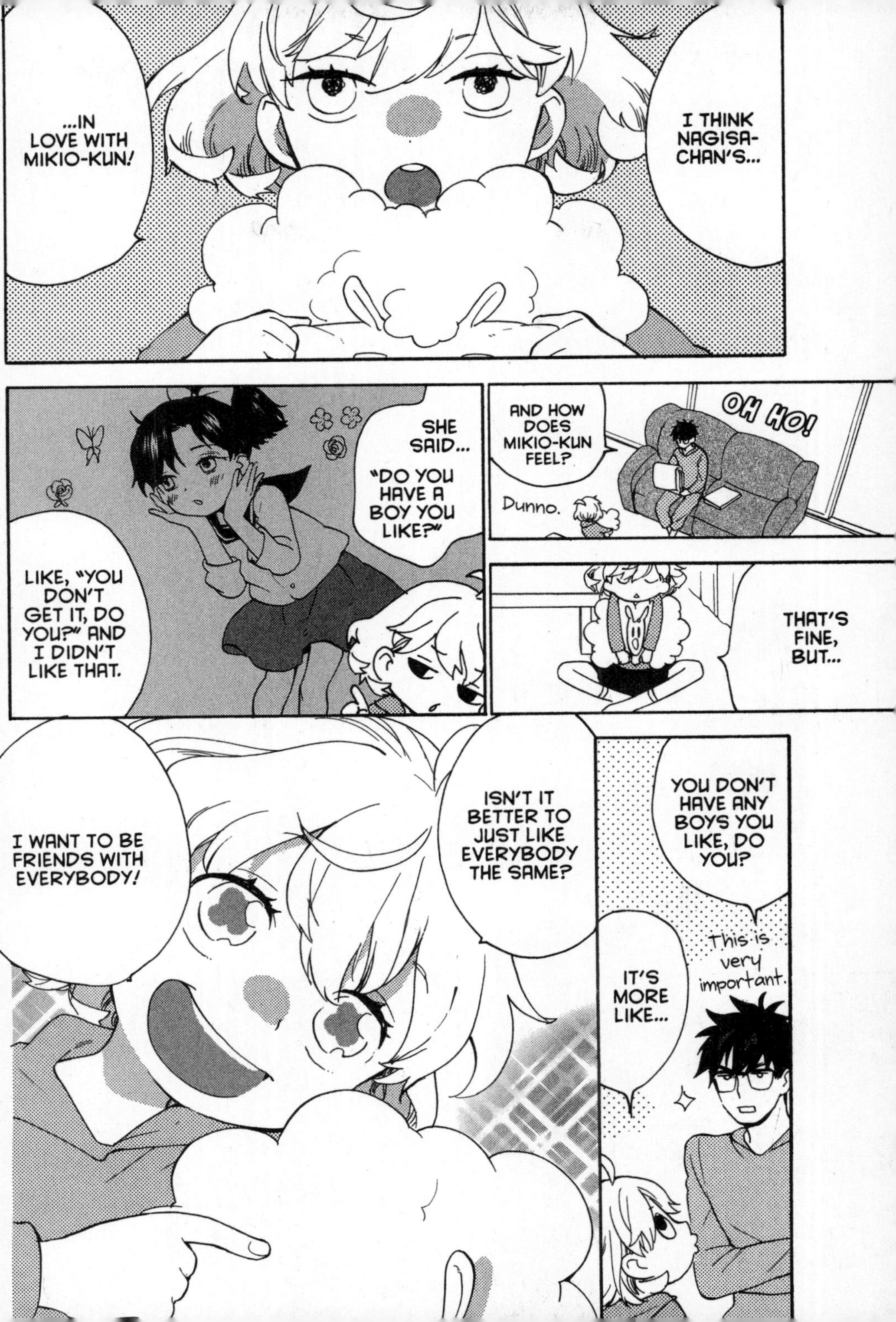
I THINK NAGISA-CHAN'S...
...IN LOVE WITH MIKIO-KUN!
OH HO!
AND HOW DOES MIKIO-KUN FEEL?
Dunno.
THAT'S FINE, BUT...
SHE SAID... "DO YOU HAVE A BOY YOU LIKE?"
LIKE, "YOU DON'T GET IT, DO YOU?" AND I DIDN'T LIKE THAT.
YOU DON'T HAVE ANY BOYS YOU LIKE, DO YOU?
This is very important.
IT'S MORE LIKE...
ISN'T IT BETTER TO JUST LIKE EVERYBODY THE SAME?
I WANT TO BE FRIENDS WITH EVERYBODY!

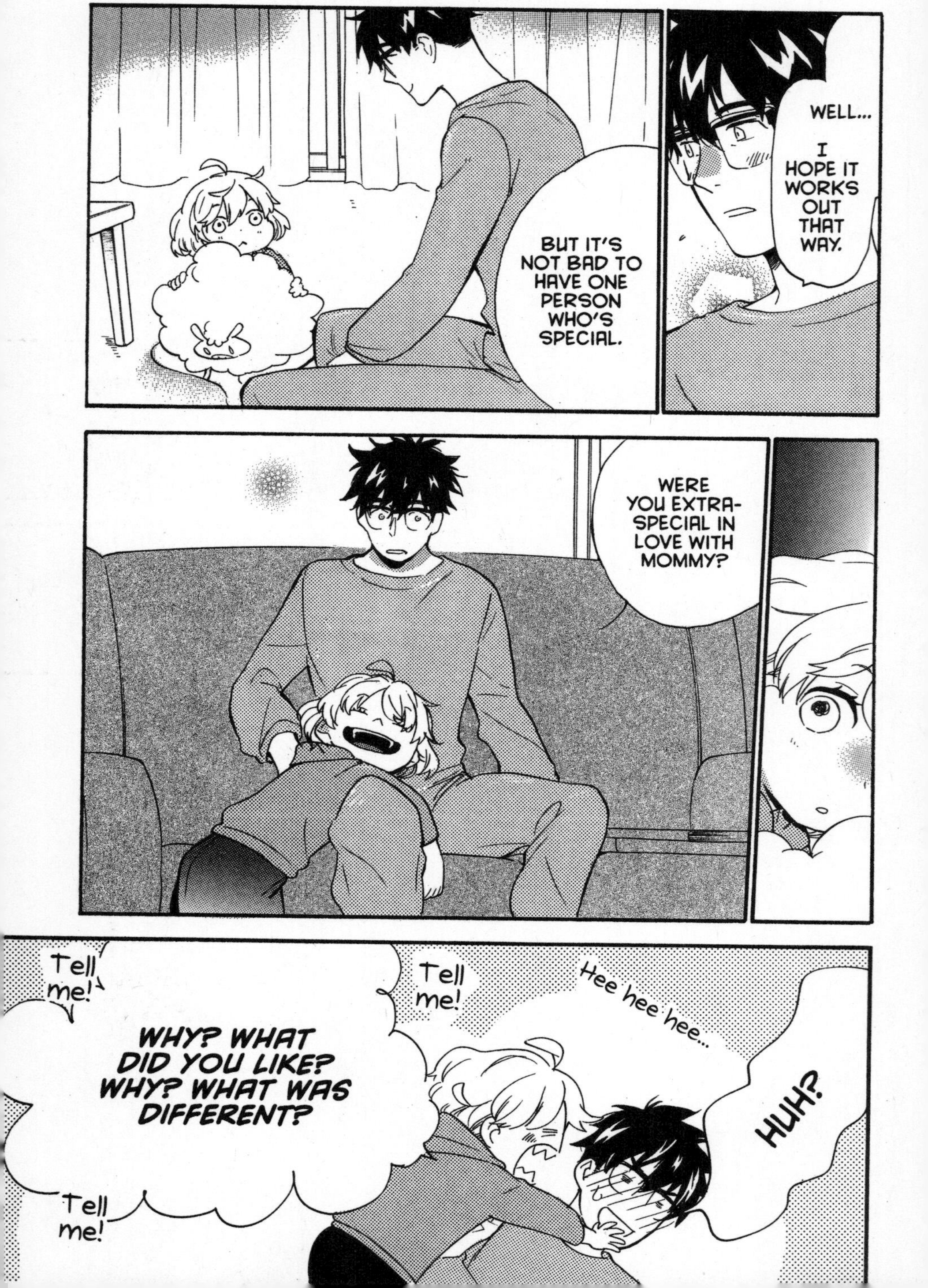
WELL...
I HOPE IT WORKS OUT THAT WAY.
BUT IT'S NOT BAD TO HAVE ONE PERSON WHO'S SPECIAL.
WERE YOU EXTRA-SPECIAL IN LOVE WITH MOMMY?
HUH?
Hee hee hee...
Tell me!
Tell me!
WHY? WHAT DID YOU LIKE? WHY? WHAT WAS DIFFERENT?
Tell me!

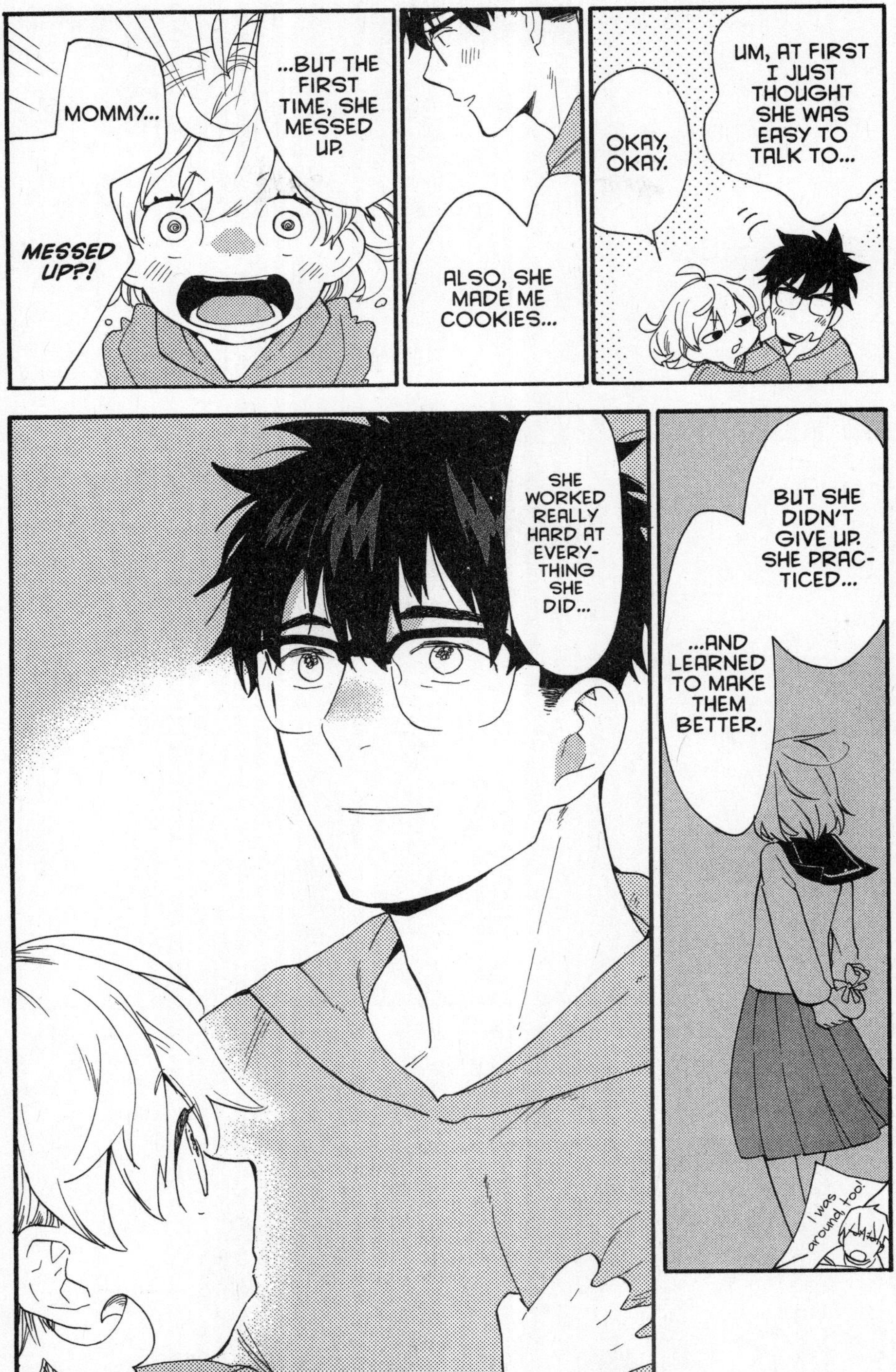
UM, AT FIRST I JUST THOUGHT SHE WAS EASY TO TALK TO...
OKAY, OKAY.
ALSO, SHE MADE ME COOKIES...
...BUT THE FIRST TIME, SHE MESSED UP.
MOMMY...
MESSED UP?!
BUT SHE DIDN'T GIVE UP. SHE PRAC-TICED...
...AND LEARNED TO MAKE THEM BETTER.
I was around, too!
SHE WORKED REALLY HARD AT EVERY-THING SHE DID...

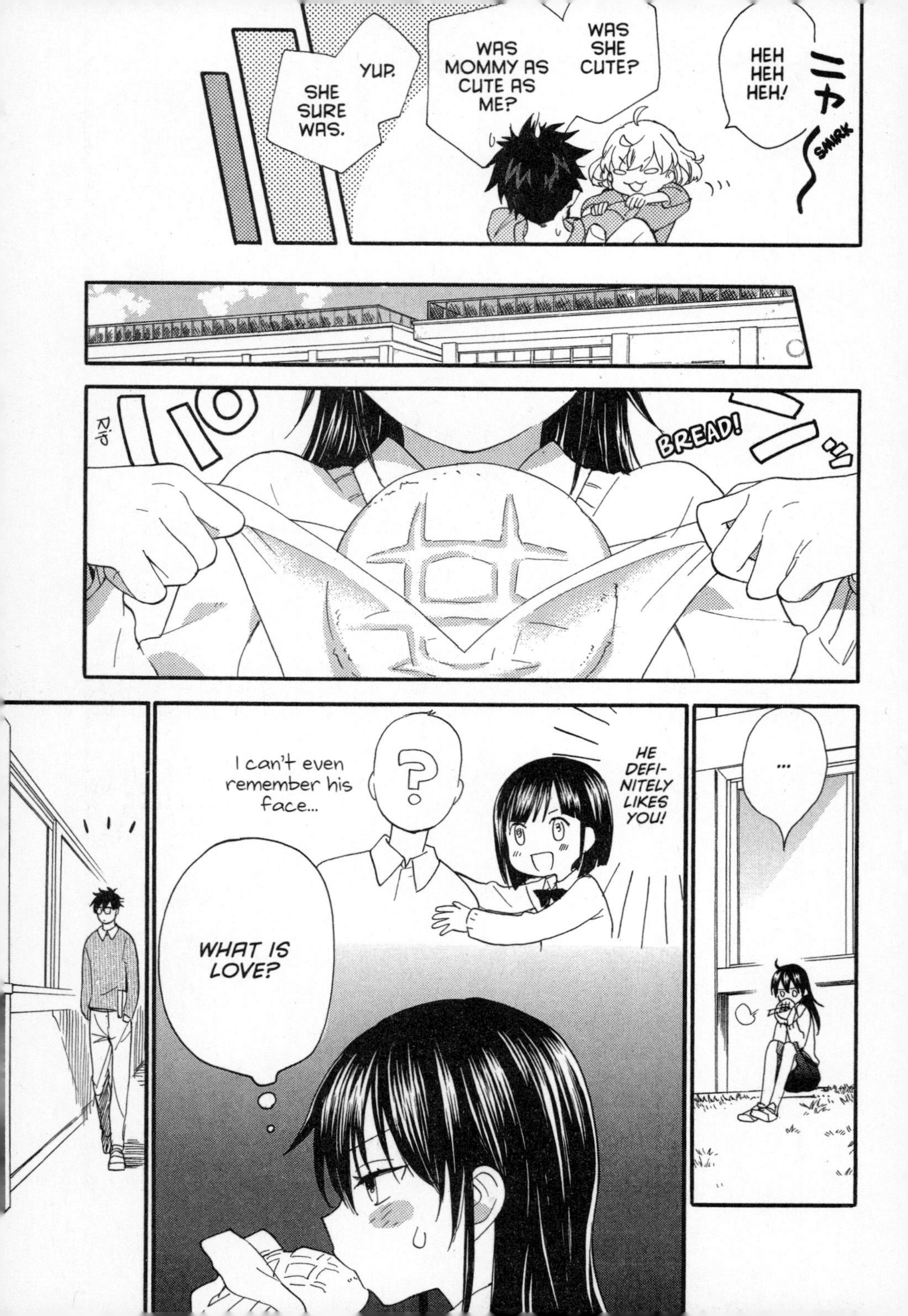

HEH HEH HEH!
ニヤ
SMIRK
WAS SHE CUTE?
WAS MOMMY AS CUTE AS ME?
YUP.
SHE SURE WAS.
BREAD!
RIP
...
HE DEFINITELY LIKES YOU!
I can't even remember his face...
WHAT IS LOVE?

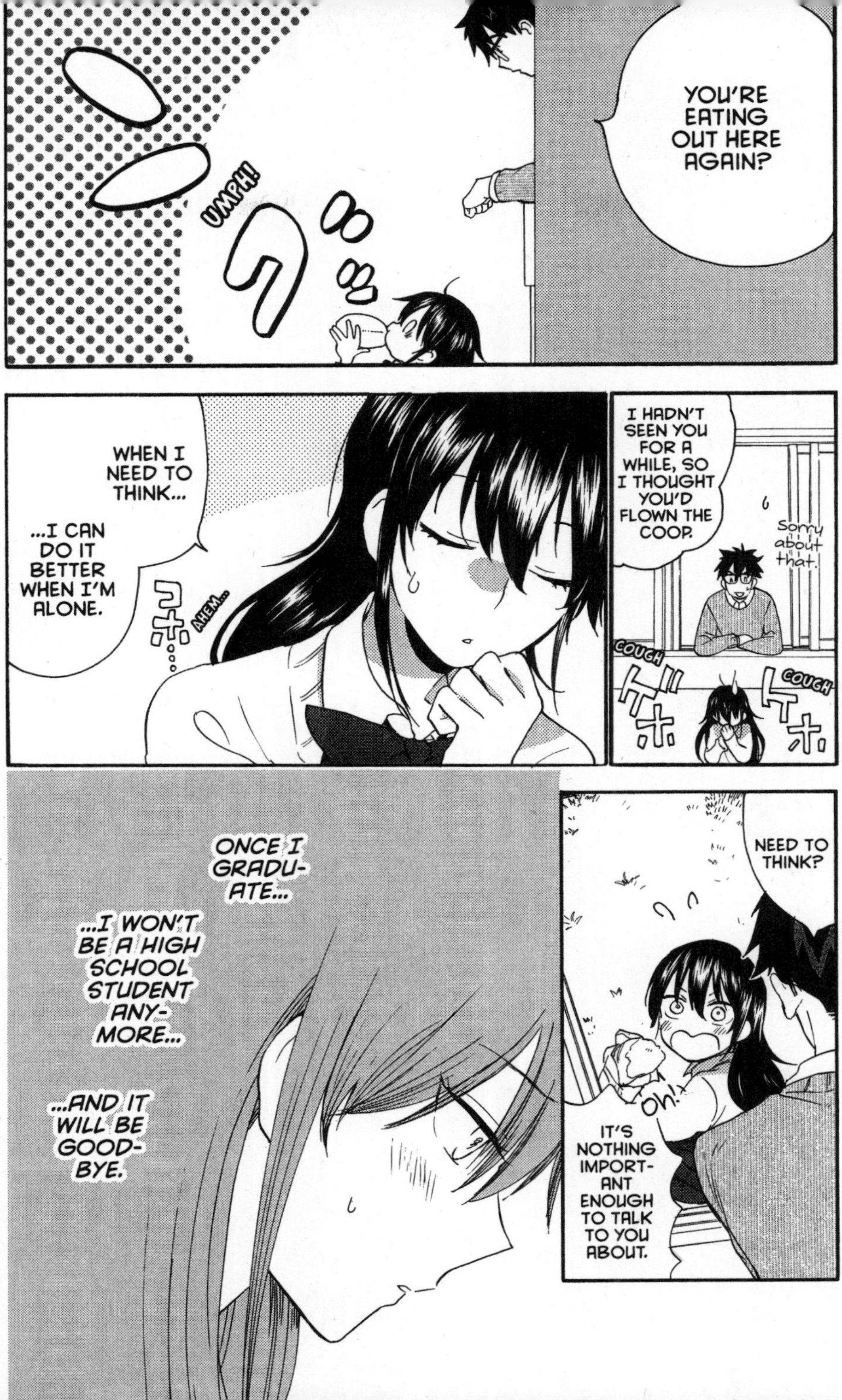
YOU'RE EATING OUT HERE AGAIN?
UMPH!
I HADN'T SEEN YOU FOR A WHILE, SO I THOUGHT YOU'D FLOWN THE COOP.
Sorry about that.
COUGH
COUGH
WHEN I NEED TO THINK...
...I CAN DO IT BETTER WHEN I'M ALONE.
AHEM...
NEED TO THINK?
Oh!
IT'S NOTHING IMPORTANT ENOUGH TO TALK TO YOU ABOUT.
ONCE I GRADUATE...
...I WON'T BE A HIGH SCHOOL STUDENT ANYMORE...
...AND IT WILL BE GOODBYE.

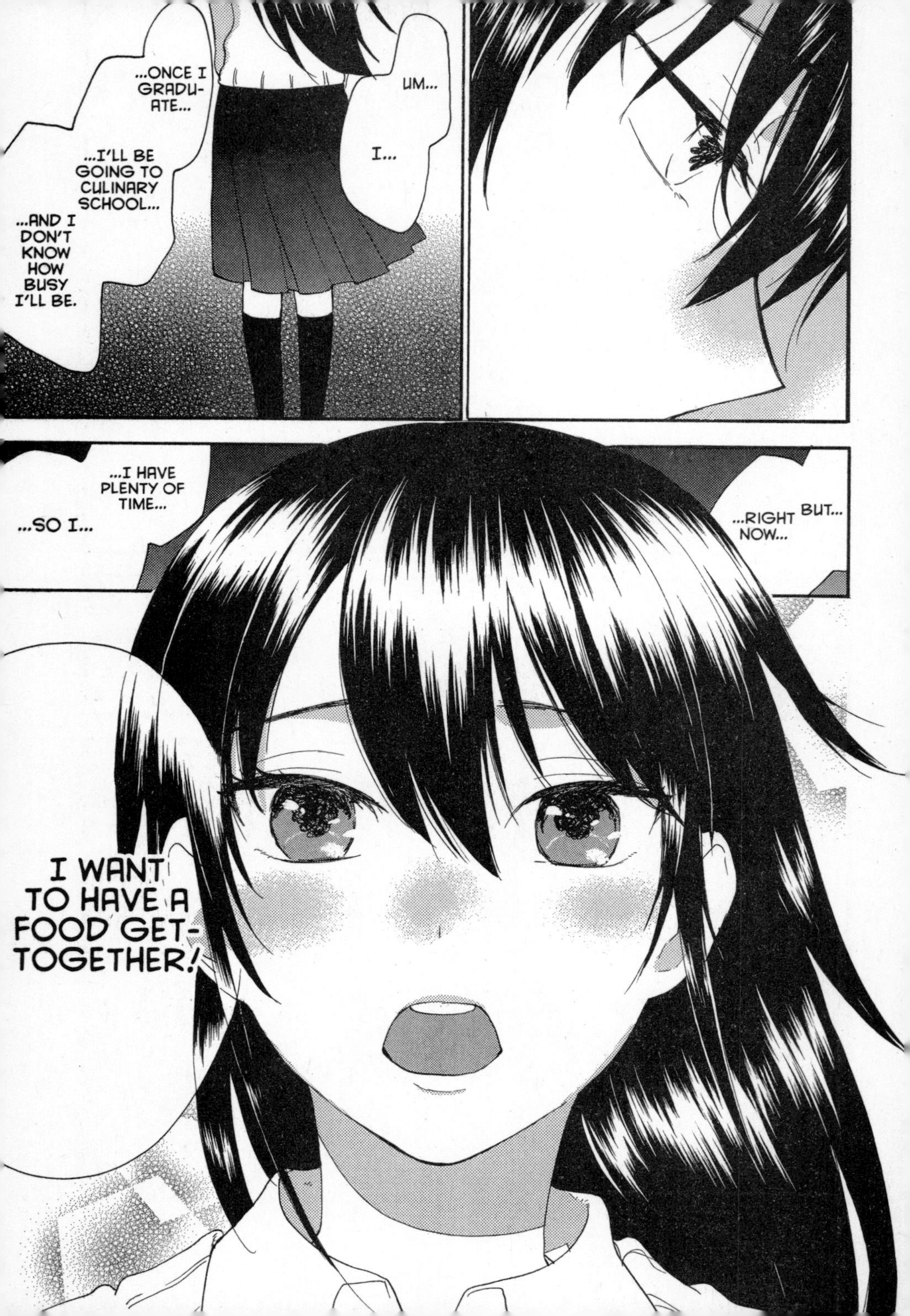
UM...
I...
...ONCE I GRADUATE...
...I'LL BE GOING TO CULINARY SCHOOL...
...AND I DON'T KNOW HOW BUSY I'LL BE.
BUT...
...RIGHT NOW...
...I HAVE PLENTY OF TIME...
...SO I...
I WANT TO HAVE A FOOD GET-TOGETHER!

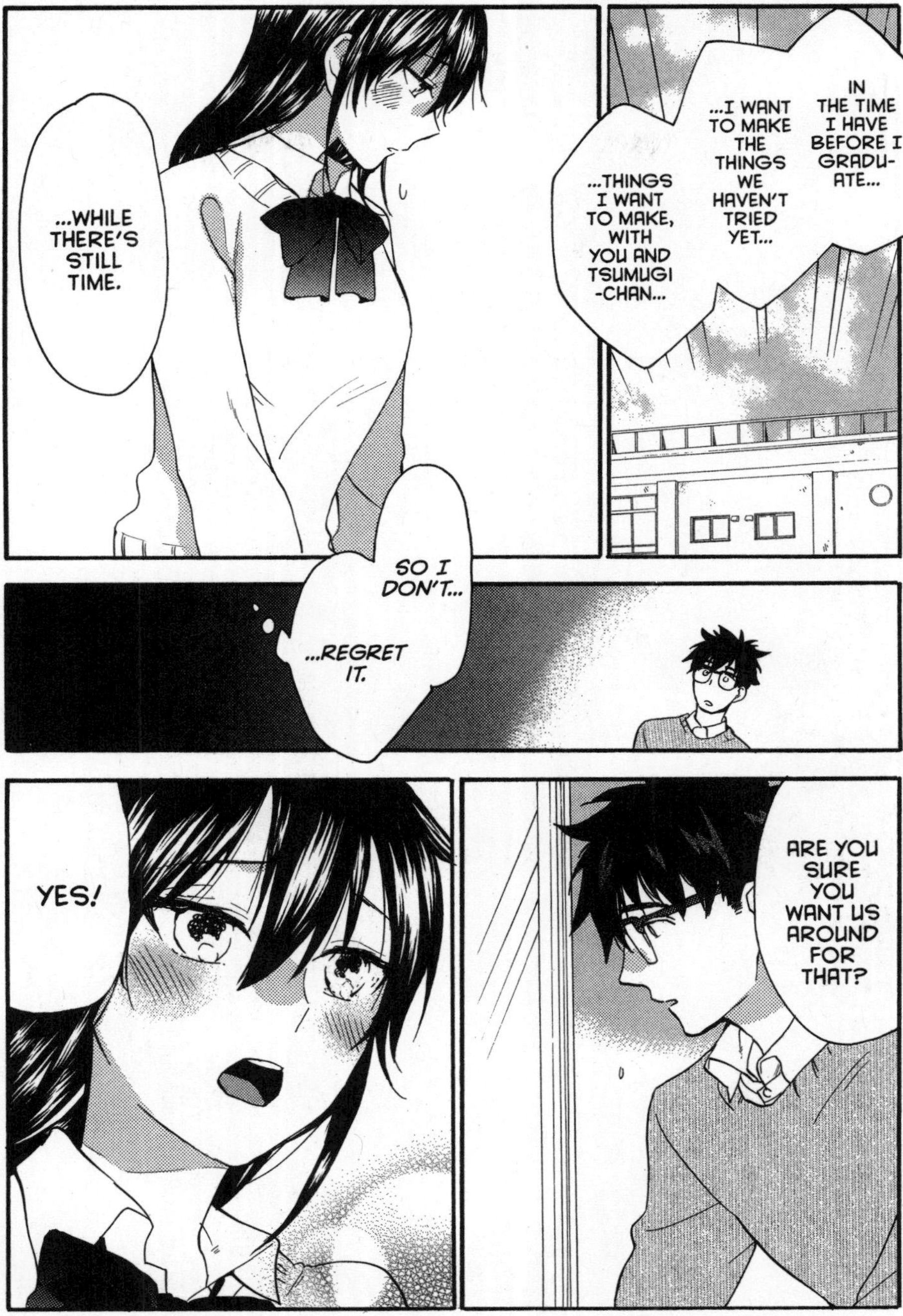
IN THE TIME I HAVE BEFORE I GRADU-ATE...
...I WANT TO MAKE THE THINGS WE HAVEN'T TRIED YET...
...THINGS I WANT TO MAKE, WITH YOU AND TSUMUGI -CHAN...
...WHILE THERE'S STILL TIME.
SO I DON'T...
...REGRET IT.
ARE YOU SURE YOU WANT US AROUND FOR THAT?
YES!

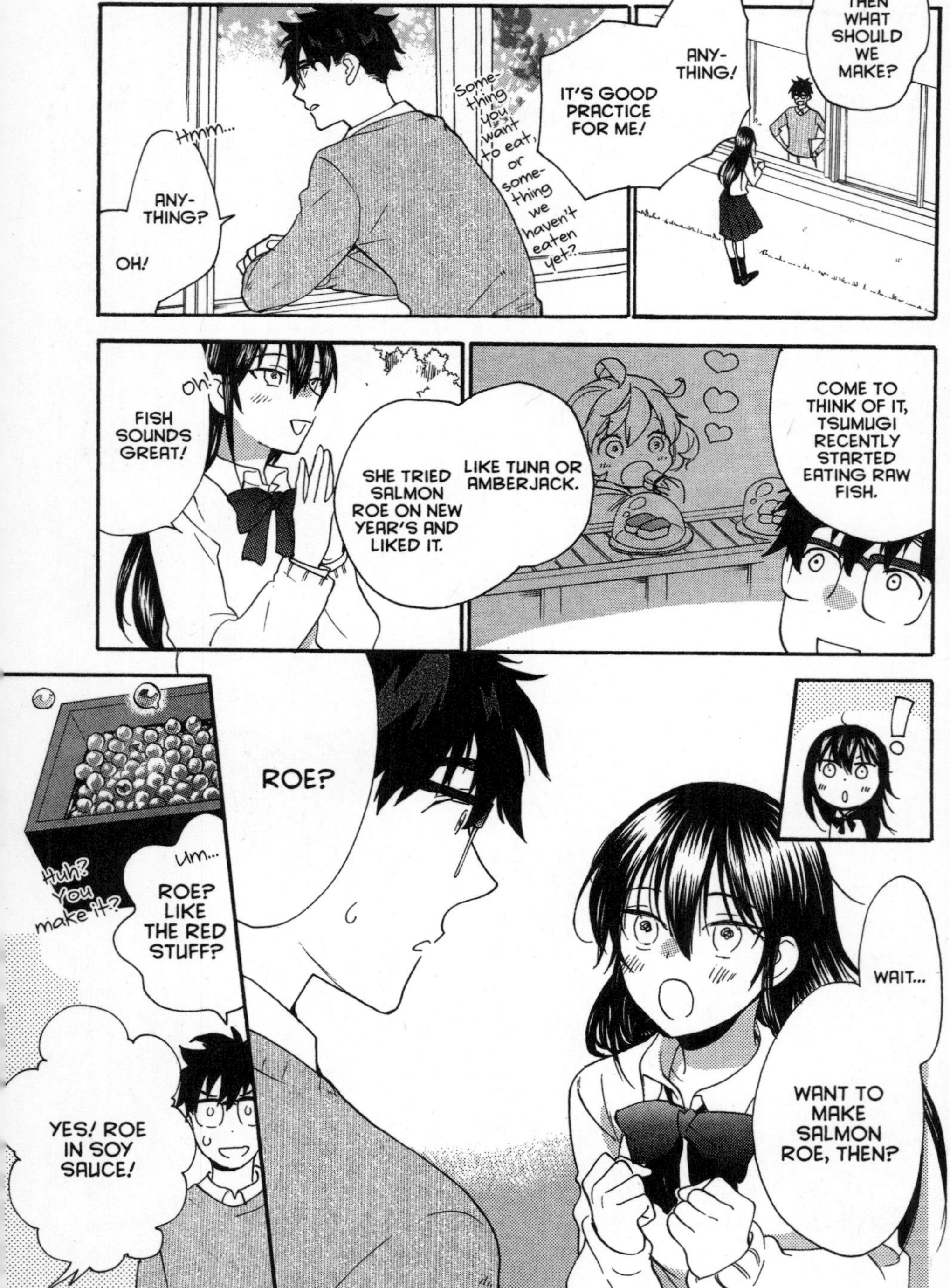
THEN WHAT SHOULD WE MAKE?
ANY-THING!
IT'S GOOD PRACTICE FOR ME!
Some-thing you want to eat, or some-thing we haven't eaten yet?
Hmm...
ANY-THING?
OH!
COME TO THINK OF IT, TSUMUGI RECENTLY STARTED EATING RAW FISH.
LIKE TUNA OR AMBERJACK.
SHE TRIED SALMON ROE ON NEW YEAR'S AND LIKED IT.
Oh!
FISH SOUNDS GREAT!
!
WAIT...
WANT TO MAKE SALMON ROE, THEN?
ROE?
Um...
ROE? LIKE THE RED STUFF?
Huh? You make it?
YES! ROE IN SOY SAUCE!

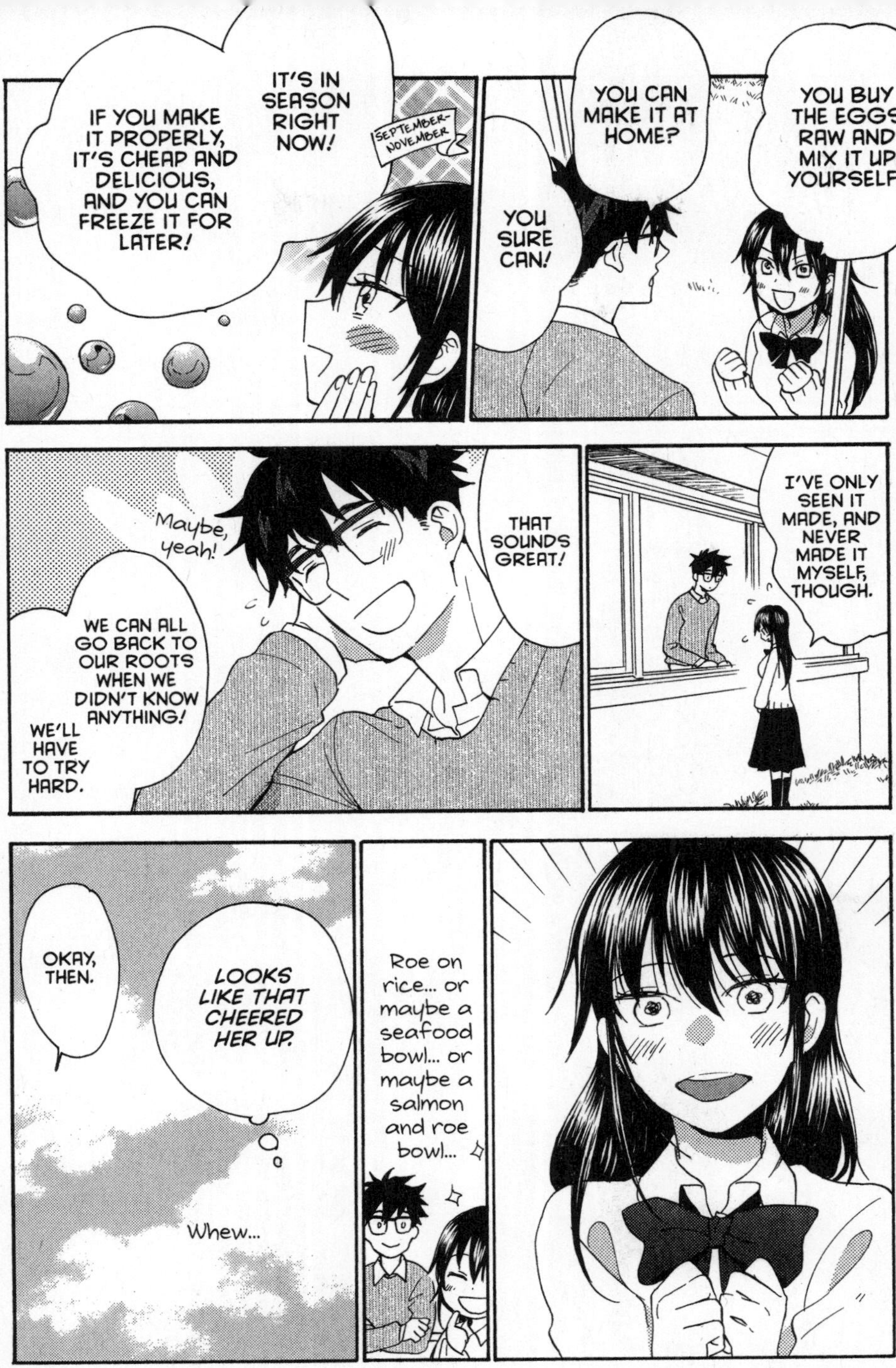
YOU BUY THE EGGS RAW AND MIX IT UP YOURSELF!
YOU CAN MAKE IT AT HOME?
YOU SURE CAN!
IT'S IN SEASON RIGHT NOW!
SEPTEMBER-NOVEMBER
IF YOU MAKE IT PROPERLY, IT'S CHEAP AND DELICIOUS, AND YOU CAN FREEZE IT FOR LATER!
I'VE ONLY SEEN IT MADE, AND NEVER MADE IT MYSELF, THOUGH.
THAT SOUNDS GREAT!
Maybe, yeah!
WE CAN ALL GO BACK TO OUR ROOTS WHEN WE DIDN'T KNOW ANYTHING!
WE'LL HAVE TO TRY HARD.
Roe on rice... or maybe a seafood bowl... or maybe a salmon and roe bowl...
LOOKS LIKE THAT CHEERED HER UP.
OKAY, THEN.
Whew...

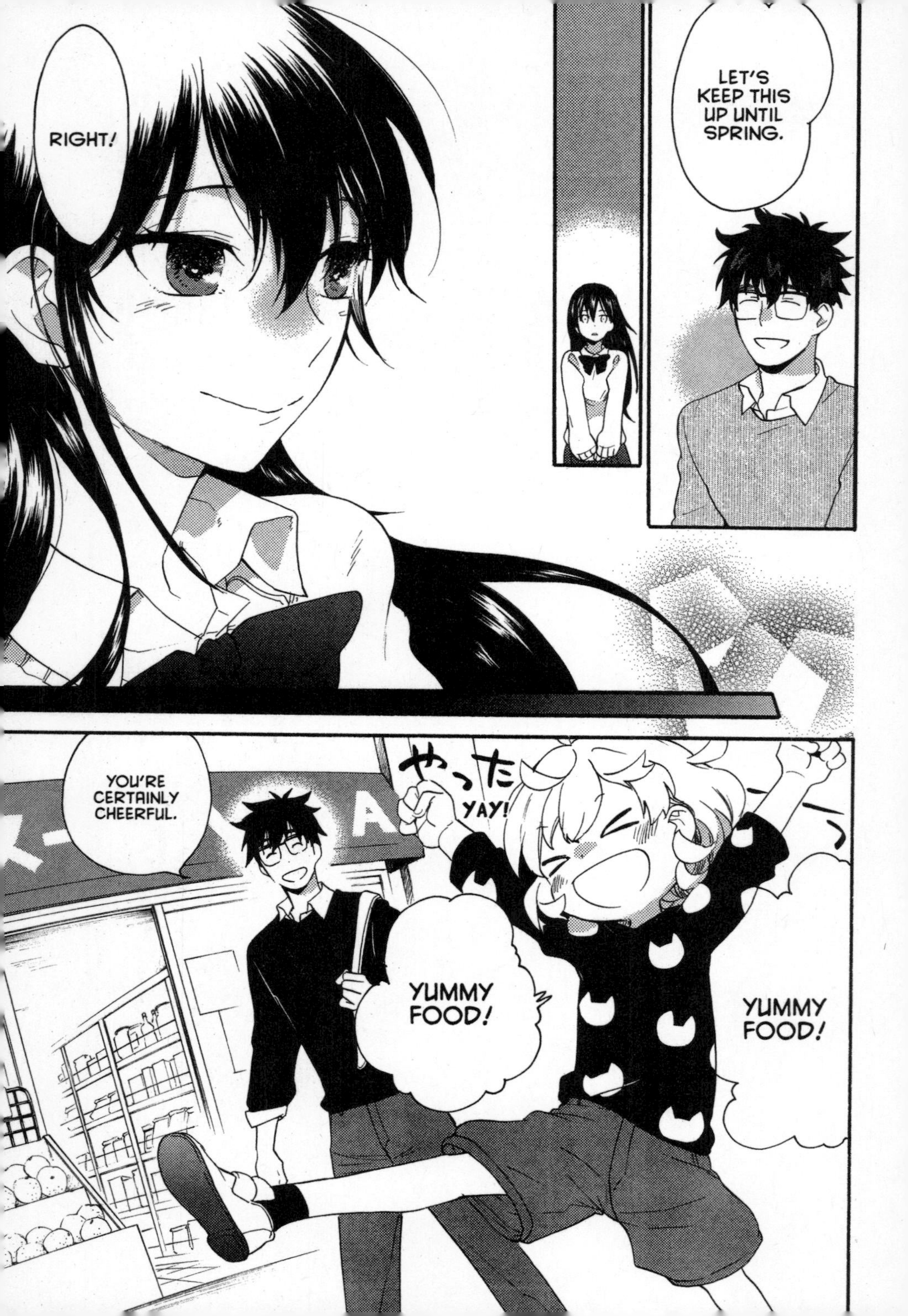
LET'S KEEP THIS UP UNTIL SPRING.
RIGHT!
やった
YAY!
YOU'RE CERTAINLY CHEERFUL.
YUMMY FOOD!
YUMMY FOOD!

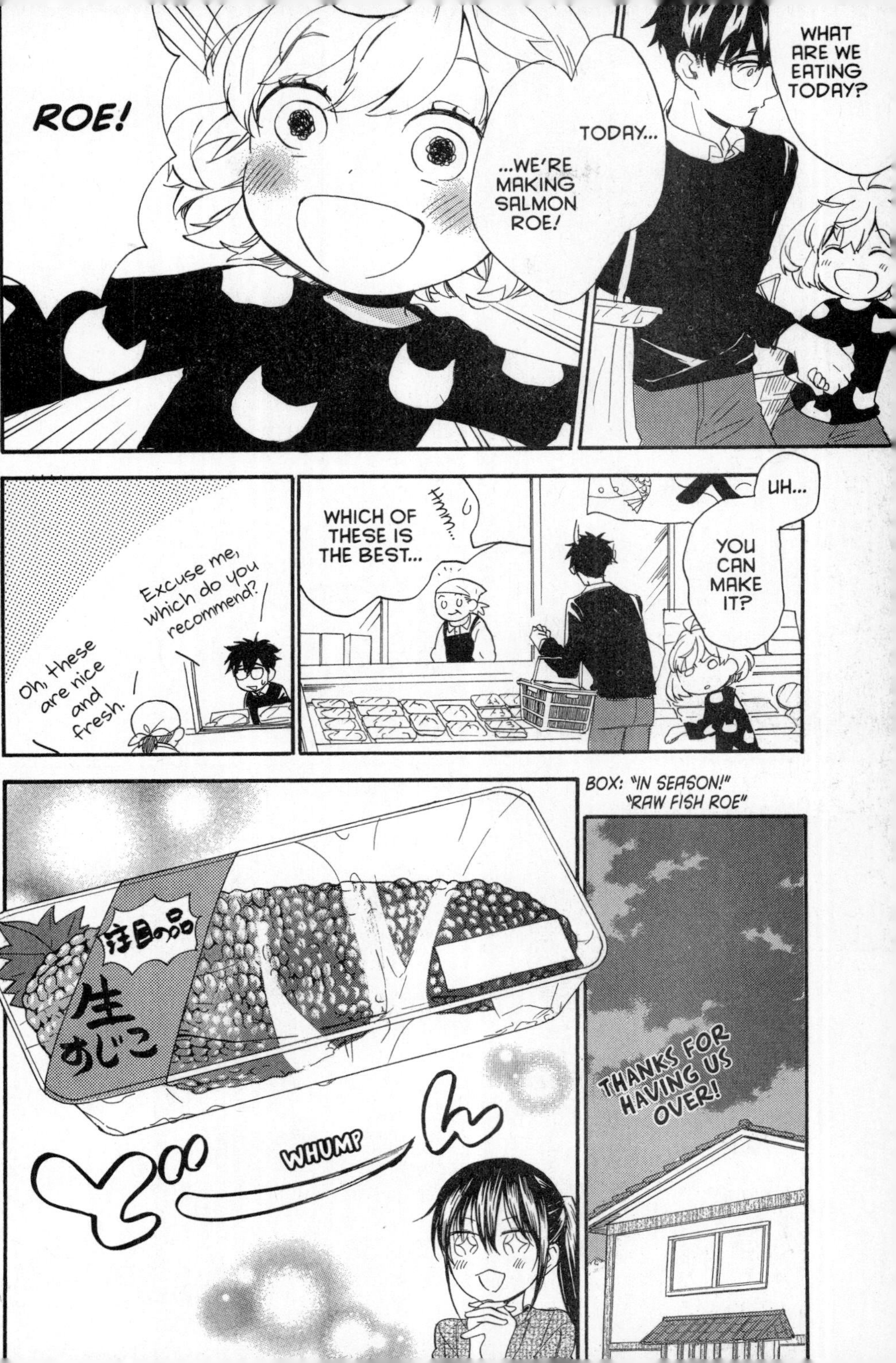
WHAT ARE WE EATING TODAY?
TODAY...
...WE'RE MAKING SALMON ROE!
ROE!
UH...
YOU CAN MAKE IT?
Hmm...
WHICH OF THESE IS THE BEST...
Excuse me, which do you recommend?
Oh, these are nice and fresh.
BOX: "IN SEASON!" "RAW FISH ROE"
THANKS FOR HAVING US OVER!
注目の品
生すじこ
WHUMP

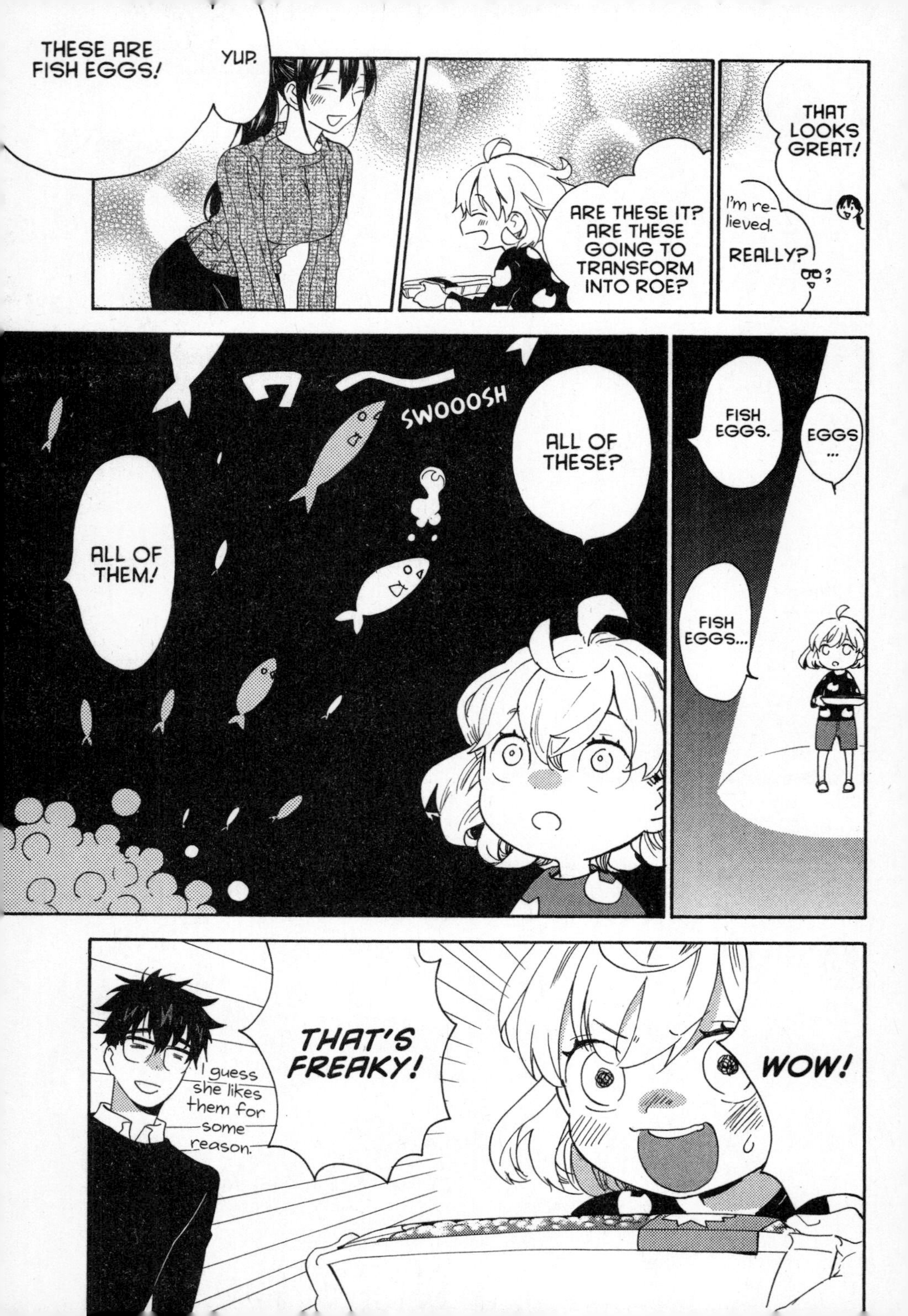
THAT LOOKS GREAT!
I'm relieved.
REALLY?
ARE THESE IT? ARE THESE GOING TO TRANSFORM INTO ROE?
THESE ARE FISH EGGS!
YUP.
FISH EGGS.
EGGS ...
FISH EGGS...
ALL OF THESE?
SWOOOSH
ALL OF THEM!
WOW!
THAT'S FREAKY!
I guess she likes them for some reason.

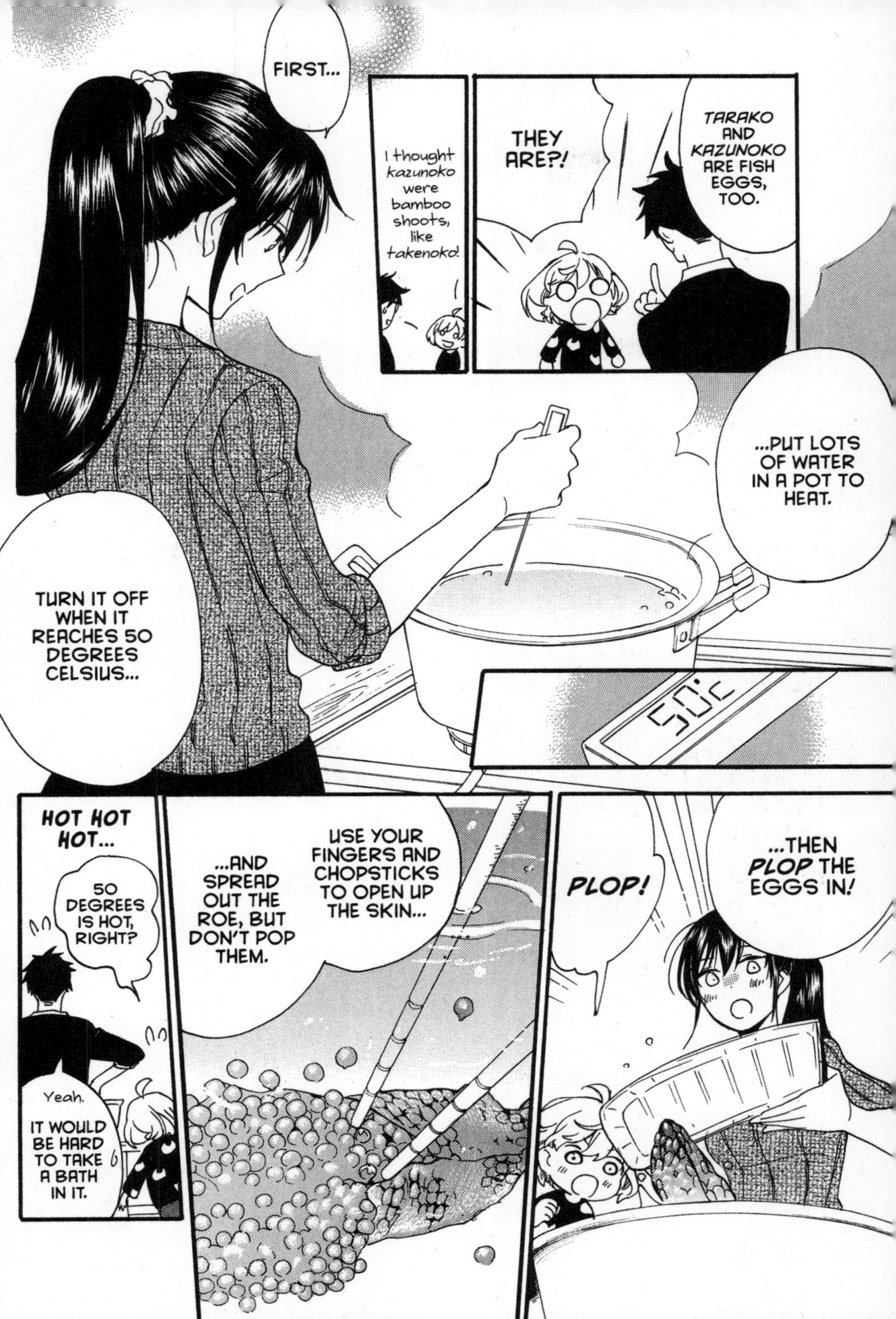
TARAKO AND KAZUNOKO ARE FISH EGGS, TOO.
THEY ARE?!
I thought kazunoko were bamboo shoots, like takenoko!
FIRST...
...PUT LOTS OF WATER IN A POT TO HEAT.
TURN IT OFF WHEN IT REACHES 50 DEGREES CELSIUS...
50°C
...THEN PLOP THE EGGS IN!
PLOP!
USE YOUR FINGERS AND CHOPSTICKS TO OPEN UP THE SKIN...
...AND SPREAD OUT THE ROE, BUT DON'T POP THEM.
HOT HOT HOT...
50 DEGREES IS HOT, RIGHT?
Yeah.
IT WOULD BE HARD TO TAKE A BATH IN IT.

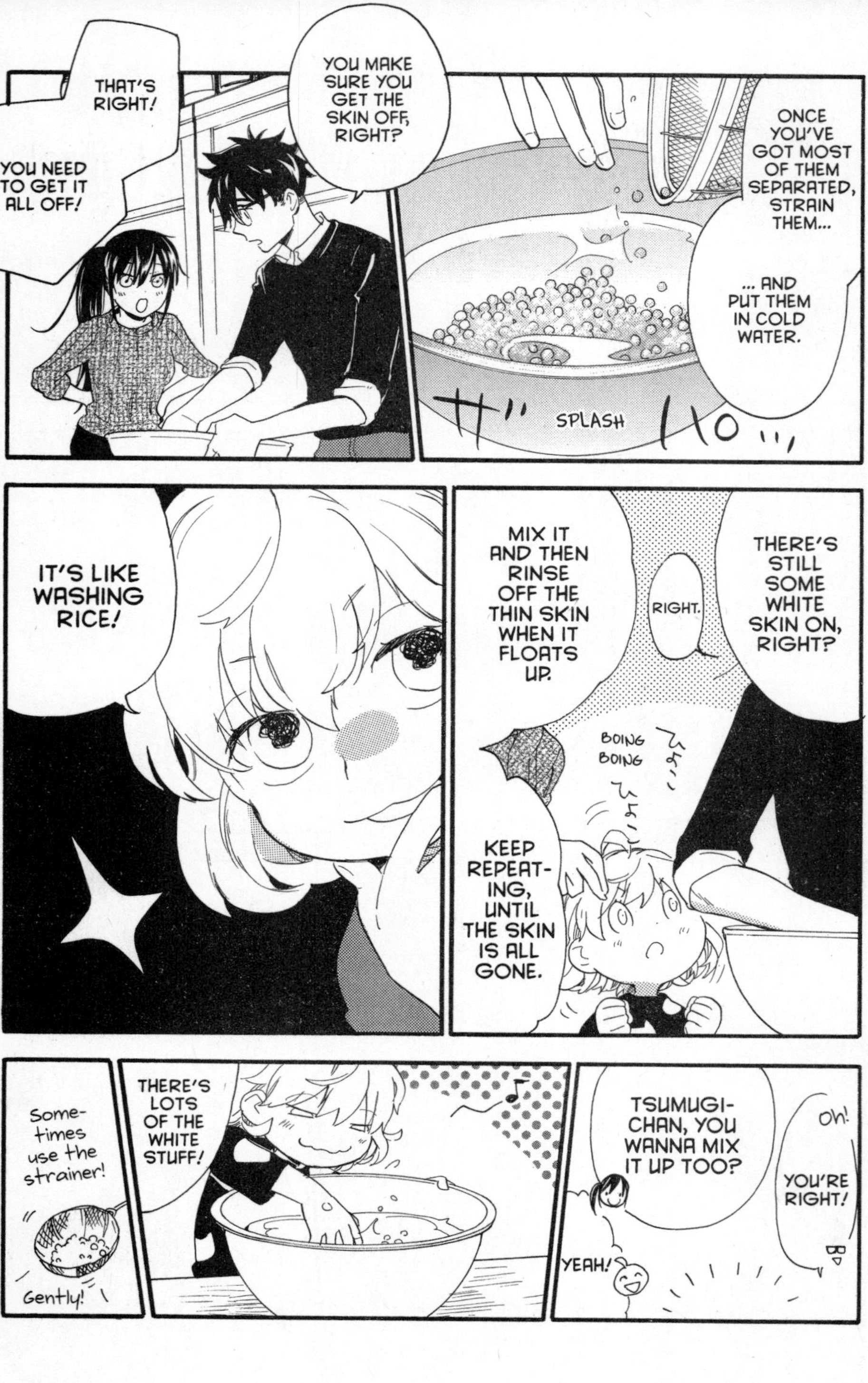
ONCE YOU'VE GOT MOST OF THEM SEPARATED, STRAIN THEM...
... AND PUT THEM IN COLD WATER.
SPLASH
YOU MAKE SURE YOU GET THE SKIN OFF, RIGHT?
THAT'S RIGHT!
YOU NEED TO GET IT ALL OFF!
THERE'S STILL SOME WHITE SKIN ON, RIGHT?
RIGHT.
MIX IT AND THEN RINSE OFF THE THIN SKIN WHEN IT FLOATS UP.
BOING BOING
KEEP REPEATING, UNTIL THE SKIN IS ALL GONE.
IT'S LIKE WASHING RICE!
Oh!
YOU'RE RIGHT!
TSUMUGI-CHAN, YOU WANNA MIX IT UP TOO?
YEAH!
THERE'S LOTS OF THE WHITE STUFF!
Some-times use the strainer!
Gently!

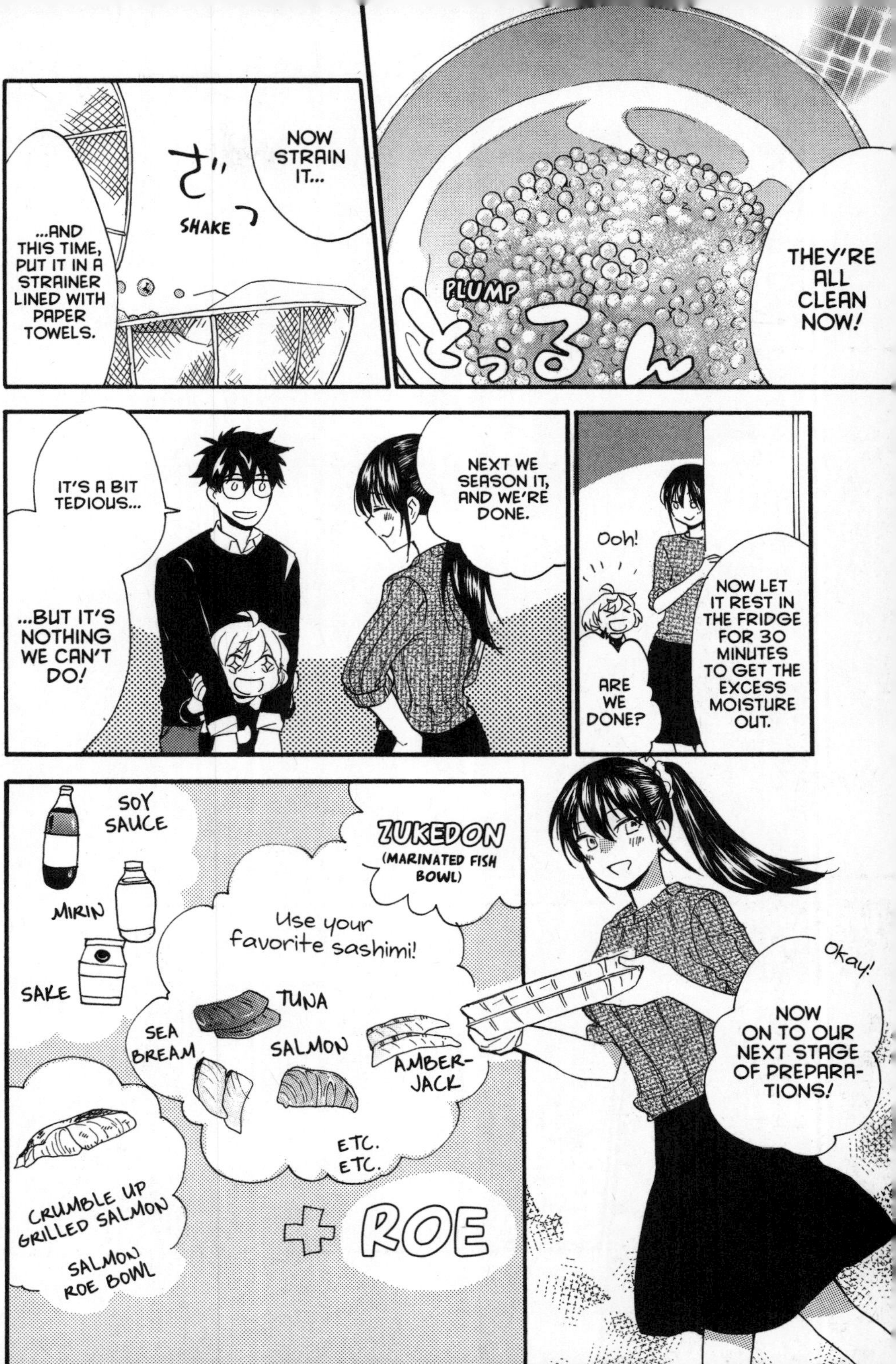
THEY'RE ALL CLEAN NOW!
PLUMP
とぅるん
NOW STRAIN IT...
ざっ
SHAKE
...AND THIS TIME, PUT IT IN A STRAINER LINED WITH PAPER TOWELS.
NOW LET IT REST IN THE FRIDGE FOR 30 MINUTES TO GET THE EXCESS MOISTURE OUT.
Ooh!
ARE WE DONE?
NEXT WE SEASON IT, AND WE'RE DONE.
IT'S A BIT TEDIOUS...
...BUT IT'S NOTHING WE CAN'T DO!
Okay!
NOW ON TO OUR NEXT STAGE OF PREPARA-TIONS!
ZUKEDON
(MARINATED FISH BOWL)
SOY SAUCE
MIRIN
SAKE
Use your favorite sashimi!
TUNA
SEA BREAM
SALMON
AMBER-JACK
ETC. ETC.
CRUMBLE UP GRILLED SALMON
SALMON ROE BOWL
+ ROE

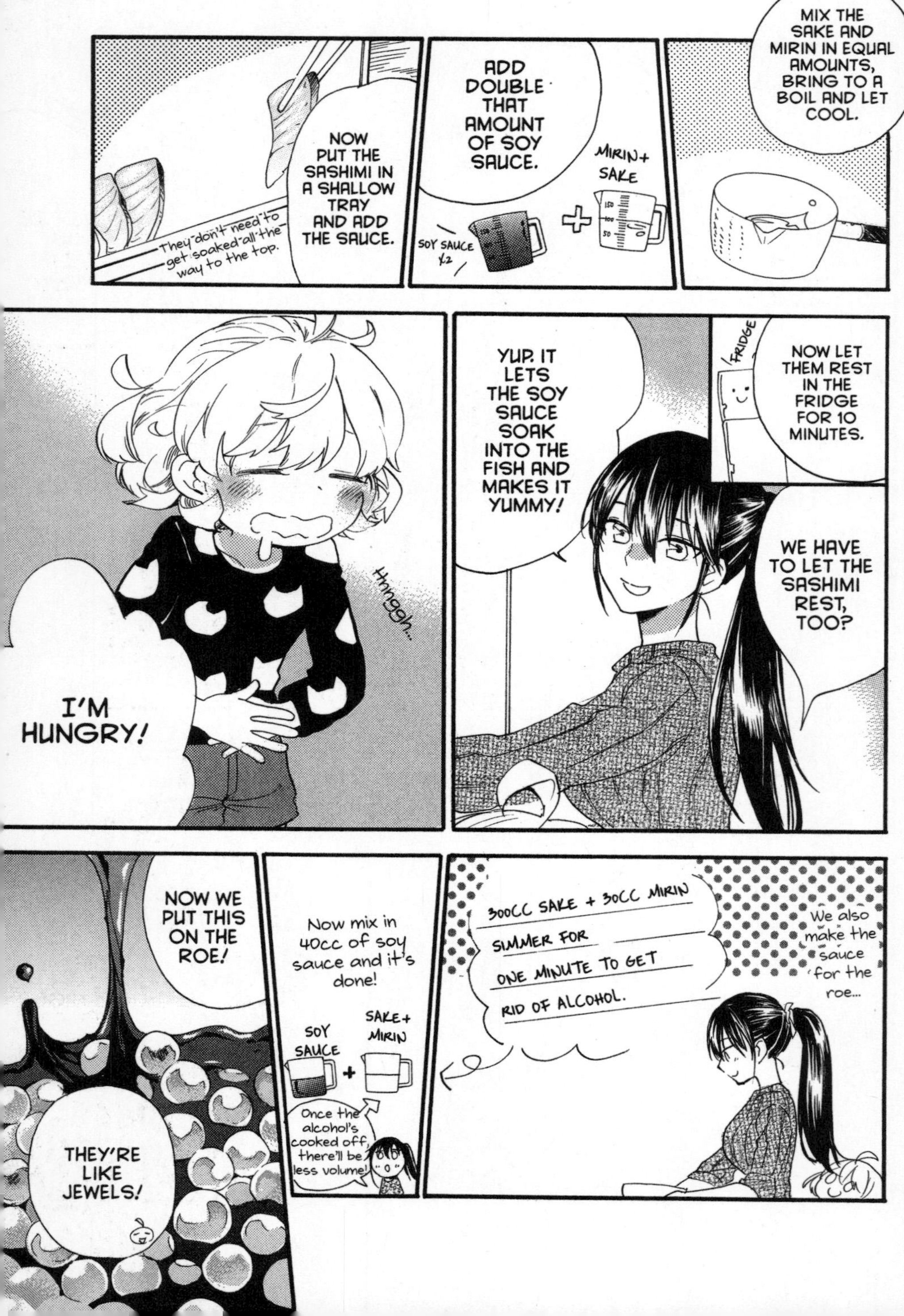
MIX THE SAKE AND MIRIN IN EQUAL AMOUNTS, BRING TO A BOIL AND LET COOL.
ADD DOUBLE THAT AMOUNT OF SOY SAUCE.
MIRIN+ SAKE
SOY SAUCE x2
NOW PUT THE SASHIMI IN A SHALLOW TRAY AND ADD THE SAUCE.
They don't need to get soaked all the way to the top.
FRIDGE
NOW LET THEM REST IN THE FRIDGE FOR 10 MINUTES.
WE HAVE TO LET THE SASHIMI REST, TOO?
YUP. IT LETS THE SOY SAUCE SOAK INTO THE FISH AND MAKES IT YUMMY!
Hnnggh...
I'M HUNGRY!
We also make the sauce for the roe...
300CC SAKE + 30CC MIRIN
SIMMER FOR
ONE MINUTE TO GET
RID OF ALCOHOL.
Now mix in 40cc of soy sauce and it's done!
SOY SAUCE
SAKE+ MIRIN
Once the alcohol's cooked off, there'll be less volume!
NOW WE PUT THIS ON THE ROE!
THEY'RE LIKE JEWELS!

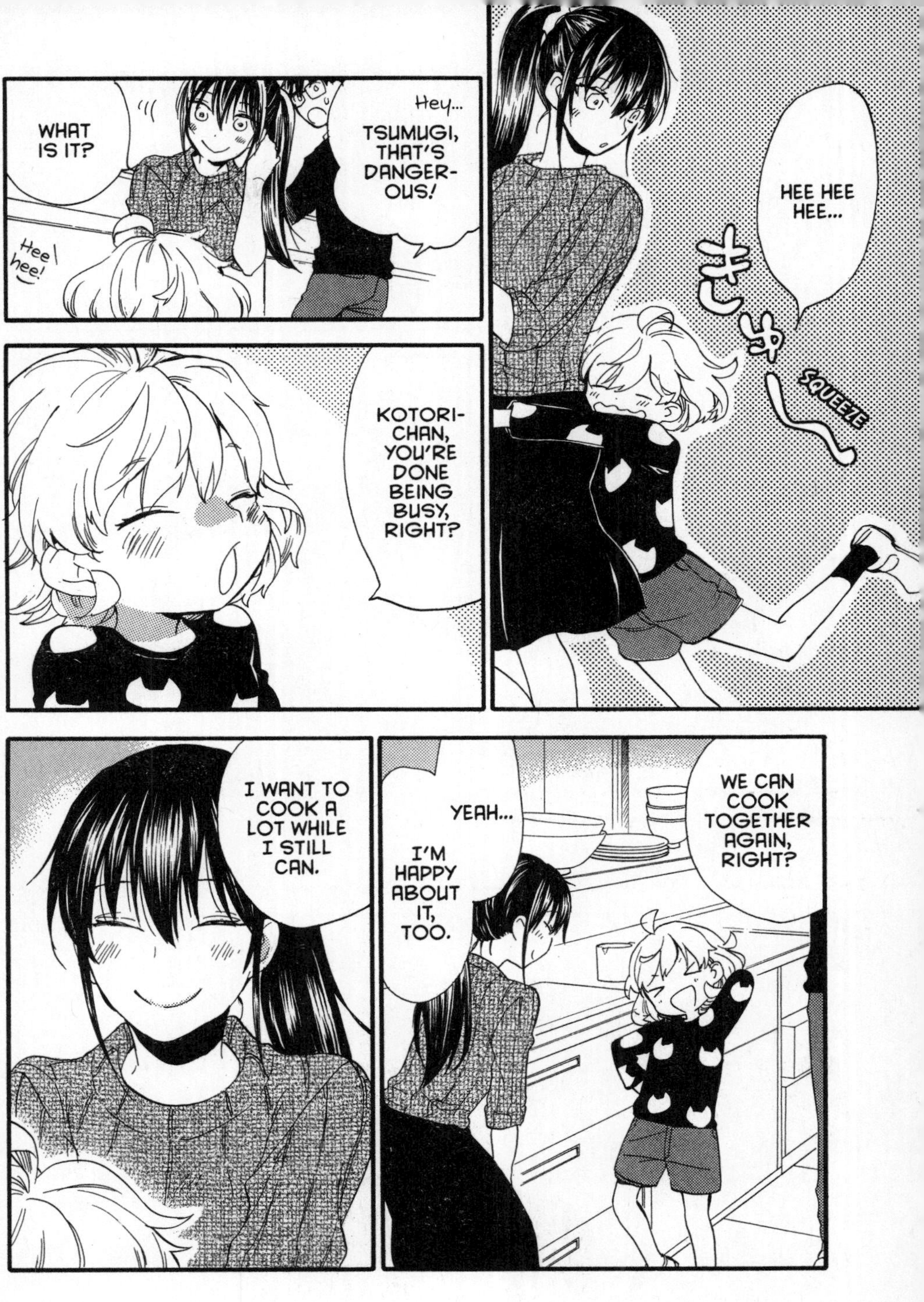
HEE HEE HEE...
SQUEEZE
Hey...
TSUMUGI, THAT'S DANGER-OUS!
WHAT IS IT?
Hee hee!
KOTORI-CHAN, YOU'RE DONE BEING BUSY, RIGHT?
WE CAN COOK TOGETHER AGAIN, RIGHT?
YEAH...
I'M HAPPY ABOUT IT, TOO.
I WANT TO COOK A LOT WHILE I STILL CAN.

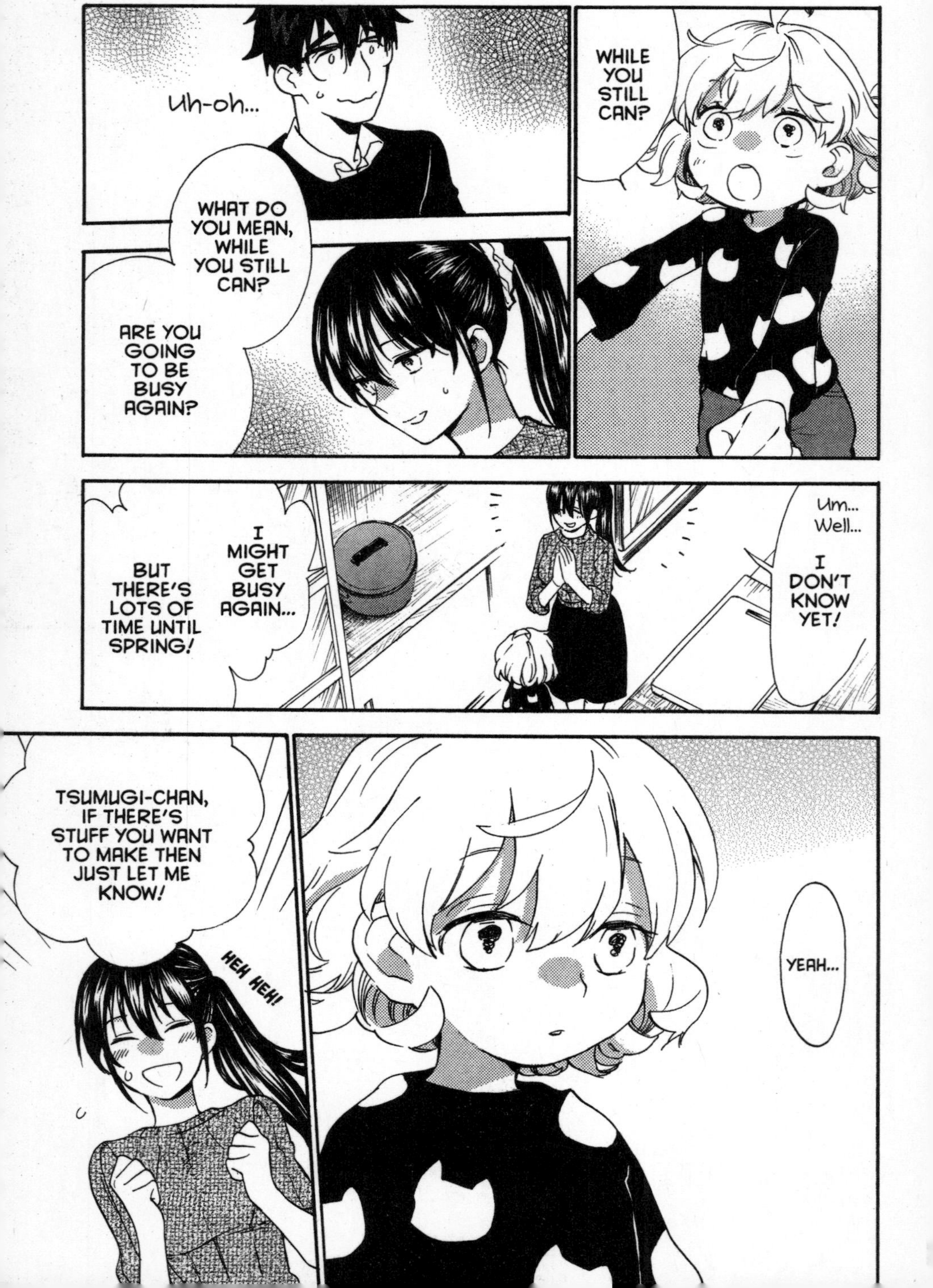
WHILE YOU STILL CAN?
Uh-oh...
WHAT DO YOU MEAN, WHILE YOU STILL CAN?
ARE YOU GOING TO BE BUSY AGAIN?
Um... Well...
I DON'T KNOW YET!
I MIGHT GET BUSY AGAIN...
BUT THERE'S LOTS OF TIME UNTIL SPRING!
YEAH...
TSUMUGI-CHAN, IF THERE'S STUFF YOU WANT TO MAKE THEN JUST LET ME KNOW!
HEH HEH!

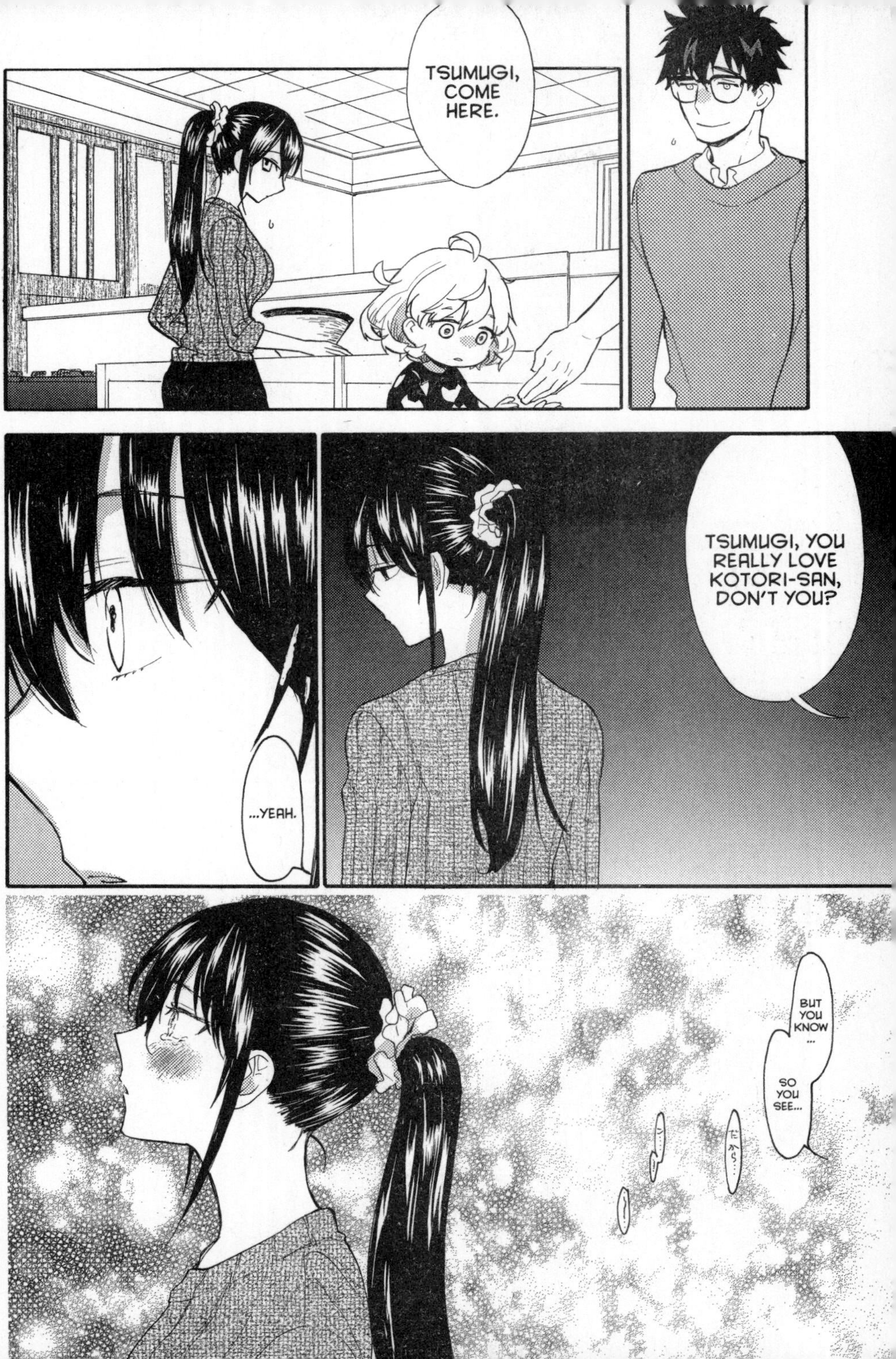
TSUMUGI, COME HERE.
TSUMUGI, YOU REALLY LOVE KOTORI-SAN, DON'T YOU?
...YEAH.
BUT YOU KNOW...
SO YOU SEE...

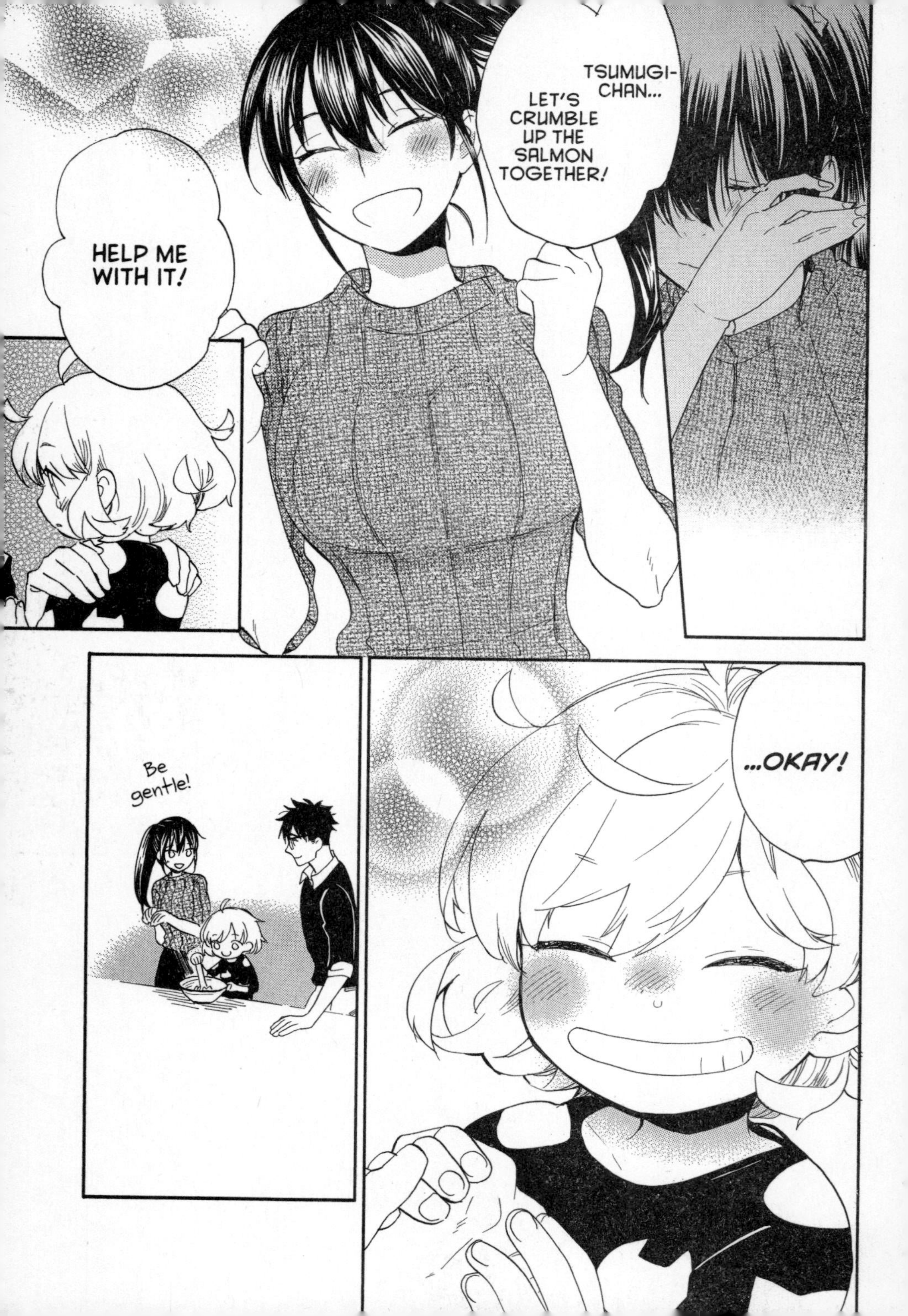
TSUMUGI-CHAN... LET'S CRUMBLE UP THE SALMON TOGETHER!
HELP ME WITH IT!
...OKAY!
Be gentle!

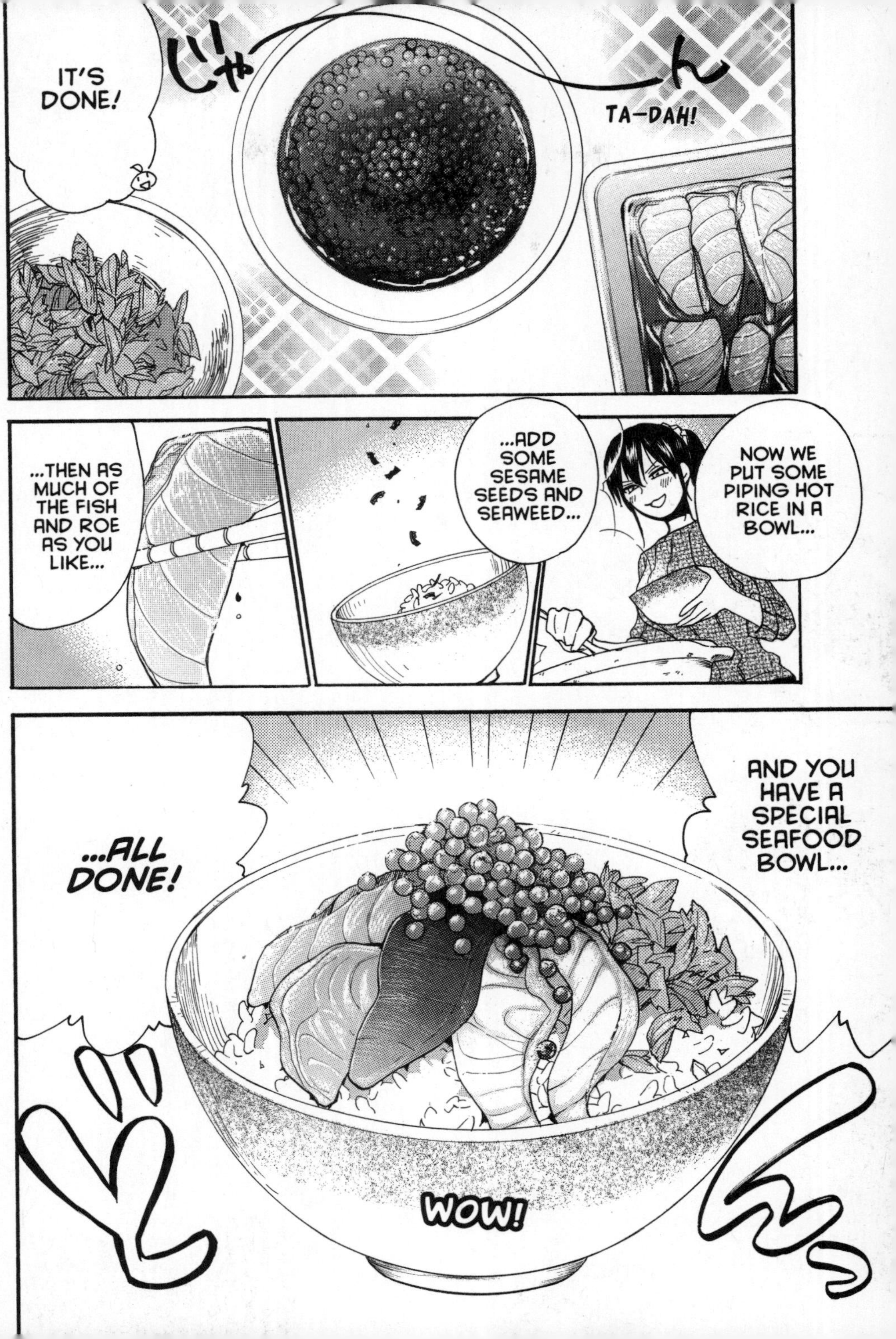
じゃーん
TA-DAH!
IT'S DONE!
NOW WE PUT SOME PIPING HOT RICE IN A BOWL...
...ADD SOME SESAME SEEDS AND SEAWEED...
...THEN AS MUCH OF THE FISH AND ROE AS YOU LIKE...
AND YOU HAVE A SPECIAL SEAFOOD BOWL...
...ALL DONE!
WOW!

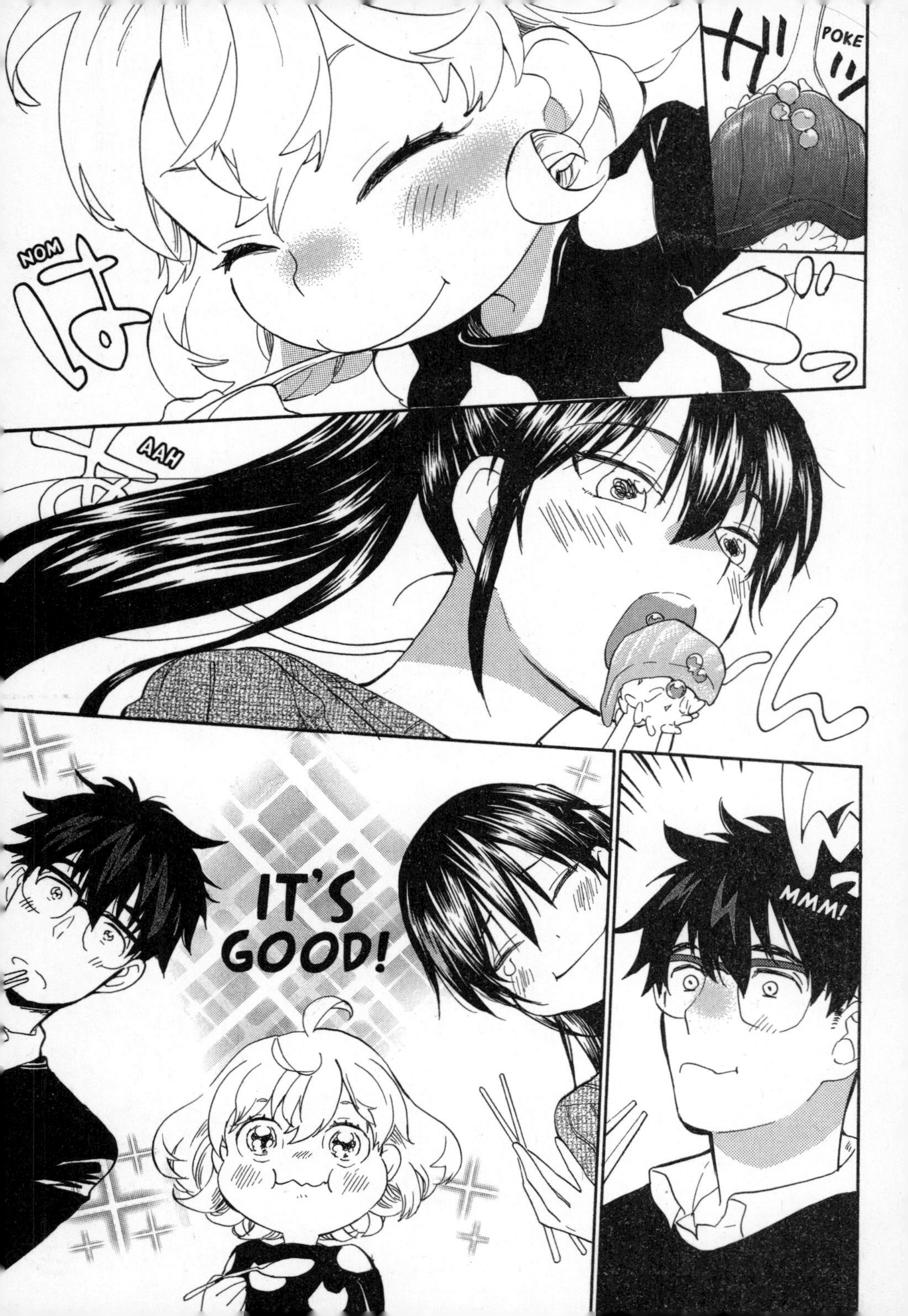
POKE
NOM
AAH
MMM!
IT'S GOOD!

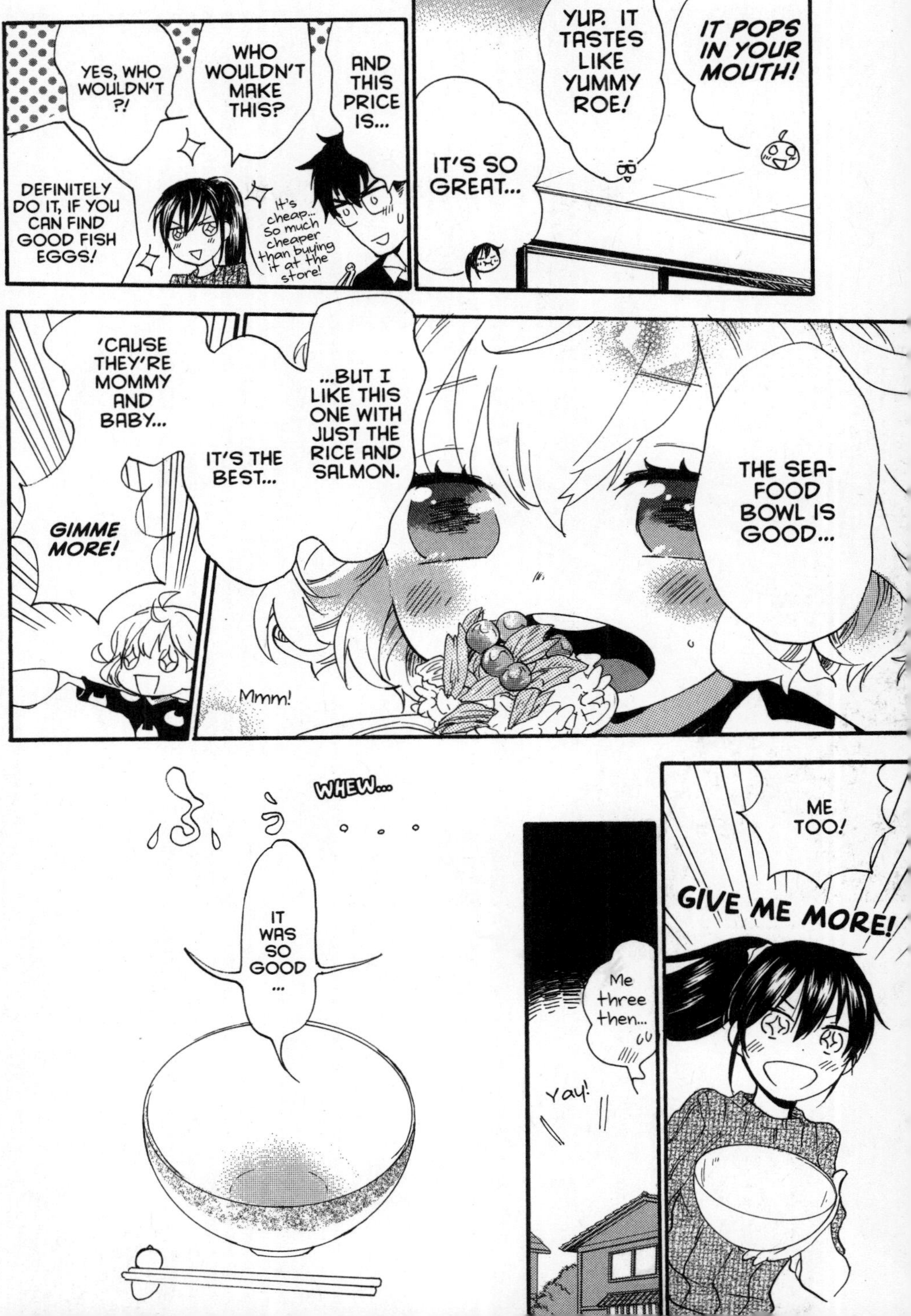
IT POPS IN YOUR MOUTH!
YUP. IT TASTES LIKE YUMMY ROE!
IT'S SO GREAT...
AND THIS PRICE IS...
WHO WOULDN'T MAKE THIS?
YES, WHO WOULDN'T ?!
DEFINITELY DO IT, IF YOU CAN FIND GOOD FISH EGGS!
It's cheap... So much cheaper than buying it at the store!
THE SEA-FOOD BOWL IS GOOD...
...BUT I LIKE THIS ONE WITH JUST THE RICE AND SALMON.
IT'S THE BEST...
Mmm!
'CAUSE THEY'RE MOMMY AND BABY...
GIMME MORE!
ME TOO!
GIVE ME MORE!
Me three then...
Yay!
ふぅ
WHEW...
IT WAS SO GOOD ...

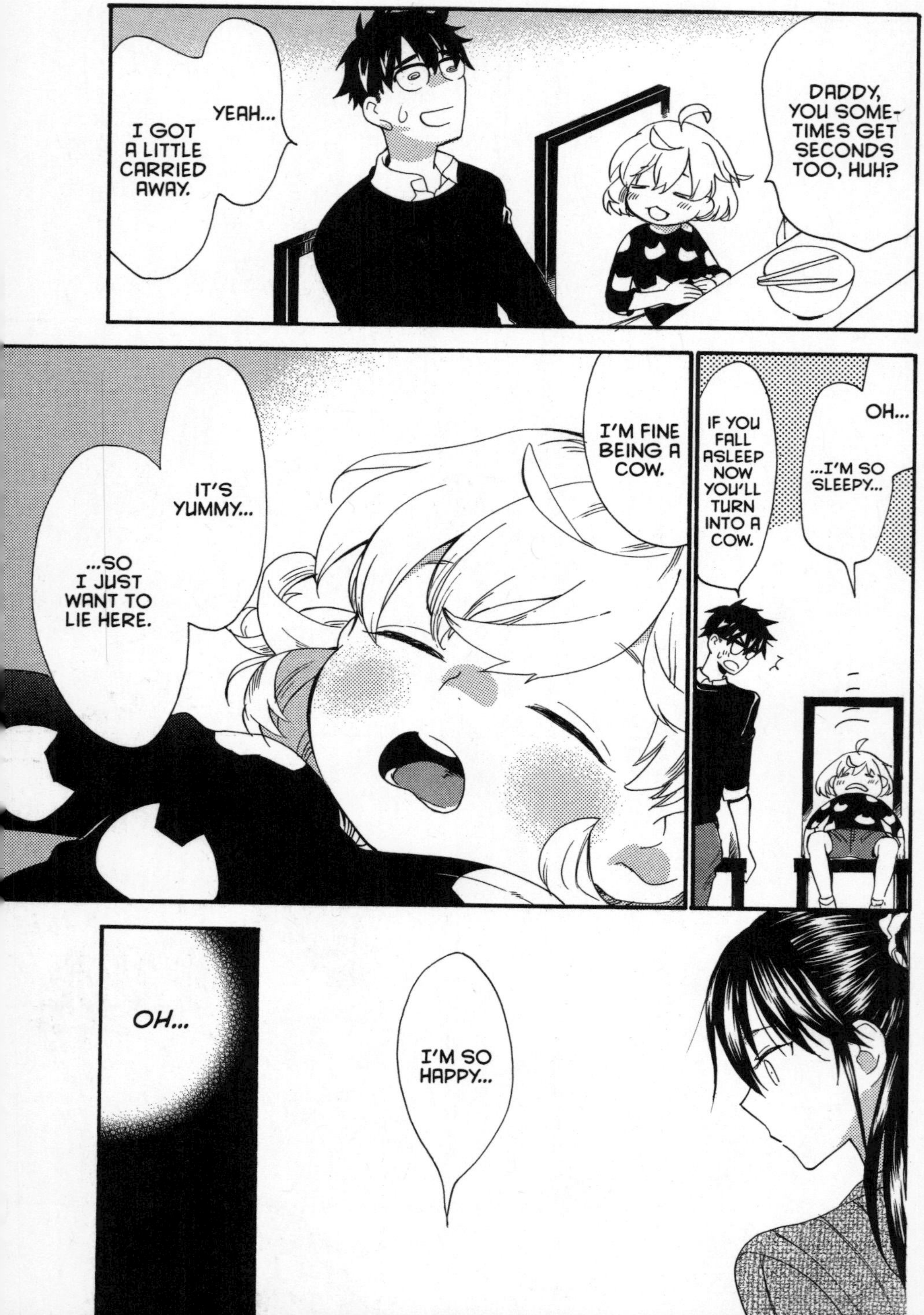
DADDY, YOU SOME-TIMES GET SECONDS TOO, HUH?
YEAH... I GOT A LITTLE CARRIED AWAY.
OH...
...I'M SO SLEEPY...
IF YOU FALL ASLEEP NOW YOU'LL TURN INTO A COW.
I'M FINE BEING A COW.
IT'S YUMMY...
...SO I JUST WANT TO LIE HERE.
I'M SO HAPPY...
OH...

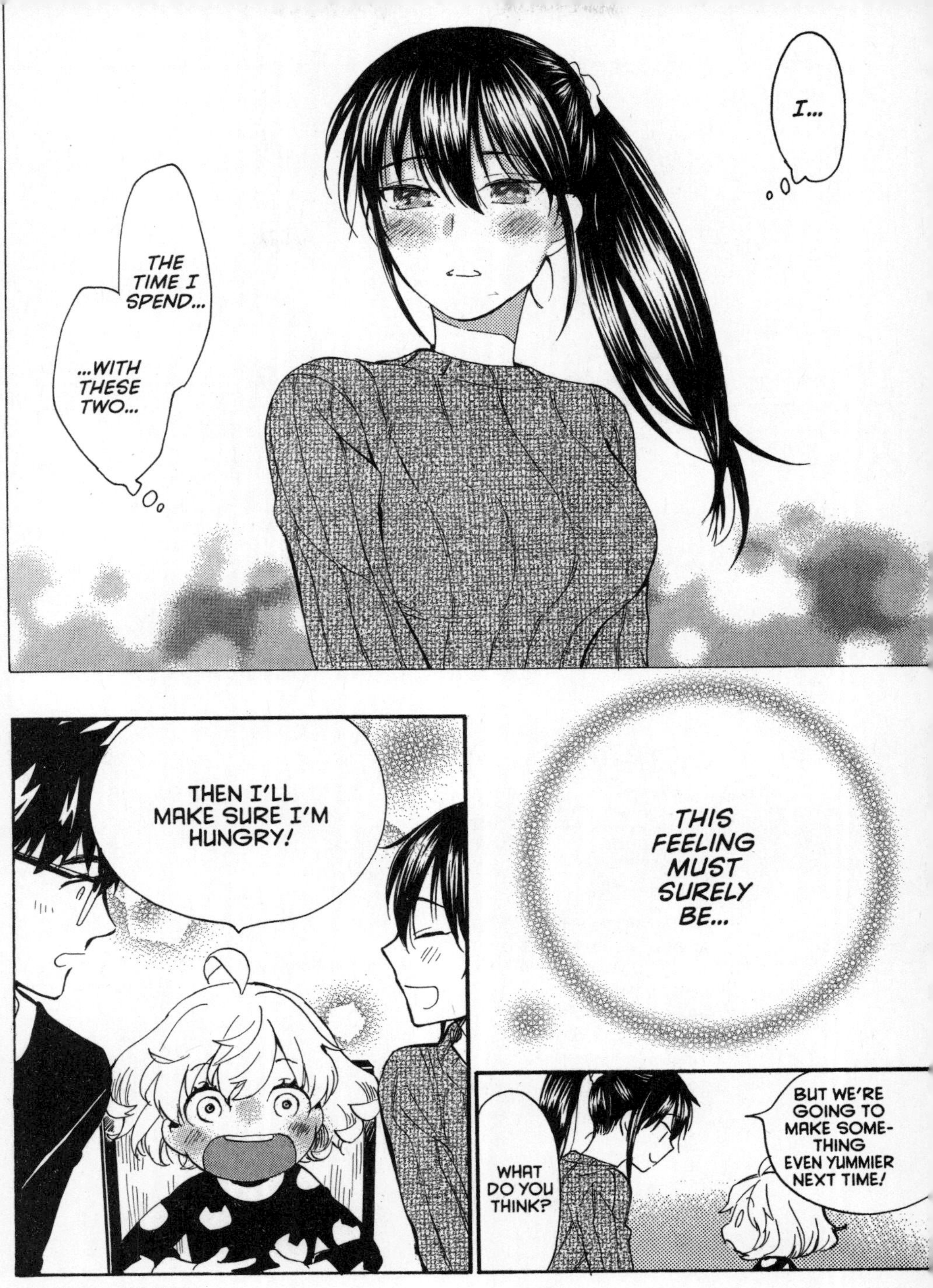
I...
THE TIME I SPEND...
...WITH THESE TWO...
THIS FEELING MUST SURELY BE...
BUT WE'RE GOING TO MAKE SOME-THING EVEN YUMMIER NEXT TIME!
WHAT DO YOU THINK?
THEN I'LL MAKE SURE I'M HUNGRY!

TO BE CONTINUED...

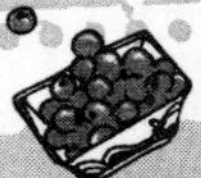

SALMON ROE WITH SOY SAUCE

☆Ingredients☆
→ 200g raw salmon roe
→30cc sake
→ 40cc soy sauce
→ 30cc mirin

Preparation

1. Heat a lot of water in a pan. Turn off the heat when it reaches about 50°C and put the salmon roe in.

2. Open the skins with chopsticks and a spoon, exposing the bead of the roe. Remove what you can and transfer the rest to a colander. Rinse them under cold water.

3. Remove the large skins. The smaller skins will run off with the water. Repeat the washing process until all skins have been removed.

☆POINT☆ It's easier to sometimes to pick remaining skins out of the colander. The skins will leave a pungent smell, so make sure you remove them all!

4. Remove from colander and transfer roe to a plate that has been lined with kitchen paper towels. Put in the fridge for 30 minutes to remove any excess moisture.

5. Boil the mirin and sake in a pan. Reduce the heat when it starts boiling. Leave for 1 minute to remove the alcohol.

Mirin and sake can catch fire on a high heat, so be careful!

6. Once (5) has cooled add the 40cc of soy sauce.

7. Combine (4) and (6). Leave for 1 hour and you're done.

They'll keep in the fridge for a few days and the sauce can also be frozen!

ZUKE-DON (MARINATED TUNA ON RICE)

☆Ingredients☆
→ Sashimi: such as maguro (raw tuna), buri (Japanese amberjack), tai (sea bream), ika (squid), salmon, etc.
→ Salmon roe
→ Soy sauce, sake, mirin

Preparation

1. Heat up the sake and mirin of the same ratio.

2. Let (1) cool and add twice the amount of soy sauce.

3. Lay the sashimi out on a tray and cover with (2). You don't need to fill the tray. Shake the tray, making sure everything is covered in sauce.

4. Let sit in the fridge for 10 minutes.

5. Fill a donburi bowl with rice and lay nori over the rice. Lay the marinated sashimi over and garnish with salmon roe.

You can also add as much green onion, sesame seeds, perilla, etc., as you like!

Grilled salmon goes really well with salmon roe~

Cow!

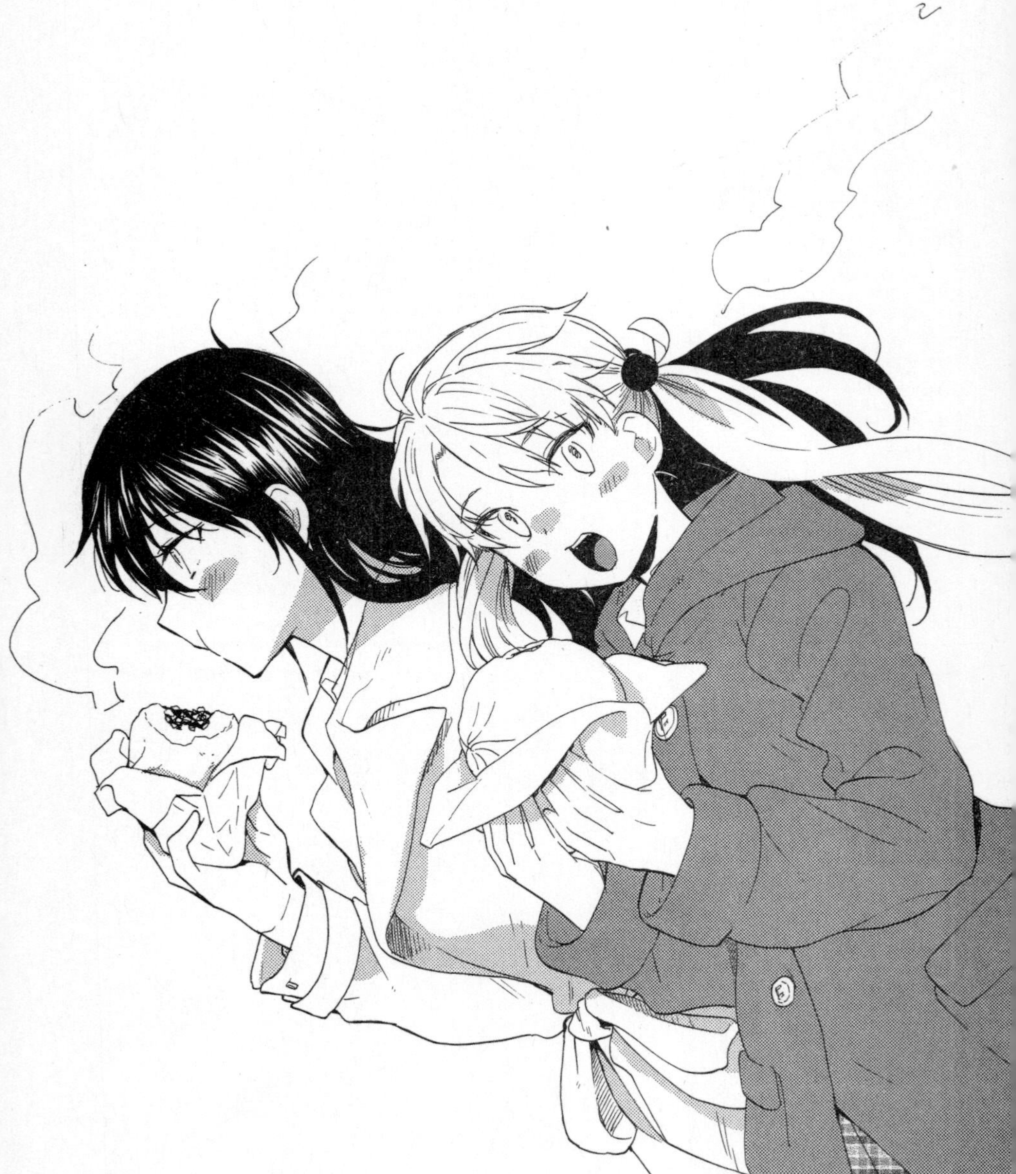

Chapter 49 | Sunset at the Beach and Piping-Hot Oden

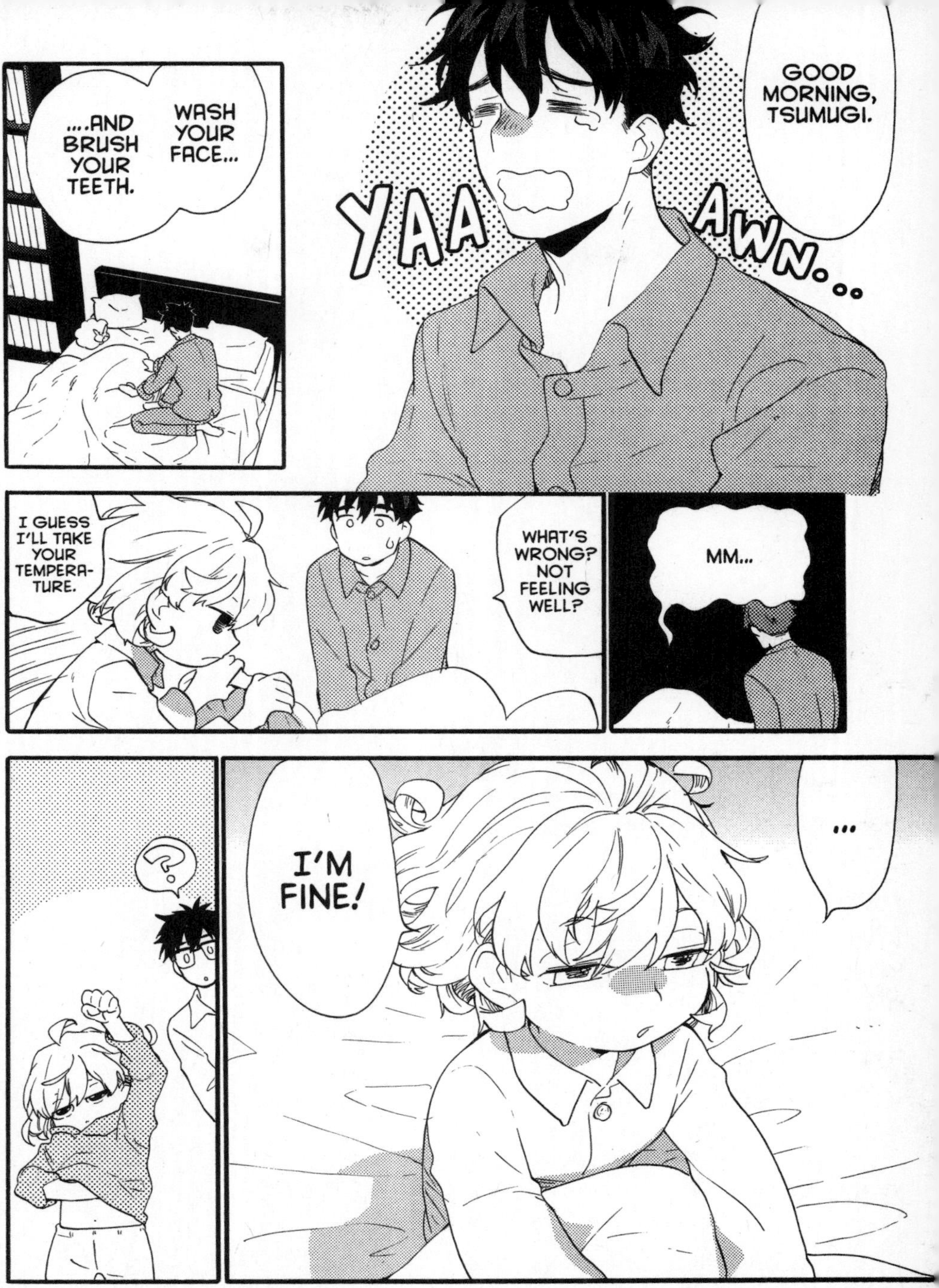
GOOD MORNING, TSUMUGI.
YAAAWN...
WASH YOUR FACE...
...AND BRUSH YOUR TEETH.
MM...
WHAT'S WRONG? NOT FEELING WELL?
I GUESS I'LL TAKE YOUR TEMPERA-TURE.
...
I'M FINE!
?

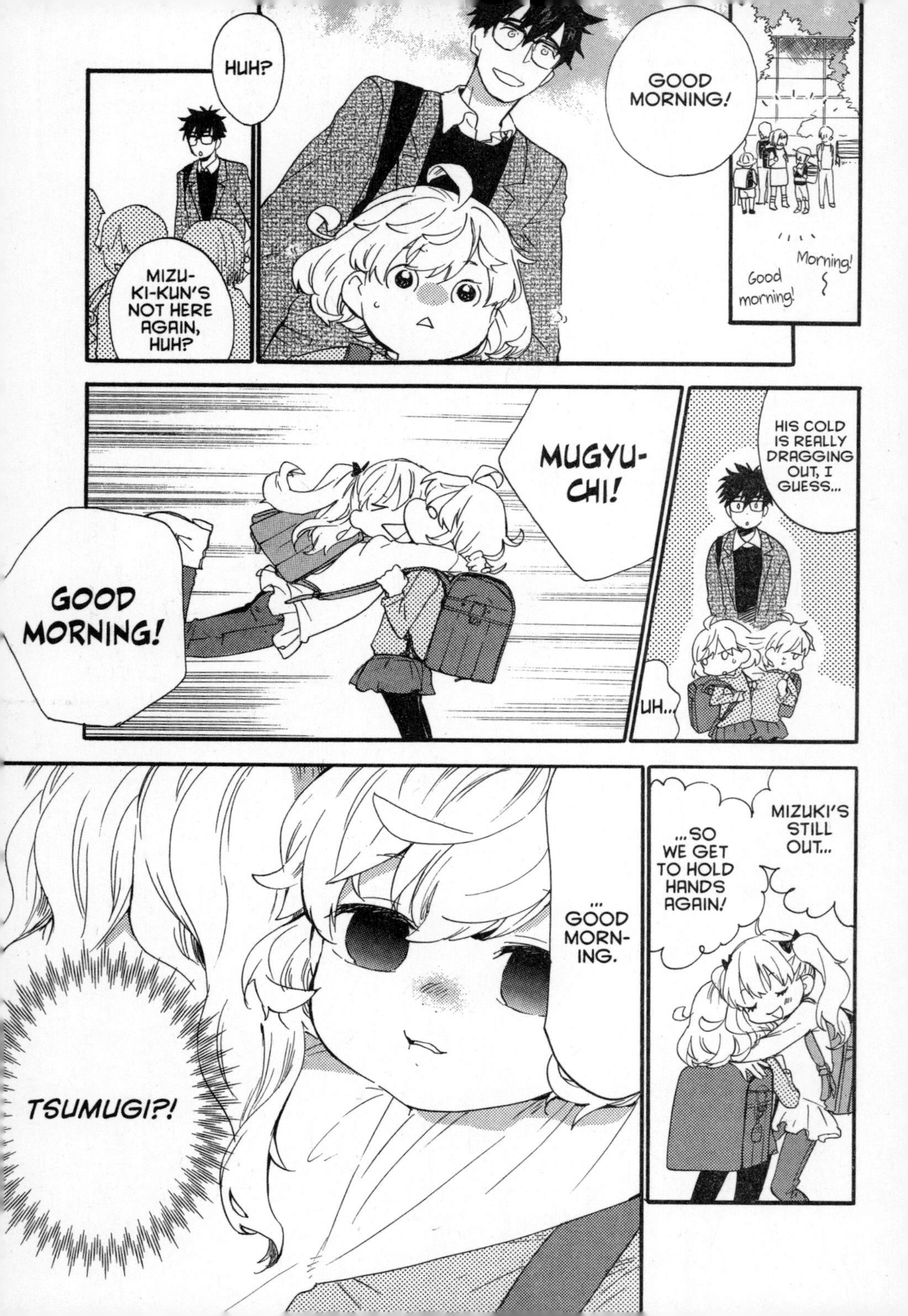
Morning!
Good morning!
GOOD MORNING!
HUH?
MIZU-KI-KUN'S NOT HERE AGAIN, HUH?
HIS COLD IS REALLY DRAGGING OUT, I GUESS...
UH...
MUGYU-CHI!
GOOD MORNING!
MIZUKI'S STILL OUT...
...SO WE GET TO HOLD HANDS AGAIN!
...GOOD MORN-ING.
TSUMUGI?!

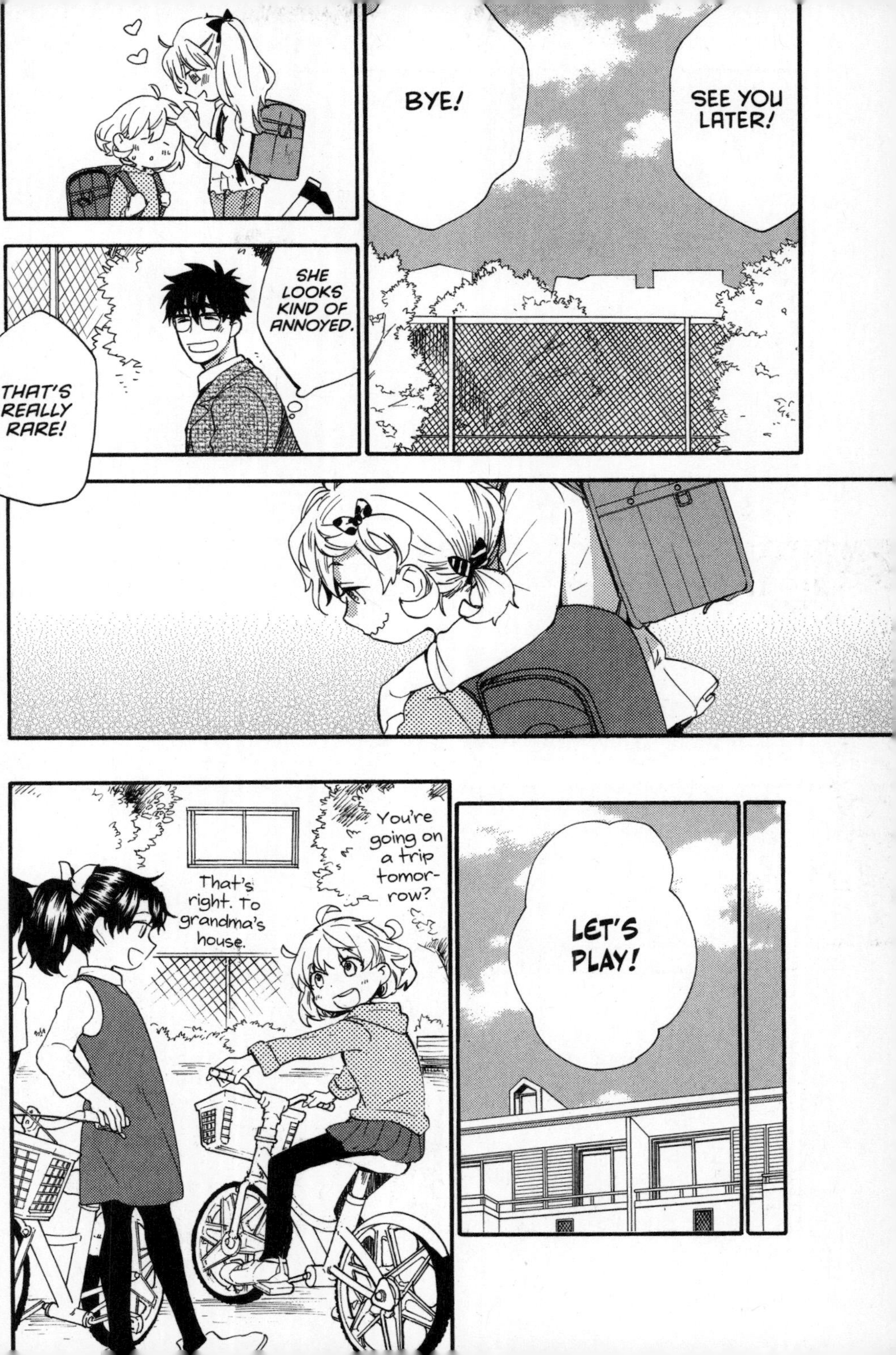
SEE YOU LATER!
BYE!
SHE LOOKS KIND OF ANNOYED.
THAT'S REALLY RARE!
LET'S PLAY!
You're going on a trip tomorrow?
That's right. To grandma's house.

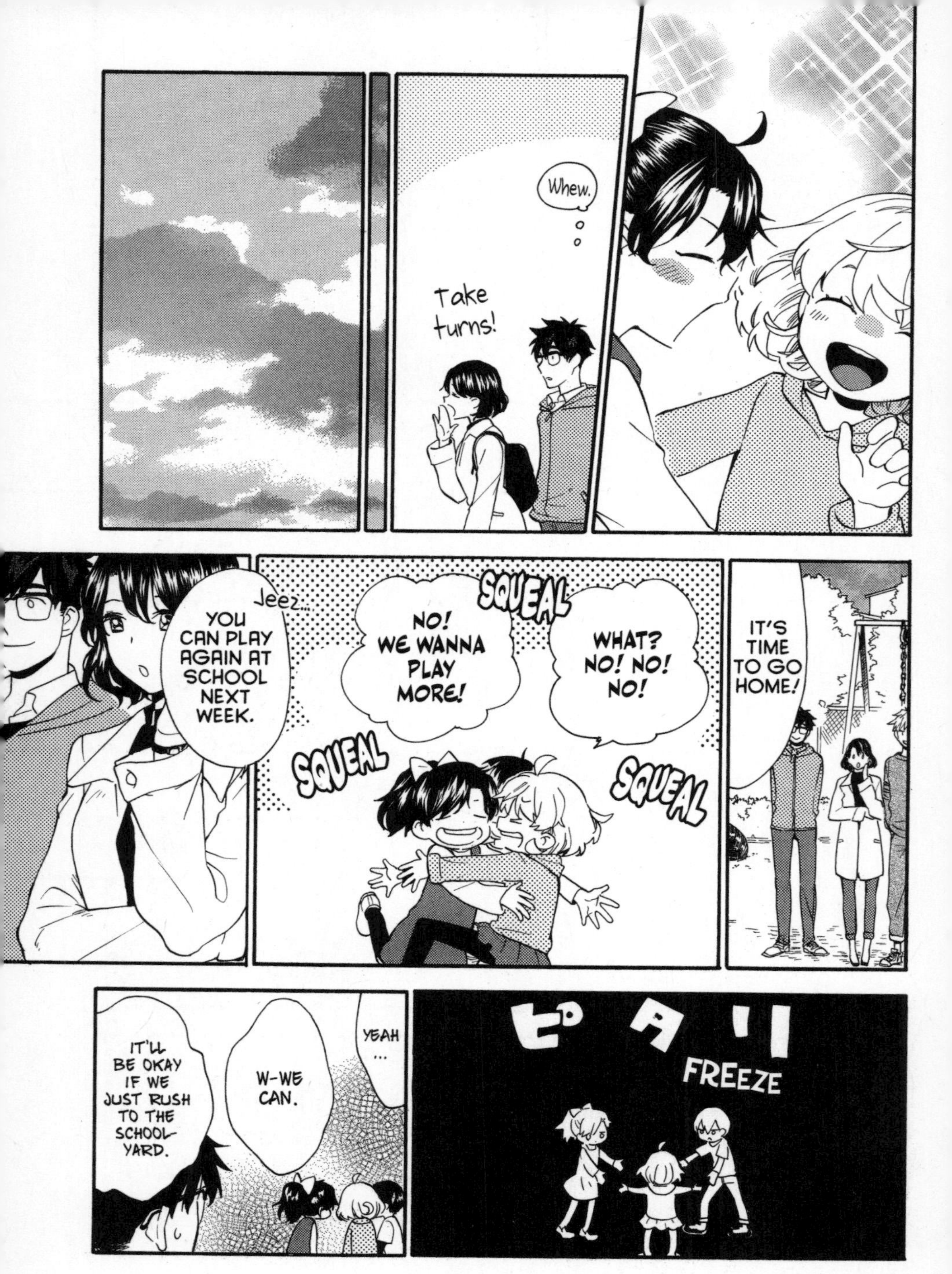
Whew.
Take turns!
IT'S TIME TO GO HOME!
SQUEAL
WHAT? NO! NO! NO!
SQUEAL
NO! WE WANNA PLAY MORE!
SQUEAL
Jeez...
YOU CAN PLAY AGAIN AT SCHOOL NEXT WEEK.
ピタリ
FREEZE
YEAH ...
W-WE CAN.
IT'LL BE OKAY IF WE JUST RUSH TO THE SCHOOL-YARD.

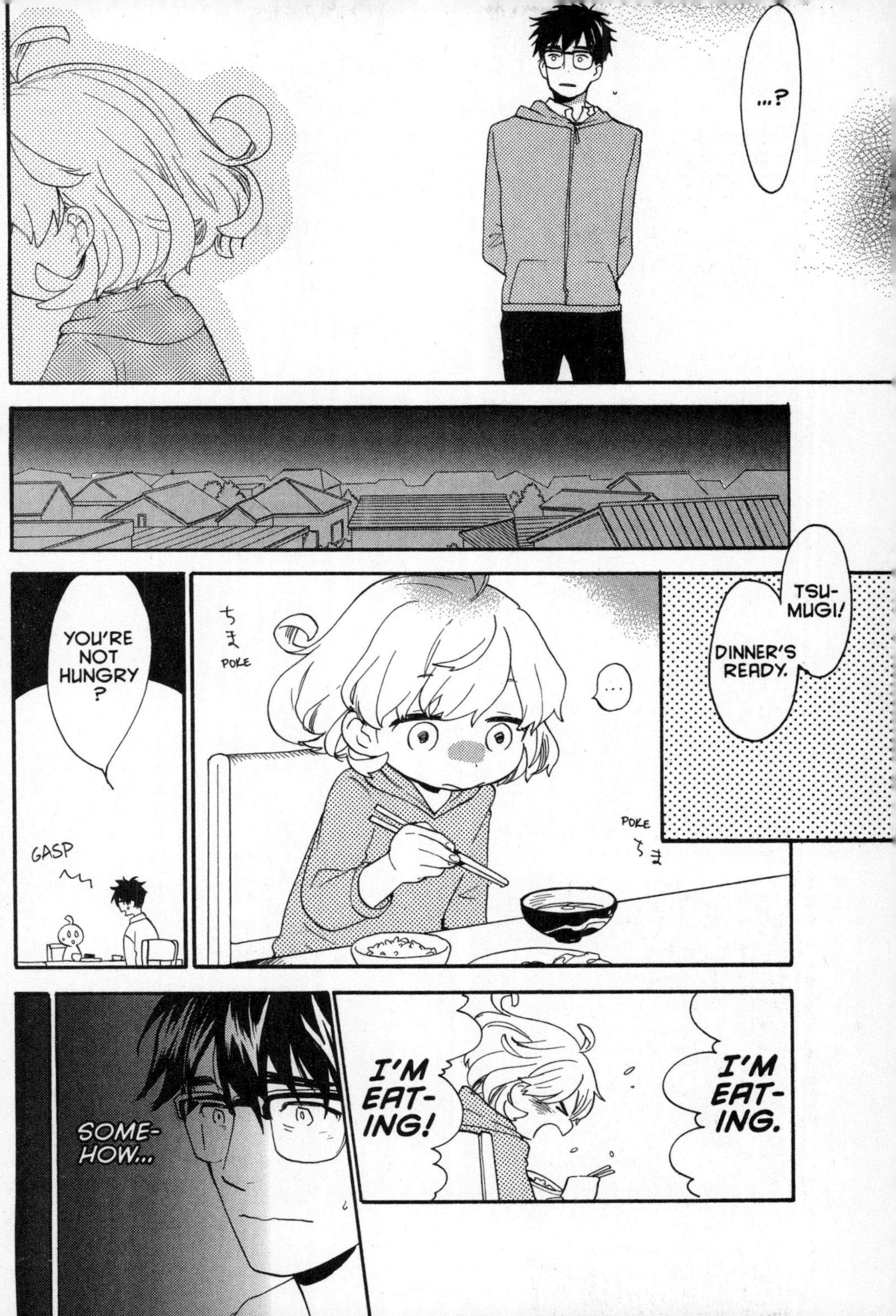
...?
TSU-MUGI!
DINNER'S READY.
ちま
POKE
...
POKE
ちま
YOU'RE NOT HUNGRY?
GASP
I'M EAT-ING.
I'M EAT-ING!
SOME-HOW...

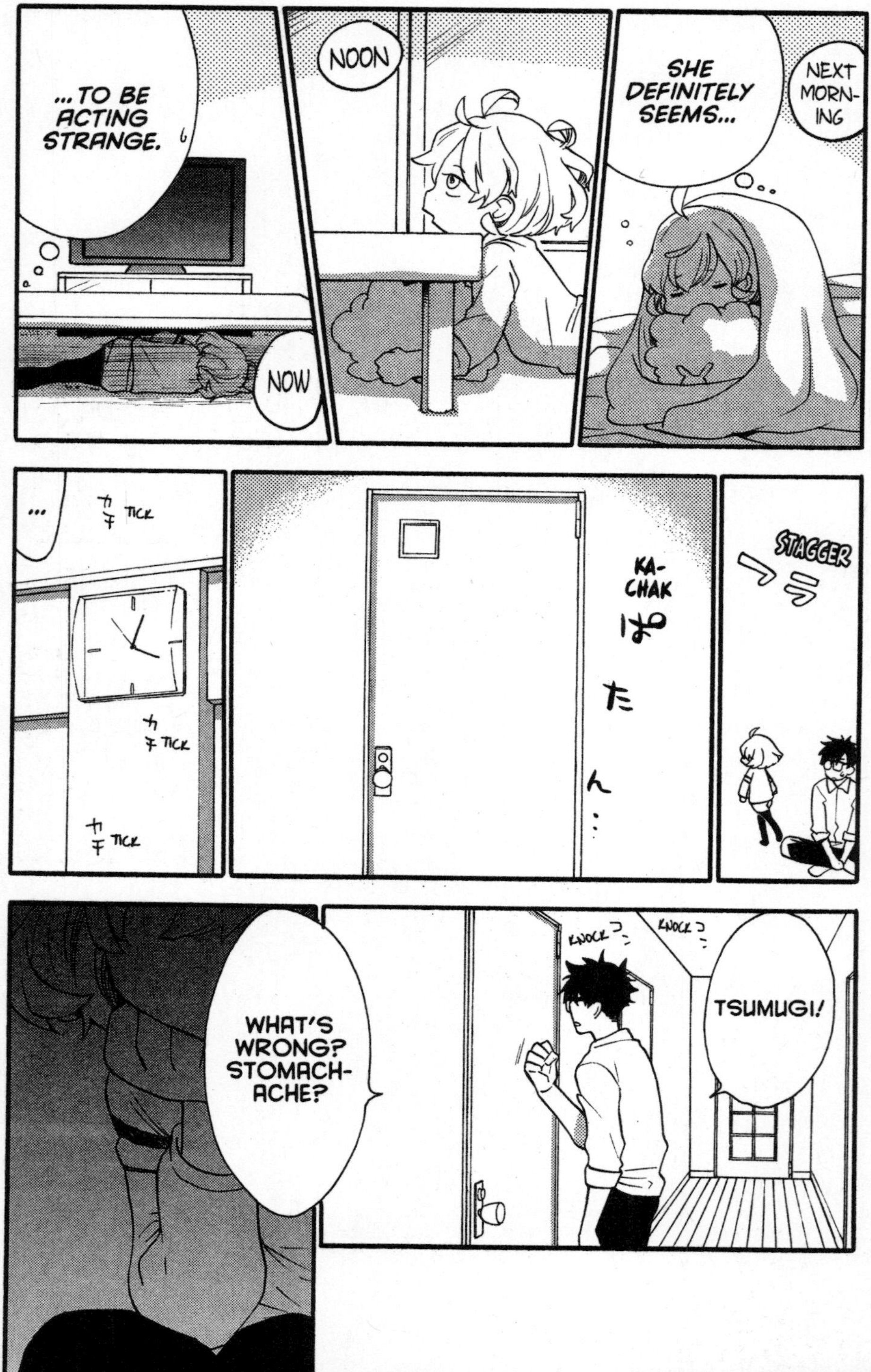

NEXT MORNING
SHE DEFINITELY SEEMS...
NOON
NOW
...TO BE ACTING STRANGE.
STAGGER
フラ
KA-CHAK
ぱたん…
...
カチ TICK
カチ TICK
カチ TICK
KNOCK
KNOCK
TSUMUGI!
WHAT'S WRONG? STOMACHACHE?

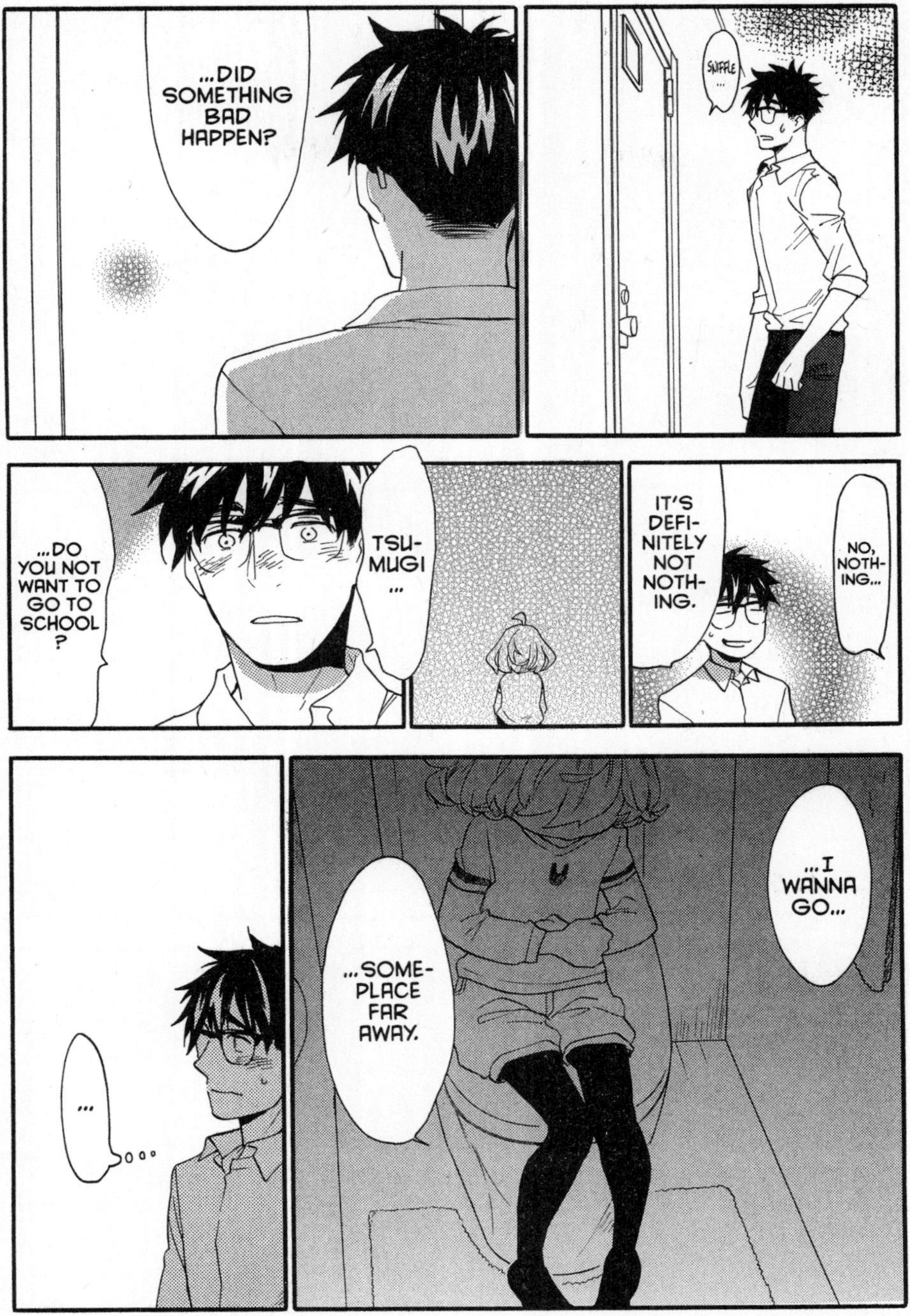
SNIFFLE...
...DID SOMETHING BAD HAPPEN?
NO, NOTHING...
IT'S DEFINITELY NOT NOTHING.
TSUMUGI...
...DO YOU NOT WANT TO GO TO SCHOOL?
...I WANNA GO...
...SOMEPLACE FAR AWAY.
...

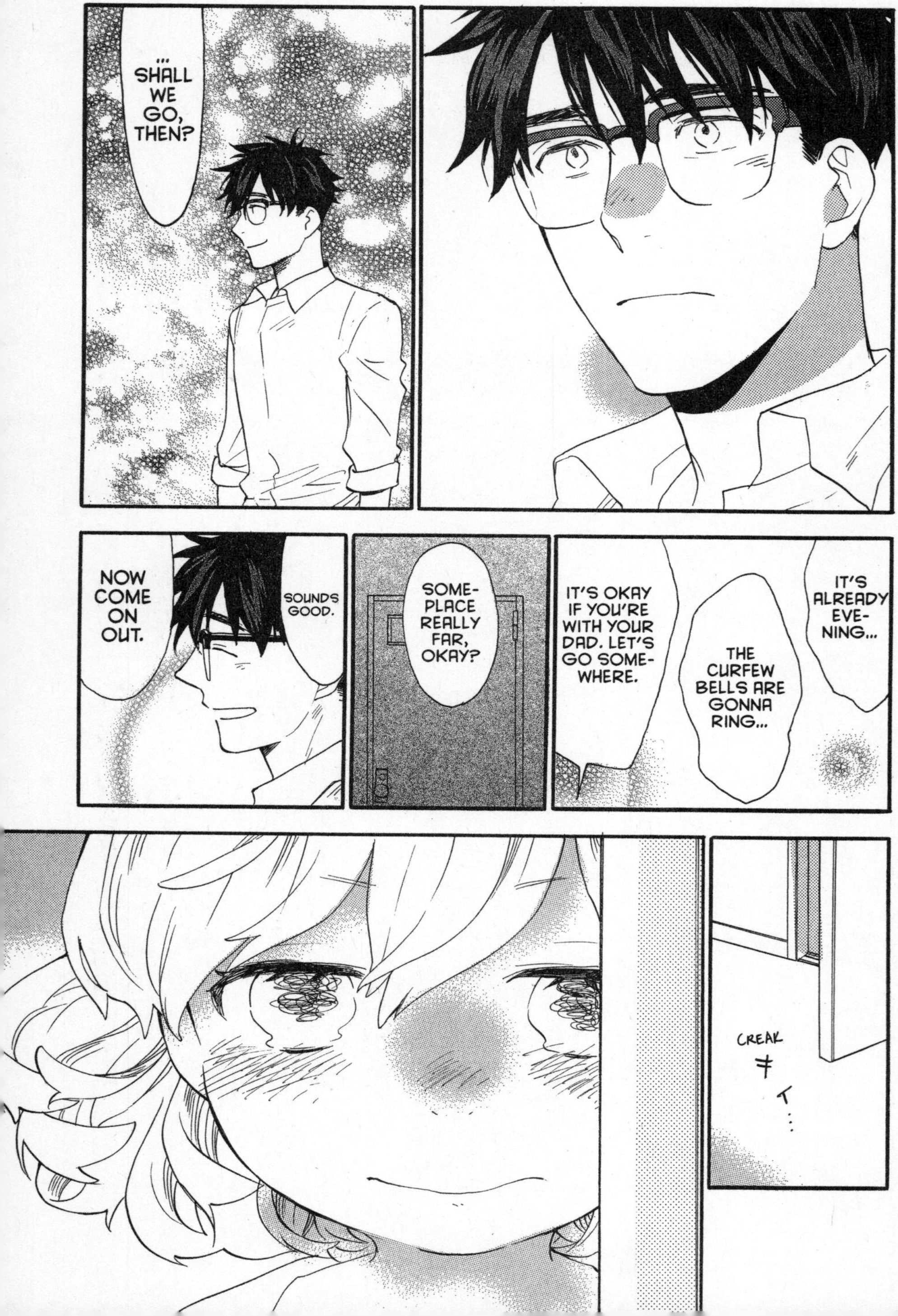

...SHALL WE GO, THEN?
IT'S ALREADY EVE-NING...
THE CURFEW BELLS ARE GONNA RING...
IT'S OKAY IF YOU'RE WITH YOUR DAD. LET'S GO SOME-WHERE.
SOME-PLACE REALLY FAR, OKAY?
SOUNDS GOOD.
NOW COME ON OUT.
CREAK
キイ...

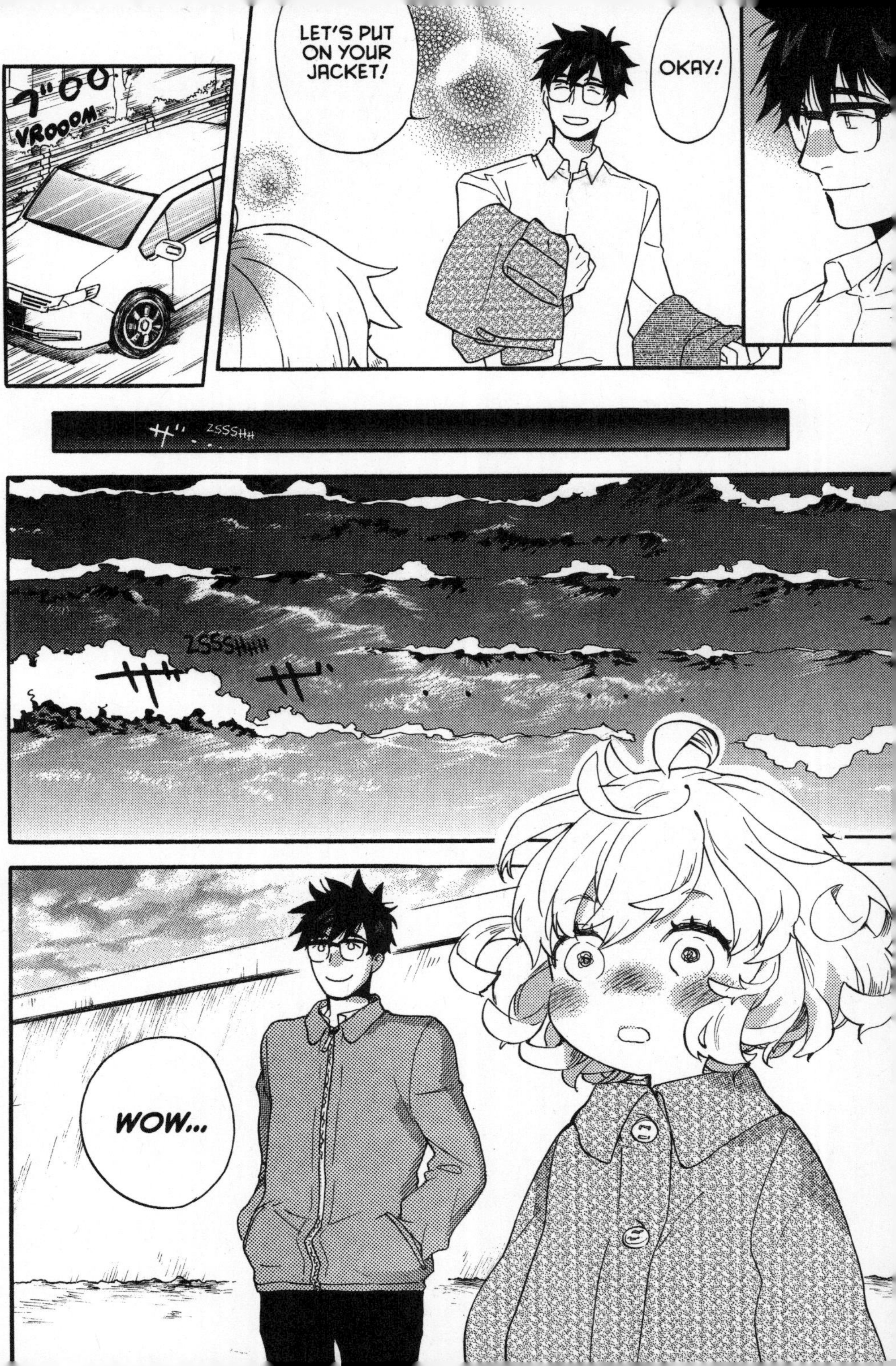
OKAY!
LET'S PUT ON YOUR JACKET!
VROOOM
ZSSSHH
ZSSSHHH
WOW...

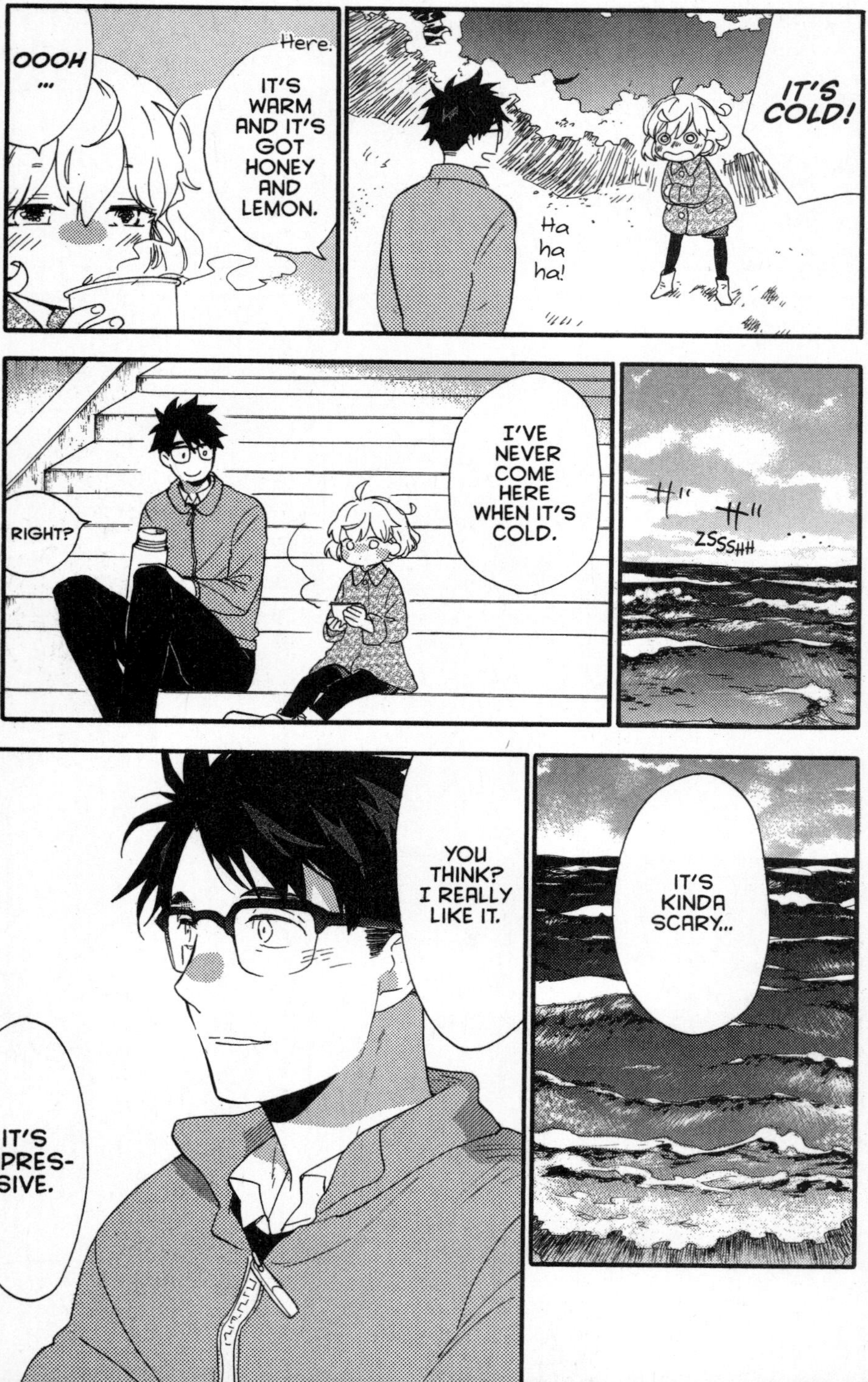
IT'S COLD!
Ha ha ha!
Here.
IT'S WARM AND IT'S GOT HONEY AND LEMON.
OOOH...
ZSSSHH
I'VE NEVER COME HERE WHEN IT'S COLD.
RIGHT?
IT'S KINDA SCARY...
YOU THINK? I REALLY LIKE IT.
IT'S IMPRESSIVE.

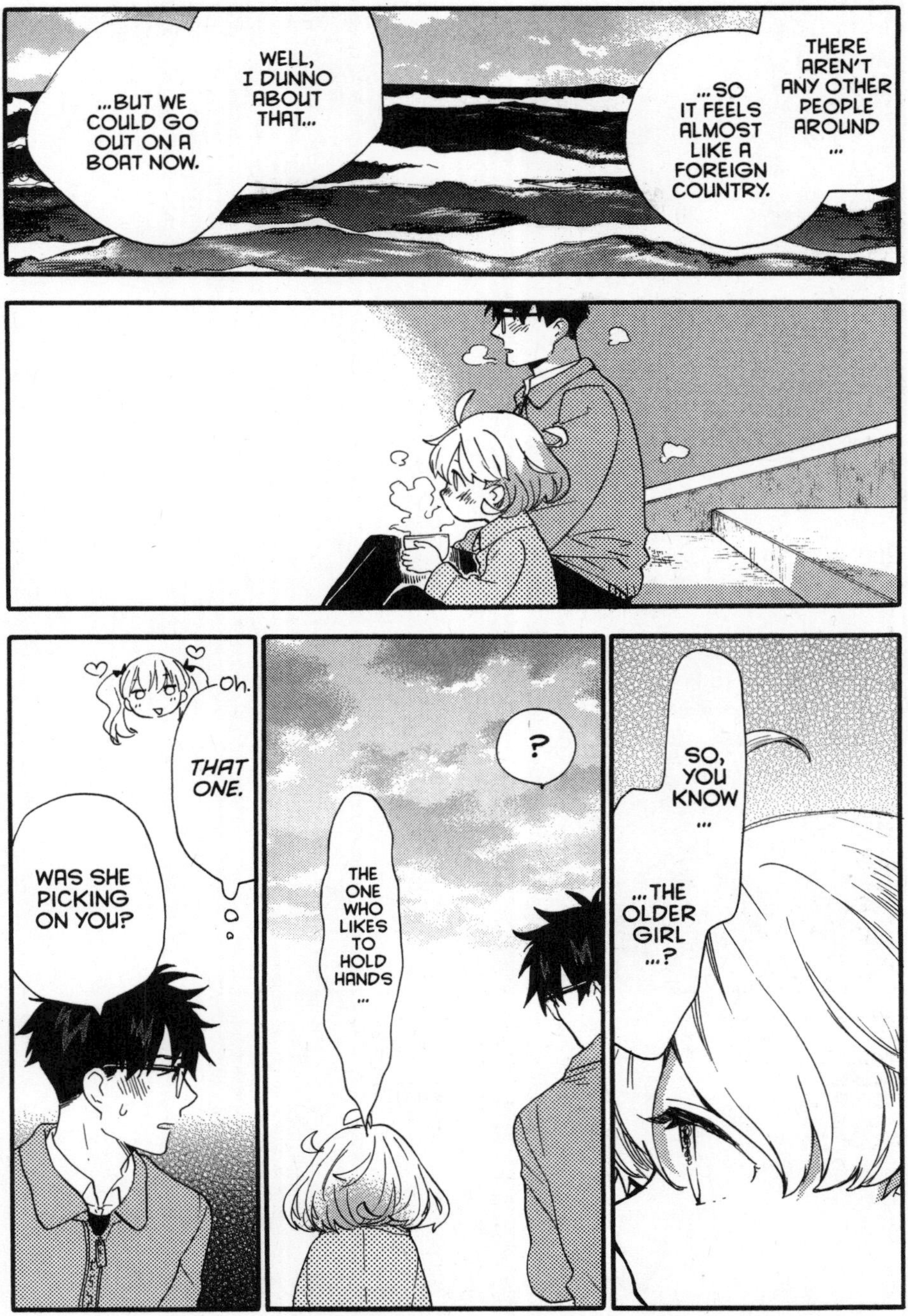
THERE AREN'T ANY OTHER PEOPLE AROUND ...
...SO IT FEELS ALMOST LIKE A FOREIGN COUNTRY.
WELL, I DUNNO ABOUT THAT...
...BUT WE COULD GO OUT ON A BOAT NOW.
SO, YOU KNOW ...
...THE OLDER GIRL ...?
?
THE ONE WHO LIKES TO HOLD HANDS ...
Oh.
THAT ONE.
WAS SHE PICKING ON YOU?

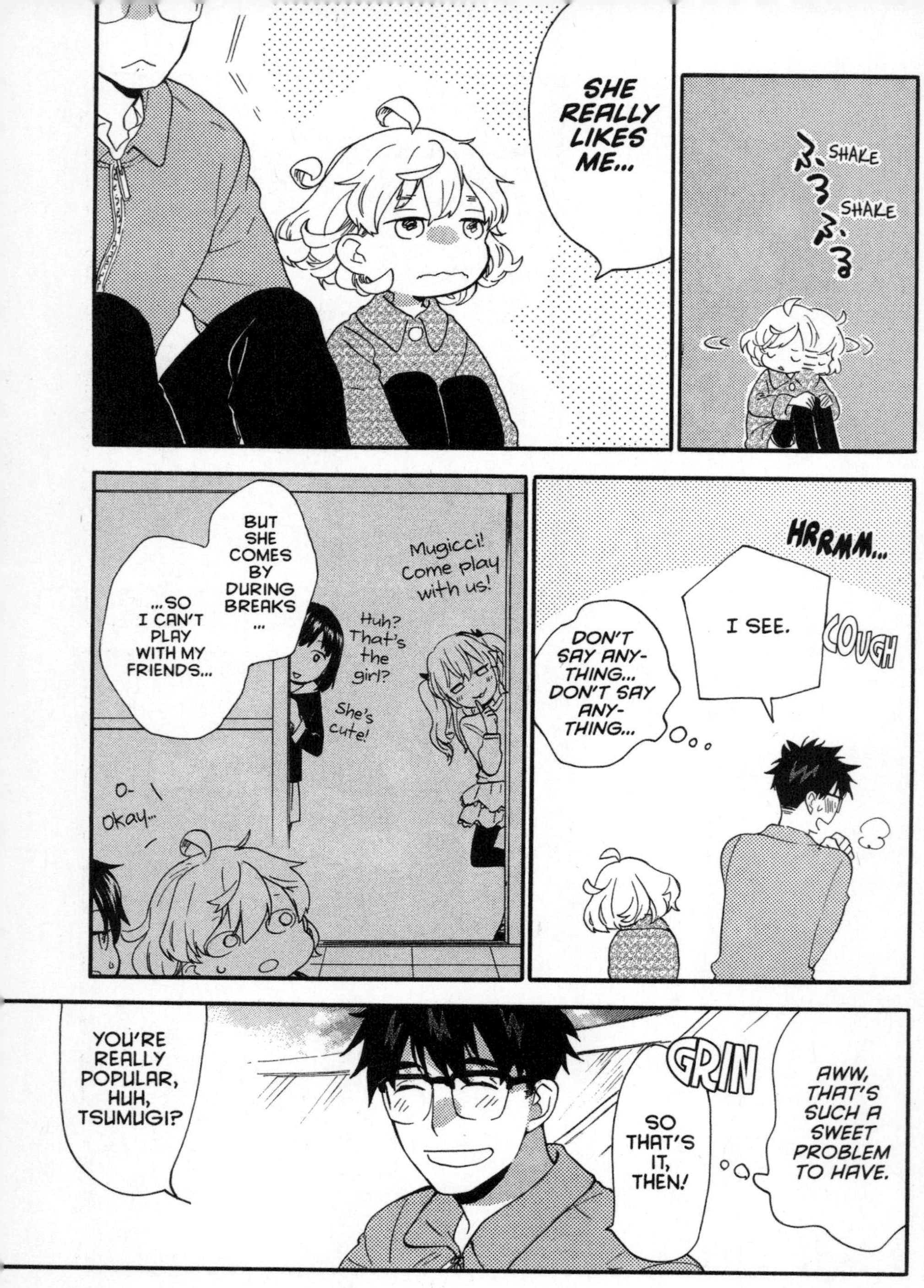
ぷるぷる
SHAKE
SHAKE
SHE REALLY LIKES ME...
HRRMM...
I SEE.
COUGH
DON'T SAY ANYTHING... DON'T SAY ANYTHING...
BUT SHE COMES BY DURING BREAKS...
...SO I CAN'T PLAY WITH MY FRIENDS...
Mugicci! Come play with us!
Huh? That's the girl?
She's cute!
O- Okay...
AWW, THAT'S SUCH A SWEET PROBLEM TO HAVE.
GRIN
SO THAT'S IT, THEN!
YOU'RE REALLY POPULAR, HUH, TSUMUGI?

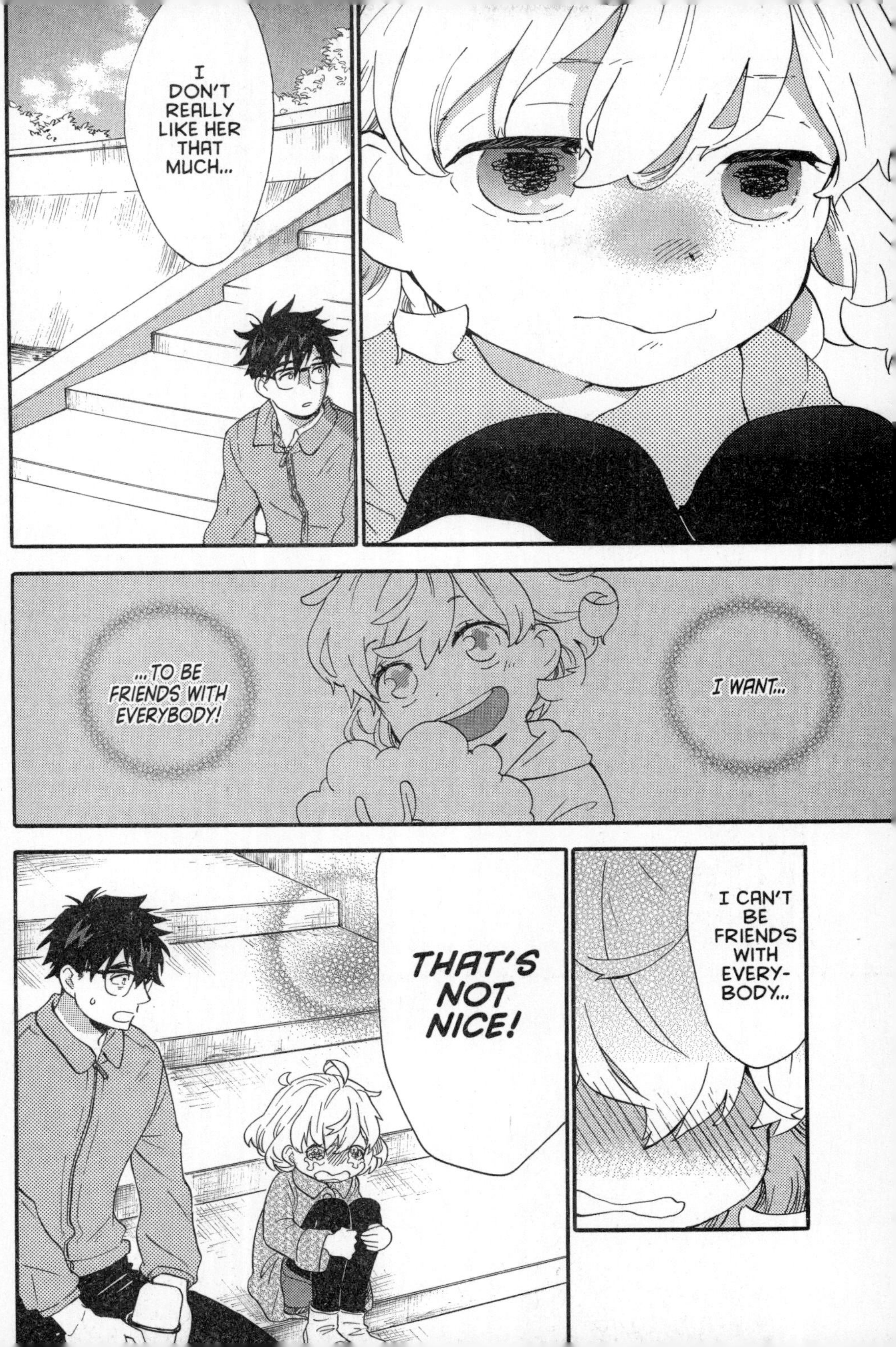
I DON'T REALLY LIKE HER THAT MUCH...
I WANT...
...TO BE FRIENDS WITH EVERYBODY!
I CAN'T BE FRIENDS WITH EVERY-BODY...
THAT'S NOT NICE!

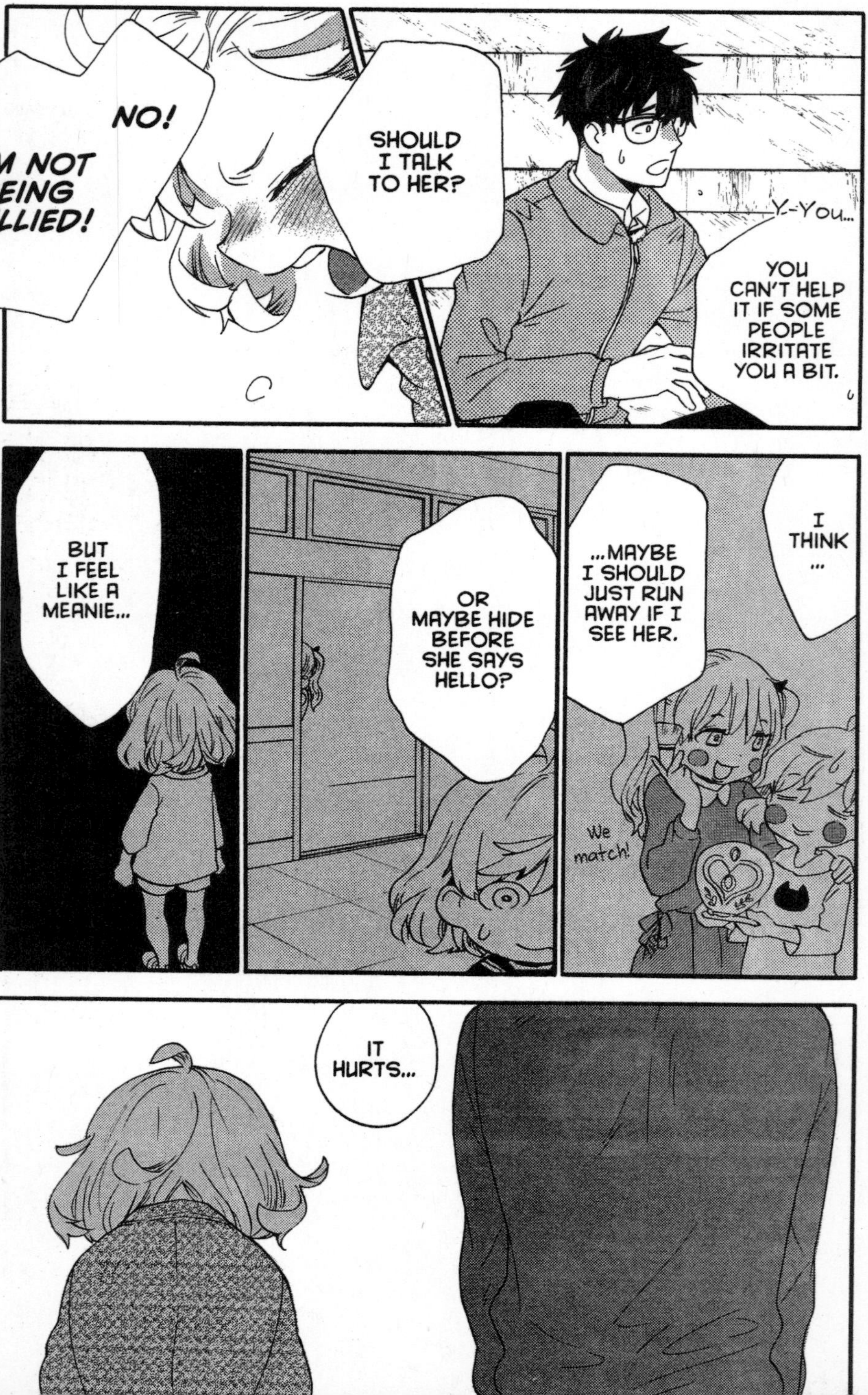
Y-You...
YOU CAN'T HELP IT IF SOME PEOPLE IRRITATE YOU A BIT.
SHOULD I TALK TO HER?
NO!
I'M NOT BEING BULLIED!
I THINK ...
...MAYBE I SHOULD JUST RUN AWAY IF I SEE HER.
We match!
OR MAYBE HIDE BEFORE SHE SAYS HELLO?
BUT I FEEL LIKE A MEANIE...
IT HURTS...

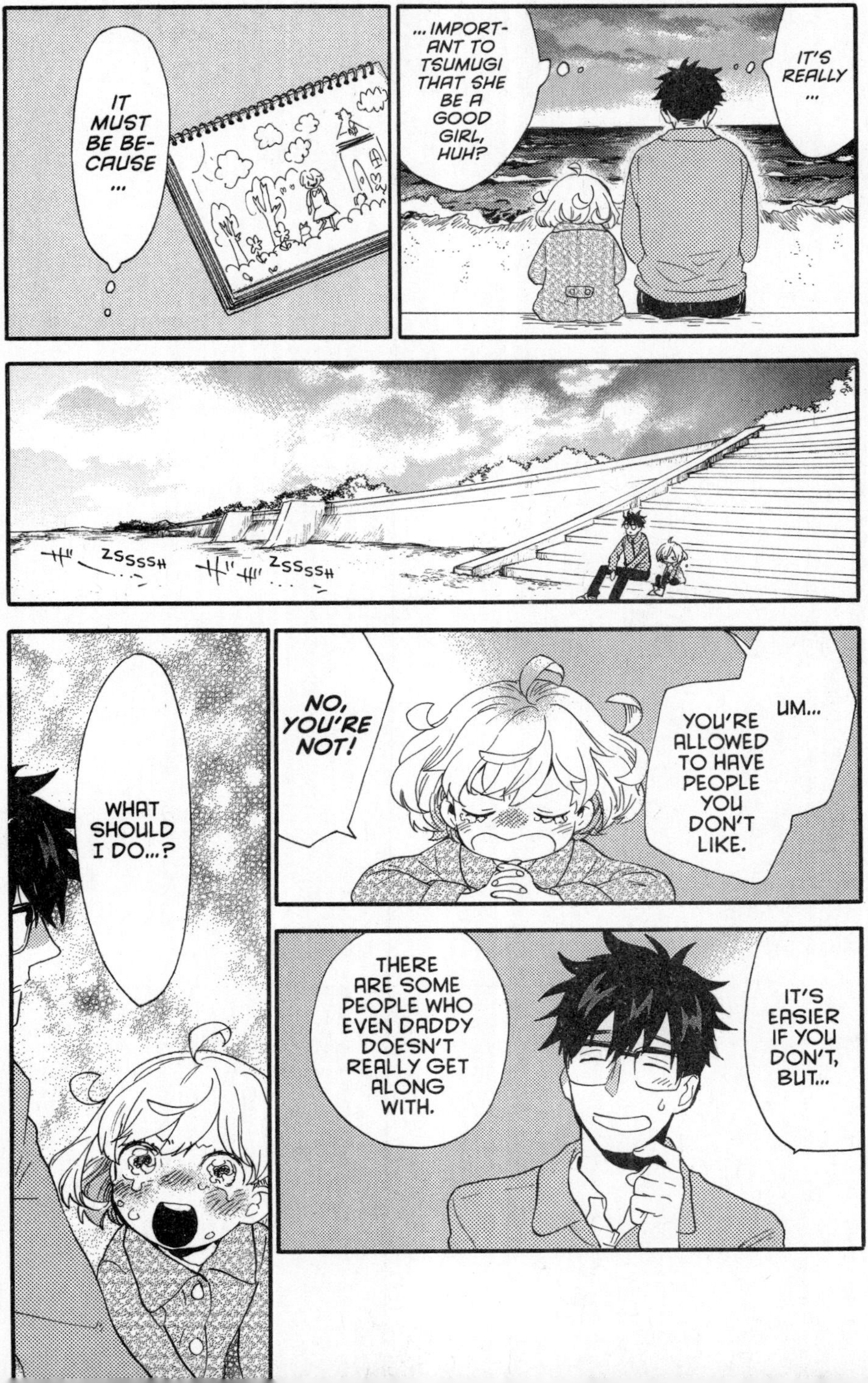
IT'S REALLY ...
... IMPORTANT TO TSUMUGI THAT SHE BE A GOOD GIRL, HUH?
IT MUST BE BE-CAUSE ...
ZSSSSH
ZSSSSH
UM...
YOU'RE ALLOWED TO HAVE PEOPLE YOU DON'T LIKE.
NO, YOU'RE NOT!
IT'S EASIER IF YOU DON'T, BUT...
THERE ARE SOME PEOPLE WHO EVEN DADDY DOESN'T REALLY GET ALONG WITH.
WHAT SHOULD I DO...?

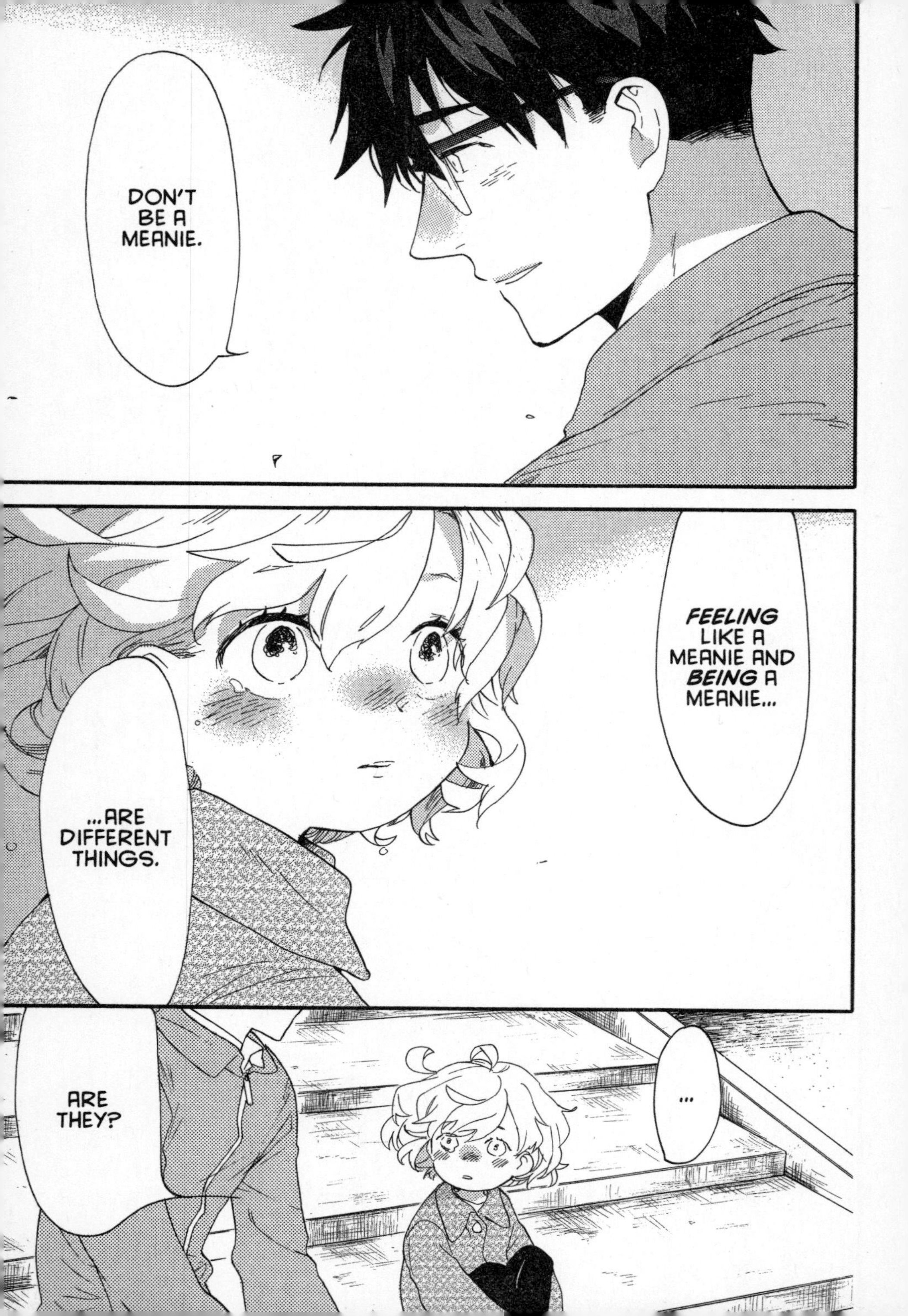
DON'T BE A MEANIE.
FEELING LIKE A MEANIE AND *BEING* A MEANIE...
...ARE DIFFERENT THINGS.
...
ARE THEY?

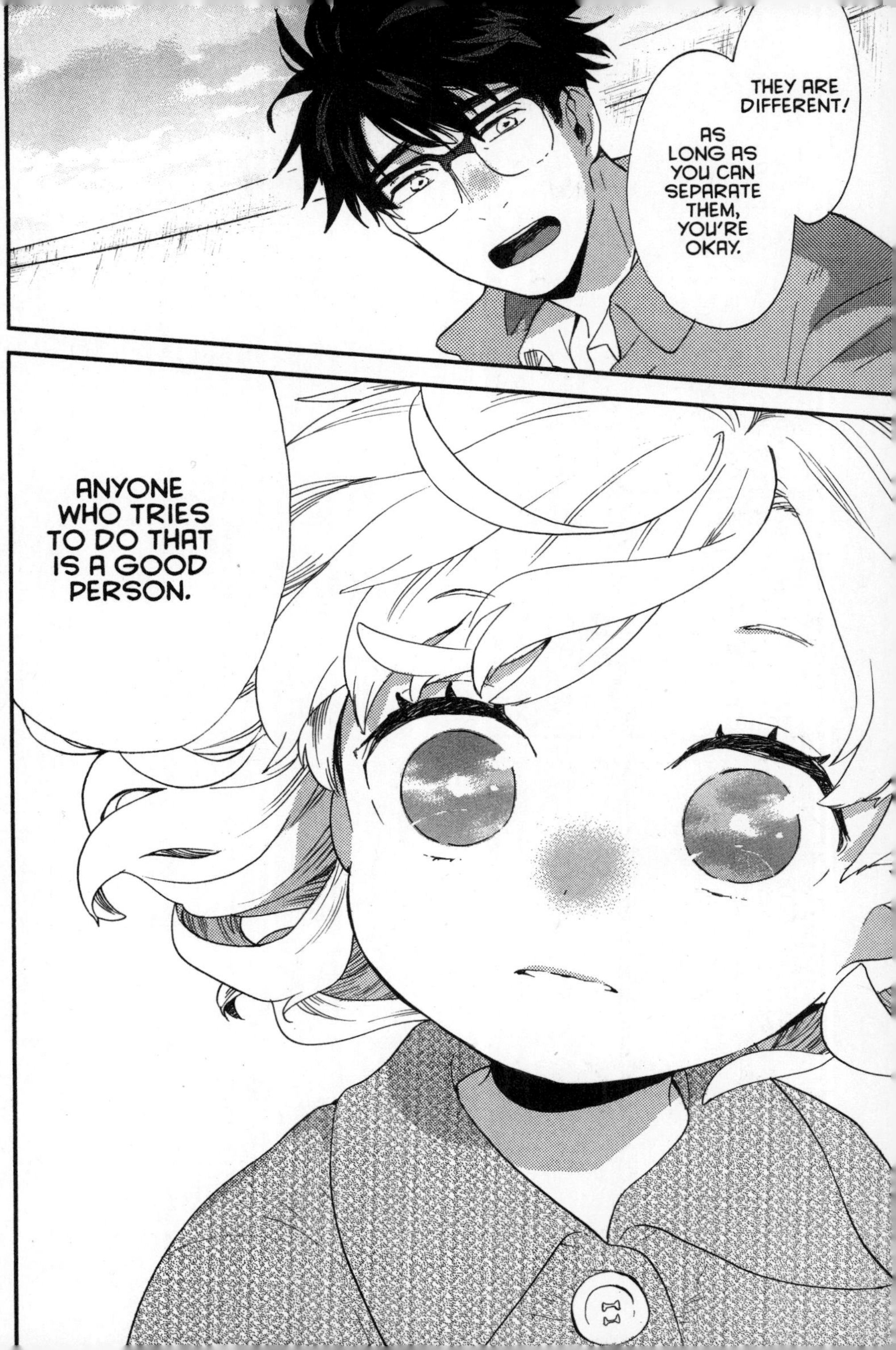
THEY ARE DIFFERENT!
AS LONG AS YOU CAN SEPARATE THEM, YOU'RE OKAY.
ANYONE WHO TRIES TO DO THAT IS A GOOD PERSON.

I FEEL LIKE A MEANIE, TOO, A LOT OF THE TIME...
...BUT THAT'S HOW I WANT TO BE!
I DIDN'T KNOW THAT.
OH...
THE BEACH IS COLD, BUT FOR SOME REASON...
YEAH.
IT FEELS KIND OF WARM.
ぐるるる～
GURGLE
GURGLE

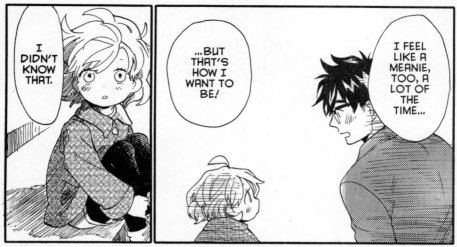

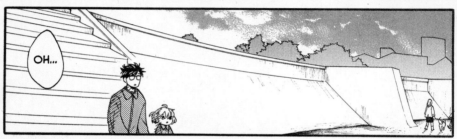

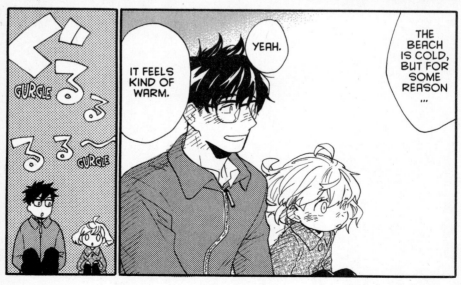

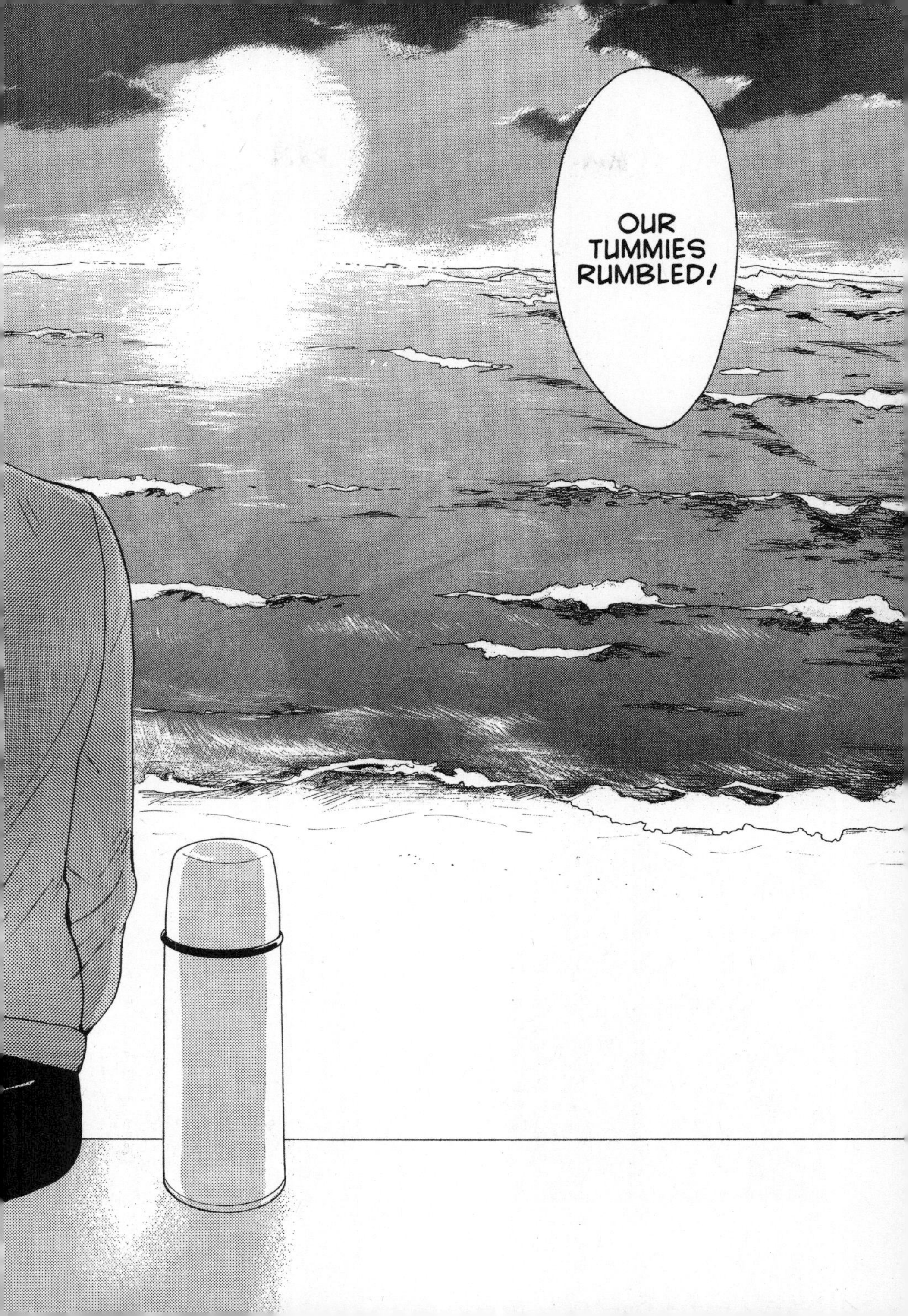
OUR TUMMIES RUMBLED!

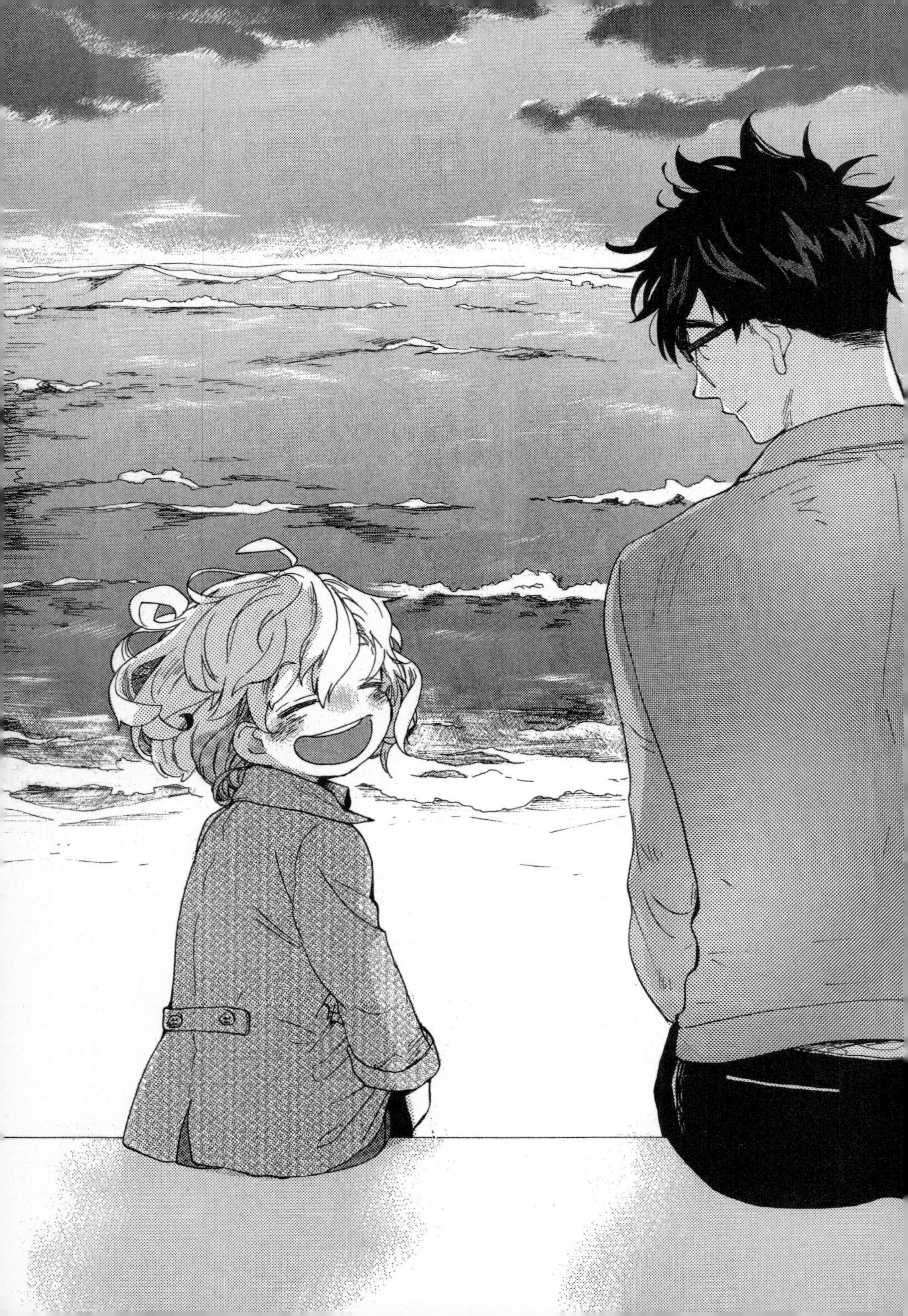

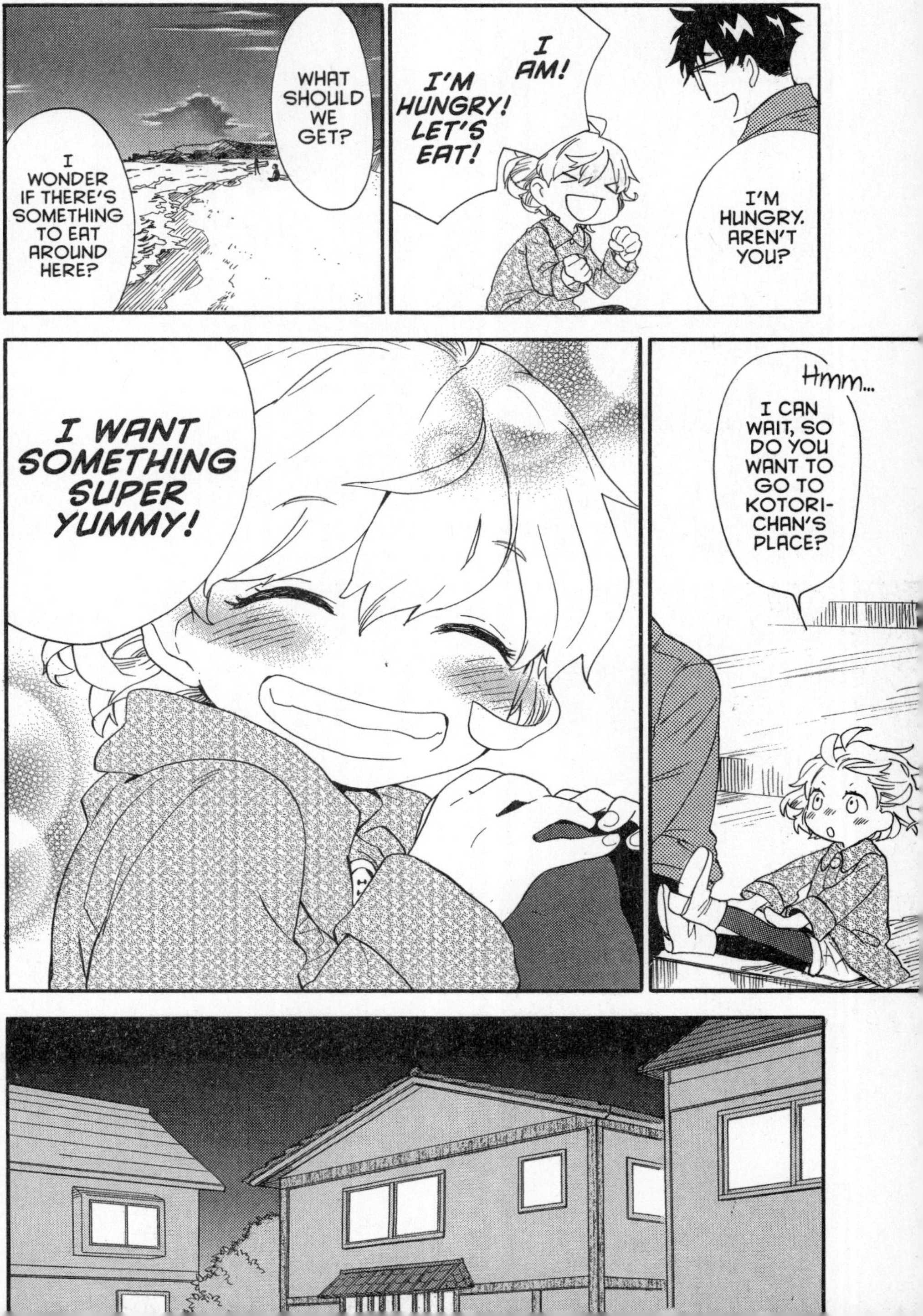
I'M HUNGRY. AREN'T YOU?
I AM! I'M HUNGRY! LET'S EAT!
WHAT SHOULD WE GET?
I WONDER IF THERE'S SOMETHING TO EAT AROUND HERE?
Hmm...
I CAN WAIT, SO DO YOU WANT TO GO TO KOTORI-CHAN'S PLACE?
I WANT SOMETHING SUPER YUMMY!

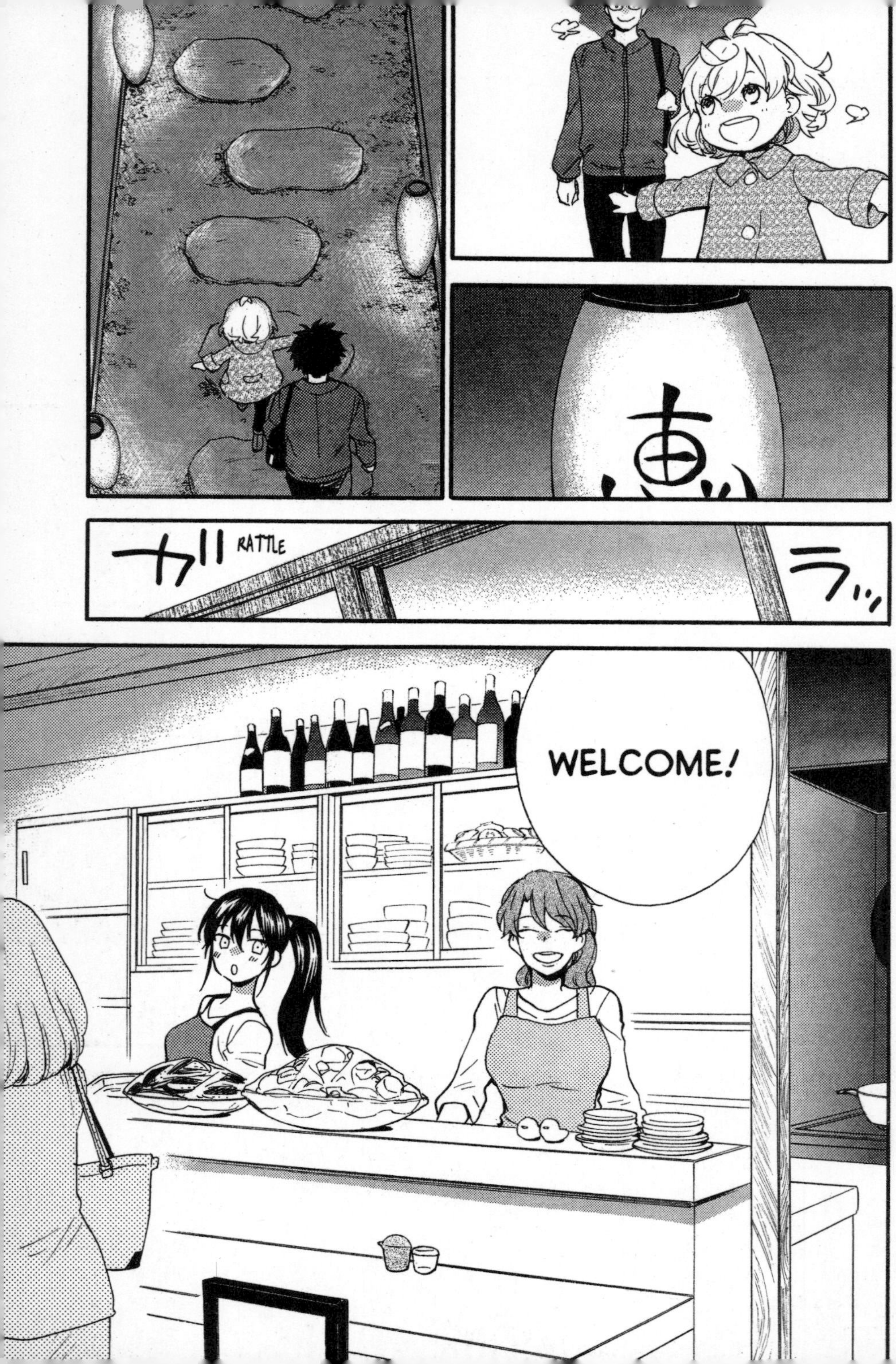
ガラッ
RATTLE
WELCOME!

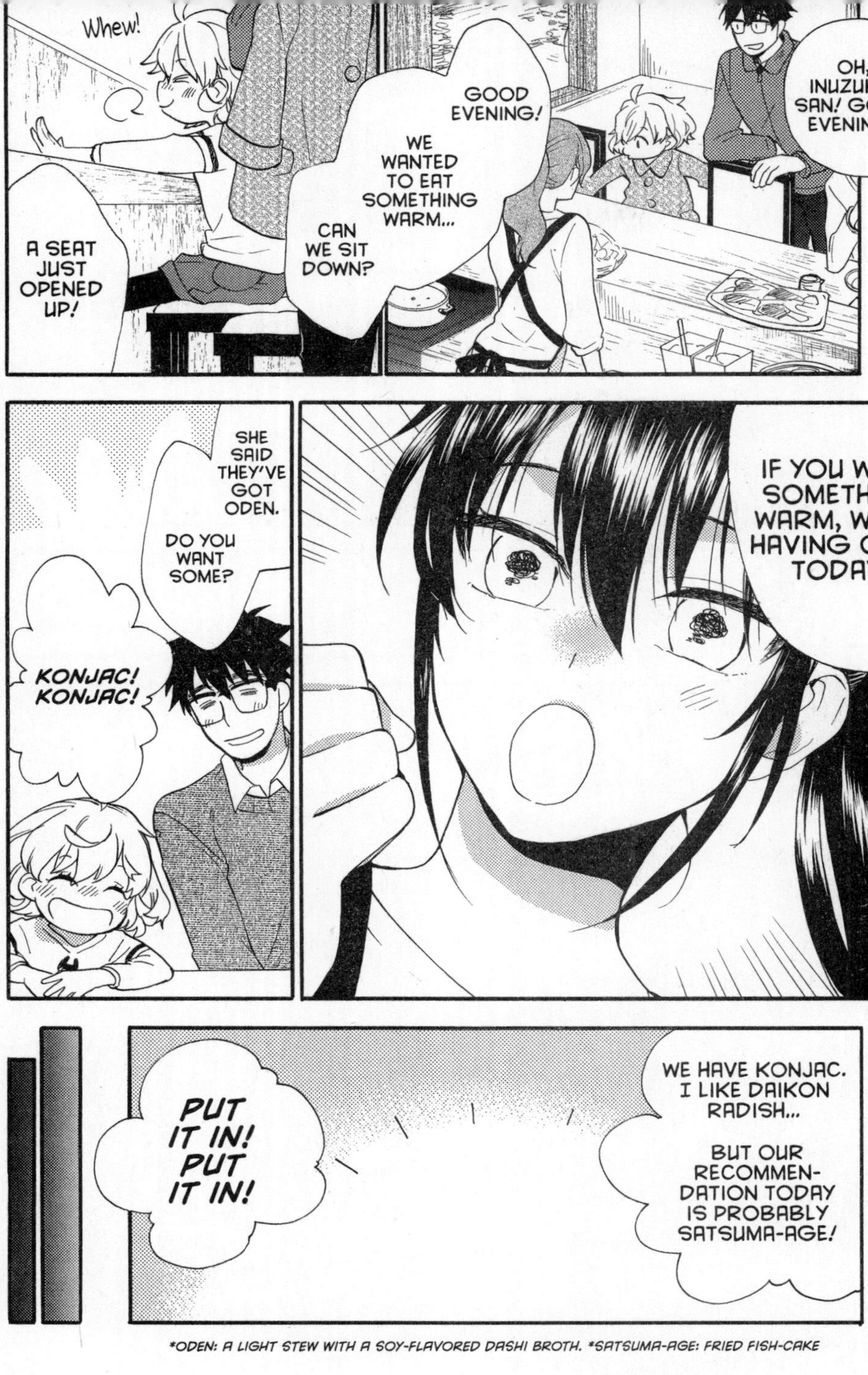
OH, INUZUKA-SAN! GOOD EVENING!
GOOD EVENING!
WE WANTED TO EAT SOMETHING WARM...
CAN WE SIT DOWN?
Whew!
A SEAT JUST OPENED UP!
IF YOU WANT SOMETHING WARM, WE'RE HAVING ODEN TODAY!
SHE SAID THEY'VE GOT ODEN.
DO YOU WANT SOME?
KONJAC! KONJAC!
WE HAVE KONJAC. I LIKE DAIKON RADISH...
BUT OUR RECOMMENDATION TODAY IS PROBABLY SATSUMA-AGE!
PUT IT IN! PUT IT IN!

*ODEN: A LIGHT STEW WITH A SOY-FLAVORED DASHI BROTH. *SATSUMA-AGE: FRIED FISH-CAKE

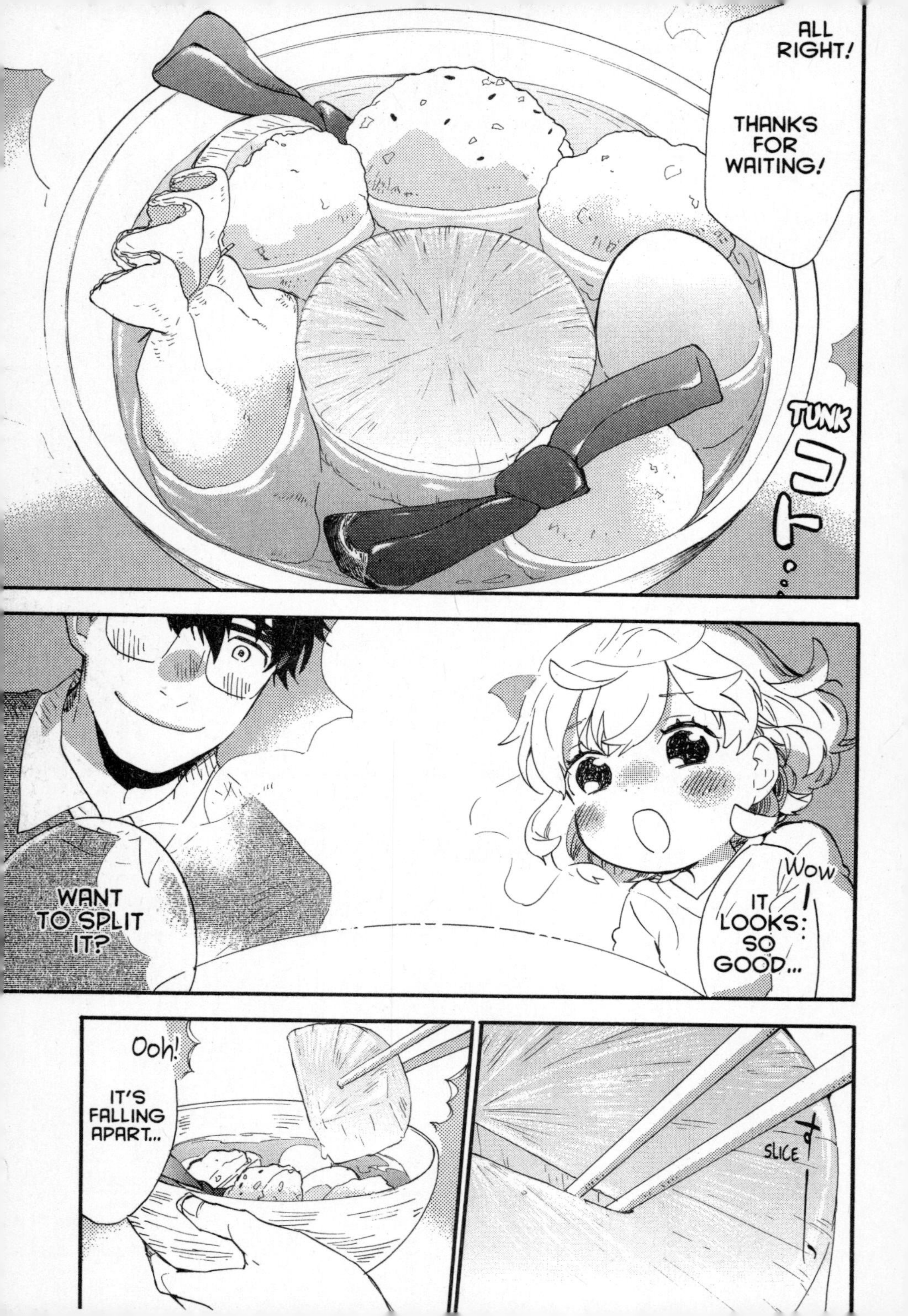
ALL RIGHT!
THANKS FOR WAITING!
TUNK
コト...
Wow!
IT LOOKS SO GOOD...
WANT TO SPLIT IT?
SLICE
す
Ooh!
IT'S FALLING APART...

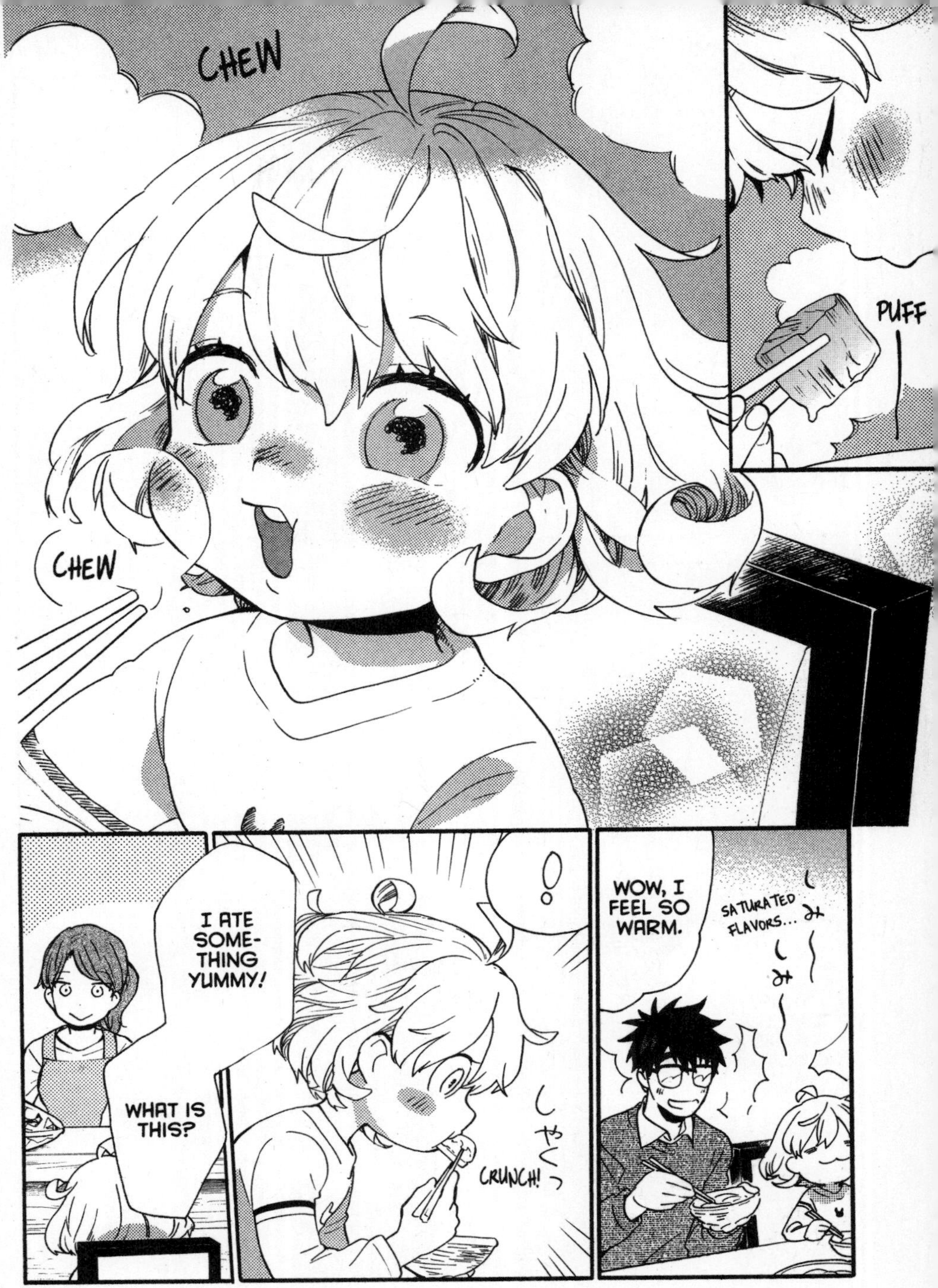
PUFF
CHEW
CHEW
WOW, I FEEL SO WARM.
SATURATED FLAVORS...
しみ〜
しみ〜
!
しゃくっ
CRUNCH!
I ATE SOMETHING YUMMY!
WHAT IS THIS?

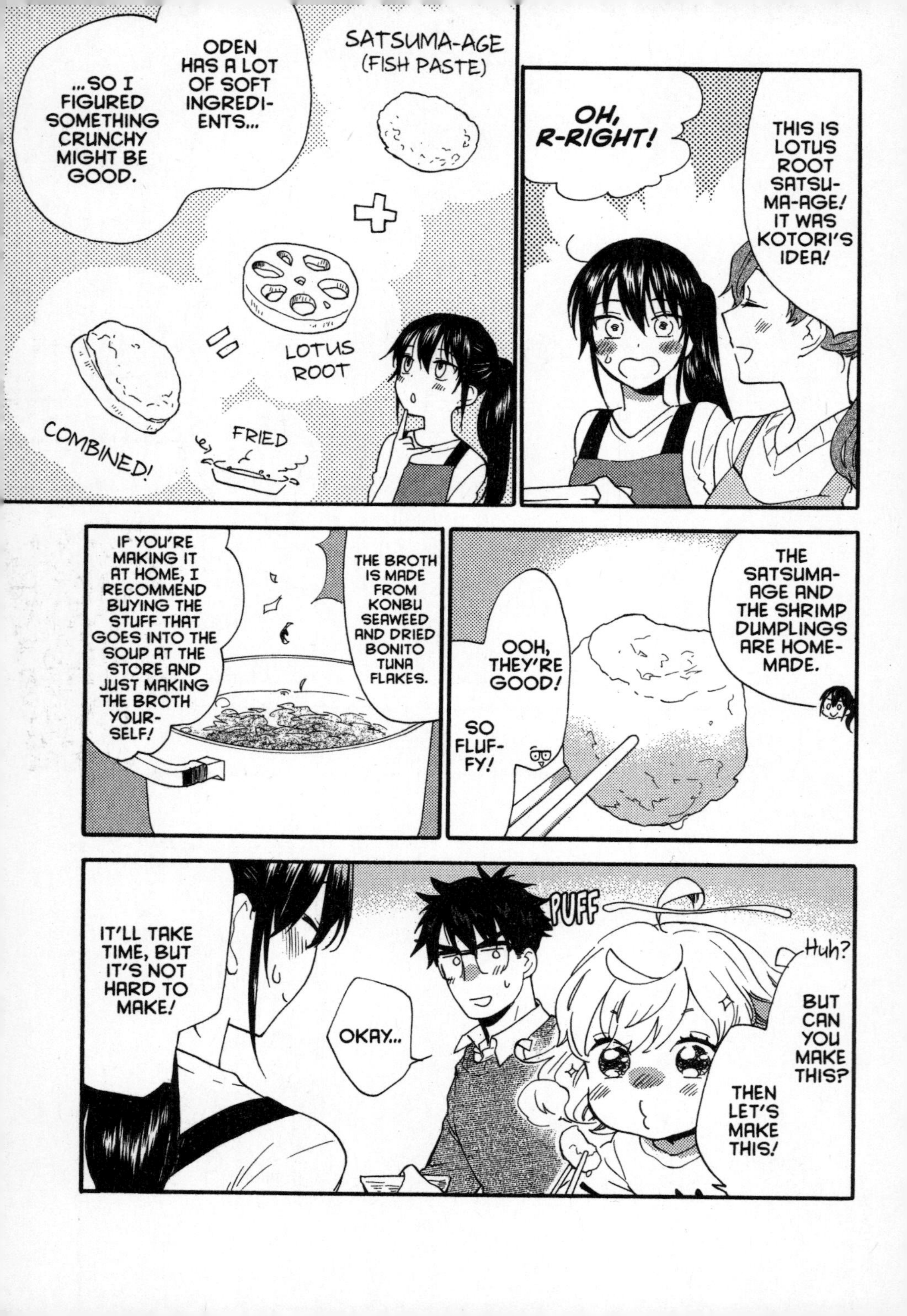
THIS IS LOTUS ROOT SATSUMA-AGE! IT WAS KOTORI'S IDEA!
OH, R-RIGHT!
SATSUMA-AGE (FISH PASTE)
ODEN HAS A LOT OF SOFT INGREDIENTS...
...SO I FIGURED SOMETHING CRUNCHY MIGHT BE GOOD.
+
LOTUS ROOT
=
COMBINED!
FRIED
THE SATSUMA-AGE AND THE SHRIMP DUMPLINGS ARE HOMEMADE.
OOH, THEY'RE GOOD!
SO FLUFFY!
THE BROTH IS MADE FROM KONBU SEAWEED AND DRIED BONITO TUNA FLAKES.
IF YOU'RE MAKING IT AT HOME, I RECOMMEND BUYING THE STUFF THAT GOES INTO THE SOUP AT THE STORE AND JUST MAKING THE BROTH YOURSELF!
Huh?
BUT CAN YOU MAKE THIS?
THEN LET'S MAKE THIS!
PUFF
OKAY...
IT'LL TAKE TIME, BUT IT'S NOT HARD TO MAKE!

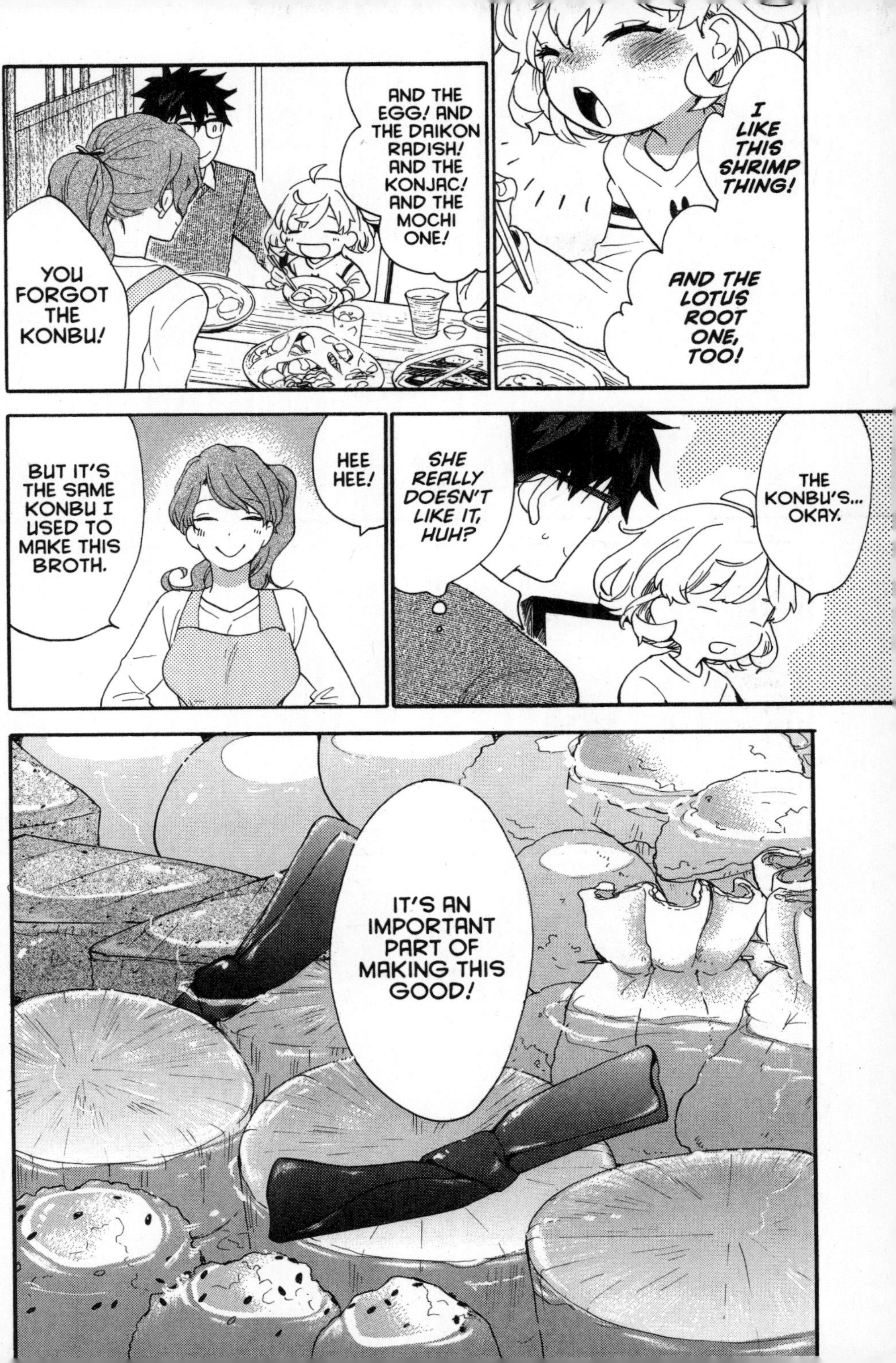
I LIKE THIS SHRIMP THING!
AND THE LOTUS ROOT ONE, TOO!
AND THE EGG! AND THE DAIKON RADISH! AND THE KONJAC! AND THE MOCHI ONE!
YOU FORGOT THE KONBU!
THE KONBU'S... OKAY.
SHE REALLY DOESN'T LIKE IT, HUH?
HEE HEE!
BUT IT'S THE SAME KONBU I USED TO MAKE THIS BROTH.
IT'S AN IMPORTANT PART OF MAKING THIS GOOD!

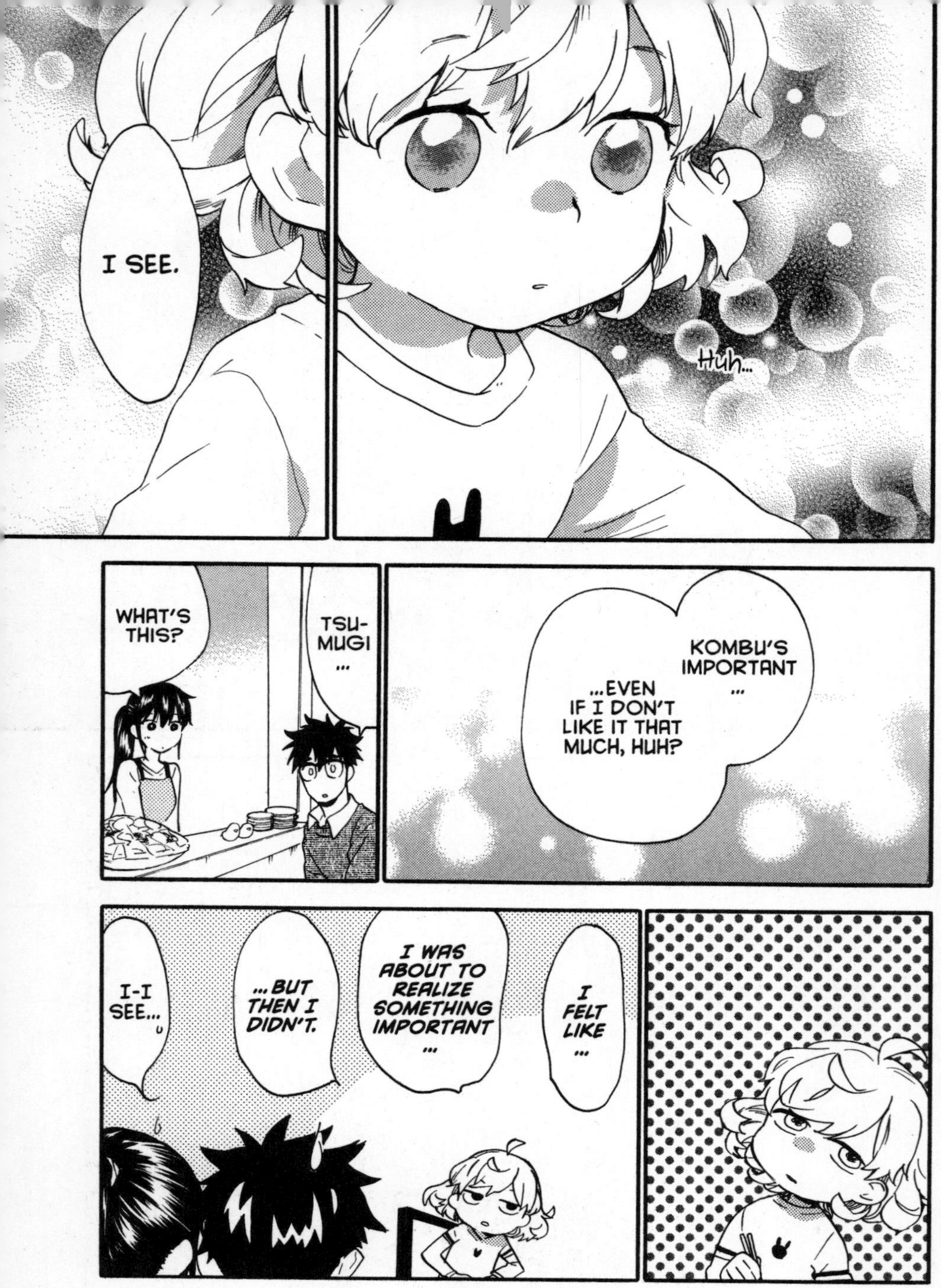
Huh...
I SEE.
KOMBU'S IMPORTANT...
...EVEN IF I DON'T LIKE IT THAT MUCH, HUH?
TSU-MUGI...
WHAT'S THIS?
I FELT LIKE...
I WAS ABOUT TO REALIZE SOMETHING IMPORTANT...
...BUT THEN I DIDN'T.
I-I SEE...

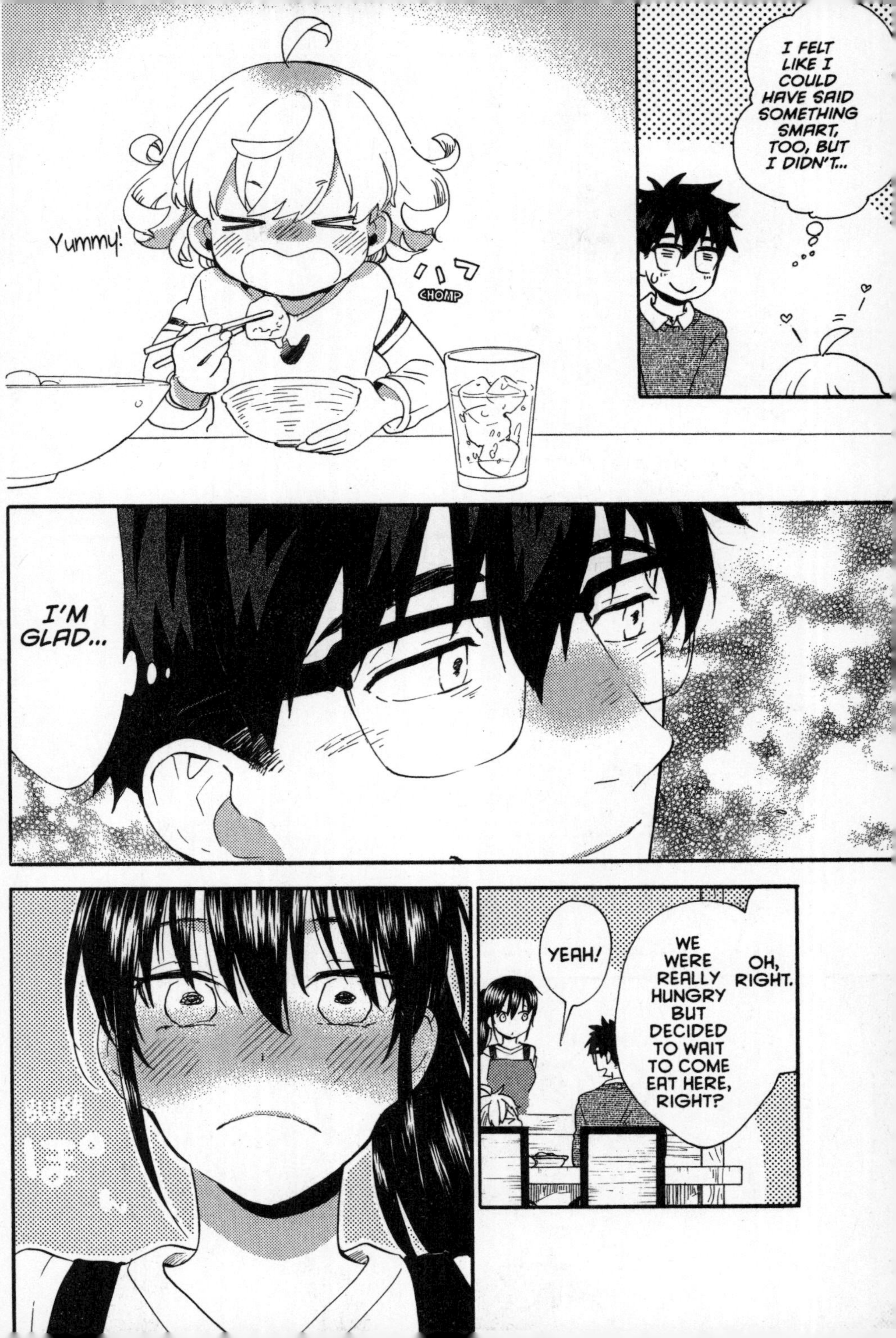
I FELT LIKE I COULD HAVE SAID SOMETHING SMART, TOO, BUT I DIDN'T...
Yummy!
CHOMP
I'M GLAD...
OH, RIGHT.
WE WERE REALLY HUNGRY BUT DECIDED TO WAIT TO COME EAT HERE, RIGHT?
YEAH!
BLUSH

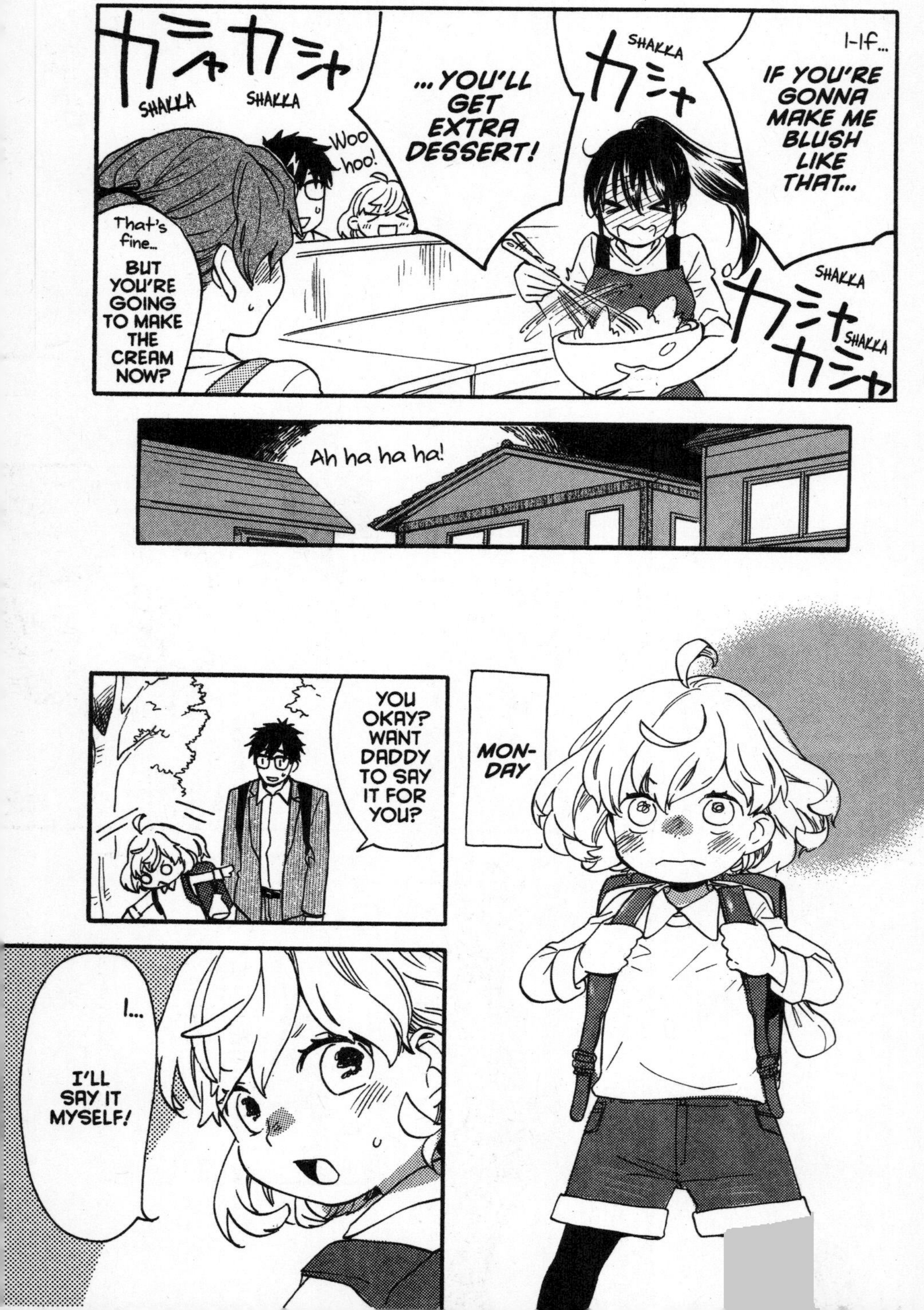
I-If...
IF YOU'RE GONNA MAKE ME BLUSH LIKE THAT...
SHAKKA
カシャ
...YOU'LL GET EXTRA DESSERT!
カシャカシャ
SHAKKA SHAKKA
Woo hoo!
That's fine...
BUT YOU'RE GOING TO MAKE THE CREAM NOW?
SHAKKA SHAKKA
カシャカシャ
Ah ha ha ha!
MON-DAY
YOU OKAY? WANT DADDY TO SAY IT FOR YOU?
I...
I'LL SAY IT MYSELF!

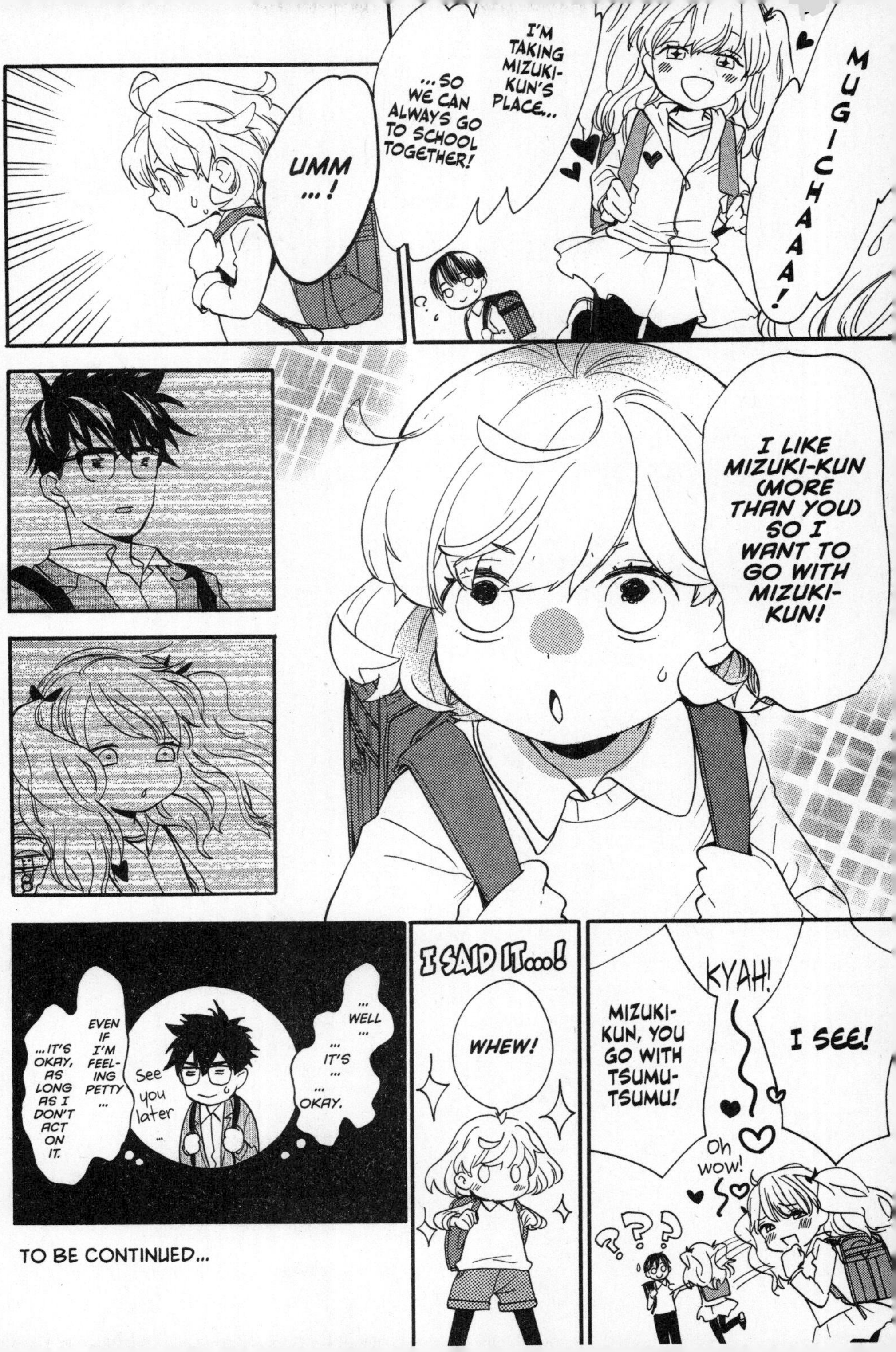
MUGICHAAAA!
I'M TAKING MIZUKI-KUN'S PLACE...
...SO WE CAN ALWAYS GO TO SCHOOL TOGETHER!
UMM ...!
I LIKE MIZUKI-KUN (MORE THAN YOU) SO I WANT TO GO WITH MIZUKI-KUN!
I SEE!
KYAH!
MIZUKI-KUN, YOU GO WITH TSUMU-TSUMU!
Oh wow!
I SAID IT...!
WHEW!
...WELL...
...IT'S...
...OKAY.
See you later...
EVEN IF I'M FEELING PETTY...
...IT'S OKAY, AS LONG AS I DON'T ACT ON IT.

TO BE CONTINUED...

ODEN

☆Ingredients (serves 4) ☆

12cm daikon
3 pieces Hidaka-kombu (each approx. 15 cm)
4 eggs
2 pieces kirimochi (rectangular mochi)

1 block konnyaku
2 pieces aburaage (deep fried tofu)
Anything else, like ganmodaki
(fried tofu fritter)

☆Broth☆
2 liters water
2 tablespoons usukuchi (thin) soy sauce
½ tablespoon salt

40g bonito flakes
2 tablespoons mirin

Preparation

1. Soak the Hidaka-kombu water for 1 hour.
2. Peel the daikon. Cut into 3cm length sections and lightly score an x with a kitchen knife. Boil daikon in water until tender and easily pierced with a skewer and then transfer to cold water.
3. Score both sides of the konnyaku, then boil in water. After boiling for 5 minutes drain the konnyaku and cut it into your desired shape.
4. Take stock from step one and put over medium heat. Just before boiling remove the kombu and add the bonito flakes. Remove from heat and let sit for 2 minutes. Strain broth with cheesecloth. Add soy sauce, mirin, and salt.
5. Cut kombu strips into 3-4 equal sized pieces and then tie into a knot.
6. Soft boil the eggs and then remove the shells.
7. Add the daikon, konnyaku, and kombu to the stock and return stock to the heat. When boiling drop to low heat and simmer for 20 to 30 minutes. [insert] If the daikon goes soft that's OK! [insert] Add the eggs and remove from heat.
8. Cut the aburaage into two equal parts. Full pockets of aburaage with sliced mochi. Pin closed with a toothpick.
9. Boil fried tofu fritter, fried fishcake, shrimp fritters and then drain.
10. Add steps (8) and (9) to the broth and return to heat. After boiling add any remaining ingredients. Keep warm on low heat and enjoy!

★Ganmodoki / Fried tofu fritters★

200g firm tofu
Pinch of salt

15g Japanese yam
Black sesame – to taste

1. Wrap tofu with a cloth. Weigh down and allow it to sit for at least 1 hour. Lightly squeeze tofu to drain excess water, and then mash with mortar and pestle.
2. Shred the Japanese yam and add to the tofu. Add salt and black sesame and mix well.
3. Split mixture into 4 parts and add to 170 °C oil. Lower heat and fry for 4-5 minutes.

★Satsuma-age / fried fish cake ★ Ebi-shinjo / Shrimp fritters ★

Satsuma-age / fried fish cake
160g cod (deboned and skinned)
2 g salt   8g sugar
Ebi-shinjo / Shrimp fritters
60g cod (deboned and skinned)
100g shrimp (shelled)
30g egg whites   2g salt

3cm lotus root

8g sugar

1. Cut lotus root into 4 equal pieces and add to water.
2. Mince the cod and blend with food processor.
3. De-vein the shrimp. Dry with paper towel and then mince and blend with food processor.
4. Add portion of cod for satsuma-age along with seasoning to mortar and mix well.
5. Drain the lotus root. With oiled hands cover the lotus root with the mixture from step 4.
6. Add the remaining cod, the shrimp, egg whites, and seasoning for the ebi-shinjo to the mortar. Mix well.
7. With oiled hands take the mixture from step 6 and shape into 4 equal discs.

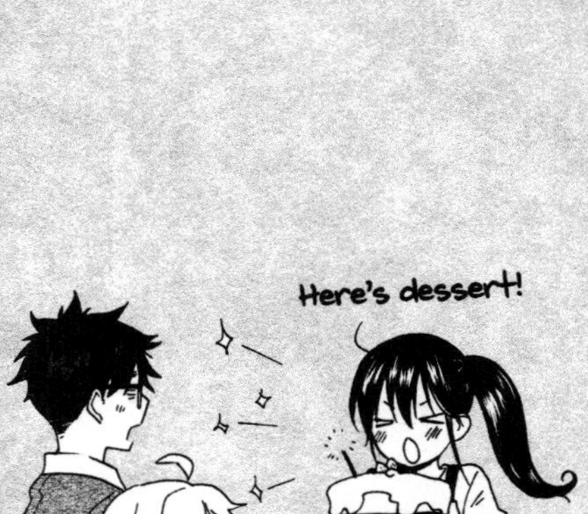
Here's dessert!
TA-DA!

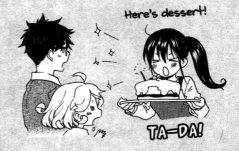

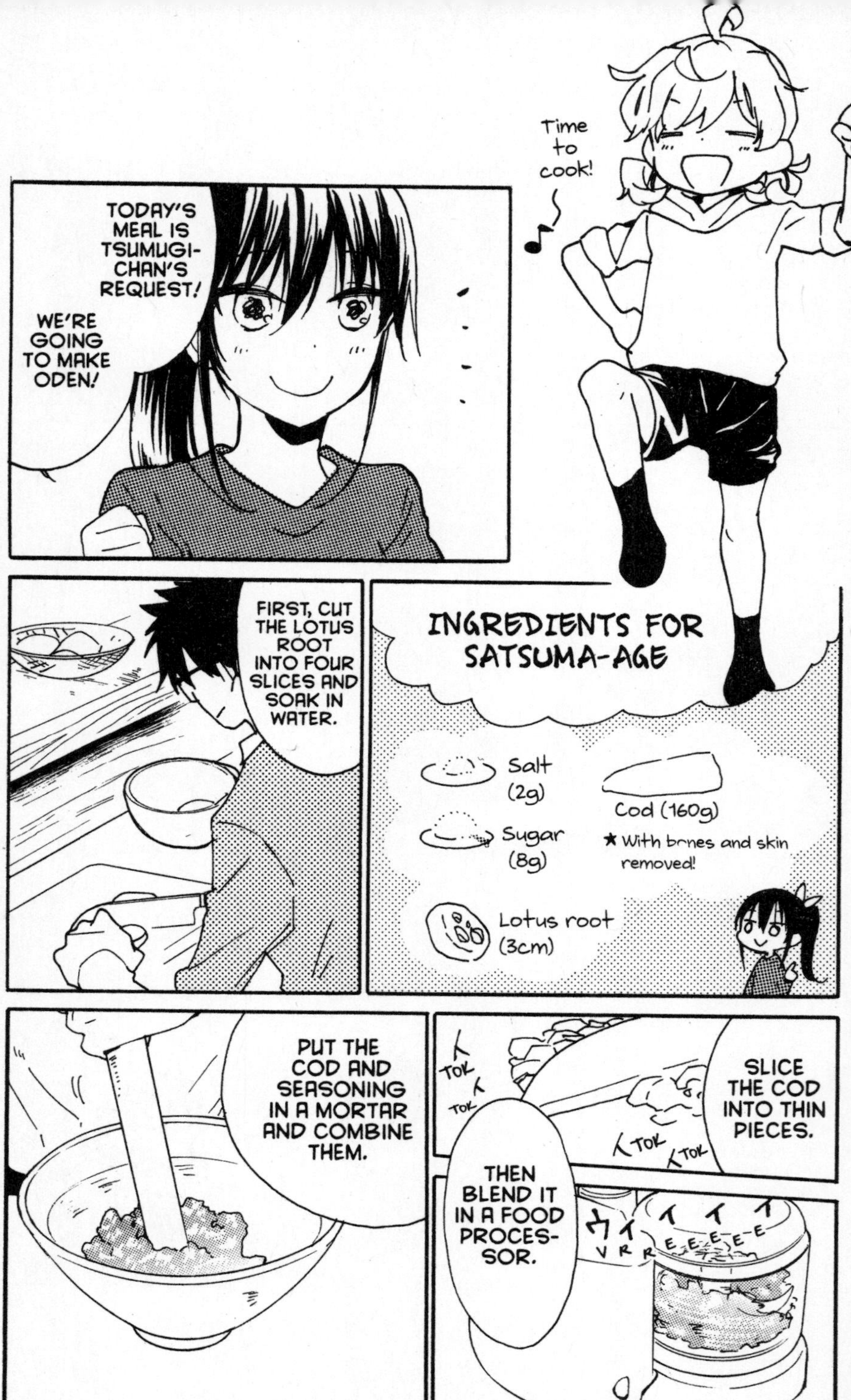
Time to cook!
TODAY'S MEAL IS TSUMUGI-CHAN'S REQUEST!
WE'RE GOING TO MAKE ODEN!
INGREDIENTS FOR SATSUMA-AGE
Salt (2g)
Cod (160g)
Sugar (8g)
★ With bones and skin removed!
Lotus root (3cm)
FIRST, CUT THE LOTUS ROOT INTO FOUR SLICES AND SOAK IN WATER.
SLICE THE COD INTO THIN PIECES.
TOK
TOK
TOK
TOK
THEN BLEND IT IN A FOOD PROCES-SOR.
ウィイイイ
VRREEEEEE
PUT THE COD AND SEASONING IN A MORTAR AND COMBINE THEM.

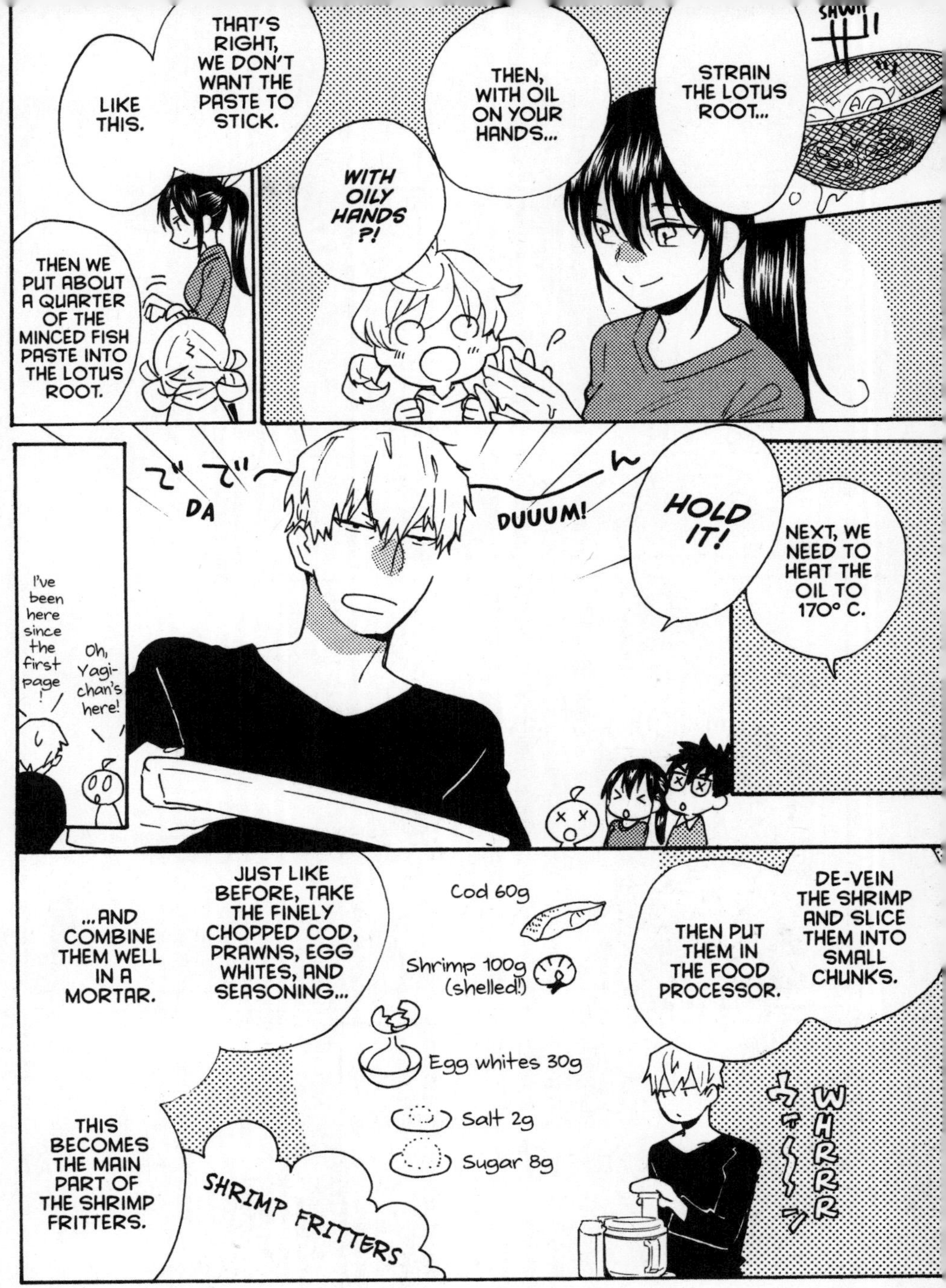
STRAIN THE LOTUS ROOT...
THEN, WITH OIL ON YOUR HANDS...
WITH OILY HANDS ?!
THAT'S RIGHT, WE DON'T WANT THE PASTE TO STICK.
LIKE THIS.
THEN WE PUT ABOUT A QUARTER OF THE MINCED FISH PASTE INTO THE LOTUS ROOT.
NEXT, WE NEED TO HEAT THE OIL TO 170° C.
HOLD IT!
DA
DUUUM!
Oh, Yagi-chan's here!
I've been here since the first page!
DE-VEIN THE SHRIMP AND SLICE THEM INTO SMALL CHUNKS.
THEN PUT THEM IN THE FOOD PROCESSOR.
WHRRR
Cod 60g
Shrimp 100g (shelled!)
Egg whites 30g
Salt 2g
Sugar 8g
JUST LIKE BEFORE, TAKE THE FINELY CHOPPED COD, PRAWNS, EGG WHITES, AND SEASONING...
...AND COMBINE THEM WELL IN A MORTAR.
SHRIMP FRITTERS
THIS BECOMES THE MAIN PART OF THE SHRIMP FRITTERS.

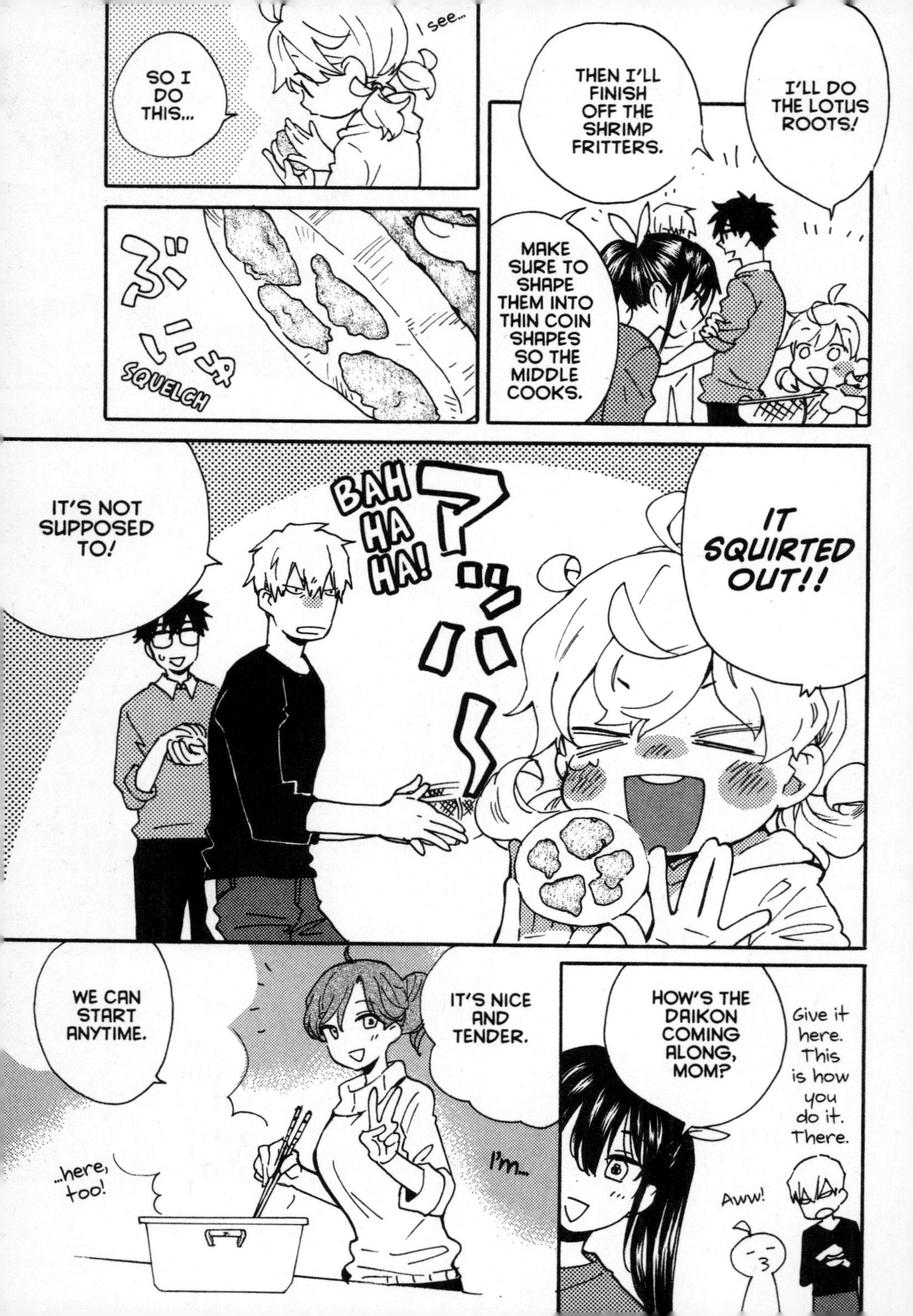
I'LL DO THE LOTUS ROOTS!
THEN I'LL FINISH OFF THE SHRIMP FRITTERS.
MAKE SURE TO SHAPE THEM INTO THIN COIN SHAPES SO THE MIDDLE COOKS.
SO I DO THIS...
I see...
SQUELCH
IT SQUIRTED OUT!!
BAH HA HA!
IT'S NOT SUPPOSED TO!
HOW'S THE DAIKON COMING ALONG, MOM?
Give it here. This is how you do it. There.
Aww!
I'm...
IT'S NICE AND TENDER.
WE CAN START ANYTIME.
...here, too!

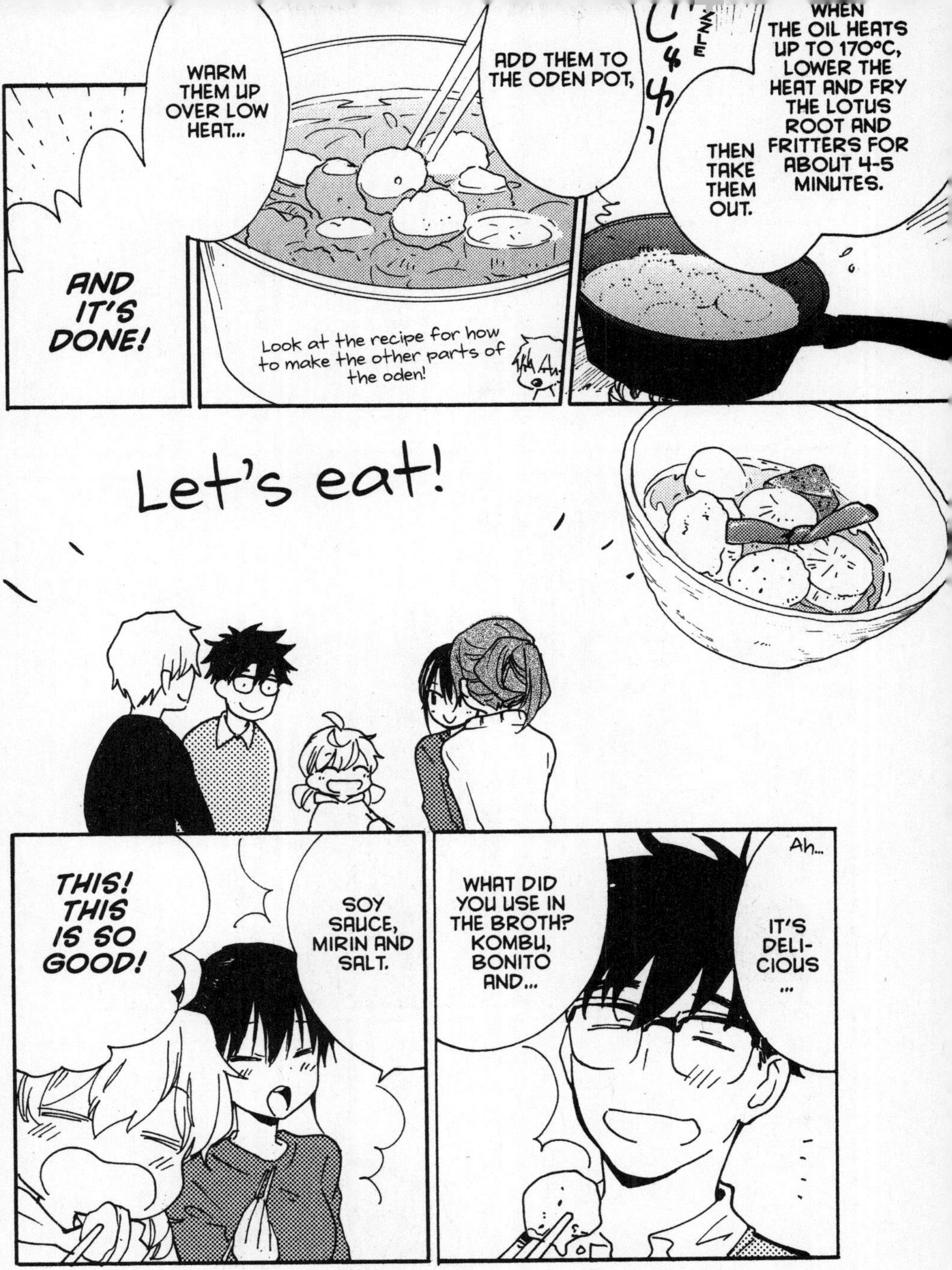
WHEN THE OIL HEATS UP TO 170°C, LOWER THE HEAT AND FRY THE LOTUS ROOT AND FRITTERS FOR ABOUT 4-5 MINUTES.
THEN TAKE THEM OUT.
じゅわっ
ADD THEM TO THE ODEN POT,
WARM THEM UP OVER LOW HEAT...
Look at the recipe for how to make the other parts of the oden!
AND IT'S DONE!
Let's eat!
Ah...
IT'S DELICIOUS ...
WHAT DID YOU USE IN THE BROTH? KOMBU, BONITO AND...
SOY SAUCE, MIRIN AND SALT.
THIS! THIS IS SO GOOD!

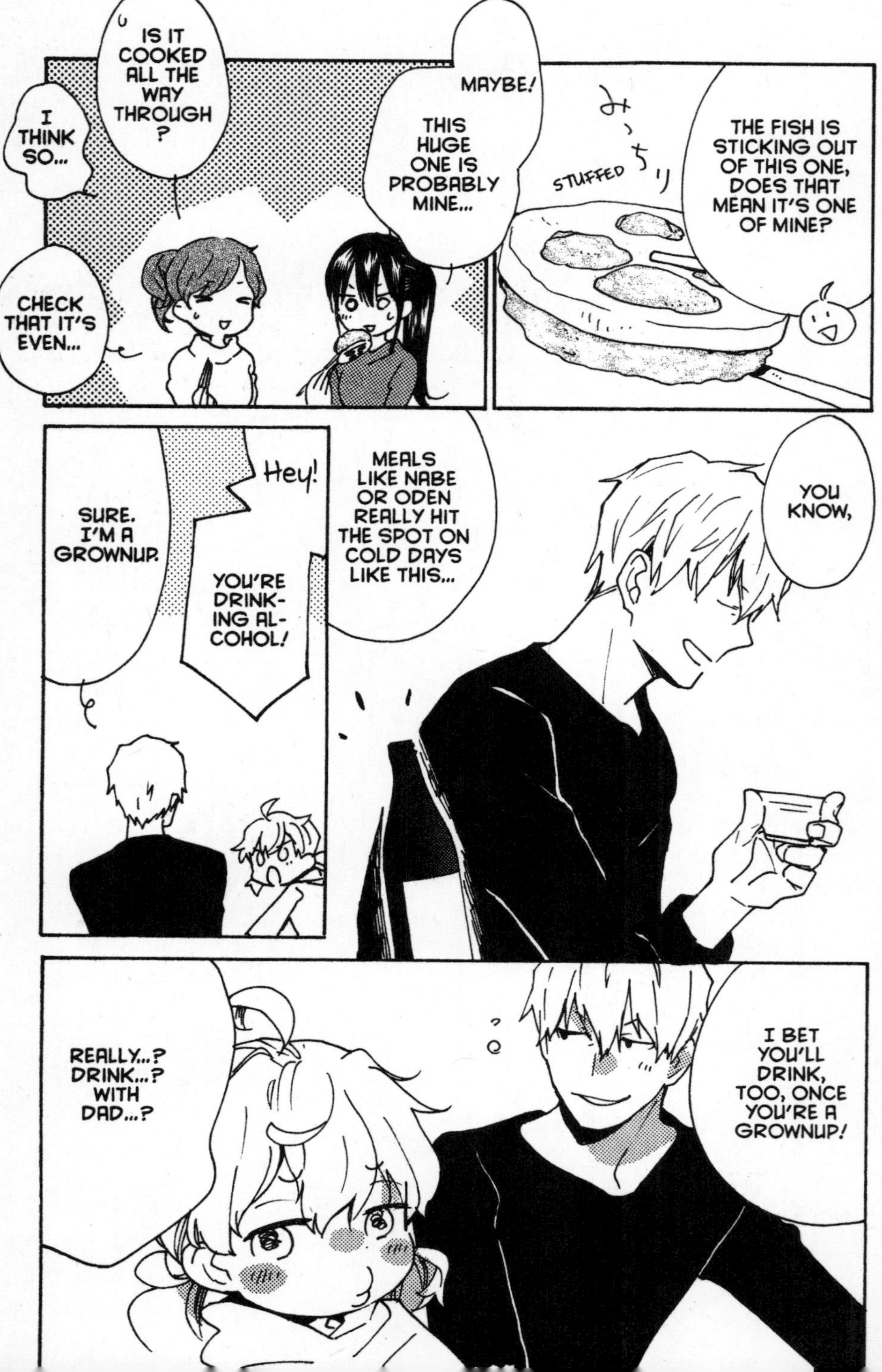
みっちり
STUFFED
THE FISH IS STICKING OUT OF THIS ONE, DOES THAT MEAN IT'S ONE OF MINE?
MAYBE!
THIS HUGE ONE IS PROBABLY MINE...
IS IT COOKED ALL THE WAY THROUGH?
I THINK SO...
CHECK THAT IT'S EVEN...
YOU KNOW,
MEALS LIKE NABE OR ODEN REALLY HIT THE SPOT ON COLD DAYS LIKE THIS...
Hey!
YOU'RE DRINK-ING AL-COHOL!
SURE. I'M A GROWNUP.
I BET YOU'LL DRINK, TOO, ONCE YOU'RE A GROWNUP!
REALLY...? DRINK...? WITH DAD...?

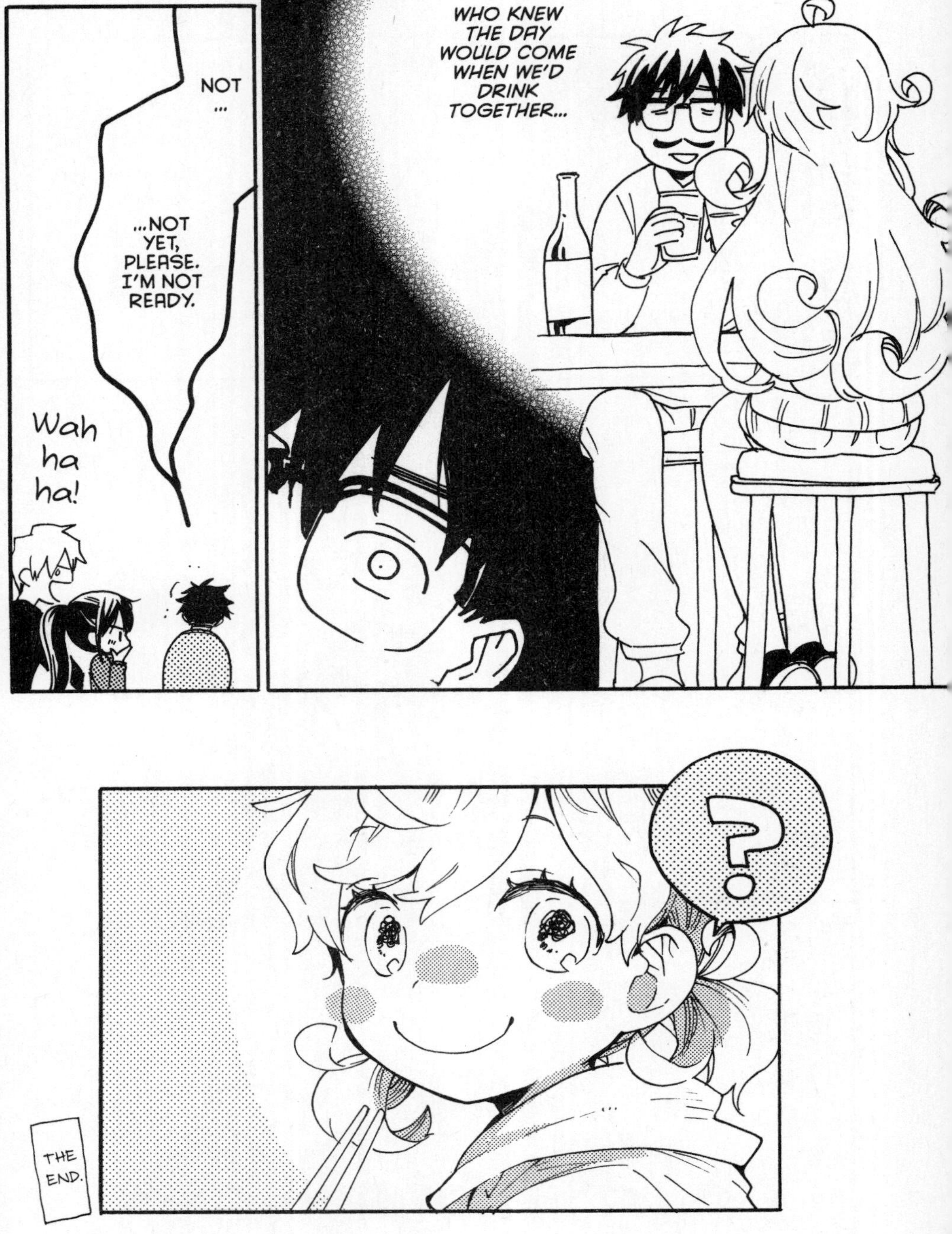
WHO KNEW THE DAY WOULD COME WHEN WE'D DRINK TOGETHER...
NOT ...
...NOT YET, PLEASE. I'M NOT READY.
Wah ha ha!
?
THE END.

Afterword

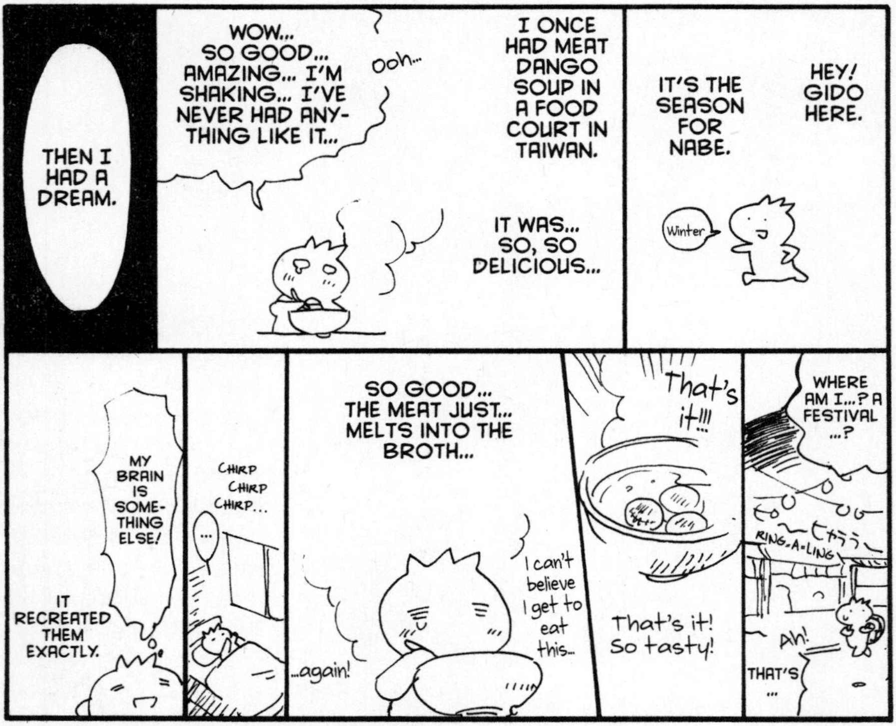
HEY! GIDO HERE.
IT'S THE SEASON FOR NABE.
Winter
I ONCE HAD MEAT DANGO SOUP IN A FOOD COURT IN TAIWAN.
IT WAS... SO, SO DELICIOUS...
WOW... SO GOOD... AMAZING... I'M SHAKING... I'VE NEVER HAD ANY-THING LIKE IT...
ooh...
THEN I HAD A DREAM.
WHERE AM I...? A FESTIVAL ...?
RING-A-LING
Ah!
THAT'S ...
That's it!!!
That's it! So tasty!
SO GOOD... THE MEAT JUST... MELTS INTO THE BROTH...
I can't believe I get to eat this...
...again!
CHIRP CHIRP CHIRP...
...
MY BRAIN IS SOME-THING ELSE!
IT RECREATED THEM EXACTLY.

NEXT VOLUME, IT'S FINALLY TIME FOR...!

THANK YOU ALL SO MUCH !

W-YAMA-SAN, TSURU-SAN, GON-CHAN, M-CHAN, CHII-CHAN, MY FAMILY.

T-DAI-SAMA, K-YAMA-SAMA, ABE JUN-SAMA

★ GATHERING REFERENCE PICTURES: RABOU-SAMA FROM THE RESTAURANT.

★ EDITING THE FOOD: OBIRYOKU YOU-SAMA

GIDO AMAGAKURE

Aho-Girl

\\'ahô,g rl\\ *Japanese, noun.*
A clueless girl.

**Anime now
available on
Crunchyroll!**

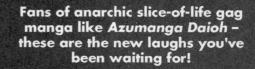

**Fans of anarchic slice-of-life gag
manga like *Azumanga Daioh* –
these are the new laughs you've
been waiting for!**

Yoshiko Hanabatake is just your average teenage girl. She
hangs out. She goes to school. She doesn't like studying. She's
got the usual ambitions - win the lottery, play around all day,
and never have any responsibilities. And she likes bananas. She
really, really likes bananas. Okay, maybe she's not average.
Maybe she's below average. Way below average. Fortunately,
Yoshiko can rely on her old friend Akkun to keep her in line.
Assuming he doesn't strangle her first.

   **AHO-
GIRL**

KC
KODANSHA
COMICS

DELUXE EDITION

BATTLE ANGEL ALITA

After more than a decade out of print, the original cyberpunk action classic returns in glorious 400-page hardcover deluxe editions, featuring an all-new translation, color pages, and new cover designs!

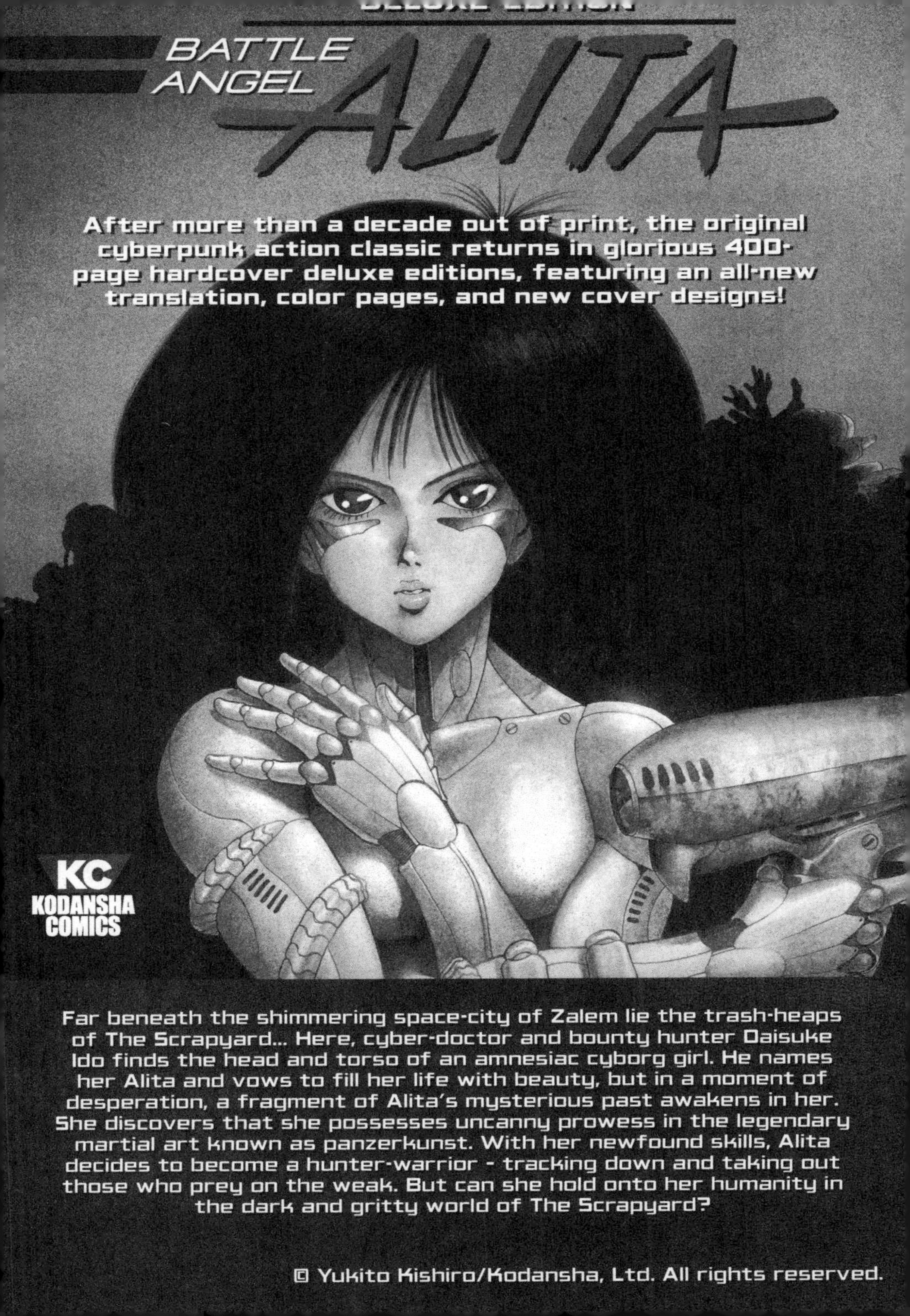

KC KODANSHA COMICS

Far beneath the shimmering space-city of Zalem lie the trash-heaps of The Scrapyard... Here, cyber-doctor and bounty hunter Daisuke Ido finds the head and torso of an amnesiac cyborg girl. He names her Alita and vows to fill her life with beauty, but in a moment of desperation, a fragment of Alita's mysterious past awakens in her. She discovers that she possesses uncanny prowess in the legendary martial art known as panzerkunst. With her newfound skills, Alita decides to become a hunter-warrior - tracking down and taking out those who prey on the weak. But can she hold onto her humanity in the dark and gritty world of The Scrapyard?

17 years after the original *Cardcaptor Sakura* manga ended, CLAMP returns with more magical adventures from a beloved manga classic!

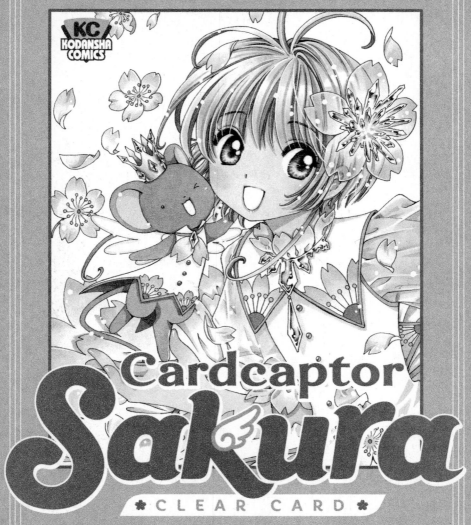

Cardcaptor Sakura

✿ CLEAR CARD ✿

Sakura Kinomoto's about to start middle school, and everything's coming up cherry blossoms. Not only has she managed to recapture the scattered Clow Cards and make them her own Sakura Cards, but her sweetheart Syaoran Li has moved from Hong Kong to Tokyo and is going to be in her class! But her joy is interrupted by a troubling dream in which the cards turn transparent, and when Sakura awakens to discover her dream has become reality, it's clear that her magical adventures are far from over...

The award-winning manga about what happens inside you!

"Far more entertaining than it ought to be... what kid doesn't want to think that every time they sneeze a torpedo shoots out their nose?"
—Anime News Network

Strep throat! Hay fever! Influenza! The world is a dangerous place for a red blood cell just trying to get her deliveries finished. Fortunately, she's not alone...she's got a whole human body's worth of cells ready to help out! The mysterious white blood cells, the buff and brash killer T cells, even the cute little platelets—everyone's got to come together if they want to keep you healthy!

Cells at Work!

By Akane Shimizu

From the creator of
No Game No Life

Naoto is a brilliant amateur mechanic who spends his days tinkering with gears and inventions. And his world is a playground—a massive, intricate machine. But his quiet life is disrupted when a box containing an automaton in the shape of a girl crashes into his home. Could this be an omen of a breakdown in Naoto's delicate clockwork planet? And is this his chance to become a hero?

CLOCKWORK PLANET

Praise for the manga and anime

"Immediately fast-paced and absorbing." - *Another Anime Review*

"A compelling science fiction world... Wildly fun and dynamic characters...The perfect manga for those who have read it all."
- *Adventures in Poor Taste*

Now available in print and digitally!

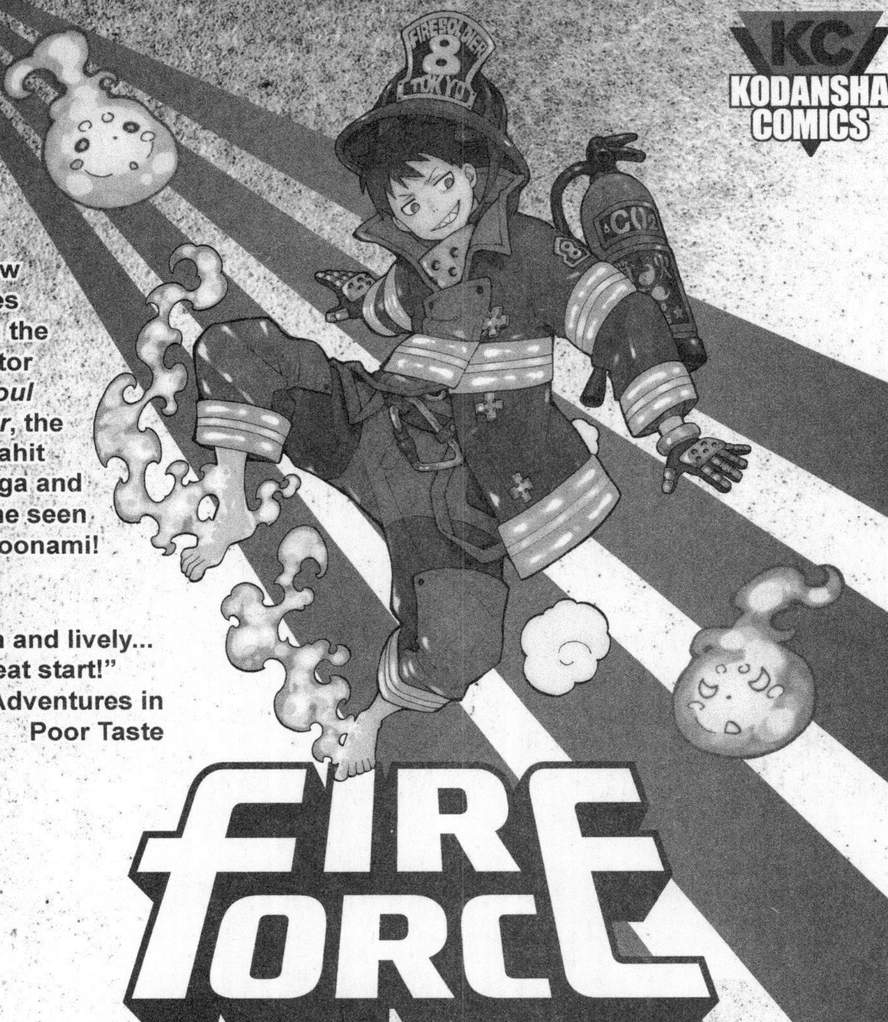

KC
KODANSHA
COMICS

A new series from the creator of *Soul Eater*, the megahit manga and anime seen on Toonami!

"Fun and lively... a great start!"
-Adventures in Poor Taste

FIRE FORCE

By Atsushi Ohkubo

The city of Tokyo is plagued by a deadly phenomenon: spontaneous human combustion! Luckily, a special team is there to quench the inferno: The Fire Force! The fire soldiers at Special Fire Cathedral 8 are about to get a unique addition. Enter Shinra, a boy who possesses the power to run at the speed of a rocket, leaving behind the famous "devil's footprints" (and destroying his shoes in the process). Can Shinra and his colleagues discover the source of this strange epidemic before the city burns to ashes?

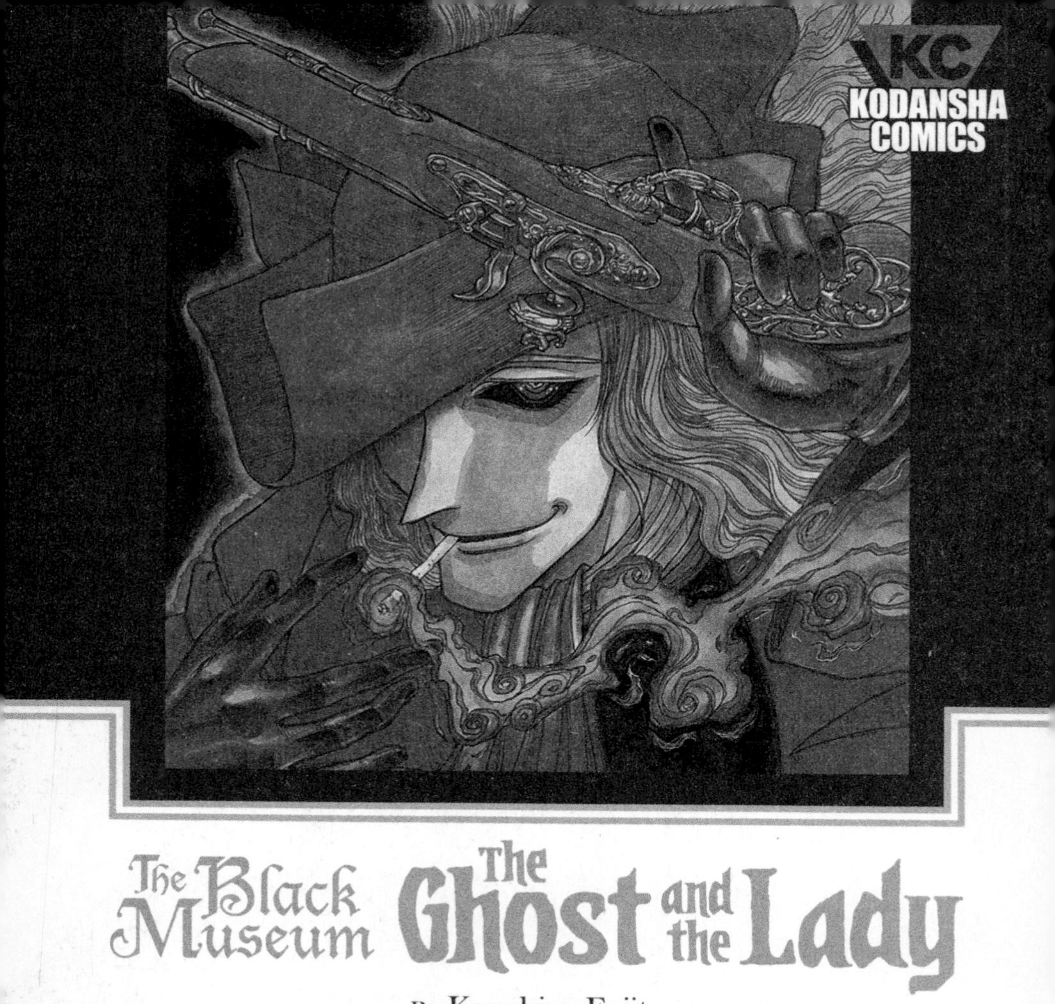
KC
KODANSHA COMICS

The Black Museum
The Ghost and the Lady

By Kazuhiro Fujita

Deep in Scotland Yard in London sits an evidence room dedicated to the greatest mysteries of British history. In this "Black Museum" sits a misshapen hunk of lead—two bullets fused together—the key to a wartime encounter between Florence Nightingale, the mother of modern nursing, and a supernatural Man in Grey. This story is unknown to most scholars of history, but a special guest of the museum will tell the tale of The Ghost and the Lady...

Praise for Kazuhiro Fujita's *Ushio and Tora*

"A charming revival that combines a classic look with modern depth and pacing... **Essential viewing both for curmudgeons and new fans alike.**" — Anime News Network

"**GREAT!** The first episode of Ushio and Tora captures the essence of '90s anime." — IGN

HAPPINESS

—ハピネス—

By Shuzo Oshimi

From the creator of *The Flowers of Evil*

Nothing interesting is happening in Makoto Ozaki's first year of high school. His life is a series of quiet humiliations: low-grade bullies, unreliable friends, and the constant frustration of his adolescent lust. But one night, a pale, thin girl knocks him to the ground in an alley and offers him a choice. Now everything is different. Daylight is searingly bright. Food tastes awful. And worse than anything is the terrible, consuming thirst...

Praise for Shuzo Oshimi's *The Flowers of Evil*

"A shockingly readable story that vividly—one might even say queasily—evokes the fear and confusion of discovering one's own sexuality. Recommended." —The Manga Critic

"A page-turning tale of sordid middle school blackmail." —Otaku USA Magazine

"A stunning new horror manga." —Third Eye Comics

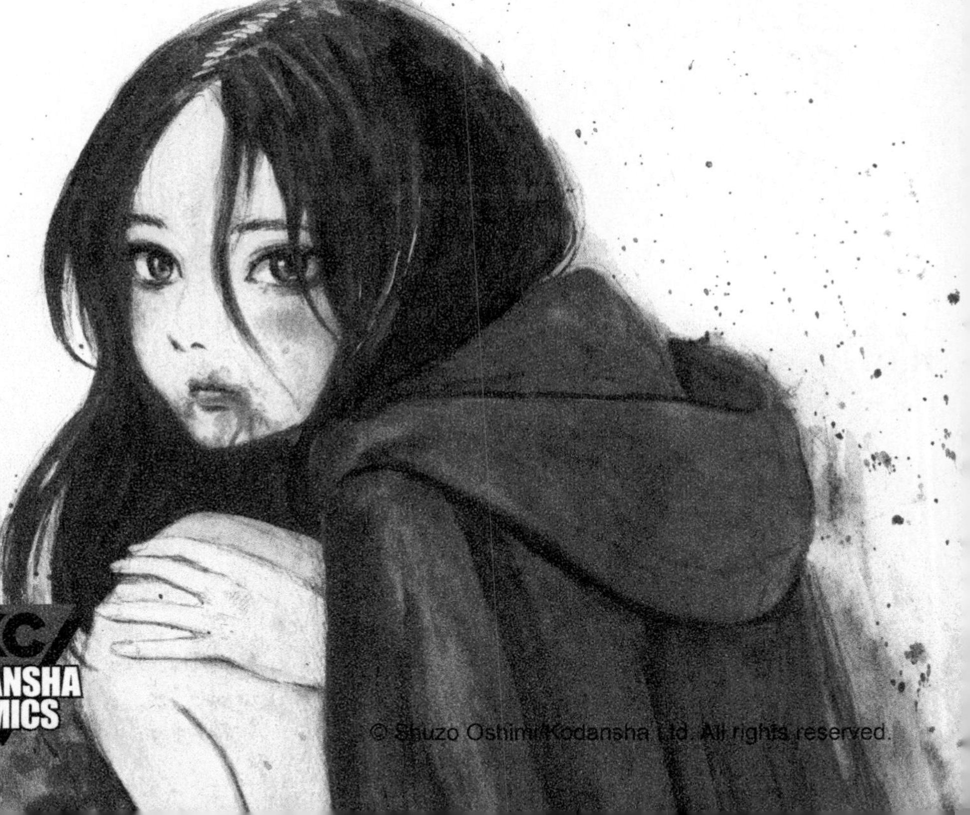

KC KODANSHA COMICS

KC
KODANSHA
COMICS

Japan's most powerful spirit medium delves into the ghost world's greatest mysteries!

Story by Kyo Shirodaira, famed author of mystery fiction and creator of *Spiral*, *Blast of Tempest*, and *The Record of a Fallen Vampire*.

Both touched by spirits called yôkai, Kotoko and Kurô have gained unique superhuman powers. But to gain her powers Kotoko has given up an eye and a leg, and Kurô's personal life is in shambles. So when Kotoko suggests they team up to deal with renegades from the spirit world, Kurô doesn't have many other choices, but Kotoko might just have a few ulterior motives...

IN/SPECTRE

STORY BY KYO SHIRODAIRA
ART BY CHASHIBA KATASE

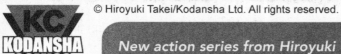

> *New action series from Hiroyuki Takei, creator of the classic shonen franchise Shaman King!*

In medieval Japan, a bell hanging on the collar is a sign that a cat has a master. Norachiyo's bell hangs from his katana sheath, but he is nonetheless a stray — a ronin. This one-eyed cat samurai travels across a dishonest world, cutting through pretense and deception with his blade.

By

Hiroyuki Takei

Based on the critically acclaimed classic horror manga

The first new *Parasyte* manga in over 20 years!

NEO PARASYTE f

BY ASUMIKO NAKAMURA, EMA TOYAMA, MIKI RINNO, LALAKO KOJIMA, KAORI YUKI, BANKO KUZE, YUUKI OBATA, KASHIO, YUI KUROE, ASIA WATANABE, MIKIMAKI, HIKARU SURUGA, HAJIME SHINJO, RENJURO KINDAICHI, AND YURI NARUSHIMA

A collection of chilling new *Parasyte* stories from Japan's top shojo artists!

Parasites: shape-shifting aliens whose only purpose is to assimilate with and consume the human race... but do these monsters have a different side? A parasite becomes a prince to save his romance-obsessed female host from a dangerous stalker. Another hosts a cooking show, in which the real monsters are revealed. These and 13 more stories, from some of the greatest shojo manga artists alive today, together make up a chilling, funny, and entertaining tribute to one of manga's horror classics!

KODANSHA COMICS

"I'm pleasantly surprised to find modern shojo using cross-dressing as a dramatic device to deliver social commentary... Recommended."

-Otaku USA Magazine

The prince in his dark days

By Hico Yamanaka

A drunkard for a father, a household of poverty... For 17-year-old Atsuko, misfortune is all she knows and believes in. Until one day, a chance encounter with Itaru–the wealthy heir of a huge corporation–changes everything. The two look identical, uncannily so. When Itaru curiously goes missing, Atsuko is roped into being his stand-in. There, in his shoes, Atsuko must parade like a prince in a palace. She encounters many new experiences, but at what cost...?

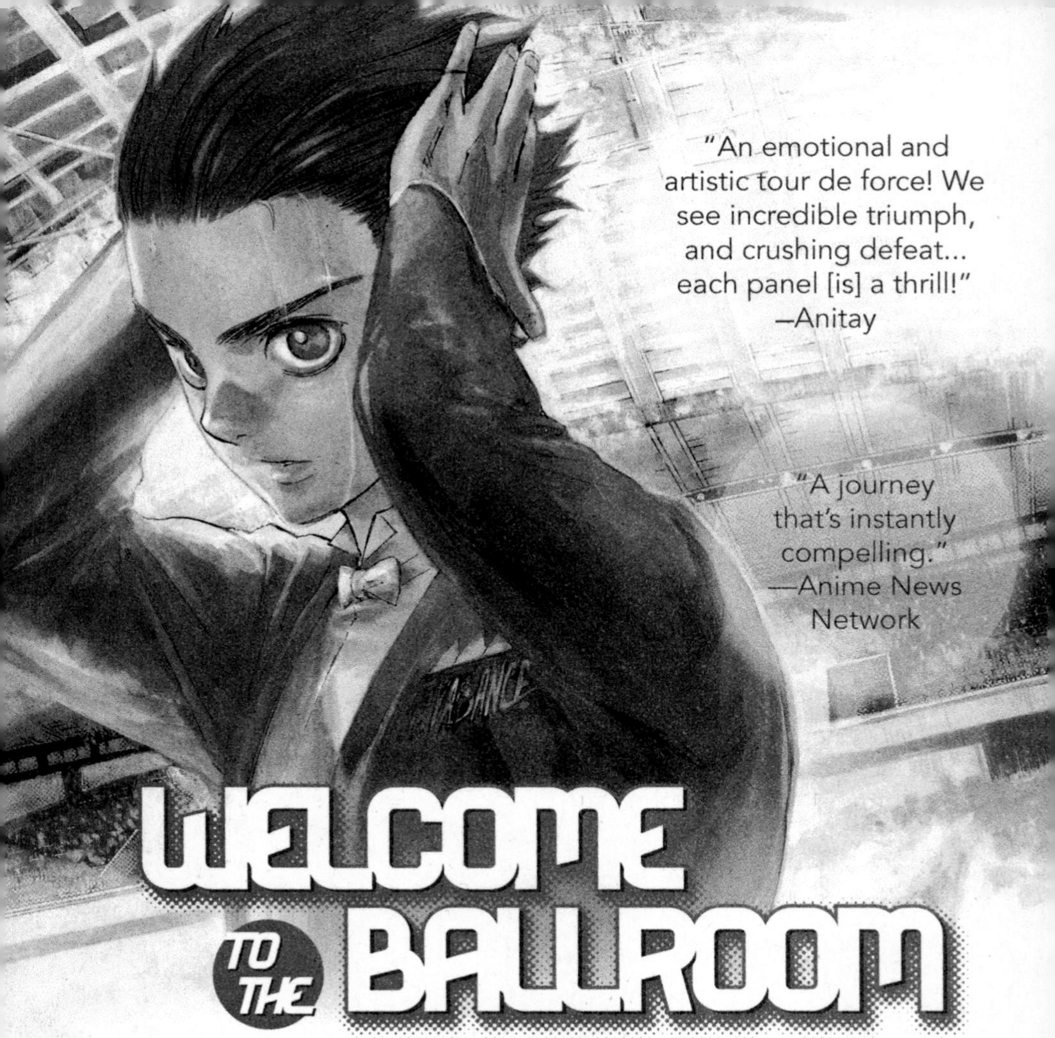
"An emotional and artistic tour de force! We see incredible triumph, and crushing defeat... each panel [is] a thrill!"
–Anitay
"A journey that's instantly compelling."
—Anime News Network

WELCOME TO THE BALLROOM

By Tomo Takeuchi

Feckless high school student Tatara Fujita wants to be good at something—anything. Unfortunately, he's about as average as a slouchy teen can be. The local bullies know this, and make it a habit to hit him up for cash, but all that changes when the debonair Kaname Sengoku sends them packing. Sengoku's not the neighborhood watch, though. He's a professional ballroom dancer. And once Tatara Fujita gets pulled into the world of ballroom, his life will never be the same.

KC KODANSHA COMICS

Sweetness & Lightning volume 10 is a work of fiction. Names, characters, places, and incidents are the products of the author's imagination or are used fictitiously. Any resemblance to actual events, locales, or persons, living or dead, is entirely coincidental.

A Kodansha Comics Trade Paperback Original.

Published in the United States by Kodansha Comics, an imprint of Kodansha USA Publishing, LLC, New York.

Publication rights for this English edition arranged through Kodansha Ltd., Tokyo.

First published in Japan in 2018 by Kodansha Ltd., Tokyo, as *Ama-ama to Inadzuma* volume 10.

ISBN 978-1-63236-569-9

Printed in the United States of America.

www.kodanshacomics.com

9 8 7 6 5 4 3 2 1

Translation: Adam Lensenmayer
Additional Translation: Jennifer O'Donnell
Lettering: Carl Vanstiphout
Editing: Paul Starr
Editorial Assistance: Tiff Ferentini
Kodansha Comics Edition Cover Design: Phil Balsman